rick stein's
Guide to
the food heroes
of Britain

rick**stein's**

Guide to
the food heroes
of Britain **BBC**

Where to Buy the Best Produce
in Britain & Ireland

Chief Researcher: Christina Burnham

This book was published to accompany the television
series entitled *Rick Stein's Food Heroes: Another Helping*
The series was produced for BBC Television
by Denham Productions
Producer and Director: David Pritchard
Assistant Producer: Arezoo Farahzad
Executive Producer for the BBC: Andy Batten-Foster

First published in 2003 by BBC Books,
Second edition published in 2005
BBC Books, BBC Worldwide Limited
80 Wood Lane
London W12 0TT

ISBN 0 563 52240 2

Commissioning Editor: Vivien Bowler
Project Editor: Rachel Copus
Copy Editor: Deborah Savage
Book Art Director: Sarah Ponder
Designed by Ben Cracknell Studios
Illustrations by Ruth Murray
Production Controller: Kenneth McKay
Database Development: Mark Ginns

Set in Helvetica Neue
Printed and bound in Great Britain by The Bath Press Ltd
Cover printed by The Bath Press Ltd

contents

introduction	6
how to use this book	10
bread	16
dairy and eggs	52
delicatessens and specialist food shops	100
drinks	144
fish	174
fruit and vegetables	210
game	256
meat	274
poultry	362
acknowledgements	384
index by location	386
alphabetical index	396

introduction

Food Heroes is about producers who believe that food should taste of where it comes from; should, in other words, have local character and honesty of flavour. Nothing is perfect though, and little stays the same for long. Producers retire, or go bankrupt, or simply decide to give up the struggle against the ever-increasing tide of cheap imported food. Others, rarely, allow standards to slip, and so with this in mind, we have updated the Food Heroes guide.

It has proved an illuminating experience, with plenty of positive stories emerging, and a few disappointments. The owner of an organic shop selling local produce in Newcastle, for example, told of how the guide had given a real boost to the demand for local food in an area which, until now, had seemed to lag behind others in terms of interest in good quality, locally produced food. The basic point of the guide has been to encourage a general awareness of small-scale, locally produced foods and we have had a large number of letters and emails from producers who have been helped by inclusion in the book.

Conversely, we heard tales of long-established family businesses closing permanently due to illness or retirement simply because the younger generation have seen the long hours and hard work that producing the best quality food entails, and they decided that there are easier ways to earn a living. They are certainly right, which makes the people that we list seem all the more heroic.

Despite so much change, much has stayed the same, and we should celebrate this. You'll see many of the same entries that were featured in the last edition; they are still quietly labouring away, producing the same great food, and they deserve their mention as much as ever.

We have also added an index of producers to make the navigation through the guide easier and we have replaced the maps with a listing of entries by area and town, since we thought the maps were not clear enough. I never fail to get a thrill of certainty every time I buy produce from one of my Food Heroes and realize that it does taste better. The butter produced by Cream of Cumbria at Howberry Farm, outside Carlisle, has a sweet creaminess that makes spreading it on some crusty bread a special occasion. The meat from

Lishman's in Ilkley makes you realize why great roast beef and Yorkshire pudding depends on a quality butcher like David Lishman who looks for succulence, tenderness and flavour enhanced by the presence of fat, both on the surface and marbled throughout the flesh. The book concentrates on people like him and primary producers who have a commitment to quality and flavour and a determination to produce food properly; and who care more about that rather than selling high volumes. They have a feeling for the traditions and heritage of food, for animal welfare and good husbandry, for flavour and eating pleasure, everything, it seems that modern farming has largely left behind.

It's all too easy to blame supermarkets for mediocrity in food but they are trying to target excellence in their own way with premium ranges like Tesco's Finest and Sainsbury's Taste the Difference. Marks and Spencer too must be praised for a determination to go for quality over price and a commitment to animal welfare, evidence of which can be found in their refusal to sell anything but free range eggs, both fresh and in their cooked food. There are signs that all of the chains are starting to take the concept of buying locally seriously: Asda buy lots from producers each of which supplies to only one or two stores, Tesco stocks literally thousands of locally obtained items, and Waitrose has a clear policy of supporting small, local producers. Nevertheless they all lean heavily in the direction of large volume simply because they need the quantity to supply all their outlets. This book's raison d'être is that small is beautiful.

Variety is the spice of life and in this guide you will find vegetable growers who offer literally hundreds of varieties of vegetables throughout the season, varieties that are grown for their taste rather than their ability to survive weeks in cold rooms before display. You will also find meat producers who rear a dazzling array of rare-breed pork, lamb and beef, with textures and flavours that you are very unlikely to find in the supermarkets. There are delis brimming with foods from artisan producers, foods that will never find their way onto supermarket shelves because they are made in quantities too small to satisfy the supermarkets' requirements.

The guide will enable you to find them and enrich your life in the process, but I had a second reason for writing it – to do my bit to support small producers. Sadly most people think food should be ever cheaper; price is normally the governing factor in what consumers buy. The best food costs money to produce. Every week in this country, small farms go bust often because the cost of producing the food is more than we are prepared to pay for. On the continent, small, artisan producers of high quality foods are revered; tradition, heritage, and most of all, taste, are afforded great respect, and people are happy to pay realistic prices for their produce. We need to have that respect here too.

Mass produced food can often be seen to exact a high price from the environment, on rural economies, on the survival of traditional cultures and skills. Many of the producers featured here address these problems, painstakingly maintaining traditional methods, and passing them on through their families and staff, when a modern approach would almost certainly create more profit. Many of the producers have a keen awareness of the environmental impact of their production, and endeavour to minimise any adverse effects. There are delis and farm shops that, when selling imported foods, choose to stock 'fair trade' produce – they want small-scale producers abroad to make a fair living from their skills, too. Some producers go much further – take the Camphill Communities, for example, where market gardens and bakeries are run to enable people with developmental disabilities to learn a trade and earn a living. These centres produce fantastic traditional breads and tasty organic vegetables, and have a far-reaching benefit to the community, too. With so many of the producers, there is a sense that food is not just fuel for the body, but a connection to the community and the outside world.

Buying and eating produce from local producers can offer so many benefits. Food will be fresher; it won't have travelled the length and breadth of the country, from packing plant to warehouse to shop shelves. Food miles – the hot environmental topic concerning the energy wasted as foods are trucked or flown around the world – are minimised. Rural economies, which have for so long struggled, are boosted – jobs are created or retained, the culture of traditional farms and smallholdings is maintained. Farmers' markets and farm shops can add a great sense of community to villages and towns – you can actually talk to the person who produced the food on your plate, find out more about it, and tell them what you think – essentially, you are buying direct from specialists, with all their expertise and knowledge at your disposal. There is real opportunity now to get more involved in the production of what you eat, whether that be through farm shops and farmers' markets, a weekly vegetable box scheme delivered by the grower, or even joining a community supported agriculture scheme, where you pay a fee to a farm or group of farms, and then share in the entire harvest throughout the year. You'll often be surprised at the great value for money you get when you buy your food this way, but equally, you'll be paying a fair price, that enables the producers to make a realistic living.

Rick Stein

how to use this book

I've divided my guidebook into nine chapters, each consisting of producers who supply a particular type of food, such as Bread, Dairy and Eggs, Meat, Poultry etc. Each one begins with a brief introduction, telling you a little about my criteria for choosing the entries and why I believe the suppliers I have selected are manufacturing produce of the highest quality. Within these chapters the producers are organised into regions (indicated on the top left-hand side of each entry) that fall along county boundaries. The regions are broken up as follows:

SOUTH WEST

Bristol and Bath, Cornwall, Devon, Dorset, Gloucestershire, Somerset, Wiltshire

SOUTH EAST

Bedfordshire, Berkshire, Buckinghamshire, East and West Sussex, Hampshire, Hertfordshire, Kent, London, Oxfordshire, Surrey

EAST ANGLIA

Cambridgeshire, Essex, Norfolk, Suffolk

MIDLANDS

Derbyshire, Hereford and Worcester, Leicestershire, Lincolnshire, Northamptonshire, Nottinghamshire, Shropshire, Staffordshire, Warwickshire, West Midlands (including Birmingham)

NORTH WEST

Cumbria, Cheshire, Greater Manchester, Lancashire, Merseyside

NORTH EAST

Cleveland, County Durham, Humberside, Northumberland, North, South and West Yorkshire, Tyne and Wear

NORTHERN IRELAND

REPUBLIC OF IRELAND

SCOTLAND

WALES

Once you've located the region relevant to you, the entries are organised alphabetically, by the nearest town or village (indicated on the top right-hand side of each entry).

super heroes and food-fact boxes

Also included within each chapter are boxed entries, which I've called my Super Heroes. These are the businesses or individual producers who I feel stand head and shoulders above the rest in terms of the work that they do and the quality of the food that they produce. As a consequence I have marked them out and, if you are visiting a specific region, I would put them at the top of your list of places to shop. I have also included some information boxes which look at specific issues faced by the industry in question, and which I hope will influence your choice of product when you shop in the future.

locating the suppliers

Each entry includes the full postal address, but if the specific region is not familiar to you, you will need a good road atlas if you intend to visit. The index of suppliers by location (on page 386) will help you to locate suppliers in your area, and, of course, if you are on holiday, to locate any local producers you can visit. The alphabetical index will help you look up a supplier in the book, if you know its name. Entries are listed by initial letter so, for example, A.G. Millers is listed under A.

entries

Categorizing such a range of businesses is always going to be difficult. I have done my best to put each one in the section where it fits best. However, some of the producers that appear in the game section will also sell fantastic local meats and some producers in the fish section will stock local game. Equally, those in the delicatessens section might have a good in-store bakery, and some of the cheesemongers in the dairy section will have a great selection of deli goods. Each entry should be listed under its primary product or the product type for which it is best known, but don't be surprised if you find the best cheese you've ever tasted at a recommended fishmonger… that's part of the fun of discovering fresh local food for yourself.

I have included full addresses and telephone numbers for each entry and a website address where applicable. Email addresses are only included where the supplier has no website. I've included a brief description of each supplier, but the following symbols should give an 'at a glance' guide to the facilities they offer:

farm shop: Entries that display this symbol have a dedicated farm shop where you can purchase their produce and sometimes that of other local producers. You may need to phone them directly for opening times.

farmers' markets: Farmers' markets are a great way to buy fresh, local produce when it's in season. This symbol indicates that the producer in question has stalls at their local market(s). Where possible, we have listed the relevant markets, but for more information phone the producer directly.

shop: Entries whose primary function is not that of a shop, but which have a shop on site (such as a cheese factory or a mill).

farm gate sales: Many of the producers featured in the guide may not have a recognized farm shop, but they are still happy to sell to individuals. I would recommend that you phone ahead to check that someone will be available to help you.

delivery service: A local delivery service is offered.

mail order: A mail-order service is available.

box scheme: Box schemes vary greatly from producer to producer, but generally the supplier will offer either a weekly, monthly or one-off scheme whereby you can order either a specified selection of fresh, local goods or a surprise mixture, depending on what's in season.

associations and organizations –
what do they stand for?

There are a number of associations and organizations throughout the UK and Ireland who are working hard to promote good quality, often organic, food and the various businesses that produce it. For clarity, I've included the logo for the most frequently occurring organizations next to the relevant suppliers and include a key, below and opposite, to show you what each stands for.

Artisan Bakers of Northern Ireland: A small group of craft bakers situated within Northern Ireland endeavouring to uphold traditional methods of baking and traditional regional recipes.

Demeter: The association aims to help and support those wishing to put into practice the biodynamic method (see box on organic meat, page 320). With this objective in mind it keeps in close touch with biodynamic agriculture abroad and with various organizations concerned with a sustainable approach to soil, environment and health. Visit their website at www.anth.org.uk/biodynamic/demeter

Elite Guild of Butchers: A group of master butchers within Northern Ireland aiming to preserve traditional butchery skills and encouraging sourcing of local meats. Strict hygiene standards and an emphasis on personal service are also encouraged. For more information contact John Dowey at jrdowey@aol.com

Guild of Fine Food Retailers: The Guild of Fine Food Retailers is instrumental in the UK in encouraging small-scale producers of high-quality and fine foods and promoting specialist shops and delis that stock their produce. For more information visit their website at www.finefoodworld.co.uk

Guild of Q Butchers: The Guild of Q Butchers aims to tempt consumers back to buying from specialist butchers with the promise of properly hung, well-butchered meats, from named sources – often local farms – backed by rigorous hygiene standards. Visit their website at www.guildofqbutchers.co.uk

Irish Organic Farmers and Growers: An accreditation scheme for Irish organic producers, ensuring that the methods by which they produce food abide by the strict organic standards the association imposes. For more information visit their website at www.irishorganic.ie

Organic Farmers and Growers: An accreditation scheme for British organic producers, laying down a strict set of standards for food production (www.organicfarmers.uk.com).

Rare Breeds Survival Trust: The Rare Breeds Survival Trust (RBST) is a charity endeavouring to keep alive Britain's livestock heritage. The UK and Ireland have a magnificent selection of native breeds of farm animals, but many breeds are now at critically low levels of population and many more are on the vulnerable list. These don't suit modern farming methods and are not seen as commercially viable by conventional meat producers. Thankfully, however, since the RBST was founded in 1973 we have not lost a single breed. They insist that conserving these breeds is not romantic whimsy – 'rare breeds are an essential part of greener farming systems – helping the environment, and improving the quality of the food we eat'. Visit their website on www.rbst.org.uk.

Scottish Organic Producers Association: An accreditation scheme for Scottish organic producers, ensuring that the methods by which the foods are produced attain the exacting standards of UKROFS (the UK Register of Organic Food Standards). For more information visit their website on www.sopa.org.uk

Soil Association: Most people buying organic foods do so because they are concerned about chemical residues on and in food. The Soil Association has created a body of complex and far-reaching regulations that those growers who want to be accredited must abide by and the benefits range from the environmental and the cultural through to animal welfare and health. Visit their website on www.soilassociation.org.uk

Specialist Cheesemakers' Association and CAIS: The Specialist Cheesemakers' Association was formed in 1989, in response to a threat by the Agriculture Minister to ban the sale of unpasteurized cheese. The SCA successfully managed to prevent this happening and is now firmly established as an institution championing the work of artisan and specialist cheesemakers around the country. The Association insists that it is 'vital that all members demonstrate their commitment to quality'. More information can be found on their website (www.specialistcheesemakers.co.uk). CAIS is the association for Irish farmhouse cheesemakers, endeavouring to maintain the cheese-making heritage of Ireland.

Wholesome Food Association: The costs of being accredited by the Soil Association are beyond some smaller-scale growers. The Wholesome Food Association represents these growers, giving customers a degree of assurance regarding the methods by which its members' produce has been grown or reared.

I asked the WFA about their ethical aims in food production, and they told me:

> *'The WFA is aimed mainly at the smallholder and small-scale farmer, as this group is the most disadvantaged by the current political climate, which promotes the economies of scale over the values of "small and local".'*

The basic principles members must abide by are:

> *'Wholesome food is grown and processed using sustainable, non-polluting methods as close as possible to those found in nature.'* This includes growing without artificial pesticides, herbicides or fertilizers, high animal welfare and animal feeds free from antibiotics and genetically modified organisms.

> *'Wholesome food is, wherever possible, traded and consumed within a short distance of where it was grown.'*

> *'Wholesome food is an integral part of life and community, rather than merely a commodity for profit.'*

It is important to remember that WFA producers won't send food by mail order across the country – they are passionate about keeping food local, so try to find a producer in your area (www.wholesomefood.org).

In this chapter, I have looked for craft and artisan bakeries, producing bread from scratch using time-honoured methods, with carefully sourced ingredients and a pride in their work. Sadly, these bakeries are an endangered species. Over recent years, the nation has been led to believe that bread is a cheap, basic food, worthy of little thought. Bakers who make a high-quality, tasty and nutritious product, without artificial additives and improvers, are being squeezed out of the market. Two technical 'advances' in production methods – the Chorleywood Process and the Milton Keynes Process (page 24) – are primarily responsible for the dominance of mass-produced, factory-made loaves on supermarket shelves and this dominance is bolstered by the additives put into such loaves, which create certain characteristics seen as desirable, and improve their shelf life.

bread

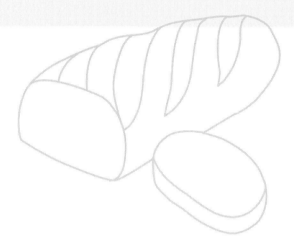

Not only are we losing the skills of traditional bread-baking – of making loaves slowly, to allow flavour and texture to develop – but we are also losing the regional heritage of bread and bakery goods. Local bakers will often bake regional specialities, such as Bedfordshire Clangers, Kent Huffkins cakes, or Cornish Hevva cake; if we lose those local bakers, the chances are that all that cultural diversity will be lost, too. Perhaps if we stopped thinking of bread as a cheap fuel and instead recognized the value of a loaf baked slowly, with proper time devoted to the development and fermentation of the dough, with local ingredients, using skills and knowledge passed down for generations, the tide would turn, and those dying baker's skills would once more be revered.

Leakers Bakery Ltd

29 East Street, Bridport, Dorset DT6 3JX   T: 01308 423296

Interesting breads are made at Leakers by baker Aidan Chapman, including cider and cheese cottage loaf and lemon polenta. Many are organic; all are baked on the premises. Wheat- and yeast-free breads and cakes are also available daily. Leakers specialize in slow fermentation, using local ingredients wherever possible.

Hobbs House

superhero

Office: Unit 6, Chipping Edge Estate, Hatters Lane, Chipping Sodbury, Bristol BS37 6AA
Shops: 39 High Street, Chipping Sodbury, Bristol BS37 6BA AND 2 North Parade, Yate,
Bristol BS37 4AN   T: 01454 321629 (OFFICE, FOR MAIL-ORDER ENQUIRIES); 01454 317525
(CHIPPING SODBURY); 01454 320890 (YATE)   W: www.hobbshousebakery.co.uk
🥖 shop   ✉ mail order

An award-winning bakery using traditional techniques. Local ingredients are used when possible. See their Super Hero box, page 20, for more information. There is also a branch in Nailsworth, see page 20.

The Otterton Mill Bakery

Otterton Mill, Otterton, nr Budleigh Salterton, Devon EX9 7HG   T: 01395 568031
W: www.ottertonmill.com
🥖 shop

The old restored mill at Otterton uses traditional stones to grind local organic wheat. The flour is then made into an imaginative and ever-expanding range of breads, including rye, spelt, tomato and herb bread, walnut bread and olive bread, all made by hand, without improvers or additives. Next door is a restaurant, with an outdoor terrace, providing a range of meals using only local Devon ingredients.

H M Pearce

Station Road, Kelly Bray, nr Callington, Cornwall PL17 8ER   T: 01579 383362

This is the home of one of the most famous Cornish saffron cakes. The recipe is from generations ago, the ingredients are chosen with incredible attention to detail, and the result is one of the best saffron cakes you'll ever taste.

The Bread Pancheon

Grafton House, High Street, Chipping Campden, Gloucestershire GL55 6AT
T: 01386 849090

🍞 **farmers' markets**

A specialist French bakery, with a fantastic choice of artisan breads. None of the breads here happen quickly – dough fermentation times are rarely less than 16 hours, and everything is made from scratch. The real specialities are the French varieties and the ryes and sourdoughs.

Seeds Bakery & Health Stores

22, Duke Street, Dartmouth, Devon TQ6 9TZ   T: 01803 833200

Hand-made breads and cakes made using organic ingredients: all the breads are 100% organic. Ingredients are chosen carefully; local free-range eggs are used, as is unhydrogenated fat. The shops (there is another branch in Totnes, see page 23) also stock local organic vegetables and milk.

Common Loaf Bakery

Stentwood Farm, Dunkeswell, nr Honiton, Devon EX14 4RW   T: 01823 681155
w: www.commonloaf.com

🍞 **farmers' markets**

The Common Loaf Bakery does not use wheat in its breads but only spelt, an old variety of grain, and rye. This is because the bakers here feel that wheat has been 'over-hybridized' and now contains too much gluten. All the breads are hand-made and come in a great selection of varieties, including sourdough, wholegrain with soaked seeds (easier to digest and more flavoursome), and Parmesan focaccia. Their bread is available from Bristol, Taunton, Honiton, Totnes, Tiverton and Exeter farmers' markets, as well as local shops – call for details.

super hero

THE WELLS FAMILY, owners of Hobbs House Bakery, Chipping Sodbury, Yate and Nailsworth (see pages 18 and below)

Hobbs House Bakery has won many awards for its traditionally made breads. The mission statement of this family-run business is 'to produce honest bread with passion'; keen to retain traditional methods, they have even installed an old-fashioned wood-fired oven at their Nailsworth bakery and café. Packaging is kept to an absolute minimum for environmental reasons, organic breads are becoming an ever bigger part of their range (they've won Organic Food Awards for the last seven years running) and local ingredients are sourced wherever possible.

Three generations of the Wells family are involved in the bakery and this, no doubt, is a key part of their desire to maintain a sense of community spirit in food production. Clive Wells told me that at Hobbs House, they 'mourn greatly the loss of the village bakery and corner shop, and are keen to support local village shops which are so vital to the community'. He went on to lament bread from large-scale bakeries, where products are made to a price rather than with quality as the primary concern. A loaf of Hobbs House sourdough or organic spelt bread shows clearly that this bakery aims to reverse that trend and more than adequately substantiates their slogan – 'discover real bread'.

SOUTH WEST   **NAILSWORTH**

Hobbs House   `super hero`

4 George Street, Nailsworth, Gloucestershire GL6 0AG   T: 01453 839396
w: www.hobbshousebakery.co.uk
✉ **mail order**

See the Super Hero box, above, for more information. There are also branches in Chipping Sodbury and Yate, near Bristol, see page 18.

SOUTH WEST   **NEWENT**

The Authentic Bread Company

Strawberry Hill, Newent, Gloucestershire GL18 1LH   T: 01531 828181
w: www.authenticbread.co.uk
✉ **mail order**

Organic, traditionally baked bread in varieties including rye, walnut, spelt and classic continental types. No flour improvers are used, the dough is allowed to ferment naturally, twice, and Authentic Bread states that 'taste rather than cost is paramount'. Call to find out where your nearest stockist is, or buy mail order from Graig Farm (see page 358).

Stein's Patisserie

1 Lanadwell Street, Padstow, Cornwall PL28 8AN   T: 01841 532700

There's no reason why I shouldn't include my bakery, since we make good sourdough bread, pain levain, wholewheat with walnuts, white tin loaves, foccacia and granary bread, all made with slowly developed dough. We bake five different varieties of Cornish pasty including steak, smoked haddock, and crab with saffron, which naturally we think are rather good, and lots of pretty cakes and pastries, which we sell in our small patisserie, right in the centre of Padstow. The bread is also available at our deli on the quayside below the Seafood School.

Portreath Bakery

3 The Square, Portreath, Cornwall TR16 4LA   T: 01209 842612

A bakery with a really imaginative range of breads and pasties, made with locally produced ingredients wherever possible. Good examples of saffron cake and Hevva cake are available.

Lydia's Cottage Industry

Southfields Piece, Carnkie, Redruth, Cornwall TR16 6SG   T: 01209 217352
🛒 farmers' markets

Old-fashioned methods and ingredients are the key to the breads, cakes and preserves from Lydia's Cottage Industry. Local ingredients are used as far as possible and there are gluten-free, wheat-free, sugar-free and dairy-free varieties to try. Available from the Country Market in Truro, Perranporth Country Market, and Carnon Downs Village Market.

super hero

TOBY AND LOUISE TOBIN-DOUGAN, of St Martin's Bakery, Higher Town, St Martin's, Isles of Scilly (see below).

Using mostly organic, mostly local produce, Toby and Louise of St Martin's Bakery make specialist continental-style breads and English loaves by hand, using old-fashioned methods. Croissants are made from scratch and quiches are available, filled with local salmon and grey mullet (caught and smoked by the couple themselves) or home-grown vegetables. The Cornish pasties they make contain home-grown potatoes and beef reared on the island. They are even trying their hands at cheesemaking. In a part of the world where 'food miles' could be a problem, Toby and Louise seem to have a talent for self-sufficiency – and the food they produce is all the fresher and tastier for it. And the couple are keen to share their skills – also on offer are baking courses in which customers can learn to bake traditional foods with local produce in the gorgeous setting of the Scilly Isles. Toby and Louise are also part of a new collaboration between producers on St. Martins. 'Scillonian Fayre' is a mail-order service offering a great variety of Scilly Isles produce, direct to your door. Call the bakery for details.

SOUTH WEST   SCILLY ISLES

St Martin's Bakery and Scillonian Fayre   super hero

Higher Town, St Martin's, Isles of Scilly TR25 0QL   T: 01720 423444
w: www.stmartinsbakery.co.uk
✉ **mail order**

Continental-style breads and English loaves, all made using old-fashioned techniques. See the Super Hero box, above, for more information.

SOUTH WEST   SHAFTESBURY

N R Stoate and Sons

Cann Mills, Shaftesbury, Dorset SP7 0BL   T: 01747 852475
✉ **farm gate sales**

There has been a mill on this site since before the Domesday Book was written and the Stoate family are keen to retain the heritage of traditional milling in the watermill that now stands here. Using 19th-century French burr stones makes a soft flour, ideal for traditional bread-making. Using local wheat whenever possible, the range includes organic flours and is available to buy direct from the mill. Cann Mills is a member of the Traditional Corn Millers Guild.

Sunshine Health Shop

25 Church Street, Stroud, Gloucestershire GL5 1JL   T: 01453 763923
w: www.sunshinehealth.co.uk
✉ **mail order**

Sunshine Health Shop is supplied with great organic bread from its own bakery, with an interesting range that includes all the regular types as well as spelt, oat and sourdough breads and a unique recipe – 'Sunshine loaf' – a dense, nutty wholemeal bread made with English flour. The breads are all made without improvers – as Ray, the owner, says – 'a good thing doesn't need improving'.

Shipton Mill

Long Newnton, Tetbury, Gloucestershire GL8 8RP   T: 01666 505050
E: enquiries@shipton-mill.com
✉ **mail order**

Around 60 varieties of stoneground flour are produced at Shipton Mill, the majority of which are organic. There are some really unusual varieties that you are unlikely to find elsewhere, such as organic chestnut flour and an Egyptian pasta flour called *kamut*. Mail order is available (ask for Flour Direct when you call), and the staff are also happy to give advice on baking questions.

Seeds Bakery & Health Stores

35 High Street, Totnes, Devon TQ9 5NP   T: 01803 862526

For details see under the Dartmouth branch on page 19.

FOOD HEROES OF BRITAIN

Carley's

34–36 St Austell Street, Truro, Cornwall TR1 1SE T: 01872 277686
W: www.carleys.co.uk

🚚 **delivery service** 📦 **box scheme**

Carley's stocks all kinds of organic produce – locally grown
vegetables, cheese and their own sauces and chutneys – but it
is the bread that makes this shop really special. Made on the
premises, there are all the basics, plus continental varieties and
some made with spelt. They all have the slightly heavier feel and
closer texture of proper home-made bread, and fantastic flavour.

food facts

MODERN BREAD

Lifestyles have changed a great deal in recent decades and we no longer shop
for food on a daily basis. This means that our foods need to have a longer
shelf life. We also want food to be cheap, and both these issues have caused
most modern bread to be very different from traditional loaves. The baking
industry has come up with two processes to enable bakers to produce longer
lasting and cheaper bread. The first is the Chorleywood Process, introduced in
the 1960s. As is so often the case with new food technologies, it is a way of
cutting down the time it takes to make a product, so that more food can be
made in less time, more cheaply. A traditional baker will allow his dough time
to ferment and develop and it is during this time that the flavour unfolds and
the flour becomes more digestible. Many artisan bakers will make dough the
night before baking, leaving it overnight to develop. The result will be a loaf of
satisfying texture and complex flavour. The Chorleywood method cuts this time
to less than an hour, by agitating the dough at high speed, which mellows the
gluten mechanically with the help of dough modifiers, such as ascorbic acid
and potassium bromate. In this way, the bread can be made quickly, but it will
lack some of the flavour and texture of a traditionally made loaf. We buy
70–80% of our bread from large commercial bakeries, so most of us are
eating bread made using the Chorleywood Process.

The second process is the Milton Keynes Process, which produces 'bake
off' breads. The dough is made in large bakeries and shipped to smaller
bakeries, which then bake the dough as needed. This type of dough is made
specifically for a long shelf life, and means that smaller bakeries need fewer
fully trained bakers, as half the work is already done. Both these processes
result in cheaper bread, but the casualty, as always, is flavour.

Long Crichel Bakery

Long Crichel, Wimborne, Dorset BH21 5SJ   T: 01258 830852   E: finebread@lineone.net

Very traditional methods are employed at this bakery, even down to the wood-fired oven that all the breads are baked in. An interesting range of both speciality breads and the more basic loaves, all organic. The dough is made for most of the breads at least 12 hours in advance, to allow proper development, and no additives are used at all.

The Old Farmhouse Bakery

Steventon, nr Abingdon, Oxfordshire OX13 6RP   T: 01235 831230

Katherine Bitmead specializes in old-fashioned, home-baked breads, using high-quality ingredients including locally milled flour. The breads, including the traditional cottage loaves, are all made by hand. To complement the range she also stocks a selection of farmhouse cheeses, home-made pies, cakes and quiches.

Bakers Basket

Woodway Farm, Bicester Road, Long Crendon, Aylesbury, Buckinghamshire HP18 9EP
T: 01844 202717
farmers' markets

Using local flour and baking from scratch, Ian Forster makes all manner of breads – from the basic white, brown and granary loaves, to rye bread, focaccias with pesto and black olives, and ciabatta. He even makes Danish pastries from scratch, too, and some of the breads are organic. Available only from farmers' markets around Oxfordshire – call for details, or see the Thames Valley Farmers Markets association website www.tvfm.org.uk.

Bread & Co

The Bakery, Tuthill Park, Wardington, nr Banbury, Oxfordshire OX17 1RY
T: 01295 758489   W: www.breadandco.co.uk
farmers' markets

Bread & Co is a young bakery producing a range of hand-crafted bread, from classic English recipes, using traditional time-honoured methods. Simplicity is the key here – for almost every variety of bread baked here, only four ingredients are used: flour, water, wild yeast, and salt. Old and traditional types of grain are used – spelt, rye and barley as well as wheat – and the dough is allowed to slowly develop to create a rich flavour and satisfying texture. Bread & Co even have plans to grow their own grain, such is their attention to detail. Find them at Stratford-on-Avon, Moreton-in-Marsh, Southam and Kenilworth markets.

SOUTH EAST · BEACONSFIELD

H P Jung

6 The Broadway, Beaconsfield, Buckinghamshire HP9 2PD T: 01494 673070
w: www.hpjung.com

A bakery and café specializing in continental breads, using recipes the owner brought back from many years training on the Continent. Everything is hand-made, and specialities include rye, corn and olive breads.

SOUTH EAST · BRIGHTON

Infinity Foods Bakery

25 North Road, Brighton BN1 1YA T: 01273 603563 w: www.infinityfoods.co.uk

---

A workers' co-operative of just four bakers, Infinity Foods produces breads from 100% organic ingredients. The interesting varieties include rye, sourdough, spelt, linseed, walnut and sunflower seed breads and focaccia – 30 varieties are made in all.

SOUTH EAST · BRIGHTON

Real Pâtisserie

43 Trafalgar Street, Brighton BN1 4ED T: 01273 570719 w: www.realpatisserie.co.uk
🛒 **farmers' markets**

Very traditional French-style breads and cakes are sold here, with a great choice of four different kinds of croissant and really authentic pastries and brioches. Buy direct from the shop or from many Sussex farmers' markets.

SOUTH EAST · COBHAM

The Pâtisserie

38 Station Road, Stoke D'Abernon, Cobham, Surrey KT11 3HZ T: 01932 863926
w: www.thepatisserie.co.uk

Long proving times and the stone-soled oven at The Pâtisserie combine to make tasty, traditional breads. Some are organic, and some are salt-free. Continental types of bread are well represented and also rye and sourdough.

Marsh Mellow Bakery

11 High Street, Dymchurch, Kent TN29 0NH   T: 01303 873297

farmers' markets

Using wheat grown and milled in the south east, Marsh Mellow Bakery make imaginative breads, including their Devil's Breath chilli bread. The breads are all hand-made with great attention to detail, with an expanded range for this year. Buy direct from the shop, and from Rye, Rolvenden, Egerton, Capel-le-Ferne and Cranbrook farmers' markets.

Oscar's Bakery

3 Limes Place, Preston Street, Faversham, Kent ME13 8PQ   T: 01795 532218

farmers' markets

A husband-and-wife team run this traditional bakery, producing classic British breads and Irish batch and rye breads. Nothing is rushed – the doughs used are traditional sponge doughs – and the flour is grown and milled locally. The bread can also be found at Cliftonville, Meopham, Lenham, and Rochester farmers' markets, and Harriet's Deli in Canterbury.

Cyrnel Bakery

Lower Road, Forest Row, East Sussex RH18 5HE   T: 01342 822283

farmers' markets

Cyrnel Bakery produce a big choice of breads, many of which are organic. Local ingredients are used wherever possible, including locally milled flour and free-range eggs from a nearby farm. The bread is available direct from the shop, or from several Sussex farmers' markets – call for details.

Flour Power City

57 North Street, Guildford, Surrey GU1 4AH T: 01483 561713
W: www.flourpowercity.com

Organic breads without additives, often using unusual grains, are the order of the day here. Organic cakes are on offer too, and everything is made by hand. Flour Power City is accredited by the Organic Food Federation.

Baker & Spice

47 Denyer Street, London SW3 2LX ALSO AT 75 Salusbury Road, Queens Park, London NW6 6NH T: 020 7589 4734 (DENYER ST); 020 7604 3636 (SALUSBURY ROAD)
W: www.bakerandspice.com

Traditional British breads, baked without additives. A true artisan bakery.

Born and Bread Organic Bakery

East Dulwich Deli, 15–17 Lordship Lane, London SE22 8EW T: 020 8693 2525
🛒 shop

Born and Bread use a French 20 ton wood-fired oven – the only one of its kind in the UK – to make a range of beautiful, hand-moulded artisan breads. Using all organic flour, the loaves range from the classic white and wholemeal, to focaccia, rye, and a traditional French baguette (renamed here the 'Kentish Flute'). Available direct from the shop, or from La Fromagerie (see page 67).

Breads Etcetera

Unit 1 Charterhouse Works, Eltringham Street, London SW18 1TD T: 07811 189545
W: www.breadsetcetera.com

Is this the smallest artisan bakery in London? The two members of staff at Breads Etcetera believe so. Rustic, hand-made loaves are produced here without commercial yeast, using organic flours. No artificial additives are used and time is of the essence – the dough is allowed plenty of time to develop before baking. Many London delis stock the bread – call to find your nearest.

super hero

THE CELTIC BAKERS, London (see below)

The Celtic Bakers have thought of every way possible to make their bread as ethically as they can. Not only is it 'real' bread – properly fermented, with no artificial additives and baked thoroughly on the oven bottom, but every measure has been taken to ensure it is environmentally friendly. The range is impressive, too – all the regulars, plus spelt, pain levain (a traditional French loaf made with natural leaven rather than commercial yeast), rye and sourdough. There is a real sense of openness about the company – absolutely nothing is hidden from its customers. Sarah at The Celtic Bakers is adamant that this is the bakery's policy. 'We feel that the message about honesty about what goes in bread is really important – down to the sunflower oil we line tins with (which in theory we don't have to mention in the ingredients because it's a "processing aid"). We choose to mention our processing aids because our customers might be allergic to them so they ought to know.' The website is a great education about the bread.

SOUTH EAST   LONDON

The Celtic Bakers

42b Waterloo Road, Cricklewood, London NW2 7UH   T: 020 8452 4390
w: www.thecelticbakers.co.uk
farmers' markets

Bread baked at The Celtic Bakers is all organic and the techniques used are environmentally friendly. See the Super Hero box, above, for more information.

SOUTH EAST   LONDON

& Clarkes

122 Kensington Church Street, London W8 4BH   T: 020 7229 2190
w: www.sallyclarke.com

A great range of traditional British and continental breads, all baked without artificial colours, preservatives or improvers and also available from Carluccio's, Selfridges and Harvey Nichols.

De Gustibus

53 Blandford Street, London W1H 3AF ALSO AT 53–55 Carter Lane, London EC4V 5AE
and 4 Southwark Street, London SE1 0JE T: 020 7486 6608 (BLANDFORD ST);
020 7236 0056 (CARTER LANE); 020 7407 3625 (SOUTHWARK ST)
W: www.degustibus.co.uk

De Gustibus's bread is legendary. Their range of hand-made breads
is incredible – recipes from America, Ireland, the continent, Eastern
Europe and the Mediterranean have all been sought, and some of
the more unusual breads include Old Milwaukee rye, honey and
lavender, savoury potato bread, Portuguese cornbread and potato
and yoghurt bread. Imagination and skill blended perfectly.

Flourish Bakery and Patisserie

Unit 7 Morrison Yard, 551a High Road, Tottenham, London N17 6SB
T: 0208 801 9696 W: www.flourishbakery.com
🗞 **farmers' markets**

At Flourish, traditional baking methods – long fermentations, hand-
moulding, no nasty additives – are used to make artisan breads, and
then an added helping of imagination takes these breads one step
further. Pain à l'ancienne and green peppercorn bread rub shoulders
with fresh pineapple and coconut or pear and chocolate Danish
pastries – all the benefits of tradition, with a dash of modern
funkiness! Find Flourish at Notting Hill and Pimlico farmers' markets.

The Lighthouse Bakery

64 Northcote Road, London SW11 6QL T: 020 7228 4537 W: www.lighthousebakery.co.uk

Classic British loaves and speciality continental breads rub
shoulders at the Lighthouse Bakery, all made with traditional
methods. Organic flour is used in many of the breads, but artificial
additives and improvers never are.

Neal's Yard Bakery

6 Neal's Yard, Covent Garden, London WC2H 9DP T: 020 7836 5199

Organic breads are made by hand on site at Neal's Yard Bakery, which produces a wide variety of loaves, some of which are wheat free. There is also a café, with lots of home-made dishes, and sandwiches made with their own breads.

The Old Post Office Bakery Ltd

76 Landor Road, London SW9 9PH   T: 020 7326 4408

All the breads made at the Old Post Office are accredited organic by the Soil Association. This bakery has been producing organic, hand-made, hand-kneaded breads for over 18 years, long before the organic movement was as well known as it is now. No improvers or additives are used and a particular speciality is the range of sourdough breads.

Poilâne

46 Elizabeth Street, London SW1W 9PA   T: 020 7808 4910

This French bakery is famous for its sourdough, baked on site in a wood and brick oven, an exact replica of a Roman oven. The shop is an off-shoot of the justly famous Parisian bakery that has been an institution for those seeking the best bread in Paris since Pierre Poilâne opened it in 1932.

Origin Foods

Unit 5, Bell Farm Industrial Park, Nut Hampstead, Royston, Hertfordshire SG8 8ND
T: 01763 849993
farmers' markets

100% organic, hand-made breads, including sourdoughs and unusual varieties such as hazelnut and raisin, and rosemary. No additives or flour improvers are used and the bakers allow proper fermentation times, starting baking at midnight to have bread ready for the morning. Available from many local farmers' markets – call for details.

Sarre Windmill

Canterbury Road, Sarre, Kent CT7 0JU   T: 01843 847573
🛒 **shop**

The wheat milled at Sarre comes from fields nearby, grown specially for them. One of only a handful of working, commercial windmills in the UK, the old-fashioned stonegrinding method produces tasty flour – the stones don't get hot, which can affect the flavour adversely. There is also a bakery and café on site.

Slindon Bakery

Slindon, West Sussex BN18 0RP   T: 01243 814369 OR 07741 053764
E: atc121@msn.com
🍴 **farmers' markets**

Traditional British breads such as the Sussex Kibble, milk and cottage loaves, and a Roman Army bread (made with spelt flour) are hand-made here with local ingredients and, always, English flour. Available from many farmers' markets in Hampshire, Sussex, Dorset and Surrey – call for details.

Artisan Bread

Units 16 & 17 John Wilson Business Park, Whitstable, Kent CT5 3QZ   T: 01227 771881
W: www.artisanbread.ltd.uk
✉ **mail order**

Artisan Bread mill their own grain for flour, often using unusual varieties. No yeast or tap water is used (only spring water), and minimal salt. Gluten-free breads are available. This is the UK's first biodynamic bakery. Call or check out the website to find your nearest stockist or order by mail.

The Winchester Bakery

37 Byron Avenue, Winchester, Hampshire SO22 5AT   T: 01962 859498
🍴 **farmers' markets**

Alison Reid makes proper bread – dense and heavy, a world away from the pre-cut fluffy loaves many of us buy at supermarkets.

She makes around 16 different loaves, which include the basics, plus rye bread, continental varieties and a sourdough using a 12-hour fermentation period. Alison's bread is available from Winchester, Basingstoke and Romsey farmers' markets.

All Natural Bakery

Unit 3, Sentinel Works, Northgate Avenue, Bury St Edmunds, Suffolk IP32 6AZ
T : 07956 026630   w: www.allnaturalbakery.co.uk
✉ mail order

Michael Goetze sacrifices a lot of sleep to produce great bread – he seldom leaves the bakery before 2am, and is usually back at 6am. Sourdough bread is the speciality at the All Natural Bakery, made slowly with great attention to detail, using the best quality flour he can find. The spelt bread he makes is, unusually, made with a white spelt flour, giving a lighter bread than most other spelts. He also makes gluten-free and yeast-free bread, and other wheat-free varieties, all organic or biodynamic. Find Michael's bread at many farm shops and delis around East Anglia (check the website for details), or by mail order.

The Mill Bakery

Harkers Lane, Swanton Morley, Dereham, Norfolk NR20 4PA   T: 01362 637212
w: www.themillbakery.co.uk

A craft bakery making traditional English breads, with an organic range and some of the less-well-known spelt and rye types. The Mill is accredited by the Organic Food Federation.

North Elmham Bakery

Eastgate Street, North Elmham, Dereham, Norfolk NR20 5HD   T: 01362 668548
E: northelmhambakery@btinternet.com

North Elmham Bakery is run by Norman Ollie, a tireless campaigner for 'real bread'. Everything here is made the old-fashioned way, with no short cuts and no additives. The bread is available from other outlets in Norfolk – call for details.

The Metfield Organic Bakery

The Stores, The Street, Metfield, Harleston, Norfolk IP20 0LB   T: 01379 586798

Out of the 20 breads produced at the Metfield Organic Bakery, 18 are certified organic and all are patiently hand-made, without additives. Some of the loaves are wheat-free and gluten-free; some are made without yeast. Metfield Bakery bread can be found in many healthfood stores around Norfolk and Suffolk; call to find your nearest.

Fosters Mill

Swaffham Prior, Cambridgeshire CB5 0JZ   T: 01638 741009   w: www.fostersmill.co.uk
✉ **mail order**

Fosters Mill is nine miles north east of Cambridge. A country mill built in 1858 and restored to working order in 1991, it has two sets of French burr stones, producing flours solely by wind power. The mill is open to the public on the second Sunday of each month. Flour can be ordered by telephone or purchased direct from local shops (call to find out where). All flour is produced from organic wheat – wholemeal, unbleached white, brown, semolina, rye and spelt. Wheat is sourced, where possible, from local farmers and through a local organic grain merchant. The mill also produces a range of breakfast cereals. Fosters Mill is a member of the Traditional Corn Millers Guild.

Tony's Bakery

1 Peel Street, Kidderminster, Worcestershire DY11 6UG   T: 01562 636463

Tony's use bread recipes going back 130 years and hand-make their bread without using any kinds of machines. The kitchens are open, so customers can see the bread being made.

True Loaf Bakery

super hero

Mount Pleasant Windmill, Kirton in Lindsey, North Lincolnshire DN21 4NH
T: 01652 640177   w: www.trueloafbakery.co.uk

Mervin Austin bakes bread using his own flour made from English wheat. See the Super Hero box, opposite, for more information.

super hero

MERVIN AUSTIN, owner of True Loaf Bakery (opposite)

Mervin Austin mills his own flour from English wheat, which marks him out right from the start. Canadian wheat has long been considered the best for breadmaking, because it can withstand the harsh commercial milling process better, allowing the starch to remain undamaged. Mervin comes at the process of milling from a different angle – instead of choosing wheat to fit the modern process, he has chosen old-fashioned methods, with traditional French burr stones and Derbyshire peak stones. This is a more gentle process, far less damaging to the wheat. The result is tasty, more digestible bread. His respect for tradition doesn't end there – the bread is baked in a wood-fired oven, which takes two weeks to reach temperature, and scrap wood is used as fuel wherever possible to limit the ecological impact. Both the flour and bread are available from the on site shop and café; try some of the traditional Lincolnshire Plum Loaf or the recently introduced organic soda bread flour.

MIDLANDS   LUDLOW

S C Price

7 Castle Street, Ludlow, Shropshire SY8 1AS T: 01584 872815
E: pricesthebakers@btinternet.com

Traditional bakers, producing award-winning bread the old-fashioned way for maximum flavour. Flour from Shipton Mill is used (see page 23), and long fermentation times. Specialities include sourdoughs, rye, and malted grain loaves.

MIDLANDS   MELTON MOWBRAY

Paul's

66–68 Snow Hill, Melton Mowbray, Leicestershire LE13 1PD T: 01664 560572
W: www.soyfoods.co.uk
🛒 **farmers' markets** 🚚 **delivery service**

The staff at Paul's are not interested in fast food, and call their products 'slow bread' – everything is made by hand using traditional methods, with wheat from a local biodynamic farm, milled locally. Sourdoughs, spelt, rye and barley breads are the specialities, all made without any flour improvers. Find the breads at Belper and Towcester farmers' markets.

FOOD HEROES OF BRITAIN

High Lane Oatcakes

597–599 High Lane, Burslem, Stoke-on-Trent, Staffordshire ST6 7EP   T: 01782 810180
w:www.highlaneoatcakes.co.uk

✉ **mail order**

One of the oldest established bakeries making traditional
Staffordshire oatcakes, a speciality of this area. Like pancakes, but
made with oatmeal, the oatcakes are a versatile food and can be
used for sweet or savoury meals. High Lane are widely believed to
make the best Staffordshire oakcakes, having developed their recipe
over the years.

The Moody Baker Workers Cooperative

3 West View, Front Street, Alston, Cumbria CA9 3SF   T: 01434 382003

The Moody Baker sources its ingredients as locally as possible and
uses organic flour and fair-trade products. Everything is hand-made
and there is a constantly changing repertoire of breads, so there are
always new products to try. A regional speciality available here is
Miner's Pie – a pastry with a seven-eighths savoury filling and one-
eighth sweet.

The Broughton Village Bakery

Princes Street, Broughton-in-Furness, Cumbria LA20 6HQ   T: 01229 716284

☎ **farmers' markets**

The bread at Broughton Village Bakery is made using mainly organic
local ingredients – the free-range eggs used in the cakes are laid
half a mile away and flour comes from The Watermill (see page 38
and the Super Hero box opposite). The breads available range from
the traditional to the imaginative: try basil and tomato bread, with
fresh basil and fresh tomatoes, not the dried kind, or All-Day
Breakfast bread, containing local bacon, eggs and cheese. The
cinnamon rolls are even made with organic cinnamon. There is a
café at the bakery, and the produce can also be found at Kendal,
Orton and Ulverston farmers' markets. The bakery is not open every
day, so call first.

Hazelmere Café and Bakery

1 & 2 Yewbarrow Terrace, Grange-over-Sands, Cumbria LA11 6ED   T: 01539 532972
E: hazelmeregrange@yahoo.co.uk

A fantastic range of breads, cakes, deli goods, jams, chutneys,
preserves and home-cooked meals, made predominantly with local
ingredients, is available here. The breads – from basic white and
brown loaves to focaccias and rye breads – is all hand-made without
additives or improvers by craft bakers. Ian and Dorothy, the owners,
recently won an award for their Cumberland Rum Nicky, a traditional
pastry dessert made to a 250-year-old local recipe, from the times
when Cumbria had strong trade links with the Caribbean. This really
is a treasure-trove of local produce and there is also a café.

super hero

ANA AND NICK JONES, owners of The Watermill, Little Salkeld (see page 38)

Ana and Nick Jones restored the watermill at Little Salkeld in 1975, and have
been milling the finest organic and biodynamic British grains ever since. They
have a passion for local food and would like to be able to buy Cumbrian wheat
but say 'there are no organic or biodynamic farms growing wheat in Cumbria at
the moment so we get all our wheat from two biodynamic farms – one in Kent and
one in Leicestershire. I want to tell our customers about the wheat – who grows it,
the different varieties, where it comes from, why we favour the biodynamic system'.
The real secret of the quality of the flour lies in the original French stones used to
grind the wheat; the process of traditional stonegrinding allows the wheatgerm oils
to be distributed throughout the flour, giving the characteristic nutty taste.

Ana feels that many people are put off making their own bread, believing it
to be a difficult and complicated process. 'I wish more people knew how quick,
easy and satisfying it is to make bread by hand, especially if the flour has been
ground the traditional way. I run a range of breadmaking, baking and vegetarian
cooking workshops at the mill and people are always amazed at what fun it is
and how easy too.' She is more than willing to offer help and advice to
customers embarking on their first home-made loaves. 'I feel that "small is
beautiful" when it comes to business, and put lots of care and commitment into
the process, the product, and into getting to know and help our customers to
get the best from our special flours'.

The wide range of flours, including spelt, wheat, rye, barley, flour mixes, and
all kinds of oat products, are available by mail order or from the mill, and there
is a tea room on site, with at least four or five different types of bread available.

Staff of Life

2 Berrys Yard, 27 Finkle Street, Kendal, Cumbria LA9 4AB   T: 01539 738606

Using flours from The Watermill (see below and the Super Hero box on page 37), Simon Thomas makes a great range of Mediterranean breads and sourdoughs, including a damson sourdough. Overnight fermentation for the breads allows the flavour to develop fully and the rye breads take even longer – they are allowed three or four days to develop.

The Village Bakery

Melmerby, Penrith, Cumbria CA10 1HE   T: 01768 881811   w: www.village-bakery.com
✉ **mail order**

This is one of the country's biggest organic bakeries, with a great choice of bread varieties, including some for those with wheat or yeast intolerances and there is a restaurant at the bakery, too. Village Bakery breads are available in branches of Waitrose and Sainsbury.

The Watermill super hero

Little Salkeld, Penrith, Cumbria CA10 1NN   T: 01768 881523   w: www.organicmill.co.uk
✉ **mail order**

A restored watermill milling the finest organic grains. See the Super Hero box, page 37, for more information.

Potts Bakers

Stanley Road, Stairfoot, Barnsley, South Yorkshire S70 3PG   T: 01226 249175
w: www.pottsbakers.co.uk
🛒 **farmers' markets**

A craft bakery, producing a wide assortment of breads, including focaccias, rye breads, sourdoughs and some organic varieties. The breads are made using the old-fashioned long-fermentation sponge process. All are available at the shop or from Holmfirth and Penistone farmers' markets.

Jo's Home Baked Bread

33 Rye Terrace, Hexham, Northumberland NE46 3DX T: 01434 608456
E: joburrill@btopenworld.com

🗪 **farmers' markets**

Jo Burrill started baking because she couldn't find bread locally that she liked and now she sells her imaginative, home-baked breads at Barnard Castle and Hexham farmers' markets. Using organic ingredients as far as possible, she bakes sourdoughs as well as regular white, wholewheat and granary breads, spelt bread, and her own speciality, Hadrian's Wall Roman Loaf.

Café Royal

8 Nelson Street, Newcastle-upon-Tyne NE1 5AW T: 0191 231 3000

If you pop into Café Royal, you'll find more than a good cup of coffee – you'll be able to pick up a loaf of delicious, continental-style, artisan bread. All hand-made, with no additives or improvers, sourdoughs are the speciality – the loaves are allowed over twelve hours of fermentation time, giving great flavour and texture.

Thomson's Bakery

385 Stamfordham Road, Westerhope, Newcastle upon Tyne NE5 5HA
T: 0191 286 9375 W: www.geordiebakers.co.uk

Thomson's bake some very unusual breads – brown ale bread (using the native brew) is a favourite, Spanish orange bread, soda breads and their own-recipe ciabatta are all popular. All the breads are made by hand and giving training to employees in traditional skills is integral to the policy of this bakery.

Davills Pâtisserie

24 West Gate, Ripon, North Yorkshire HG4 2BQ T: 01765 603544

The name Davills Pâtisserie could make you think you were going to find all manner of continental confectionery in this bakery but Davills is far better than that – it is a traditional artisan bakery, offering proper craft breads, all made by hand with locally milled British flour.

Heatherlea

94-96 Main Street, Bangor BT20 4AG   T: 028 9145 3157

A member of the Artisan Bakers of Northern Ireland, Heatherlea specialise in traditional griddle breads and classic wheaten bread.

Café Paul Rankin (Roscoff Bakery)

12–14 Arthur Street, Belfast BT1 4GD ALSO AT 27–29 Fountain Street, Belfast BT1 5EA and Castle Court Shopping Centre BT1 1DD   T: 028 9031 0108 (ARTHUR STREET); 028 9031 5090 (FOUNTAIN STREET); 028 9024 8411 (CASTLE COURT)

The Paul Rankin cafés are also outlets for the Roscoff Bakery, a traditional artisan Irish bakery. Everything is hand-made, and alongside the continental-style breads are native Irish varieties, such as soda and wheaten breads.

Ditty's Home Bakery

44 Main Street, Castledawson BT45 8AB. ALSO AT 3 Rainey Street, Magherafelt, Co. Londonderry BT45 5DA   T: 028 7946 8243 (CASTLEDAWSON); 028 7963 3944 (MAGHERAFELT)
w: www.dittysbakery.com

Robert Ditty bakes traditional Irish breads including soda and potato breads. See the Super Hero box, page 42, for more information. There is also a branch in Magherafelt.

Kitty's of Coleraine

3 Church Lane, Coleraine, Co. Londonderry BT52 1AG   T: 028 7034 2347

A branch of Hunter's of Limavady, see page opposite.

Camphill Organic Farm Shop & Bakery

8 Shore Road, Holywood, Co. Down BT18 9HX
T: 028 9042 3203

From entirely Soil-Association-accredited organic ingredients,
Rob Van Duin makes some unusual types of bread – sourdough, rye
bread, and bread from the old-fashioned spelt grain. Classic Irish
wheaten breads are available too.

Hunter's

5–9 Market Street, Limavady, Co. Londonderry BT49 0AB. ALSO AT 34 Main Street,
Ballykelly, Co. Londonderry BT49 9HS   T: 028 7772 2411 (LIMAVADY) AND
028 7776 6228 (BALLYKELLY)

All the classic Northern Irish breads can be found here – wheaten,
soda, and so on – all made by hand to old recipes. There is also
plenty of new produce to try – continental-style breads and cakes,
such as blueberry and cinnamon. There is a branch in Ballykelly as
well as Kitty's in Coleraine (see opposite).

The Country Kitchen Home Bakery

57–59 Sloan Street, Lisburn, Co Down BT27 5AG   T: 028 9267 1730
E: countrykitchen@bakery5759.fsnet.co.uk

A 4–5 year apprenticeship is required before you can call yourself a
baker at the Country Kitchen, testament to the level of skill required
to produce the breads and cakes. Great breads and really
imaginative cakes are made here.

The Corn Dolly Home Bakery

12 Marcus Square, Newry, Co. Down BT34 1AE   T: 028 3026 0524

Another great Irish artisan bakery, a member of Robert Ditty's group
(see his Super Hero entry on page 42). While the Corn Dolly
specializes in classic Irish breads, like batch bread and soda farls,
they are also trying their hands at continental breads, and the
ciabattas and focaccias, made with the same attention to detail.
There is also a branch in Warrenpoint (see page 42).

super hero

ROBERT DITTY, owner of Ditty's Home Bakery, Castledawson and Magherafelt
(see page 40)

Robert Ditty has a passion for keeping alive the traditions of Northern Irish baking. His two shops are filled with the heritage of his country – wheaten breads, soda breads, potato breads – all baked to the perfection that 30 years' experience allows. Ditty's is not a backward-looking establishment, though; Robert is always striving to bring new things to Irish taste buds, and he and a gang of equally enthusiastic Irish bakers often get together, swapping ideas and offering constructive criticism to ensure that artisan baking in Ireland remains part of modern culture. Instead of professional rivalry and secrets, this small guild of bakers (Artisan Bakers of Northern Ireland) is refreshingly eager to share knowledge in an effort to heighten the public's awareness of craft baking. Robert runs baking workshops at his premises, which attract amateur bakers from miles away, all keen to learn the secrets of traditional Irish baking. These workshops are so popular that they are usually booked up a year in advance.

NORTHERN IRELAND   NEWTOWNARDS

Knotts Cake and Coffee Shop

45 High Street, Newtownards BT23 7HS   T: 028 9181 9098

This artisan bakery sells all the classic Irish breads, but they also create a great selection of all-butter cakes, including some really rich boiled fruit cakes. The integral café offers plenty of wholesome savoury food, too, including a classic Irish stew, served in traditional hearty portions.

NORTHERN IRELAND   WARRENPOINT

The Corn Dolly Home Bakery

28 Church Street, Warrenpoint, Co. Down BT34 3HN   T: 028 4175 3596

A sister shop to Corn Dolly Home Bakery in Newry (see page 41).

The Stoneoven

Kingshill, Arklow, Co. Wicklow   T: 0402 39418

From this tiny bakery come some rare finds – pumpernickel, pure rye breads, organic spelt bread, 100% sourdoughs, and even 'grey bread' from the baker's native Cologne in Germany. All are made by hand with the kind of attention to detail you just don't get in big industrial bakeries.

Organico

Glengarriff Road, Bantry, Co. Cork   T: 027 51391

A mainly organic shop with a strong commitment to buying local or fair-trade produce. There is plenty of good food to choose from here, with organic fruit and vegetables, groceries and even locally made vegetarian sushi, but a big attraction is the bakery on the premises. The baker, Rachel Dare, uses organic ingredients to produce hand-made loaves, the specialities being the classic soda bread and an HRT Cake, for women of a certain age! There is also a café offering meals made with fair trade and organic ingredients.

Barron's Bakery

The Square, Cappoquin, Co. Waterford   T: 058 54045

Reputed to be the one of the oldest bakeries in Ireland, Barron's still use Scotch brick ovens instead of stone ovens to bake their hand-made breads. Traditional breads such as soda bread, barm brack, turnovers and blaas are the staples here. No mechanization is used at Barron's – as Esther Barron says, 'Bread-making is beyond science.' There is a teashop at the bakery, too.

Arbutus Bread

Rathdene, Montenotte, Cork   T: 086 3805 065   E: arbutus@iol.ie
🛒 farmers' markets

Fantastic hand-made breads, using long proving times and a range of French and Irish stoneground flours. West Cork brown soda bread, red wine and walnut bread, ryes, sourdoughs and continental varieties are all made, and are available from On The Pigs Back (see their entry on page 345), or from Midleton, Bantry, Kenmare, Dingle, Dungarvan, Cobh, Clonakilty and Macroom farmers' markets.

REPUBLIC OF IRELAND   DUBLIN

The Bakery

Pudding Row, Temple Bar, Dublin 8   T: 016 729882

The kitchens at The Bakery are open plan and customers can watch the breads and cakes being made – no pre-mixed products or short cuts here, just the skills of trained bakers proudly on display. There are all the great Irish breads, with the soda and wheaten breads made the old-fashioned way, with buttermilk, not yeast, not to mention foccacias, rye breads, croissants, Danish pastries and pains au chocolat – all hand-made.

REPUBLIC OF IRELAND   GALWAY

Goya's

Kirwan's Lane, Galway   T: 091 567010   W: www.goyas.ie

All the breads and pastries here are made by hand and with the best ingredients. The sweet pastries are what Goya's are renowned for, but they also do a good range of Irish breads.

SCOTLAND   ABERDEEN

Newton Dee Bakery

Newton Dee Village, North Deeside Road, Bieldside, nr Aberdeen AB15 9DX
T: 01224 868243 OR 01224 868701   W: www.newtondee.org.uk

Part of the Camphill Trust centre for adults with learning disabilities, Newton Dee Bakery produces some unusual breads using organic flour and grains. Everything is hand-made, with many breads receiving an overnight fermentation to allow the flavour to develop. Sourdoughs and rye breads are a speciality and Clara, the baker, makes a Spanish farmhouse-style bread, using her grandparents' recipe.

BREAD

Campbell's Bakery

59 King Street, Crieff, Perthshire PH7 3HB   T: 01764 652114
w: www.campbellsbakery.com

🧺 shop

Campbell's Bakery are busy encouraging Perthshire residents to try some unusual varieties of bread – specialities include ryebreads, brioche, focaccias, bagels and seeded loaves. Everything is hand-made, using long fermentation times. All the regular types of bread are available here, too, but it is with their less-well-known varieties that Campbells really shine.

food facts

THE IMPORTANCE OF THE RIGHT FLOUR

I can remember trying to bake some baguettes from a Julia Child recipe in the late 1970s and realizing that the only way I could hope for a good result was to try to get unbleached flour from France. Today the range of flours available is much more impressive. The bakers in this guide go to enormous lengths to locate the best flour, realizing that it makes a huge difference to the end result.

Many insist that Canadian hard wheat makes the best flour for bread. The hardness of the wheat is governed by the protein content: the higher it is, the stronger the flour. A stonger flour leads to a more elastic gluten structure in the dough, which traps more air and produces a lighter loaf. There are some millers in the UK, however, who grind traditional soft British wheats, such as spelt (an ancient grain), with great success, and mention the special nuances of flavour that local grain gives to bread – spelt imbues the bread with a pleasing nutty flavour, for instance. The Watermill at Little Salkeld in Cumbria (page 38) is a good example. Here, old British flours made from native grains are being revived, such as maslin flour (a mixture of soft wheat and rye), which was widely used in the Middle Ages but had been forgotten about until recently.

How flour is milled makes a difference to flavour, too. The modern way, using high-speed, steel rollers to crush the grain, is said by many to denature flour by excluding all the bran and wheat germ. The speed also produces a lot of heat, which can compromise the taste by damaging enzymes in the flour. The traditional way, using huge stones, doesn't produce heat and allows a little natural imperfection in the finished flour.

Au Gourmand

1 Brandon Terrace, Edinburgh EH3 5EA   T: 0131 624 4666

Classic French breads made by hand on the Au Gourmand premises
include baguettes, sourdoughs, walnut, olive and almond breads.
The bakery is part of a café and deli where a respect for the
traditions of French food is to the fore.

The Engine Shed Bakery

19 St Leonard's Lane, Edinburgh EH8 9SD and at 123 Bruntsfield Place, Edinburgh EH10
4EQ   T: 0131 662 0040 (ST LEONARD'S LANE); 0131 229 6494 (BRUNTSFIELD PLACE)
W: www.engineshed.org.uk

All the breads made at the Engine Shed, a training centre for people
with disabilities which has a small craft bakery, are organic, with
some made with biodynamic flour. All the usual kinds of bread are
available and also some more unusual loaves – rye sourdough, with
100% rye, grain molasses bread, herb bread, and oatbread. The
breads are available from the shop at Bruntsfield Place. The Engine
Shed is accredited by the Organic Food Federation.

McPhies   super hero

1527 Shettleston Road, Glasgow G32 9AS   T: 0141 778 4732

Jim and Craig McPhies are craftsman bakers using traditional
techniques. See the Super Hero box, opposite, for more information.

Star Continental Bakery

158 Fore Street, Glasgow G14 0AE   T: 0141 959 7307

Continental breads such as focaccia, ciabatta and panini rub
shoulders with Russian rye and sourdoughs at this speciality bakery.
There is no machinery involved – everything is made by hand and
baked in old stone ovens. Star Continental is really a wholesaler but,
if you phone, their friendly staff will tell you where to find the bread
or – if you are lucky – they might sell you some from the door.

super hero

JIM AND CRAIG MCPHIES, owners of McPhies Bakery, Glasgow (see opposite)

McPhies, a family-run bakery, is wholeheartedly resisting pressure to change from the traditional methods by which their bread is produced. Using wheat from Scottish millers, McPhies produce hand-made breads with very little mechanization. While this inevitably leads to long hours for the bakers, they have no intention of making life easier for themselves by turning to a modern, time-saving mode of baking. Jim McPhies and his son, Craig, are adamant that the skills of the craftsman baker will not be submerged in the tide of modernization. At a time when craft baking skills are becoming more and more marginalized, the McPhies family is determined that its bakery will be staffed only by those with a commitment to real baking and a thorough training in the discipline. Young bakers joining the company can expect a full schooling in the ways of a traditional bakery; an apprenticeship to become a baker at McPhies lasts three years, testament to the level of skill that is the backbone of this company.

SCOTLAND   INVERURIE

J G Ross

Elphinstone Road, Inverurie, Grampian AB51 3UR   T: 01467 620764

'Butteries' are a very popular north-east Scottish breakfast food similar to a croissant, and were developed for fishermen to take on the boats, as they last longer than bread. The bakers at J G Ross still make them by hand – they say that you just don't get as good a buttery if it is machine made. Though they make all kinds of breads, it is for their butteries that they are best known.

SCOTLAND   PITTENWEEM

Adamson's Bakery

12 Routine Row, Pittenweem, KY10 2LG   T: 01333 311336

Adamson's is famous for its oatcakes, made in the best Scottish tradition. So good are they that you will find them in Iain Mellis's cheese shops and Neal's Yard Dairy in London (see their separate entries in the dairy section, pages 90, 92, 94 and 67).

FOOD HEROES OF BRITAIN

The Island Bakery

Main Street, Tobermory, Isle of Mull PA75 6PU   T: 01688 302225
w: www.islandbakery.co.uk
✉ mail order

Hand-crafted loaves, with great attention to detail, including rye,
soda and pumpkin breads, appear here alongside regular kinds
of loaves. The choice is constantly changing to keep customers
interested. The Island Bakery has a second string to its bow, in the
guise of Island Bakery Organics (01688 302223), producing hand-
made, award-winning biscuits from organic ingredients. Made in
small batches, with generous lashings of butter and chocolate,
the biscuits are the kind you would like to make at home but know
you'll never get round to. These are available from the bakery or
from many outlets around the UK, including Harvey Nichols and
Selfridges, and by mail order.

Lewis Fine Foods

Unit 2, Village Farm Industrial Estate, Pyle, Bridgend CF33 6BJ   T: 01656 749441

For details, see under the Porthcawl branch on page 51.

Allen's Bakery

Rear of 11 Arran Place, Roath, Cardiff CF24 3SA   T: 02920 481219
E: johnbakerboy@aol.com

Hand-made bread, some organic, from traditional British varieties to
focaccias, ciabattas and sourdoughs. A good range of flavoured
breads is also available – walnut, garlic, onion and rosemary – and
customers can watch the bread being made from the counter.

Popty'r Dref

Upper Smithfield Street, Dolgellau, Gwynedd LL40 1ET   T: 01341 422507

A craft bakery, using locally milled unbleached flours to produce
classic breads. Everything is made by hand, including the famous
bara brith. There is now a deli section.

Pantri Nolwenn

35 Barham Road, Trecwn, Haverfordwest, Pembrokeshire SA62 5XX   T: 01348 840840
🝰 farmers' markets

Using organic ingredients, Pantri Nolwenn make artisan (hearth-style) breads for which, in keeping with the tradition of the craft, spelt is the grain of choice. Other rustic grains include oat, rye and barley, so people with wheat intolerances are well catered for. All of the leavened breads use an 18-hour fermentation period and no commercial yeast is used. There are wholemeal and brown, fruit and nut loaves, the ever popular olive bread and other savouries, rye breads and many more. Spreads for the breads are also featured, such as hummus and baba ghanoush, all unpasteurized. There is also a mouthwatering choice of cookies and cakes. All available from Haverfordwest and Fishguard farmers' markets and some local outlets.

Wigmore's Bakery

9 St Mary's Street, Monmouth NP25 3DB   T: 01600 712083
🝰 farmers' markets

Using local ingredients as much as possible and employing an old-fashioned overnight resting period for the dough, Wigmore's make a good range of breads. All the regulars can be found (whites, browns and wholemeals), as well as sourdoughs, a Stilton and walnut bread and a classic bara brith cake. Find the produce at the bakery itself or at Usk farmers' market. Wigmore's was voted Tastiest Bakery in Wales 2004.

Bacheldre Watermill

Churchstoke, Montgomery, Powys SY15 6TE   T: 01588 620489
w: www.bacheldremill.co.uk
✉ mail order

Matt and Anne Scott took over Bacheldre Mill two years ago, and since then they have been busy producing award-winning artisan flours. There is a good range, from classic unbleached white, to spelt, durum and rye. The flour is all organic, all milled with French Burr stones, a slow and gentle method that allows the wheat germ to remain within the flour, giving a wonderful flavour and texture, and it is milled to order which means that the flour is always very fresh.

food facts

ADDITIVES IN BREAD AND FLOUR

Most of us think of bread as a fairly unadulterated food; simply made from a few basic ingredients. So it should be, but many of the loaves available have been made quickly, to a price, with a longer shelf life in mind. This inevitably means that they need a range of additives. Flour improver is the first – often this additive is used to increase the volume of the bread, to get a bigger loaf, and to make the bread softer. Enzymes can be used to speed the baking process. Emulsifiers are sometimes used so that the dough can withstand the industrial treatment it will receive in the large-scale bakeries. Preservatives, mould-inhibitors and crumb softeners will be required to extend shelf life. A good local baker has no need for artificial additives – he will bake the bread from scratch in the morning, and it will be sold to customers who understand that the bread is designed to be eaten that day, or the next.

Millers in this country are forced to put additives into their flour – a preparation of artificial chalk and iron – and this goes for organic millers, too. This law is a somewhat anachronistic attempt to ensure that the population does not suffer from rickets or other diseases related to poor diet. Many organic millers are very unhappy with this regulation – they maintain that there is no need for these additives, and that they are absolutely contrary to what organic produce is all about. The Traditional Corn Millers Guild is at the forefront of the protest, and represents many millers who are upholding the skills, traditions and heritage of the milling industry in Britain. Some of the mills we feature in this guide are members. For more information, contact Fosters Mill (01638 741009).

WALES   PEMBROKE

The Golden Crust Bakery

Lamphey, Pembroke, Pembrokeshire SA71 5NR   T: 01646 672102

Ian White at The Golden Crust is proud of the bread he bakes. He uses the best-quality flour he can, saying, 'quality of bread depends on quality of flour', and bakes using a traditional fermentation cycle, leaving the dough to develop for varying periods to create different styles of bread. The third generation of bakers in his family, he is still using original family recipes.

super hero

MICHAEL HALL, owner of Y Felin Mill, St Dogmaels (see below)

At last count, Y Felin was one of only a handful of working watermills in Wales and it has been around a very long time – since the 12th century. It has been completely renovated and visitors can see the original mechanisms at work – milling stones made of rock from France and Derbyshire. Michael Hall, the miller, is passionate about the flour he mills, and wherever possible, he uses Welsh grain. Although the mill itself is very traditional, Michael is distinctly forward-thinking in terms of the flour he produces; alongside organic wholemeal, he mills wholemeal mixed with seeds and herbs and even a garlic and chive flour. Organic spelt flour, 100% rye, gluten-free flour and even a mix for Irish soda bread is available – there really is everything a home baker could want here. The on-site tearoom sells bread made with all the varieties of flour. With so few traditional mills still working, Michael feels that his mill 'is an endangered species and needs tender loving care'. The survival of such vital parts of our food heritage depends on dedicated people like Michael.

WALES   PORTHCAWL

Lewis Fine Foods

8 Well Street, Porthcawl, Bridgend CF36 3BE   T: 01656 783300

Hand-made speciality breads, including focaccia, brioches, rye bread, walnut bread, basic white and wholemeal bread, and speciality Welsh cakes. Some of the produce is organic.

WALES   ST DOGMAELS

Y Felin   super hero

St Dogmaels, Pembrokeshire SA43 3DY   T: 01239 613999   w:www.yfelin.com
🛒 **farmers' markets** 🏪 **shop**

A working water mill making its own flour and with a shop and café on site. See the Super Hero box, above, for more information.

CHAPTER

2

The majority of cheese bought in this country is in the form of rectangular blocks which come from industrial-scale dairies. Here, automated processes producing large quantities of cheese very cheaply have superseded the traditional art of cheesemaking. In recent years, however, there has been a small but growing renaissance of farmhouse, or artisan cheesemakers; producers using old-fashioned methods, making individual 'truckles' or wheels of cheese instead of bigger blocks and choosing their ingredients with the utmost care. Many cheesemakers insist that cows grazing the richest pasture produce the finest, tastiest milk. Many of the artisan cheesemakers we feature use the milk of their own single herd of animals, and they feel this gives the cheese a distinctiveness. The larger quantities of milk required for larger-scale cheesemaking are likely to be from mixed herds spread over a wide area. The choice of a specific breed of cow or sheep can result in a defined regional feel to some farmhouse cheeses; Ayrshire cows in Scotland, or Jerseys further south. Llanboidy Cheesemakers (see the entry on page 99) use the milk of their own rare-breed Red Poll cows – they are believed to be the only cheesemakers in Europe to use milk from this breed. Time is of the essence, too – the traditional cheesemaker will never hurry the process and will give his or her cheese the right length of time to mature; I have also included some

dairy and eggs

cheesemongers here who have their own maturing rooms, such is their dedication to keeping the cheese in perfect condition.

While large-scale commercially produced cheese is a consistent product, artisan cheeses change with the seasons, according to the pasture the animals are grazing and the weather. Industrial dairies tailor the milk they use to fit their processes; craftsmen cheesemakers are less rigid and will adjust the process to suit the milk they have, often making minute adjustments according to different seasonal conditions. Some cheesemakers only use summer milk, when the cows are grazing on fresh grass; they say the silage the cows eat over the winter has a detrimental effect on the flavour of the milk. Instead of producing cheese using a mechanized process, small dairies offer a hand-made product, in which the cheesemaker uses his or her skill and intuition to time every process to produce the best result. These variants result in a lack of uniformity; cheese bought from an artisan cheesemaker one month may have a slightly different taste or texture the next. In an age of standardization, these inconsistencies could be seen as imperfections but, really, we should see it as a link with our natural heritage. This section is not just about cheese, however, there are also producers of milk, cream and yoghurt, eggs and ice cream, all doing things very differently to the big commercial producers of these foods.

FOOD HEROES OF BRITAIN

Bath Soft Cheese Company

Park Farm, Kelston, Bath BA1 9AG   T: 01225 331601   W: www.bathsoftcheese.co.uk
✉ **mail order**

In conversion to organic status, Park Farm have won both gold and silver medals at the British Cheese Awards. The soft cheese is made to an 1801 recipe, using the pasteurized cows' milk of the farm's own herd. Available by mail order and from shops and delis.

The Fine Cheese Co.

29–31 Walcot Street, Bath, BA1 5BN   T: 01225 448748   W: www.finecheese.co.uk
✉ **mail order**

The product list of the Fine Cheese Company reads like the British Cheese Award winners' list. Plenty of British artisan cheeses, and a good selection of continentals, too.

Paxton & Whitfield

1 John Street, Bath BA1 2JL   T: 01225 466403   W: www.paxtonandwhitfield.co.uk

A cheesemonger with a 200-year-history and a great selection of artisan cheeses – plenty of British cheeses are represented. There are other branches in London and Stratford-upon-Avon (see pages 68 and 75).

Forge Farm

Tregreenwell, nr St Teath, Bodmin, Cornwall PL30 3JJ   T: 01840 212348
🛒 **farmers' markets**

Eggs are the speciality here – hen, duck, goose and quail, all free-range and available from Truro and Wadebridge farmers' markets.

Lower Bodiniel Farm

Bodmin, Cornwall PL31 2PF   T: 01208 74136   E: rosemarybryantx@hotmail.co.uk
✉ **farm gate sales**

Really tasty organic free-range eggs from birds raised in small flocks. Available from the farm gate or from Carley's in Truro (see page 24).

(see page 24)

Modbury Farm

Burton Bradstock, Bridport, Dorset DT6 4NE   T: 01308 897193
E: timgarry@btinternet.com
⬇ **farm shop**

Organic Jersey milk and cream (unpasteurized), home-grown organic seasonal vegetables and other local produce are sold in the Garry family's farm shop, along with pork, sausages and bacon from organically reared, rare-breed Saddleback pigs. Open all day, every day.

Cerney Cheese

Chapel Farm, North Cerney, Cirencester, Gloucestershire GL7 7DE   T: 01285 831312
🛒 **farmers' markets**

A recent winner of the Supreme Champion medal at the British Cheese Awards, Cerney Cheese produces goats' cheese in two varieties – a mild, black-ash-covered pyramid and a stronger rind variety, rind-washed in grape brandy and wrapped in vine leaves. Available from Stroud, Cheltenham, Cirencester, Stow-on-the-Wold, Winchcombe and Bourton-on-the-Water farmers' markets, and also Fortnum & Mason in London and Paxton & Whitfield (see pages 54, 68 and 75).

Woolsery Cheese

The Old Dairy, Up Sydling, Dorchester, Dorset DT2 9PQ   T: 01300 341991
🛒 **farmers' markets**

Woolsery Cheese is a consistent award-winner at the British Cheese Awards. The cheeses are made with goats' and cows' milk, all from local farms; a feta-style goats' cheese, a full-fat hard, a semi-soft and a soft goats' cheese are joined by a Cheddar-style and a semi-hard cows' milk cheese. Available from many local farmers' markets; call for details.

Cornish Farmhouse Cheeses

Menallack Farm, Treverva, nr Falmouth, Cornwall TR10 9BP   T: 01326 340333
E: menallack@FSBdial.co.uk
🥄 **farm shop**

Menallack Farm produces a varied range of their own cheeses, using local cows', goats' and ewes' milk, and buffalo milk from Devon. All unpasteurized, 19 varieties are produced in all, in small batches, and customers at the farm shop can watch the process by visiting the cheese room and participate in talks, tours and group tastings.

Not content to just stock their own cheese, the Minson family also fill their farm shop with almost every other Cornish farmhouse cheese currently being made.

Little Bosoha

Trenear, Helston, Cornwall TR13 0HG   T: 01326 572409
📧 **farm gate sales**

Free-range eggs from a small flock with acres of fertilizer-free pasture to range on. The yolks are a deep golden yellow, great for baking.

Pengoon Farm

Nancegollan, Helston, Cornwall TR13 0BH   T: 01326 561219
🥄 **farm shop**

From a herd of just a half-dozen Jersey cows, Mr and Mrs East make traditional clotted cream and farmhouse butter, and untreated milk and free-range eggs are also available, direct from the farm.

Blissful Buffalo

Belland Farm, Tetcott, Holsworthy, Devon EX22 6RG   T: 01409 271406
W: www.blissfulbuffalo.fsnet.co.uk
🥄 **farmers' markets**

Mozzarella and a selection of hard cheeses made from the farm's own herd of water buffalo. The milk from these animals is higher in calcium and lower in cholesterol than cows' milk. Blissful Buffalo cheeses are available from lots of Devon farmers' markets, including Cullompton, Crediton, Kingsbridge, Exmouth, Tavistock, Launceston and Totnes.

Middle Campscott Farm

Lee, Ilfracombe, Devon EX34 8LS   T: 01271 864621   w: www.middlecampscott.co.uk
📠 **farm gate sales** 📧 **mail order**

A range of four hand-made cheeses, using unpasteurized milk from the farm's own flocks of goats and sheep. Middle Campscott Farm cheeses have won four British Cheese Award medals and one at the World Cheese Awards. Available from Ilfracombe and Barnstaple Pannier markets, and Combe Martin and Lynton farmers' markets.

West Hill Farm

West Down, Ilfracombe, North Devon EX34 8NF   T: 01271 815477
w: www.westhillfarm.org
📠 **farm gate sales**

Recent winners of two Taste of the West awards, West Hill Farm offers a rare chance to get your hands on milk that has not undergone homogenization, the process that breaks up the fat globules in the milk so that the fat is evenly distributed throughout. Why would you want unhomogenized milk? Sue Batstone of West Hill Farm says that 'homogenization is a very fierce process', it changes the structure of the milk and hence its flavour. Health concerns have been raised with homogenized milk – some people believe that it renders the fat globules small enough to pass directly into the bloodstream.

The milk from West Hill has old-fashioned flavour and texture. Also available are organic clotted cream and a cream Sue has developed herself – she calls it 'crusty cream' – which is like clotted cream, but has been air dried, not cooked, so it has a fresher flavour.

Helsett Farm

Lesnewth, Boscastle, Cornwall PL35 0HP   T: 01840 261207

28 flavours of hand-made ice cream heaven, made with milk and cream from the farm's own organic dairy herd. This is ice cream on a small scale, and it tastes all the better for it, with unusual flavours like saffron, honey and lavender and peppered strawberry

accompanying the more traditional flavours. Find Helsett Farm ice cream at Di's Dairy, Oughs, Rosuick Farm Shop near Helston, VG Deli at Launceston, or Bangors Organic Tea Rooms at Poundstock near Bude.

SOUTH WEST   LISKEARD

Cornish Cheese Co.

Cheesewring Dairy, Knowle Farm, Upton Cross, Liskeard, Cornwall PL14 5BG
T: 01579 363660   w: www.cornishcheese.co.uk
✉ mail order

High on Bodmin Moor, Philip and Carol Stansfield use the milk from their own dairy herd to produce five varieties of cheese, the most famous being Cornish Blue, a Gorgonzola-style rich and creamy cheese. There's also a pungent cider-washed rind cheese, a camembert-style, and a brie.

SOUTH WEST   LOSTWITHIEL

Trewithen Farm Foods

Greymare Farm, Lostwithiel, Cornwall PL22 0LW   T: 01208 872214
w: www.cornishfarmdairy.co.uk
🚩 farm gate sales ✉ mail order

Trewithen Farm make clotted cream the traditional way – the milk used comes from the farm's own herd of cows, which are, in turn, fed on home-grown feed. Farmhouse butter and buttermilk are also available, along with crème fraîche and yoghurts.

SOUTH WEST   NEWQUAY

Cornish Country Larder

The Creamery, Trevarrian, Newquay, Cornwall TR8 4AH   T: 01637 860331
w: www.ccl-ltd.co.uk

Interesting cheeses made from local Cornish milk, including an organic brie, are available from supermarkets and good delis, and the company also supplies to the trade.

SOUTH WEST   OKEHAMPTON

Curworthy Cheese

Stockbeare Farm, Jacobstowe, Okehampton, Devon EX20 3PZ   T: 01837 810587
🚩 farm gate sales

Rachel Stevens makes her own-recipe cheese, lying somewhere between a Gouda and a Cheddar, from the pasteurized milk of her own cows. She sells the cheese at different stages of maturity, from three to six months. The latter – though well matured, she points out – is not a 'gum stinger': in other words, not so strong that it will take the roof of your mouth off! Available direct from the dairy, or from specialist cheese shops, or from Waitrose branches in the South West.

Ashmore Farmhouse Cheese

Lime Tree Cottage, Ashmore, Salisbury, Wiltshire SP5 5AQ.   T: 01747 812337
✉ **farm gate sales** ✉ **mail order**

Pat and David Doble make an unpasteurized cows' milk cheese to their own Cheddar-style recipe. Made by hand in small batches, the cheese won a silver medal at the 2002 British Cheese Awards. Available by mail order or direct from the dairy.

Lyburn Farmhouse Cheesemakers

Lyburn Farm, Landford, Salisbury, Wilts SP5 2DN   T: 01794 390451
w: www.lyburncheese.co.uk
⬇ **farm shop** ☰ **farmers' markets**

The Smale family make pasteurized cheeses from the milk of their own cows and were successful at the 2002 British Cheese Awards, winning a silver medal for their Lyburn Garlic and Nettle. At the farm shop on site, visitors can watch the cheesemaking process, and seasonal organic vegetables are also on offer.

Alham Wood Cheeses

Higher Alham Farm, West Cranmore, Shepton Mallett, Somerset BA4 6DD
T: 01749 880221   w: www.buffalo-cheese.co.uk
⬇ **farm shop** ☰ **farmers' markets**

Biodynamic unpasteurized buffalo milk is the basis of Frances Wood's cheese. The main variety is Junas, based on an old mountain recipe and a bit like pecorino; a fresh cheese, good for salads, is also available. There is a viewing area at the dairy so that visitors can watch the cheesemaking, and the farm shop also offers buffalo meat and related products, all from the farm's own herd.

food facts

THE PASTEURIZATION DEBATE

Whether or not to pasteurize the milk used for cheesemaking is a hotly debated topic. Many cheesemakers say that pasteurizing milk kills not only the 'bad' bacteria that can cause food poisoning but also the 'good' bacteria responsible for flavour. For the last decade or so there has been a great deal of pressure on cheesemakers to pasteurize all cheeses and many producers have felt forced to begin pasteurization. Others are happy to pasteurize, feeling that it is a small price to pay for peace of mind against the slightest risk of contamination, in spite of the fact that unpasteurized cheeses are almost never the cause of food poisoning. In this chapter I've included cheesemakers who produce both pasteurized and unpasteurized cheeses, all of fantastic quality – it's up to you to taste and decide which you prefer.

SOUTH WEST   SHEPTON MALLET

Westcombe Dairy

Westcombe Farm, Evercreech, nr Shepton Mallet, Somerset BA4 6ER   T: 01749 831300
⬧ farm shop

Richard Calver at Westcombe Farm makes an unpasteurized, traditional Somerset Cheddar with the milk from his own cows. Maturing for a minimum of 11 months, and often for over 18 months, the cheese is a very full flavoured, traditionally cloth-bound, mature Cheddar. Westcombe Farm is part of a 'Slow Food Presidium' – an endorsement from Slow Food International of the farm's commitment to the ethics of artisan cheesemaking. At the farm there is a viewing window and farm shop.

SOUTH WEST   SHEPTON MALLET

R A Duckett

Westcombe Farm, Evercreech, nr Shepton Mallet, Somerset BA4 6ER   T: 01749 831300
▨ farm gate sales

Chris Duckett makes just one variety of cheese – a Caerphilly – but he is the third generation of his family to make it and has just been rewarded with a gold medal for it at the prestigious Nantwich Cheese Show. His cheese is made with milk from the herd at Westcombe Farm, ensuring full traceability.

Dorset Blue Cheese Company

Woodbridge Farm, Stock Gaylard, Sturminster Newton, Dorset DT10 2BD
T: 01963 23216   w: www.dorsetblue.com

Although Dorset Blue Vinny was a big part of West Country
cheesemaking history, sadly, the art of making it had been lost until
Mike Davies, after a prolonged period of trial and error, went into
small-scale production of it a few years ago. It is now available in
many good cheesemongers and delis, and Waitrose branches in
the South West.

Berkeley Farm Dairy

Swindon Road, Wroughton, Swindon, Wilts SN4 9AQ   T: 01793 812228
farm gate sales

Organic farmhouse butter, milk and cream is made from the rich milk
of the farm's herd of Guernsey cows. There is an on-site servery for
visitors to buy from, but call first.

Country Cheeses

Market Road, Tavistock, Devon PL19 0BW   T: 01822 615035
w: www.countrycheeses.co.uk
mail order

This cheese shop specialises in the wonderful cheeses of the
south west – in fact, 95% of the cheeses they stock are from the
West Country, including some that are specially made for the shop.
Alongside the cheeses are ice-creams, jams, apple juices and
desserts, all locally made. There is also a branch in Topsham
(see page 62).

The House of Cheese

13 Church Street, Tetbury, Gloucestershire GL8 8JG   T: 01666 502865
w: www.houseofcheese.co.uk
mail order

You will find 120 different types of cheese at this cheesemonger's,
many of them from small British producers.

Country Cheeses

26 Fore Street, Topsham, Devon EX3 0HD   T: 01392 877746

For details see under the Tavistock branch on page 61.

Sharpham Creamery

Sharpham Partnership, Sharpham House, Ashprington, Totnes, Devon TQ9 7UT
T: 01803 732203   W: www.sharpham.com
🥄 **farm shop**

Sharpham Farm has its own herd of Jersey cows. The owners were told many years ago that the milk would be no good for making cheese – too creamy, fat globules too big, advisers said. Twenty-one years on, the Jersey milk cheese at Sharpham is going strong. The three types available at the on-site shop are a brie-style, a triple-cream, and a harder, natural-rind variety.

Barwick Farm

Tregony, Truro, Cornwall TR2 5SG   T: 01872 530208
🛒 **farmers' markets** 🚚 **delivery service**

Nick Michell is a traditional butter-maker, a great rarity now. See the Super Hero box, opposite, for more information.

Ben's Hens

Little Callestock Farm, Zelah, Truro, Cornwall TR4 9HB   T: 01872 540445
📬 **farm gate sales**

Organic free-range eggs from a flock of fewer than 50 birds are available direct from the farm. The Down family also have accommodation available, where guests can enjoy other organic produce from the farm.

super hero

NICK MICHELL, of Barwick Farm, Truro (see opposite)

Traditional butter-makers are a rare breed these days, and getting rarer. This makes it all the more welcome to find Nick Michell at Barwick Farm, a man with very firm ideas about the food industry. The first thing he'll tell you is that you'll never find his products in a supermarket – he believes in selling locally. The butter and clotted cream he makes are further revelation – the butter a pronounced golden yellow colour, coming as it does from the milk of the farm's own herd of Jersey cows, a breed famed for butter-making. The clotted cream is made traditionally and is that perfect balance of firm crust and smooth cream. Both products owe their quality to the unhurried nature of their production and Nick and his wife Barbara's firm belief in doing things traditionally (the only way they've ever known) – watching Nick make the butter by hand is therapeutic and he clearly finds the process both creative and satisfying. Having been almost ruined by the artificially low price being paid by wholesalers for milk, the Michells, now they have diversified, find their products in great demand and they like the fact that they sell direct to their customers, building relationships with regulars and getting feedback about the produce. A great bonus is that all the products – milk, cream, salted, unsalted and garlic butter and curd cheese – are organic. Find the Michells at Truro Saturday farmers' market and Tuesday produce market and at Wadebridge and Veryan WI markets. They also do a delivery round in St Agnes – call for details.

SOUTH WEST   TRURO

The Cheese Shop

29 Ferris Town, Truro, Cornwall TR1 3JH   T: 01872 270742
W: www.thecheeseshop.co.uk
🛒 **shop** ✉ **mail order**

Stephen Gunn is everything you could hope for in a cheesemonger – he meticulously matures the cheese he sells in his own maturing room, supports and advises local small-scale cheese producers, and has a background in biology, giving him a great understanding of the cheese-making process. His shop has a delightful feel, incorporating a few tables at which customers can enjoy carefully chosen cheese plates. There's always help and advice on choosing cheese, with a great choice of raw milk artisan cheeses, and a deli section of both traditional and unusual delicacies to tempt you.

food facts

ARE ALL HENS THE SAME?

No, they're not and, if you're lucky, opening a box of eggs from a good egg producer can be quite a surprise. Blue eggs, chocolate brown, pale green, dazzling white – when an egg producer keeps different breeds of hen, the resulting eggs can be an explosion of colour. Not only does this make the box of eggs such an aesthetic pleasure, it also means that some of the more unusual or traditional breeds are being kept alive, sustaining the biodiversity in farm breeds of this country. The Rare Breeds Survival Trust recognizes that several poultry breeds are in danger of disappearing, including the Derbyshire Redcap and the Scots Grey. The more small-scale producers move away from high-egg-producing cross breeds and hybrids and start rearing these endangered breeds, the more likely it is the breeds will survive. It would be such a shame if eggs went the way of so many foodstuffs – governed by uniformity and price. The only way to prevent that is to search out local producers for whom the quality of their eggs, and the quality of life for their hens, is paramount.

SOUTH WEST | TRURO

Lynher Dairies Cheese Company Ltd

Ponsanooth, Truro, Cornwall TR3 7JQ   T: 01872 870789   W: www.cornishyarg.co.uk

Lynher Dairies make the famous award-winning Cornish Yarg, easily identifiable with its jacket of nettle leaves. Made with the milk of the Lynher and Pengreep herds, the company now produce eight cheese varieties in all. Widely available in cheese shops and delis around the country, or why not visit the original dairy at Liskeard and take a tour?

SOUTH WEST | TRURO

Trevaylor

Killiow, Kea, Truro, Cornwall TR3 6AG   T: 01872 864949
✉ farm gate sales

Organic free-range eggs from small flocks are available from the farm gate, the Country Store in Redruth, and Carleys in Truro.

Keens Cheddar (S H & G H Keen)

Moorhayes Farm, Verrington Lane, Wincanton, Somerset BA9 8JR   T: 01963 32286
E: keenscheddar@hotmail.com

farm gate sales

The Keen family are part of the 'Slow Food Presidium' for Cheddar cheese (see Westcombe Dairy, page 60), for their commitment to traditional Cheddar-making. The Cheddar is unpasteurized, from their own milk. The cloth-bound cheese is matured on the farm for 12 months, and is available direct (call first) or from Waitrose.

J A & E Montgomery Ltd

Manor Farm, Woolston Rd, North Cadbury, Yeovil, Somerset BA22 7DW
T: 01963 440243

Montgomery's Cheddar is something of a legend, having scooped many medals at the British Cheese Awards. Made with the unpasteurized milk of the farm's own cows, the cheese is made using traditional methods and could be described as fruity and spicy. The family also make a raclette-style cheese from Jersey milk, believed to be the only one of its kind made in the UK. The cheeses can be found at lots of good cheesemongers or, if you are in the vicinity, the village shop two doors down from Montgomery's dairy.

The Cheese Kitchen

108 Castle Road, Bedford MK40 3QR   T: 01234 217325

The Cheese Kitchen specializes in British artisan cheeses, with over 70 types on offer at any one time.

Meadow Cottage Farm

Churt Road, Headley, Borden, Hampshire GU35 8SS   T: 01428 712155

farm gate sales

Farm-gate sales of organic unhomogenized, unpasteurized milk, cream and award-winning ice cream, from the farm's own herd of Jersey cows. In 2004, Meadow Cottage Farms summer fruit ice cream won a silver Great Taste medal.

Lower Basing Farm

Cowden, Kent TN8 7JU   T: 01342 850251

⤵ **farm shop**

Disappointed in the cheese offered by her local supermarket, Maureen Browning decided to have a go at making her own. Alongside her Caerphilly type cheese, there is also goat meat, goats' milk ice cream and home-grown vegetables.

Crockham Hill Cheeses

Hurst Farm, Dairy Lane, Crockham Hill, Kent TN8 6RA   T: 01732 866516

Most Wensleydale is made using cows' milk but originally it would have been made with ewes' milk, which produces a creamier, less crumbly cheese. This unpasteurized ewes' milk Wensleydale, from a recipe dating from the 1920s, is available from many local outlets (call for details), or from Neal's Yard in London (see opposite).

Twineham Grange Farms Ltd

Bob Lane, Twineham, Haywards Heath, Sussex RH17 5NH   T: 01444 881394
w: www.tgfonline.com

✉ **mail order**

Cheesemakers trained by an Italian master-cheesemaker make English vegetarian alternatives to Parmesan and ricotta, using local milk. Available by mail order and Vegetarian Society accredited.

Nut Knowle Farm

World's End, Gun Hill, Horam, East Sussex TN21 0LA   T: 01825 872214
w: www.nutknowlefarm.com

▧ **farmers' markets** ▨ **farm gate sales**

The Jenners of Nut Knowle Farm believe they were the first in the UK to milk their own goats for commercial cheesemaking, and now they have a good range of cheeses, many with similarities to Camembert. All hand-made, the cheeses are allowed to mature well before being sold – mainly at local farmers' markets. The Jenners run their own farmers' markets at Henfield, Eastbourne and Rottingdean.

The Horsham Cheese Shop

20 Carfax, Horsham, West Sussex RH12 1EB   т: 01403 254272
w: www.horshamcheeseshop.co.uk
✉ **mail order**

Lots of artisan cheeses, with a pleasing selection of Sussex produce. Over 250 types of cheese are stocked here.

Golden Cross Cheese Company

Greenacres Farm, Whitesmith, Lewes, East Sussex BN8 6JA   т: 01825 872380
🖾 **farm gate sales**

Greenacres Farm produces a mould-ripened, lightly charcoaled goats' milk cheese, which recently won first prize at the Nantwich Cheese Show. Using the milk from the farm's own goats, the cheese is made by hand in small batches. Buy direct from the farm – call first.

La Fromagerie

30 Highbury Park, London N5 2AA ALSO AT 2–4 Moxon Street, London W1U 4EW
т: 020 7359 7440 (HIGHBURY PARK); 020 7935 0341 (MOXON STREET)
w: www.lafromagerie.co.uk
🚚 **delivery service**

An Aladdin's cave of artisan produce, with some unusual cheeses from the UK and the continent. There is a café at the Moxon Street shop. La Fromagerie is a member of the *Guilde des Fromagers*.

Neal's Yard Dairy

17 Shorts Gardens, London WC2H 9UP ALSO AT 6 Park Street, Borough Market, London SE1 9AB   т: 020 7240 5700 (SHORTS GARDENS); 020 7645 3554 (PARK STREET)
E: mailorder@nealsyarddairy.co.uk
✉ **mail order**

A cheesemonger selling British and Irish cheeses that are selected direct from the farms, matured in cellars beneath the shop and sold when they are as near to their peak as possible.

Paxton & Whitfield

93 Jermyn Street, London SW1Y 6JE   T: 020 7930 0259   w: www.paxtonandwhitfield.co.uk

For details see under the Bath branch on page 54. There is also a branch in Stratford-upon-Avon (see page 75).

Old Plaw Hatch Farm

Sharpthorne, West Sussex, RH19 4JL   T: 01342 810201
E: oldplawhatchfarm@hotmail.com
➥ **farm shop**

The farm shop stocks cream and yoghurt, as well as the farm's own organic Cheddar-type cheese, made from local unpasteurized milk. Visitors can watch the cheese being made. Home-grown and local biodynamic vegetables are also stocked, as well as biodynamic meat.

Hunts Hill Barn

Moon's Green, Wittersham, nr Tenterden, Kent TN30 7PR   T: 01797 270327
▭ **farmers' markets** ▭ **farm gate sales**

The orchard at Hunts Hill Barn produces 28 different varieties of apple, some of which are used to make single-variety juices. The orchards are also home to hens and geese, which range freely, enjoying a diet of fallen apples and insects alongside their regular feed. The eggs and juice are available either direct from the farm or from Rye farmers' market and Tenterden Farmers' Fayre.

Tenterden Cheesemakers

Forstall Farm, Tenterden, Kent TN30 7DF   T: 01580 765111
w: www.tenterdencheese.co.uk
▭ **farm gate sales** ✉ **mail order**

Unpasteurized farmhouse cheese made using milk from the farm's own prize-winning herd of pedigree Guernsey cows. Three different cheeses are made – a semi-hard, a range of fresh soft cheese (including the silver medal winner, Belle's Garlic) and a mozzarella type. The Whitehead family who farm at Forstall won Young Farmers of the Year in 2003.

Sussex High Weald Dairy

Putlands Farm, Duddleswell, Uckfield, East Sussex TN22 3BJ   T: 01825 712647
w: www.sussexhighwealddairy.co.uk

👡 **farm shop** ✉ **mail order**

From the organic milk of the farm's herd, Sussex High Weald Dairy make a range of cheeses, including a semi-hard and a cream cheese. Ewes' milk cheeses are also made here, including a halloumi-style and a feta-style cheese. Available direct from the dairy, or by mail order.

Two Hoots Farmhouse Cheese

Feathercot, School Road, Barkham, Wokingham, Berkshire RG41 4TP
T: 01189 760401   E: feathercot@tiscali.co.uk

🍴 **farmers' markets**

Sandy Rose at Two Hoots Farmhouse Cheese grew up on a dairy farm, but only turned her hand to cheesemaking recently. It turns out she's a natural, winning the coveted award of 'Best New Cheese' at the World Cheese Awards in her first year of production. She makes two varieties – Barkham Blue, which has a fine balance between the blue flavour and the rich taste of the cheese, and a new softer, stronger blue cheese called Barkham Chase. Both cheeses are made with rich Channel Island milk. Find Sandy at Reading, Basingstoke and Winchester farmers' markets.

Domini Quality Foods

Village Farm, Market Weston, Diss, Norfolk IP22 2NZ   T: 01359 221333
E: jcapon@dominifoods.fsnet.co.uk

🍴 **farmers' markets** ✉ **farm gate sales (phone first)**

Buy untreated, organic milk, cream, and sweet, hand-patted butter from the small Domini herd of Jersey cows, directly from the farm or from Wyken farmers' market at Stanton each week.

Suffolk Meadow Ice Cream

Rendham Hall, Rendham, Saxmundham, Suffolk IP17 2AW   T: 01728 663440

🛒 **farmers' markets**

Hand-made farmhouse ice cream, made with the milk of the farm's own award-winning dairy herd. There is a big choice of flavours, including the more unusual lemongrass, mascarpone and mocha. Suffolk Meadow ice creams are available from local farm shops or at Easton, Woodbridge and Felixstowe farmers' markets.

Mrs Temple's Cheese

New Farm, Wells-next-the-Sea, Norfolk NR23 1NE   T: 01328 710376
E: mrstemplescheese@farmersweekly.net

🛒 **farmers' markets**

Catherine Temple was taught to make cheese and butter by her mother and grandmother and still uses the same methods to make by hand her five varieties of cows' milk cheese. The milk comes from the family's own herd and the cheeses are available from Kings Lynn, Swaffham, Aylsham, Dereham, Wymondham and Fakenham farmers' markets. Catherine won a silver medal at the 2003 British Chesse Awards.

Fred W Reade & Sons

Ulceby Grange, Alford, Lincolnshire, LN13 0HE   T: 01507 466987
E: tlj@lincolnshirepoacher.freeserve.co.uk

🛒 **farmers' markets**

Reade & Sons are famous for their Lincolnshire Poacher cheese, a tangy Cheddar-style cheese that is a previous winner of Supreme Champion at the British Cheese Awards. Made from the unpasteurized milk of the farm's own cows, the cheese is available from many markets in the area, including Nottingham, Derby, Spalding and Boston. Farmhouse butter and free-range eggs are also available. In all, Reade & Sons attend around 28 farmers' markets per month in the East Midlands area. Call for details.

Keys Hill Poultry Farm

Sandy Lane, Wildmoor, Bromsgrove, Worcestershire B61 0RB   T: 0121 453 3370

⊠ **farm gate sales**

Free-range hens' eggs, laid on the morning of purchase, are available from the farm gate.

Ram Hall Dairy Sheep

Ram Hall Farm, Baulk Lane, Berkswell, nr Coventry, West Midlands CV7 7BD
T: 01676 532203   W: www.ram-hall.co.uk

A hard ewes' milk cheese, similar to a pecorino in texture, but matured for much longer, and two soft, mould-ripened cheeses are made at Ram Hall Farm. The unpasteurized milk from the farm's own flock of sheep is used and Ram Hall have won British Cheese Awards for the last seven years running. Available from local Waitrose branches.

Neal's Yard Creamery

Caeperthy, Arthurs Stone Lane, Dorstone, Herefordshire HR3 6AX   T: 01981 500395

Charlie Westhead makes a range of small, hand-made soft cheeses from locally produced cows' and goats' milk, as well as Greek-style yoghurts and crème fraîche. Both the cows' milk cheese and the yoghurt are organic. The methods used are very labour-intensive – everything is done by hand because there are no machines at this dairy. All the cheeses are unpasteurized. Available from specialist cheese shops, including Neal's Yard Dairy in London, page 67; (Charlie's dairy is the production arm of this shop) and the Fine Cheese Co. in Bath (page 54).

Bridge Farm Organic Foods

Bridge Farm, Snitterby Carr, Gainsborough, Lincolnshire DN21 4UU   T: 01673 818272

🛒 **farmers' markets**   ⊠ **farm gate sales**

Bridge Farm is run with a high regard for conservation and produces organic goats' milk and cheeses from the farm's own goats, free-range eggs and organic vegetables in season. Open days are occasionally held, to allow visitors to see how the farm works. Buy the produce direct from the farm gate, or from Lincoln (Castle Square) and Brigg farmers' markets.

Shepherd's

9 High Town, Hay-on-Wye, Herefordshire HR3 5AE   T: 01497 821898

The ice cream served at Shepherd's ice-cream parlour is made with ewes' milk, from the milk of one local herd – great for ice-cream lovers with an intolerance to cows' milk. Up to 40 flavours are made (16 are available at any one time), some using local fruit – the flavours are original and inventive.

Birdwood Farmhouse Cheesemakers

Birdwood, Huntley, Gloucestershire GL19 3EJ   T: 01452 750248

farmers' markets

A one-woman cheesemaking enterprise, with an interesting choice of cheeses including a Double Gloucester, a Scottish Dunlop style, a blue cheese called Birdwood Blue Heaven, and her own recipe Forester. All the milk used is cows' milk, from the farm's own herd. Available from Stroud, Cirencester, Cheltenham and Gloucester farmers' markets.

---

food facts

UNTREATED MILK

The milk most of us buy will be pasteurized and homogenized. The pasteurizing kills all bacteria, including some responsible for flavour, and homogenization breaks up the fat globules to distribute them evenly throughout the milk. This is quite a harsh process and many dairy farmers firmly believe it affects the taste of the milk – and not for the better. By its very nature, standardization eliminates character. Sometimes, it's good to taste milk in its natural form and we list some producers who sell untreated milk and cream, turning back the clock to offer dairy produce as it tasted generations ago.

Just Rachel Desserts

The Old Dairy, Churches Farm, Eggs Tump, Bromsberrow, Ledbury, Herefordshire HR8 1SA
T: 01531 650639   w: www.justrachel.com
✉ mail order

The ice creams at Just Rachel are very different to those you are
likely to find in supermarkets – from the imaginative flavours
(most popular is the damson and sloe gin variety) to the quality of
ingredients (fresh farm cream from Herefordshire and local fruits),
everything tells you that this is a unique, hand-made delicacy, not
a uniform mass-produced food. The other puddings available here
are made with the same attention to detail and careful sourcing of
ingredients, and the result is indulgent food with a wonderful sense
of both season and location.

Monkland Cheese Dairy

The Pleck, Monkland, Leominster, Herefordshire HR6 9DB   T: 01568 720307
w: www.mousetrapcheese.co.uk
🛒 shop

A few years ago, Monkland Dairy resurrected an old local cheese,
Little Hereford, using a 1918 recipe. Unpasteurized, the cheese is
brine-bathed for 24 hours and then left to mature for four months.
Available direct from the dairy or from Monkland's three shops in
Ludlow, Hereford and Leominster, where other British artisan
cheeses are stocked.

The Cheese Society

1 St Martins Lane, Lincoln LN2 1HY   T: 01522 511003
w: www.thecheesesociety.co.uk
🛒 shop ✉ mail order

Lots of British cheese, including produce from some of Britain's most
famous artisan cheesemakers – Mrs Kirkham's Lancashire, Dorset
Blue Vinny, and Stinking Bishop. As well as selling cheese by mail
order, The Cheese Society has a shop and café at its Lincoln base.

super hero

CLARE DRAPER, of The Chicken Came First, Newport (see below)

The free-range hens that Clare Draper keeps are lucky birds. Their welfare is Clare's over-riding concern: they have a great deal of space to peck and scratch, as hens should; they're not cooped up in tiny cages and force-fed high-protein foods – they are fed hot organic porridge with apple and sultanas for breakfast in the winter, and they are not slaughtered when their egg production begins to decline as they age (as happens in most commercial egg production). The birds are an unusual mix of breeds, including Brown Leghorns, Gold Legbars and the exotically named Lavender Araucana, which lays blue eggs.

Clare's customers are also rewarded well for her unusual approach to food production: 'When people open a box of these eggs, they marvel at the rich chocolate brown, snowy white and jewel-like blue shells. Cracking an egg, they are often astonished by the rich, intense colour of the yolk and when they eat it, they discover how 'real' eggs are supposed to taste.' She says that the quality of the eggs is all down to the natural, GM- and chemical-free diet (the eggs are organic), and the fact that the hens live as they naturally would – 'the philosophy of good food going hand-in-hand with animal welfare is terrifically important to me'.

Clare runs a local delivery round distributing the eggs, but customers are welcomed on to the smallholding and can even feed the hens, collect the eggs, or if they are really keen, help weave willow field shelters for the birds. Such is the interest locally that Clare produces a newsletter to tell people what's going on with the birds. She has a very simple mission with her food production: 'If I can stop one consumer buying a battery egg, then I shall be a happy woman.' Call Clare if you'd like to get on to her delivery round, or buy the eggs direct from the farm, or from Booth's supermarket in Knutsford, Newport Health Centre, or Mortimer and Bennett in London (0208 995 4145).

MIDLANDS   NEWPORT

The Chicken Came First   super hero

Lynton Mead, Outwoods, Newport, Shropshire TF10 9EB T: 01952 691418
E: clareword@btconnect.com

✉ farm gate sales   🚚 delivery service

Free-range, organic eggs from Clare Draper look and taste wonderful. See the Super Hero box, above, for more information.

Colston Bassett Dairy

Harby Lane, Colston Bassett, Nottingham NG12 3FN T: 01949 81322
w: www.colstonbassettdairy.com

🛒 **shop**

Colston Basset Dairy is one of the best-known Stilton-makers in the
UK and a member of the Stilton Cheesemakers Association.

Cropwell Bishop Creamery

Nottingham Road, Cropwell Bishop, Nottingham NG12 3BQ T: 0115 989 2350
w: www.cropwellbishopstilton.com

✉ **mail order**

The producers of award-winning Cropwell Bishop blue Stilton
and blue Shropshire cheeses are also members of the Stilton
Cheesemakers Association. Cropwell Bishop Stilton was Supreme
Champion at the 2003 British Cheese Awards.

Paxton & Whitfield

13 Wood Street, Stratford-upon-Avon, Warwickshire CV37 6JF T: 01789 415544
w: www.paxtonandwhitfield.co.uk

The third branch, after Bath and London (pages 54 and 68).

September Organic Dairy

Whitehill Park, Weobley, Herefordshire HR4 8QE T: 01544 312910
w: www.september-organic.co.uk

🥄 **farm shop** ✉ **mail order**

September Dairy makes 14 different varieties of ice cream,
all with the organic milk, cream and eggs produced on the farm,
supplemented with local and fair-trade ingredients. Unusual
flavours are the order of the day – blackberry-and-apple crumble,
brown bread, tayberry and elderflower cream, to name just a few.
Ingredients are sourced as locally as possible and the farm is run
with a commitment to environmentally sound practices. Available
from local Waitrose branches.

Appleby's of Hawkstone

Broadhay, Prees, Whitchurch, Shropshire SY13 2BJ   T: 01948 840387
W: www.applebysofhawkstone.co.uk

The Appleby family are the last cheesemakers to be producing a
cloth-bound, unpasteurized, mature Cheshire cheese. The milk
comes from their own cows, and the cheese is made entirely by hand.
Available from many cheesemongers – Iain Mellis in Scotland and
Neal's Yard in London (see pages 90, 92, 94 and 66).

Ansteys of Worcester

Broomhall Farm, Worcester WR5 2NT   T: 01905 820232   W: www.ansteys.com
🧺 **shop** ✉ **mail order**

Ansteys were the first cheesemakers to create a Worcester territorial
cheese, which they named Old Worcester White, and have since
followed this with Double Worcester cheese and a Worcestershire
Sauce cheese. All are hand-made with local milk, in the traditional
truckle form, and are hard, cloth-bound cheeses. Available mail
order, or from their shop at St Peters Garden Centre (call for details).

Lightwood Cheese

Lower Lightwood Farm, Cotheridge, Worcester WR6 5LT   T: 01905 333468
W: www.lightwoodcheese.co.uk
⬇ **farm shop** 🛒 **farmers' markets** ✉ **mail order**

Phil Holland took over Lightwood Cheese at the end of 2003,
although he is firmly upholding the traditional nature of this dairy,
using the same ancient recipes to make a variety of unpasteurized
cheeses. He has added farmhouse butter and buttermilk to the
product range, and a soft, Vignotte-style cheese, Lightwood Chaser.
Find Phil at many local farmers' markets, including Cheltenham,
Worcester, Hereford, Stratford-on-Avon and Windcombe.

Mar Goats

St Michaels Farm, Great Witley, Worcester WR6 6JB   T: 01299 896608
W: www.margoats.co.uk
⬇ **farm shop** 🛒 **farmers' markets**

The cheese at Mar Goats scooped numerous awards at the 2002 British Cheese Awards, including a gold, a silver and a bronze. The cheese is made with the unpasteurized milk of the farm's own goats – the goats feed on pesticide-free, clover-rich pasture and this produces particularly sweet milk. Mar Goats' cheeses, and also home-reared. whey-fed Saddleback pork and Welsh Mountain lamb, are available from the farm shop and Teme Valley and Stratford-on-Avon farmers' markets.

NORTH WEST   CARLISLE

Cream of Cumbria

Howberry Farm, Blackford, Carlisle, Cumbria CA6 4EN T: 01228 675558
E: tomsusan@forrester32.fsnet.co.uk
🛒 **farmers' markets**

Award-winning rich yellow farmhouse butter, hand patted and made with the milk from a local cow herd is very different from the butter you find in supermarkets and is available from all the Cumbrian farmers' markets – call for details.

NORTH WEST   CARLISLE

Thornby Moor Dairy

Crofton Hall, Thursby, Carlisle, Cumbria CA5 6QB T: 01697 345555
🛒 **farm gate sales** ✉ **mail order**

Goats', ewes' and cows' milks are the basis of the nine varieties of cheese at Thornby Moor, all unpasteurized, and from single-herd milk. There is a Cumberland farmhouse cheese, a traditional hard, cloth-bound cheese and a semi-soft, using both cows' and goats' milk.

NORTH WEST   CHESTER

The Cheese Shop

116 Northgate Street, Chester, Cheshire CH1 2HT T: 01244 346240
W: www.chestercheeseshop.com

British cheese specialists, stocking over 150 different UK cheeses, with a good selection of organic varieties.

The Cheese Shop

Unit D17 & 18, Kendal Market Hall, Westmoreland Shopping Centre, Kendal, Cumbria
LA9 4LR   T: 01539 728444   E: thecheeseshop@btopenworld.com

Of the great selection of cheeses on display here about half are
British, from small dairies making artisan cheeses, including local
varieties. Many are unpasteurized. There are also some good
continental cheeses available, including Spanish Manchego and
cave-aged Emmenthal. To complement the cheeses there are some
interesting olives and charcuterie.

Abbey Leys Farm

Peacock Lane, High Leigh, nr Knutsford, Cheshire, WA16 6NS   T: 01925 753465
w: www.abbeyleys.co.uk

▬ **farm shop**

Organic eggs from traditional-breed free-range hens (Speckledy and
Hebden Blacks) and from Khaki Campbell ducks, and a selection of
organic potatoes.

Staffordshire Cheese Company

Glenmore House, 55 Rose Bank, Leek, Staffordshire ST13 6AG   T: 01538 399733
E: jknox1066@aol.com

▬ **farmers' markets** ✉ **mail order**

A busy man, John Knox makes eight varieties of cheese, using both
goats' and cows' milk from local farms. Made using old methods,
such as muslin wrapping and wax dipping, and old recipes (one
dates back to 1860), these are very traditional cheeses. Available by
mail order, at local farmers' markets and local farm shops, butcher's
and garden centres in the Midlands – call for details.

H S Bourne

The Bank, Malpas, Cheshire SY14 7AL   T: 01948 770214
w: www.hsbourne.co.uk

▬ **farmers' markets** ✉ **mail order**

Cheesemaking has been in the Bourne family for around 200 years and they are still using the old-fashioned methods and traditional Cheshire recipes to make their artisan products. Available from Nantwich, Knutsford, Liverpool, Wrexham and Northop farmers' markets, and Borough Market in London.

The Cheese Hamlet

706 Wilmslow Road, Didsbury, Manchester M20 2DW   T: 0161 434 4781
www.cheesehamlet.co.uk

🧺 **shop** ✉ **mail order**

The Cheese Hamlet specialises in Swiss cheese, but it has an admirable range of British farmhouse cheeses too – in all, customers at this shop have a choice of over 200 types of cheese. With maturing rooms within the premises, the cheese on display is in peak condition, and the knowledgeable staff encourage tasting. There is also a good range of charcuterie, including a rare Serrano ham made from wild boar fed solely on acorns.

Ravens Oak Dairy

Burland Farm, Wrexham Road, Burland, Nantwich, Cheshire CW5 8ND
T: 01270 524624   W: www.ravensoakdairy.co.uk

Ravens Oak Dairy produces a range of award-winning organic cheeses. The cheese is made with the farm's own cows' milk and also locally produced ewes', goats' and buffaloes' milk. Although all the cheeses are pasteurized, the pasteurization method used is very gentle and many people have claimed the cheeses taste unpasteurized. They are available from Neal's Yard in London (see page 67), and specialist cheese shops.

Staffordshire Organic Cheese

New House Farm, Acton, Newcastle-under-Lyme, Staffordshire ST5 4EE   T: 01782 680366

🧺 **farm shop**

From the unpasteurized organic cows' milk of a nearby farm, the Deavilles make a Cheshire-type cheese, in plain and flavoured varieties. The most popular flavour is the unusual wild garlic. Also available is a hard cheese made with ewes' milk. The farm shop is open on Fridays and on other days by appointment.

Cotherstone Cheese Company

Quarry House Farm, Marwood, Barnard Castle, County Durham DL12 9QL

T: 01833 650351

farm gate sales

Made to an old Dales recipe that has been handed down from generation to generation, the cheese made here is reminiscent of Wensleydale. Made with cows' milk from a local farm, this cheese will never be found in supermarkets, but is available direct from the farm or from specialist farm shops.

The Swaledale Cheese Co.

Mercury Road, Gallowfields Trading Estate, Richmond, North Yorkshire DL10 4TQ

T: 01748 824932   W: www.swaledalecheese.co.uk

farmers' markets   **mail order**

The Swaledale Cheese Co. produces 11 varieties of Swaledale cheese, using local cows' milk and also goats' and ewes' milk. Traditionally hand-made and brine-soaked to an old farmhouse recipe, the plain varieties are supplemented by some flavoured varieties, including two flavoured with local ale and mead. Available by mail order, or from farmers' markets in Yorkshire – the website lists them.

Northumberland Cheese Company

Make Me Rich Farm, Blagdon, Seaton Burn, Northumberland NE13 6BZ

T: 01670 789798   W: www.northumberland-cheese.co.uk

farm gate sales   **mail order**

A range of cheeses, using local cows', goats' and ewes' milks are made here. One, the Chevington, is made to an old Northumberland recipe using rich Jersey milk. It was popular over 100 years ago and then disappeared, but Mark Robertson has resurrected it. There is a coffee shop at the dairy and visitors can taste and buy the cheeses.

Wheelbirks Farm

Stocksfield, Northumberland NE43 7HY   T: 01661 842613

E: wheelbirks@farmersweekly.net

farm gate sales

Unpasteurized milk and cream, and pasteurized ice cream are all made with milk from Wheelbirks Farm's pedigree Jersey herd. The double cream is simply separated from the milk, with no additives or processing, and local fruit is used in the ice cream. Available direct from the farm, or from local shops and restaurants.

Doddington Dairy

North Doddington Farm, Wooler, Northumberland NE71 6AN   T: 01668 283010
w: www.doddingtondairy.co.uk

This dairy farm produces a range of three cheeses and also ice cream using the milk from their own cows. Doddington cheese is a British territorial, lying somewhere between a Cheddar and a Leicester, Berwick Edge is a Gouda-style cheese and Cuddy's Cave is a natural-rinded cheese. The ice cream is free from artificial additives and the list of flavours is both long and imaginative. Available from many outlets, including Neal's Yard in London (cheese only, see page 67); see their website for full details, or phone.

Causeway Cheese Company

Unit 1, Loughgiel Millennium Centre, Lough Road, Loughgiel, Ballymena, Co. Antrim BT44 9JN   T: 028 2764 1241   w: www.causewaycheese.co.uk
📏 farmers' markets

The most popular cheese made here is the Drumkeel – similar to Wensleydale. Available plain or with flavourings such as local seaweed. Find the cheese at Belfast's St Georges Market.

Carrigbyrne Farmhouse Cheese

Carrigbyrne Farmhouse, Adamstown, Co. Wexford   T: 054 40560   w: www.carrigbyrne.com
📏 farm gate sales

Carrigbyrne is a Camembert-style cheese made with pasteurized milk from the farm's own herd of cows. Available from the farm gate (please phone first), or from Sheridans (see page 85, 86 and the Super Hero box on page 86), Caviston's (see page 200), or good specialist cheese shops. Carrigbyrne is a member of CAIS.

food facts

FREE-RANGE EGGS

Why would you bother to buy free-range eggs direct from the farm, when they are available in the supermarket? During the filming of *Food Heroes* we tested fried eggs on 15 members of staff from a hotel near Carlisle. They each tried a supermarket free-range egg, an organic free-range egg from a local farm, and a battery-farmed egg. The results were decisive, five voted for the free-range eggs, ten for the organic eggs, and none for the battery eggs.

To use the term free range a producer must allow a mimimum space per hen, but the flocks can be enormous. Our egg producers keep their hens in small flocks, which means that the birds live less stressful lives. Happy, healthier hens produce better, tastier eggs, so why not find a local egg producer and discover the difference yourself?

REPUBLIC OF IRELAND   BANTRY

Durrus Farmhouse Cheese

Coomkeen, Durrus, Bantry, Co. Cork   T: 027 61100   w: www.durruscheese.com
🔲 **farm gate sales**

One of the last remaining raw-milk, rind-washed cheeses in Cork, Durrus is a semi-soft cheese, very creamy with a hint of herbs and grass. Available direct from the farm (10am–1pm weekdays, please call first) or from Neal's Yard in London (see page 67), Iain Mellis in Scotland (see page 90, 92 and 94), Sheridans in Ireland (see pages 85, 86 and the Super Hero box on page 86) and many small cheese shops. The producer is a member of CAIS and Slow Food.

REPUBLIC OF IRELAND   BEARA

Milleens Cheese

Milleens, Eyeries, Beara, Co. Cork   T: 027 74079   E: milleens@eircom.net
🔲 **farm gate sales**

A single herd from a neighbour's farm provides the milk for Milleens cheese; grazing on herb- and clover-rich pasture, the cows produce sweet, rich milk. Winning Supreme Champion at the British Cheese Awards in 1997, CAIS members Norman and Veronica Steele make one type of cheese, a soft, rind-washed variety, which is recognized as a cheese in its own category. Available direct from the dairy, or from specialist cheese shops.

DAIRY AND EGGS

Corleggy Cheese

Corleggy, Belturbet, Co. Cavan   T: 049 952 2930

🗫 farmers' markets

Silke Cropp, a CAIS member, is proudly upholding the tradition of raw-milk cheeses in Ireland and makes a good range of cheeses, using cows', goats' and ewes' milk. She sources her milk carefully, collecting it herself from nearby farms. The range includes some soft and some hard cheeses, all available from Temple Bar market in Dublin, Leopardstown and Dun Loaghaire farmers' markets, markets around Wicklow, and Borough Market in London.

Croghan Goat Farm

Ballynadrishogue, Blackwater, Enniscorthy, Co. Wexford   T: 053 27331

🗫 farm gate sales

One of the few remaining unpasteurized goats' milk cheeses in Ireland is made on this farm, which is a member of CAIS. There is a fresh cheese, in small logs, or the most popular, the French-style Mine Gabhar cheese. A pressed variety is also made. Available from the farm gate or Sheridans (pages 85 and 86), Country Choice (page 136), Tir na nOg (page 137) or Neal's Yard (page 67).

Ardsallagh Goats' Products

Woodstock, Carrigtwohill, Co. Cork   T: 021 488 2336

🗫 farmers' markets

The Murphy family have cross-bred Saanen and Anglo-Nubian goats to find a breed that produces rich and creamy milk, and with this they make both a soft *à la louche* cheese (a slow method producing very smooth and velvety cheese), and a hard cheese, similar to Gouda but unpressed. The soft cheese comes plain, rolled in cracked black pepper, coated in wholegrain honey mustard, or rolled in chives, and the Gouda-style is available beech smoked. The cheeses are available matured to varying ages to suit everyone's palates. Find them at Midleton, Cobh, Dungarvan and Dun Laoghaire farmers' markets.

Glyde Farm Produce

Mansfieldstown, Castlebellingham, Co. Louth   T: 042 937 2343   E: glydefarm@eircom.net

🏠 **farm gate sales**

Peter Thomas will cheerfully show visitors around his dairy, where he makes Bellingham Blue, reputedly the only raw-milk blue cheese currently made in Ireland. Every part of the cheesemaking is performed by hand, as Peter feels that this way he has total control over the development of the cheese. Best eaten well matured, the cheese is sold at anything from nine months to three years old. Available direct from the dairy, or from Sheridans (see pages 85 and 86, and the Super Hero box on page 86) and Superquinn stores.

Cratloe Hills Sheep's Cheese

Brickhill, Cratloe, Co. Clare   T: 061 357185

Cratloe Hills has won many British Cheese Awards, including Best Irish Cheese. Using the milk of their own flock of sheep, Cratloe make two cheeses, a mild and a mature. A member of CAIS and run by a husband and wife team, this is a small-scale, craft dairy. The cheeses are available from Sheridans in Ireland (see below, pages 85 and 86, and the Super Hero box on page 86), Iain Mellis in Scotland (see pages 90, 92 and 94), the Cheese Shop in Chester (see page 77) and some branches of Waitrose.

Murphy's Ice Cream

Strand Street, Dingle, Co Kerry   T: 066 915 2644   W: www.murphysicecream.ie

What do you get when you combine two perfectionist ex-New Yorkers with the richest cream from Kerry? You get awesome ice cream and sorbet, in flavours so exciting they make you drool just thinking about them – Guinness and Blackcurrant, Irish Brown Bread, Bellini sorbet. And of course, there's chocolate and vanilla...but with Valrhona chocolate, and organic Mexican vanilla – the Murphy's don't use any artificial flavourings, indeed, they appear to be on a life-long search for the perfect chocolate, or the perfect recipe for home-made caramel sauce, the banana at just the perfect stage of ripeness. Check out their dessert house in Dingle, or see the website for other outlets around Ireland.

Glenilen Farm

Gurteeniher, Drimoleague, Co. Cork   T: 028 31179   W: www.glenilenfarm.com

🔲 farmers' markets

The herd of Friesian and Jersey cows at Glenilen Farm produces rich milk, which Alan and Valerie Kingston make into award-winning fromage frais, butter, fruit mousses, clotted cream, and cheesecakes, all hand-made. Available from Clonakilty, Skibbereen and Midleton farmers' markets. The farm is a member of Slow Food.

Sheridans Cheesemongers   super hero

11 South Anne Street, Dublin 2 AND ALSO 7 Pembroke Lane, Dublin 4

T: 01 679 3143 (SOUTH ANNE ST); 01 660 8231 (PEMBROKE LANE)

E: cheeseshop@eircom.net

The staff at Sheridans have an extensive knowledge of all the cheeses they sell, making shopping there a real experience. See the Super Hero box, page 86, for more information. There is also a branch in Galway (see page 86).

Coturnix Quail

Droumdrastil, Dunmanway, Co. Cork   T: 087 206 5067

The quail eggs at Coturnix are laid by birds housed in roomy open-floored barns (quail don't survive well outside in Ireland!). The birds are fed a diet of grain and grass, and are born, reared, and lay on the farm, so that total traceability is ensured. Several local outlets stock the eggs – call to find your nearest.

J & L Grubb

Beechmount, Fethard, Co. Tipperary   T: 052 31151   W: www.cashelblue.com

The Grubbs, who are CAIS members, are probably the largest of the farmhouse cheesemakers in Ireland, and they make the legendary Cashel Blue. The milk used is from the farm's own cows, and they now make Crozier Blue, using ewes' milk from their nephew's flock. This is still very much a hand-made, farmhouse cheese from a family farm, but it is widely available, even in a few supermarkets.

super hero

SHERIDANS CHEESEMONGERS, Dublin and Galway (see page 85 and below)

Sheridans is very serious about cheese. When staff join the company, they are often sent off to spend a day with one of Ireland's artisan cheesemakers, where they'll find out how the cheese is made, and even have a go at it themselves. Sheridans buys direct from the producers, from Irish farmhouse cheesemakers to olive oil producers in Spain, building relationships, visiting and learning from the producers. Shopping at any of the three shops is a real experience – customers are guided around the products, tasting and examining everything from cheese to oils to vinegars. The staff can answer any questions regarding the provenance of the foods and you can be assured that the produce is offered for sale in peak condition – the cheeses are never released from the maturing rooms until they are at their best and the shops are humidity-controlled. This is food knowledge and experience as an art form. The Pembroke Lane branch has a wine department packed with artisan wines.

REPUBLIC OF IRELAND   GALWAY

Sheridans Cheesemongers   `super hero`

14–16 Churchyard Street, Galway T: 091 564829 E: cheeseshop@eircom.net

See the Super Hero box, above, for more information. There are also two branches in Dublin (see page 85).

REPUBLIC OF IRELAND   INAGH

Inagh Farmhouse Cheese

Inagh, Co. Clare T: 065 683 6633 w: www.st-tola.ie
🏪 farmers' markets 🏠 farm gate sales

St Tola goats' cheese is made mainly with the raw, organic milk from the farm's pedigree herd of Saanen and Toggenburg goats. It comes in a log, a crottin (both soft cheeses) and a hard cheese. Due to the herb-rich pastures the goats graze near the coast, the flavour of the cheese has a suggestion of the sea with an underlying hint of peat. Available from the farm, or at Ennis farmers' market. Inagh Farmhouse Cheese is a member of CAIS and Slow Food.

Ardrahan Cheese

Ardrahan, Kanturk, Co. Cork   T: 029 78099   E: ardrahancheese.tinet.ie

Specializing in a pasteurized, semi-soft, rind-washed cheese, Ardrahan Cheese uses milk from the farm's own cows. Using traditional cheesemaking methods, Mary Burns, a CAIS member, has won an award for Best Irish Cheese at the World Cheese Awards. Widely available from Sheridans (opposite), Caviston's (page 200) and Superquinn in Ireland, and Neal's Yard (page 67), Fortnum & Mason and some branches of Waitrose.

Lavistown Cheese

Lavistown House, Kilkenny   T: (056) 776 5145
📫 **farm gate sales**

Lavistown cheese is similar to a Wensleydale, and is hand made here by the Goodwillie family. Available direct from the farm (please phone first), or from Sheridan's in Dublin and branches of Superquinn.

Killorglin Farmhouse Cheese

Ardmoniel, Killorglin, Co. Kerry   T: 066 976 1402   W: www.kerryflavours.com
📫 **farm gate sales** ✉ **mail order**

Killorglin make a raw-milk Gouda-style cheese, matured for anywhere between two months and three years. It is available either plain or flavoured with cloves, garlic and cumin, both of which have a great, long flavour. The producers also make a pasteurized version of the same cheese. Available from the farm gate, where visitors can watch the cheese being made, or by mail order.

Knockanore Farmhouse Cheese

Ballyneety, Knockanore, Co. Waterford   T: 024 97275   W: www.knockanorecheese.com
🛒 **farm shop**

CAIS members Knockanore Farmhouse Cheese was the proud recipient of a Gold Medal at the British Cheese Awards for their semi-hard, unpasteurized-milk cheese. Buy the cheese direct from the dairy, or from Sheridans (see opposite).

FOOD HEROES OF BRITAIN

Coolea Farmhouse Cheese

Coolea, Macroom, Co. Cork   T: 026 45204

⌂ **farm gate sales (office hours only)**

When the Willems family moved to Ireland from Holland many years ago, they couldn't find anything like the Gouda cheese they loved, and so Mrs Willem set about making it at home for the family. Her son took over making the cheese and now it is widely available, from Sheridans (see pages 85, 86 and the Super Hero box on page 86) and Superquinn branches in Ireland, Iain Mellis in Scotland (see pages 90, 92 and 94) and Neal's Yard in London (see page 67), and some branches of Waitrose. From a hobby to Supreme Champion at the British Cheese Awards in 2000, these CAIS-member cheesemakers have come a long way.

Gubbeen Cheese

Gubbeen House, Schull, Cork   T: 028 28231   W: www.gubbeen.com

⌂ **farmers' markets**

One of the most famous Irish artisan cheeses, hand-made with the milk of the cheesemaker's own mixed herd, which includes some rare, native Kerry cows. Gubbeen Cheese is a CAIS member.

The West Cork Natural Cheese Co.

Schull, Co. Cork   T: 028 28593   W: www.wcnc.ie

⌂ **farmers' markets**   ⌂ **farm gate sales**

The West Cork Cheese Co. use the alpine 'alpage' way of making cheese, using only the summer milk from cows fed on fresh grass – when the cows are eating silage in the winter the milk can have a bitter flavour. The two cheeses they make – Desmond and Gabriel – are both 'thermophilic', heat-treated in the early stages of production, as Parmesan-style cheeses are. Both are hard and good for cooking – Desmond has a piquant flavour and Gabriel is long-flavoured and aromatic – and are available direct from the farm or from Bantry and Cork City farmers' markets or Temple Bar market in Dublin and Neal's Yard (see page 67) in London and Sheridans (see pages 85, 86 and the Super Hero box on page 86) in Ireland. The company is a CAIS member.

Cooleeney Farmhouse Cheese

Moyne, Thurles, Co. Tipperary   T: 0504 45112   W: www.cooleeney.com

CAIS members Cooleeney produce three different cheeses using the milk of their own cows, all similar to Camembert or Brie in style and a new goats' milk cheese, using the milk from a Waterford goat herd. The goats' milk cheese is similar to a mild, velvety Brie – it's not too 'goaty', with a hint of mushroom – and won 'Best New Cheese' at the 2002 British Cheese awards. Widely available from cheese shops around Ireland and the UK.

McDonald's Cheese Shop

Westfields, Balmoral Road, Rattray, Blairgowrie, Perthshire PH10 7HY   T: 01250 872493

Caroline Robertson and her husband John are passionate about cheese and stock over 150 varieties – from Scotland, Ireland, England and Wales as well as from further afield on the continent – in their shop. There is a wealth of Scottish artisan produce here, including high-quality chocolate and even ice cream from Arran and Orkney.

The Island Cheese Company

Home Farm, Brodick, Isle of Arran KA27 8DD   T: 01770 302788
W: www.islandcheese.co.uk
🛒 farm shop   ✉ mail order

The Island Cheese Company makes ten varieties of cheese from local cows' and goats' milk, including a traditional Scottish Crowdie cheese. At the shop you can watch the cheeses being made from the viewing room, buy the company's cheese and other Scottish and English farmhouse cheeses too.

H J Errington & Co.

Walston Braehead Farm, Carnwath, Lanarkshire ML11 8NF   T: 01899 810257
✉ farm gate sales   ✉ mail order

Blue cheeses are the speciality here, made with unpasteurized ewes' and cows' milk. Ayrshire cows from a neighbour's farm and Humphrey Errington's own sheep provide the milk. Humphrey also makes a cheese called Maisie's Kebbuck, which is not blue, as a special dispensation for his mother-in-law, who doesn't like blue cheese! Humphrey is at the forefront of a movement to protect raw milk cheese.

The Hand Made Cheese Co.

Swinlees Farm, Dalry, Ayrshire KA24 5JZ T: 01294 832479

🍴 **farmers' markets**

Hazel Forsyth is not happy being called an artisan cheesemaker – she protests that it conveys 'images of hippies'! However, given that she makes small batches of her cloth-bound, Cheddar-style cheese using traditional methods, with the unpasteurized milk from local Ayrshire cows, and, as the name suggests, by hand, then artisan is what she is. Hazel's cheese is available at all the Ayrshire farmers' markets, see www.ayrshirefarmersmarket.co.uk or call Hazel for more details.

Loch Arthur Creamery

Camphill Village Trust, Beeswing, Dumfries DG2 8JQ T: 01387 760296

🍶 **farm shop**

Four types of cheese are made at the Loch Arthur Creamery, including a farmhouse cloth-bound, Cheddar type. All are made from unpasteurized organic milk, most of which comes from the farm's own herd. As Loch Arthur is a mixed farm, the farm shop also stocks organic and biodynamic meat, home-baked bread, and vegetables.

Iain Mellis (The Cheesemonger)

30a Victoria Street, Edinburgh EH1 2JW ALSO AT 6 Bakers Place, Edinburgh EH3 6SY and 330 Morningside Road, Edinburgh EH10 4DH T: 0131 226 6215 (VICTORIA ST); 0131 225 6566 (BAKERS PLACE); 0131 447 8889 (MORNINGSIDE ROAD)

w: www.ijmellischeesemonger.com

✉ **mail order**

Iain Mellis ripens the cheese he sells in his own maturing rooms, the sign of a cheesemonger truly passionate about cheese. He sells a huge range, including lots of British farmhouse cheese varieties. There is also a branch in Glasgow and one in St Andrews (see pages 92 and 94).

food facts

STORING CHEESE AT HOME

I asked the Specialist Cheesemakers Association for their advice on buying and storing cheese, and here is an abridged version of their advice.

- Buy cheese on the same day, or as near to the time you want to eat it as possible, and keep it cool, in a good larder or cool place, but preferably not the fridge.

- Hard cheeses are relatively tolerant of plastic or vacuum wrapping and fridges, but not the softer cheeses, as they ripen more quickly and tend to sweat in plastic. If soft, white, Brie-type cheeses are kept very cold they will tend to become soapy or even damp and slimy with condensation, so an interesting alternative to the fridge is to put the cheese into a Chinese bamboo steamer basket and hang it in a cool place.

- The ideal storage location is a cellar, pantry or larder, where the temperature is around 8–10°C. Realistically, however, for most people, especially in warm weather, a fridge is the only option, in which case, the carefully wrapped cheeses should be kept in plastic boxes.

- Cheese is a living product and needs to breathe. Clear plastic film can be used to protect the cut surfaces of cheese, but leave some of the rind exposed. Use clear plastic film sparingly on hard and blue cheeses and wrap softer ones in wax paper, foil or, if it's all you have, greaseproof paper.

- Draping a damp linen napkin or cheesecloth over cheese will keep it from drying out, but it only works if the cloth is kept constantly damp.

- Rounds of cheese should be cut in half and then into small wedges, rather than cutting a cheese as you would a cake. This reduces wastage significantly – triangular spaces are impossible to seal satisfactorily. Unsealed surfaces and hollow spaces provide an opportunity for dehydration or mould to damage the cheese and Bries can collapse completely.

- If you have stored cheese in the fridge, allow it to come up to room temperature for an hour or two before eating – it will taste better.

super hero

PAM RODWAY, owner of Wester Lawrenceton Farm, Moray (see below)

Pam Rodway has been making cheese for over 30 years, and is passionate about keeping the heritage of Scottish cheese alive. From the unpasteurized organic milk of her own herd of Ayrshire cows, famous for the creamy quality of their milk, she makes Dunlop, a traditional Scottish 'sweet milk' cheese. Instead of striving for uniformity, Pam takes pleasure in the way the colour and flavour of the cheese can vary subtly according to the season or the pasture the cows are grazing. She is now researching a 'lost' Scottish variety, Highland cheese, which has not been made for generations, with a view to resurrecting this old, traditional variety. Finding a defined recipe for this cheese is proving tricky; it comes from a time when cheese was usually made within the home, not commercially, with the recipe handed down from mother to daughter. Producers with such a keen sense of local history are a rare and refreshing find. Pam's cheeses can be found at Elgin farmers' market or specialist Scottish cheesemongers.

SCOTLAND   FORRES

Wester Lawrenceton Farm

Forres, Moray IV36 2RH   T: 01309 676566
🚜 farmers' markets ✉ farm gate sales

Pam Rodway makes traditional Scottish cheeses from unpasteurized organic milk. See the Super Hero box, above, for more information.

SCOTLAND   GLASGOW

Iain Mellis (The Cheesemonger)

492 Great Western Road, Glasgow G12 8EW   T: 0141 339 8998
W: www.ijmellischeesemonger.com
✉ mail order

For details, see under the Edinburgh branches on page 90. There is also a branch in St Andrews (see page 94).

Dunlop Dairy

West Clerkland Farm, Stewarton, Kilmarnock, Ayrshire KA3 5LP T: 01560 482494

⬛ **farmers' markets** ⬛ **farm gate sales**

Using ewes', goats' and cows' milk, Ann Dorward makes a range of pasteurized cheeses, including the very traditional cloth-bound Dunlop – from an old recipe – which is like a soft Cheddar. All the milk comes from the dairy's own animals. Find Ann at Edinburgh, Glasgow, Stirling and Paisley farmers' markets.

Grimbister Farm Cheese

Grimbister Farm, by Kirkwall, Orkney KW15 1TT T: 01856 761318
E: grimbister@orknet.co.uk

⬛ **farm gate sales** ⬛ **mail order**

Specializing in one type of cheese – a crumbly, unpasteurized variety – Hilda Seator uses the milk from her own herd of cows. Her cheese is available direct from the dairy, but call first.

Galloway Farmhouse Cheese

Millaries Farm, Sorbie, Newton Stewart, Dumfries and Galloway DG8 8AL
T: 01988 850224 w: www.ewetoyou.co.uk

⬛ **farm shop**

Galloway Farmhouse specializes in a Cheddar-style cheese, using raw ewes' milk and with a complex nutty flavour. Also available is a goats' milk cheese. Available from the shop at the dairy, but call first.

Kintaline Farm

Benderloch, Oban, Argyll, PA37 1QS T: 01631 720223 w: www.kintaline.co.uk AND
www.poultryscotland.co.uk

⬛ **farmers' markets** ⬛ **farm gate sales**

Kintaline Farm's Black Rock hens produce magnificent large eggs. See the Super Hero box, page 94, for more information.

super hero

KINTALINE FARM, Oban (see page 93)

Hens have a more complicated natural lifecycle than most people think and require resting periods and moulting periods in order to function properly. Most commercial egg producers take no account of this; birds are expected to lay continuously until they effectively wear out. At Kintaline Farm, things are different. The Black Rock hens are allowed to behave naturally, with acres of fresh pasture to roam on and with their natural cycles of laying and resting respected. This particular breed of hen has never been known to have salmonella in any UK flock and Kintaline's flocks produce magnificent eggs. They are not fed with high-protein feed, which can give the eggs a fishy flavour. For 2004, new breeds have been added to the flock, including Marans and Lavender Araucanas, so the eggs now come in a mix of lovely colours. The hens' eggs, as well as duck eggs and herbs, are available from the farm gate or Oban farmers' market.

Iain Mellis (The Cheesemonger)

149 South Street, St Andrews KY16 9UN T: 01334 471410
w: www.ijmellischeesemonger.com
✉ **mail order**

For details, see under the Edinburgh branches on page 90. There is also a branch in Glasgow (see page 92).

West Highland Dairy

Achmore, Stromeferry, Ross-shire IV53 8UW T: 01599 577203
w: www.westhighlanddairy.co.uk
⚊ **farm shop**

Kathy Biss of the West Highland Dairy has been making cheese for over 40 years, and her expertise is much sought-after – she has been asked by numerous institutions to conduct lectures on the finer points of cheesemaking. Eleven different cheeses are made here, all with cows' milk, and two won medals at the 2002 British Cheese Awards. Crème fraîche is also available – so rich and thick that it won't fall out of the pot if you turn it upside-down. All produce is available from the small shop at the dairy.

Highland Fine Cheeses Ltd

Blarliath Farm, Shore Road, Tain, Ross-shire IV19 1EB   T: 01862 892034

🏠 **farm shop**   ✉ **mail order**

Among other varieties, the Highland Fine Cheese Company make the traditional Scottish Crowdie, a soft and rich cheese that is an important part of the heritage of cheesemaking in Scotland.

Isle of Mull Cheese

Sgriob-Ruadh Farm, Tobermory, Isle of Mull PA75 6QD   T: 01688 302235
E: mull.cheese@btinternet.com

🏠 **farm gate sales**   ✉ **mail order**

From the milk of the assortment of cows on the farm (Ayrshires, Jerseys and Brown Swiss), Jeff Reade makes unpasteurized Cheddar-type cheeses, and there is now a choice of three ewes' milk cheeses too. Visitors are welcome and can watch the cheese being made from the viewing room, and buy the produce from the farm. Jeff was the recent winner of the BBC Radio 4 Best Food Producer award.

Bower Farm Dairy

Grosmont, Abergavenny, Gwent NP7 8HS   T: 01981 240219
W: www.bowerfarm.freeserve.co.uk

From the milk of their own herd of Jersey cows, the Collinson family make cream, clotted cream and yoghurt. Also available is free-range Gloucester Old Spot pork, from pigs reared on the farm. Available at Raglan farm shop.

Caws Cenarth

Fferm Glyneithinog, Llancwch, Boncath, Ceredigion SA37 0LH   T: 01239 710432
W: www.cawscenarth.co.uk

🏠 **farm gate sales**

Award-winning unpasteurized organic cheese from the milk of the dairy's own cows. See the Super Hero box, page 96, for more information.

super hero

THELMA ADAMS, cheesemaker at Caws Cenarth dairy, Ceredigion (see page 95)

Thelma Adams, the cheesemaker at Caws Cenarth, runs her dairy very much with an open-door policy. 'From day one I was adamant that the farm would be open to visitors to enable them to meet us and our animals and to watch the cheese being made, for them to gain a better understanding of the role played by farmers in producing the nation's food.' Thelma's son, Carwyn, is now taking the reins to allow Thelma some well-deserved time off.

The cheese is made with unpasteurized organic milk from Thelma's own herd, which is run with an emphasis on welfare – the calves are fed on their mother's milk until fully weaned. The varieties include a traditional Caerphilly, a blue cheese, and a semi-soft cheese, and the list of awards, including a gold from the British Cheese Awards, is impressive. Cheesemaking runs in the family – Thelma still makes it entirely by hand, the way she was taught by her mother and grandmother – the only difference is that Thelma uses vegetarian rennet. All the cheeses are accredited by the Soil Association. Buy on site, or from specialist cheesemongers such as Paxton & Whitfield.

WALES   CARDIGAN

Caffi Patio

super hero

Llangrannog, Cardigan Bay, Ceredigion SA44 6SL   T: 01239 654502
E: the.patiocafe@virgin.net

A café serving wonderful home-made food but especially renowned for its own Italian-style ice cream. See the Super Hero box, page 98, for more information.

WALES   CARDIGAN

Clover Jerseys

Cwrcoed Farm, Llangoedmor, Cardigan SA43 2LG,   T: 01239 621658
🔳 **farmers' markets** 🔳 **farm gate sales** ✉ **mail order**

Traditional Welsh farmhouse butter, hand-made from the Jersey milk of the farm's own herd. The butter is available in unsalted, medium-salted or the traditionally Welsh very salty versions. Buy it mail order, from the farm gate or from Cowbridge, Llandrindod Wells and Brecon farmers' markets.

Nantybwla

College Road, Carmarthen, Carmarthenshire SA31 3QS   T: 01267 237905
🛒 farmers' markets   📭 farm gate sales

Nantybwla make a great range of cheeses, all with the
unpasteurized milk of their own cows. There is a Caerphilly and a
matured Caerphilly, and a range of cheeses with flavourings – garlic
and leek, laverbread, cranberry, apricots or chives, and a smoked
variety. The cheeses have won many awards at the British Cheese
Awards, the Royal Welsh Show and the National Farmers' Union –
far too many to list. Find the cheese at Cowbridge, Penarth, Brecon,
Aberystwyth, Lampeter and Carmarthen farmers' markets, or buy it
direct from the farm.

Pant Mawr Farmhouse Cheese

Pant Mawr Farm, Rosebush, Clynderwen, Pembrokeshire SA66 7QU   T: 01437 532627
📭 farm gate sales   ✉ mail order

Pant Mawr Farm produces cheese from both cows' and goats' milk.
The goats' cheese is a soft curd cheese, available plain or in olive
oil. The cows' milk is used to make Caws Cerwyn, a fresh, young
cheese that is also available oak smoked; it is this version that won
Pant Mawr Farm a gold medal at the 2002 World Cheese Awards.
A Brie-like cheese – Caws Preseli – and a pungent, mead-washed
cheese – Caws Coch – complete the range.

Llangloffan Farmhouse Cheese

Llangloffan, Castle Morris, nr Fishguard, Pembrokeshire SA62 5ET   T: 01348 891241
W: www.welshcheese.co.uk
🥛 farm shop

The Downey family make a full-fat, unpasteurized cheese with the
milk from their own cows, and visitors can watch the cheesemaking
process in demonstrations every morning at the farm shop on site.
Breads made in the farmhouse kitchen are also available – among
the regular loaves and rolls, you'll find Italian-style breads and bara
brith (traditional fruit bread). Also on site is a new restaurant, Tides,
run by the Downey's daughter Emma, with lots of Pembrokeshire
seafood and a menu based on local organic produce. The farm is
accredited by the Organic Food Federation.

super hero

CAFFI PATIO, Cardigan Bay (see page 96)

This café has some lovely foods – home-made seafood chowder, rich with fish from Cardigan Bay, home-made soups and pizzas – but the star of the show is the home-made Italian-style ice cream. The owners, Julie and Mervyn, visit Italy regularly to learn techniques and get inspiration and it shows in the very imaginative flavours they make. They use raw local milk and cream, and the ice cream is not deep frozen – it really is 'iced cream', so it is softer and fresher than commercial ice cream. Incredibly rich and creamy, the ice cream has no artificial additives and fresh fruit, not concentrate, is used to flavour it.

WALES   HAVERFORDWEST

Caws Caerfai

Caerfai Farm, St David's, Haverfordwest, Pembrokeshire SA62 6QT   T: 01437 720548
W: www.caerfai.co.uk
⬆ **farm shop**

The farm shop at Caerfai Farm stocks some good local produce – organic vegetables, eggs and beef – but it is the home-made cheeses that are the real attraction. Unpasteurized organic milk from the farm's own cows is used to make Caerphilly cheeses, both plain and flavoured, and a Cheddar-type cheese. Call before visiting.

WALES   LLANDYSUL

Teifi Cheese

Glynhynod Farm, Llandysul, Ceredigion SA44 5JY   T: 01239 851528
⬆ **farm shop**

Winners of the Supreme Champion award at the British Cheese Awards, John and Patrice Savage make a range of cheeses, including a Gouda-style one. The cheese is made with the unpasteurized milk from the Savages' own Jersey cows. There is a farm shop on site, or find the cheeses in specialist cheese shops around the country.

WALES   NARBERTH

Drim Farm

Llawhaden, Narberth, Pembrokeshire SA67 8DN,   T: 01437 541295
▨ **farm gate sales**

Mr McNamara, the farmer at Drim Farm, is giving the West Country a run for its money when it comes to cream teas. He makes clotted cream from his own herd of Jersey cows, and it is so tasty that it has beaten more famous West Country cream-makers in competitions. Available from Haverfordwest farmers' market in the summer.

WALES   TREGARON

Gorwydd Caerphilly

Gorwydd Farm, Llanddewi Brefi, Tregaron, Ceredigion SY25 6NY   T: 01570 493516
E: morgan@gorwydd.com
🚩 farmers' markets

True specialists, the Trethowan family at Gorwydd Farm produce just one cheese – a mature Caerphilly. Using local milk, the cheese is unpasteurized and hand-made. Available from Borough Market in London or from local Welsh farmers' markets – call to find out where.

WALES   WHITLAND

Llanboidy Cheesemakers

Cilowen Uchaf, Login, Whitland, Carmarthenshire SA34 0TJ   T: 01994 448303
W: www.llanboidycheese.co.uk
✉ mail order

At Llanboidy Cheesemakers, the unpasteurized milk of rare-breed Red Poll cows is used to make a hard-pressed cheese – believed to be the only cheese in Europe made with this particular milk. The cheese is available plain or flavoured with laver bread, the Welsh seaweed. An organic range has also been developed.

food facts

FARMHOUSE BUTTER

Sadly, only a few makers of farmhouse, hand-patted butter remain. Farmhouse butter is made on a small scale, by hand, but the real key is the milk. The butter-makers we feature use the milk from one herd – often their own – and they may have chosen Jersey or Guernsey cows, famed for their rich, creamy milk, although these are not the highest yielding breeds. Farmhouse butter is usually a vibrant yellow, almost orange sometimes – this is due to the cows' diet of rich, verdant pasture, making a creamier milk. Many dairy farmers believe that using the milk from just one herd allows the characteristics of time and place – the season, and the pasture – to shine through in the end product.

This section is largely about delicatessens and specialist local food shops. I have focused on delis that endeavor to seek out and stock local, regional specialities: produce from British or Irish artisan producers. These are the stores that support small-scale producers and manufacturers and which offer unusual local foods that you are unlikely to find elsewhere. They may well sell some great-quality or hard-to-find imported produce – after all, good olive oils and balsamic vinegars are such an integral part of cooking these days, but are not produced on home turf. Alongside foreign delights, these shops will also provide a solid sense of local or regional flavour. In these times when it seems that food is becoming more and more standardized, indistinct and uniform, these shops proudly wave a flag for the obscure and the rare and are often an important part of the local community, where people can experience traditional shopping, where the foods are tasted and discussed. Often staff will personally know many of the producers that they buy from and can give customers background information. I have also listed some farm shops here, because they

delicatessens and specialist food shops

have such a vast array of different types of food on offer that they did not fit comfortably into any of the other categories.

While so much of this book is about the home-produced treasures that the UK and Ireland abound in, it would be unrealistic to deny the pleasures that some good quality imported foods bring – after all, there are many things that this country is unable to produce, and I'm not suggesting we shouldn't have access to them. So, alongside the delis, where you'll find delicacies from around the world, often from artisan producers, I've also listed a few other fine retail emporia, such as chocolate shops that have raised chocolate to an art form – after all, we are a nation of chocoholics. I hope that you discover new edible pleasures within this section. The Guild of Fine Food Retailers is instrumental in this country in encouraging small-scale producers and promoting specialist shops and delis that stock their produce. The annual Great Taste Awards that the Guild runs is a celebration of the diversity and skill of small producers in the UK and Ireland, and I have listed many winners in this section.

FOOD HEROES OF BRITAIN

Washing Pool Farm Shop

North Allington, Bridport, Dorset DT6 5HP   T: 01308 459549
w: www.washingpoolfarm.co.uk
⬤ farm shop

This farm shop is absolutely packed with produce from Dorset.
Food from over 50 local producers is represented here, from
chocolates to bread, meat and a great range of fresh fruit and
vegetables grown on the farm. There is also a restaurant on site,
again using local produce.

The Better Food Company

The Bristol Proving House, Sevier Street, Bristol BS2 9QS   T: 0117 935 1725
w: www.betterfood.co.uk; www.walledgarden.co.uk
⬤ shop

The Better Food Company offer a one-stop-shop for fantastic fresh
foods and groceries, all of which are as ethically and environmentally
sustainable as possible. There is a wonderful range of fresh fruit and
veg from the company's own two acre Victorian walled garden,
artisan bread, organic fish, farmhouse cheeses and locally reared
meat and poultry, all with an emphasis on organic.

Tamarisk Farm

West Bexington, Dorchester, Dorset DT2 9DF   T: 01308 897781 OR 01308 897784
w: www.tamariskfarm.co.uk
⬤ farm gate sales ⬤ box scheme

Conservation is an issue at the heart of this Dorset organic farm –
proper crop rotation maintains the soil's natural fertility and the
species-rich permanent pasture is well looked after. The farm
produces organic lamb, hogget, mutton and beef, a good range of
vegetables in season (sold through the box scheme) and even flour
from home-grown grains, including a rye flour, and a wheat flour
made using an old variety of wheat, good for making a firm, nutty
loaf. All are available direct from the farm. Flour is also available
from Washing Pool Farm shop (see above).

Sageberry Cheese Delicatessen

21 Cheap Street, Frome, Somerset BA11 1BN   T: 01373 462543

The staff at Sageberry Cheese are always willing to search out that elusive ingredient. A great selection of local cheeses, high-quality chocolate and locally produced smoked meats are always on display.

Lefktro UK Ltd

Somerville House, High Street, Hinton St George, Somerset TA17 8SE   T: 01460 72931
W: www.getoily.com

✉ **mail order**

A great selection of extra-virgin olive oils from around the world, plus Mediterranean foods and kitchen accessories can be found at this shop.

Honeybuns

Naish Farm, Stony Lane, Holwell, Dorset DT9 5LJ   T: 01963 23597
W: www.wemadeitourselves.com

Honeybuns produce exquisite, artisan cakes, by hand, with largely locally produced ingredients. If chocolate is required, they'll use Valrhona and the butter is traditional farmhouse – margarine is never used. The eggs are laid only two fields away – there is a distinct community feel to the business. A large selection of gluten- and wheat-free cakes is also on offer. As yet, Honeybuns have no retail outlet themselves (you can find the cakes at John Lewis cafés) but they are toying with the idea of a café on site and are happy for visitors to come along, with a day's notice.

Daylesford Organic Farmshop

Daylesford Organic Farmshop, Daylesford, Near Kingham, Gloucestershire GL56 0YG
T: 01608 731700   W: www.daylesfordorganic.com

This really is an exceptional farmshop. Beautifully designed, the shop is filled with home-produced organic foods, from rare heritage varieties of vegetables, fresh from the kitchen garden, award-winning Daylesford Cheddar and Penyston cheeses from the creamery, artisan breads made with wheat grown at Daylesford, and a full range of organic meat, including venison, Aberdeen Angus beef and lamb from indigenous breeds.

SOUTH WEST	KINGSBRIDGE

Burts Potato Chips

The Parcel Shed, Station Yard, Kingsbridge, Devon TQ7 1ES   T: 01548 852220
w: www.burtschips.com

Crisps with personality! Burts Potato Chips are made from potatoes from farms that the makers know – in fact, each bag is labelled with the field that the potatoes came from and which member of staff fried that particular batch. Burts really do take potato chips to a whole new level. Phone to find your nearest outlet.

SOUTH WEST	LISKEARD

Oughs

10 Market Street, Liskeard, Cornwall PL14 3JJ   T: 01579 343253
w: www.oughs.co.uk
✉ mail order

The best of Cornish artisan produce can be found at Oughs, from farmhouse cheeses and local bacon and ham, to Cornish wine, cider and real ales. Home made cakes, a great selection of local jams and chutneys, and wonderful Cornish ice cream are all on offer. There is a traditional tea room on the premises, and Oughs specialise in hampers packed with regional delicacies.

SOUTH WEST	MORETON-IN-MARSH

Longborough Farm Shop

Longborough, Moreton-in-Marsh, Gloucestershire GL56 0QZ   T: 01451 830469
w: www.longboroughfarmshop.com
🍴 farm shop

The knowledgeable and helpful staff at the Longborough Farm Shop will happily guide you through their incredible range of local produce – rare-breed meats, game from nearby shoots, local cheeses, even local crisps. In season, home-grown asparagus is available and in summer there is the opportunity to pick your own fruit.

Bre-Pen Farm

Mawgan Porth, Newquay, Cornwall TR8 4AL   T: 01637 860420
w www.bre-penfarm.co.uk
⚓ **farm shop**

Rod and Jill at Bre-Pen Farm pack a lot into a small space – the
farm shop is compact, but full of home-reared lamb, including
sausages and burgers, home-produced vegetables (check out
the delicious new potatoes when they are in season), home made
cakes, jams and chutneys, and plenty of other local produce, from
cheese and chocolate to cider and single-varietal apple juices.

Stein's Seafood Deli

South Quay, Padstow, Cornwall PL28 8BY   T: 01841 533466   w: www.rickstein.com
✉ **mail order**

The emphasis is on local, fresh produce. In our Deli you'll find
Cornish smoked fish and charcuterie, pâtés, sausages, dry-cured
bacons, local cheeses, and freshly made sandwiches, as well
as a range of ready-to-cook delicacies such as fish pie, seafood
thermidore, fishcakes and fish soup, rouille, and croûtons from
the Seafood Restaurant. There's also a wide selection of wines
from my winery in Australia's Hunter Valley, and we still stock the
ever popular range of jams, marmalades, chutneys and preserves,
all made in Padstow.

Enys Wartha

28 Market Jew Street, Penzance, Cornwall TR18 2HR   T: 01736 367375

A deli specializing in all things Cornish. Over two-thirds of the
produce stocked is home-produced by the owners, Michael and
Debbie Sculthorp-Wright. Specialities include free-range duck and
goose eggs, Cornish-recipe cakes, Cornish cheese and smoked
fish, and home-made pâtés and pies. There is a tearoom at the deli.

Riverford at Kitley

Yealmpton, nr Plymouth, Devon PL8 2LT   T: 01752 880925   w:www.riverford.co.uk
↳ **farm shop**

A branch of the Riverford Farm Shop. See their main entry, opposite, for more information.

Di's Dairy and Pantry

Rock Road, Rock, Cornwall   T: 01208 863531

When you first enter Di's Dairy, you might find that you just don't know what to look at first – there's so much to see. A huge chilled cabinet is packed with artisan cheeses, home-made pies, pasties and puddings, another is filled with all manner of cold meats and charcuterie. There is a wonderful selection of alcoholic drinks, including local wines and ciders, and shelves groan under the weight of home-made and locally produced preserves, chutneys and honey. Local ice cream is well represented, and there is even a choice of several varieties of Cornish butter – Di's really is a paradise for food lovers.

Truffles

72 Belle Vue Road, Salisbury, Wiltshire SP1 3YD   T: 01722 331978
✉ **mail order**

Christmas wouldn't be Christmas without a traditional 'plum' pudding, but many people don't have the time to make them, and often the ones found in supermarkets can be disappointing. Barbara at Truffles makes truly delicious Christmas puddings – generous with the brandy and sherry, packed with moist fruit, and with a lovely warm spiciness, they have the feel of old-fashioned, home-made puddings.

Emma B Delicatessen

6 West Street, Somerton, Somerset TA11 7PS   T: 01458 273444

In the face of stiff competition from supermarkets, Emma has two plans – to try to source any foods her customers ask for and to make shopping fun, instead of a chore. The rich heritage of

Somerset foods is well represented here, with over 90 varieties of cheese available at any one time, home-baked pies and quiches, and sweet-pickled garlic.

Provender Delicatessen

3 Market Square, South Petherton, Somerset TA13 5BT   T: 01460 240681
w: www.provender.co.uk

✉ **mail order**

The emphasis at Provender is on the produce of the West Country, so artisan cheeses, cider, air-dried ham and locally sourced smoked meat and fish are found here in profusion.

Hampton's Deli

1 Digbeth Street, Stow-on-the-Wold, Gloucestershire GL54 1BN   T: 01451 831733
w: www.hamptons-hampers.co.uk

A good selection of British cheeses, predominantly from small, less-well-known dairies, including the famous Stinking Bishop and the local single Gloucester. A range of French-style breads from a local bakery, home-baked raised pies and interesting oils and vinegars are all included. Tasting is encouraged.

Wellswood Village Pantry

11 Ilsham Road, Torquay, Devon TQ1 2JG   T: 01803 292315

A deli selling home-made, award-winning sausages made with local meats, locally baked bread and a great range of cheeses. The owner's policy on buying is 'if we can get it locally, we will'.

Riverford Farm Shop

Staverton, nr Totnes, Devon TQ9 6AF ALSO AT Riverford Goes to Town, High Street, Totnes TQ9 5YR   T: 01803 762523 (STAVERTON); 01803 863959 (TOTNES)
w: www.riverfordfarmshop.co.uk

🥄 **farm shop**

Owned by the Watson family, the Riverford Farm Shop is a mecca for serious food lovers and aims to be 'the complete one-stop food shop'. The store sells a wide variety of products from bread to meat, to vegetables and dairy produce and even a selection of wines. The family aim to make their customers more aware of the source of their food and believe in stocking local organic produce where possible. Other products, such as olive oils and vinegars, which cannot be bought from local firms, are all acquired from fair-trade sources. There is a second shop in Yealmpton, near Plymouth, see page 106, and a third (Riverford Goes to Town) in Totnes itself.

see page 106

SOUTH WEST   WADEBRIDGE

Porteath Bee Centre

nr Polzeath, Wadebridge, Cornwall PL27 6RA   T: 01208 863718

✉ farm gate sales

Cornish honey available as clear, set or creamed; none of the types has been heat treated, as many commercial honeys are. Visitors are welcome on site, where there is a live bee exhibition.

food facts

OLIVE OIL

The most prized type of olive oil is the result of the first cold pressing, known as extra-virgin oil. This can come in either filtered or unfiltered form; the unfiltered variety will have a slightly hazy look, while the filtered will be clear and bright. Many consider that the unfiltered oil has a purity of flavour lacking in the filtered oil. The most easily found olive oils come from Italy, Greece and Spain and the oils of each country tend to have common characteristics – Spanish oil is often fruity, with undertones of melon or even banana; Greek oils will have a more recognizable rich olive flavour, with a grassy taste, and Italian oils tend to be robust and peppery. Oils will change flavour to a degree when heated. Some purists believe that to heat fine extra-virgin oil is crass, and that it should only ever be consumed cold and raw. The olive oil industry seems to be mirroring the wine world; alongside the classic Mediterranean countries, great oils are now coming out of New World countries – Australia, the US (California), Chile and New Zealand. With lesser-known countries like Portugal and Tunisia also producing fine oils, there are so many to try.

Wells Stores at Peachcroft Farm

Twelveacre Drive, Abingdon, Oxfordshire OX14 2HP   T: 01235 535978

Wells Stores originally began as a cheese shop and still stocks an array of artisan British cheeses from small dairies. Alongside these are some great home-produced foods – free-range seasonal geese, fruit and vegetables (all produced on the farm), and even game that the owners shoot themselves. Bread from De Gustibus (see page 30), local apple juice and a host of deli items make this a treasure-trove.

Pollen Organics

Three Firs House, Bramshott Chase, Hampshire   T: 01948 840252
W: www.pollenorganics.com

🚜 **farmers' markets** ✉ **mail order**

The drive behind Pollen Organics is one we have witnessed in many of our Food Heroes – the Pollen family simply could not find sauces, dressings and pesto that they really liked, and so decided that they would make their own. The result is food that has an appealing freshness and simplicity (due in part to the total absence of additives and preservatives), and a home-made quality that has seen Pollen Organics winning many awards. Fresh, local produce is a key feature, along with an avid attention to detail and a spirit of creativity – the pesto is made with almonds, not pine nuts, and there is even a watercress pesto. Find Pollen Organics at Winchester, Petersfield, Farnham and Milford farmers' markets.

Montezuma's Chocolate

15 Duke Street, Brighton BN1 1AH   T: 01273 324979   w: www.montezumas.co.uk
✉ **mail order**

Montezuma's make wonderful hand-made chocolates. See the Super Hero box, page 110, for more information. There is also a branch in Chichester (page 111).

super hero

SIMON AND HELEN PATTINSON, of Montezuma's Chocolate, Brighton, Chichester and Solihull (see pages 109, 110 and 111)

Although Montezuma's is a young company, having only been established in 2001, it has already received high-profile acclaim, including winning a Soil Association award. Though the chocolate is organic, this is not the only key to its success. Simon Pattinson and his wife Helen, both ex-lawyers, make it their mission to find the best raw materials with which to make their chocolates and they believe they have found them in the cocoa beans they buy from organic estates in the Dominican Republic. They then make everything by hand at their headquarters in Sussex, endlessly experimenting to find the best combinations of flavours and the percentages of cocoa solids that make the chocolates the perfect balance of sweetness and bitterness. Simon told me that there is a great deal of snobbery in the chocolate industry and that many people think that the higher the level of cocoa solids in a bar, the better the chocolate. Not so, he says. Too high a percentage and the chocolate is too bitter, making it necessary to add sweet fillings or sugar to alleviate this. The excess sugar then destroys the flavour of the chocolate. Simon has settled on 73% cocoa solids for his 'Very Dark' chocolate. After a great deal of testing and trying, he feels this is the balance that allows the chocolate taste to shine through without being overly bitter. And for the non-purist, he has added some wonderful flavourings – from chilli, cinnamon and cardamom to lime, apple and ground coffee. This is a food obsession at its best!

SOUTH EAST   CANTERBURY

The Goods Shed

Station Road West, Canterbury, Kent CT2 8AN T: 01227 459153
🗂 farmers' markets

A six-day-a-week farmers' market, with local producers gathering to sell their food all under one roof. Meat – free-range and organic – cheeses, fish, beer, cider and bread are all on offer. There is an on-site bakery and a restaurant, where only foods from the stalls are used. The chef chooses his ingredients from the market each morning, and devises that day's menu accordingly. Closed Mondays.

Montezuma's Chocolate

29 East Street, Chichester PO19 1HF   T: 01243 537385
w: www.montezumas.co.uk
✉ **mail order**

See the Super Hero box, opposite, for more information. There is also a branch in Brighton (page 109).

Trencherman and Turner

52 Grove Road, Little Chelsea, Eastbourne, East Sussex BN21 4UD   T: 01323 737535
w: www.loadedtable.com

Local cheeses, including 'Scrumpy Sussex', a variety made with local cider, Sussex sparkling wine, organic ham on the bone, wild boar sausages, bacon and free-range eggs from a local farm and unusual English wines – all great foods that you won't find in supermarkets – are available here.

The Food Halls

5–9 Packhorse Road, Gerrards Cross, Buckinghamshire SL9 7QA   T: 01753 893071
w: www.thefoodhalls.co.uk

This is the sister outlet of H P Jung, the baker (see page 26), but is also an alliance of several local companies – the great continental bread is here, but there is a charcuterie section, a butchery, a pâtisserie counter and even a Champagne bar. A foodie's delight.

The Silver Palate

3 Vaughan Road, Harpenden, Hertfordshire AL5 4HU   T: 01582 713722
w: www.hotolives.com
✉ **mail order**

Georgina at The Silver Palate is a crusader for good food, and among the specialities at this large food emporium are Cypriot-style breads, lots of fair-trade produce, artisan cheeses and their own-made Turkish delight. A huge olive selection is also on display.

Roots Deli

33 Crendon Street, High Wycombe, Buckinghamshire HP13 6LJ   T: 01494 524243
w: www.rootsdeli.co.uk

✉ **mail order**

Lots of British cheeses, olive oils to taste and a strong organic
section, too, make this deli well worth a visit.

Mrs Huddleston's

5 Dingle Dell, Leighton Buzzard, Bedfordshire LU7 3JL   T: 01525 381621
w: www.mrshuddleston.com

✉ **mail order**

Mrs Huddleston scooped seven major awards at the 2004 Great
Taste Awards, including one for her English-wine jelly. She makes
mulled-wine jelly, ginger-wine jelly and a cider-and-sage jelly, all of
which are great as accompaniments to cold meats. Many of the
ingredients Mrs Huddleston uses are from local sources. Conserves,
marmalades, sauces and chutneys complete the range, and can be
bought by mail order, or from Fortnum & Mason in London or from
some branches of Waitrose. Mrs Huddleston's is a member of Slow
Food.

Abel & Cole Ltd

8–15 MGI Estate, Milkwood Road, London SE24 0JF   T: 0845 262 6262
w: www.abel-cole.co.uk

▨ **box scheme**

Abel & Cole operate an organic delivery scheme throughout London
and further afield, the mainstay of which is the incredibly fresh fruit
and veg that they source as locally as possible. Solid ethics are
behind the buying decisions here – sustainability is a key issue, and
Abel & Cole use biodegradable plastics, and will never import
anything by air. Along with the fruit and vegetables, customers are
offered sustainably caught Cornish fish, organic meat, and great
organic bread baked fresh each morning at the Old Post Office
Bakery (see their entry on page 31).

L'Artisan du Chocolat

89 Lower Sloan Street, London SW1 W8DA   T: 020 7824 8365
www.artisanduchocolat.com
✉ mail order

L'Artisan du Chocolat have been creating quite a stir among lovers
of good quality chocolate. The company won the prestigious
'Best Producer' title in the 2004 Observer Food Awards, and the
chocolatier, Gerard Coleman, has been called 'the leading light in
the world of modern chocolate'. The ingredients used here are, quite
simply, the best, beginning with Criollo or Trinitario cocoa beans from
small scale, thoughtful producers, continuing through to the spices,
herbs and fruits that are all chosen when in the peak of their season.
The flavours are a revelation: Sechuan pepper, Earl Grey tea, red
wine, chestnut honey, even tobacco. Such is this company's passion
for chocolate, there are even 11 varieties of plain dark chocolate bar
to choose from. Available direct from the shop, or by mail order.

Brindisa

32 Exmouth Market, Clerkenwell, London EC1R 4QE ALSO AT Borough Market SE1 9AH
T: 020 7713 1666 (CLERKENWELL); 020 7407 1036 (BOROUGH MARKET)
W: www.brindisa.com

The legendary Spanish deli, offering the very best of Spanish artisan
produce, from fish and charcuterie, to cheese, chocolate and oils.

The Chocolate Society

36 Elizabeth Street, London SW1W 9NZ ALSO AT 32–34 Shepherd Market,
London W14 7HQ   T: 0207 259 9222 (ELIZABETH ST); 0207 495 0302
(SHEPHERD MARKET); 01423 322230 (MAIL ORDER)   W: www.chocolate.co.uk
✉ mail order

Hand-made truffles, Valrhona bars, and organic, single-bean bars
are available from The Chocolate Society's shop. There is a small
café selling chocolate brownies, ice cream and milkshakes – all
underpinned by the highest quality chocolate. See also the entry
on page 131.

FOOD HEROES OF BRITAIN

Delectables Fine Foods

4 Ravenslea Road, Wandsworth Common, London SW12 8SB   T: 07717 296239
W: www.delectablesfinefoods.co.uk

🛒 **farmers' markets** 🚚 **delivery service** ✉ **mail order**

Delectables Fine Foods is a moveable feast of all manner of specialist foods, from French and Spanish charcuterie, lamb from Devon and free-range Norfolk pork, to British farmhouse cheeses and artisan breads. Find Delectables stalls around London – phone for details or check the website.

Forman & Field

30a Marshgate Lane, London E15 2NH   T: 020 8221 3939
W: www.formanandfield.com

✉ **mail order**

Forman & Field have brought together many traditional, small-scale producers from around the country and are offering a selection of high-quality foods with a luxurious feel. Some of the producers are people we feature individually here, such as Seldom Seen Farm, Richard Woodall and Neal's Yard (see pages 373, 374, 330 and 67). Forman & Field are offering a one-stop-shop for traditionally produced foods.

Gourmet World

101 Lonsdale Road, London SW13 9DA   T: 020 8748 0125   W: www.gourmet-world.com

✉ **mail order**

Gourmet World seek out artisan producers around Europe, finding the unusual and the small scale. Everything is high quality, produced without artificial additives.

The Oil Merchant Ltd

47 Ashchurch Grove, London W12 9BU   T: 020 8740 1335
E: the_oil_merchant@compuserve.com

✉ **mail order**

The Oil Merchant is a specialist importer of single-estate olive oils and oil-related products such as vinegars and salsas from small-scale producers throughout Europe, Australia, New Zealand and South Africa. The Oil Merchant is a member of Slow Food.

Rococo Chocolates

321 Kings Road, London SW3 5EP T: 0207 352 5857 ALSO AT 45 Marylebone High Street, London W14 5HG T: 020 7935 7780 W: www.rococochocolates.com
✉ mail order

Among the hand-made chocolates – the pinnacle of luxury, made from chocolate with a very high cocoa content – you'll find organic 'artisan' bars of dark and milk chocolate. Rococo are keen to promote the planting of rare cocoa bean plants to conserve biodiversity, and their chocolate is fairly traded.

food facts

CHOCOLATE

Fine chocolate is a very different food from the confectionery available in most corner shops. Chocolate should be a combination of both cocoa solids and cocoa butter extracted from the cocoa bean. Most well-known brands contain a remarkably low percentage of cocoa-solids – as little as 25% – and in some cases hardly qualify as chocolate at all, since the butter content is often mixed with other fats. Good quality chocolate should have at least a 50% cocoa-solid content, and much of the rest should be pure cocoa butter. The best-known cocoa bean types are Criollo, Forastero and Trinitario, which is a hybrid of the first two. The best, Criollo, comes from Central America and, like so many of the finest foodstuffs, it is in danger of dying out – it's expensive, relatively low yielding, and not particularly disease resistant. There are, however, chocolate shops that offer chocolate made from these magical beans; some even stock 'single-bean variety' chocolate – made from the highest quality beans, from one cocoa estate, not blended with cheaper beans. The resulting chocolate is a revelation, but beware – buying from the chocolate shops we've listed will ruin you for cheaper varieties forever.

The Spice Shop

1 Blenheim Crescent, London W11 2EE   T: 020 7221 4448
w: www.thespiceshop.co.uk
✉ **mail order**

The Spice Shop currently stocks around 2,500 different spices and
blends. All the blends are mixed on the premises by Birgitt, the
owner, using the best-quality spices on the market. No salt, MSG,
starch, wheat nuts or any artificial additives are used. Oils are also
available, including the highly prized Argan oil from North Africa.
This is a treasure-trove of the unusual.

Lymington Larder

7 St Thomas Street, Lymington, Hampshire SO41 9NA   T: 01590 676740
w: www.lymingtonlarder.co.uk

Charles Du Parc, the owner of this deli, sources most of his stock
from the south of England, including almost all the cheeses he sells.
The cheeses are mainly from small producers who make cheese
using milk from their herds, and he has a good selection of ewes'
and goats' milk cheeses – generally, Charles personally knows the
producers that he buys from. Other foods available include meats
and pâtés, and local free-range eggs.

The Grapevine Delicatessen

77 High Street, Odiham, Hampshire RG29 1LB   T: 01256 704466 (MAIL ORDER)
01256 701900 (DELI)   w: www.grapevine-gourmet.co.uk
✉ **mail order**

Foods from all over the continent and the Far East, but also
specialities from closer to home, sourced from specialist growers
and producers. Lots of home-made food, too.

County Delicacies

35–37 St Mary's Butts, Reading, Berkshire RG1 2LS   T: 0118 957 4653

A deli keen to support small local producers, sourcing mainly from
southern England. Berkshire ham on the bone, local cheeses, local

wine and cider, and some interesting speciality breads are the most popular products.

Angela's Delicatessen

The Square, Yarmouth, Isle of Wight PO41 0NS T: 01983 761196

A deli with a really wide scope of produce, from British artisan cheeses to organic smoked salmon, free-range local chicken, local game and dry-cured bacon. The shop is even open at 7am on Sundays to provide freshly baked bread, croissants and pains au chocolat.

The Cambridge Cheese Company

All Saint's Passage, Cambridge CB2 3LS T: 01223 846129
🛒 shop

Over 150 types of cheese are available at the Cambridge Cheese deli, offered at the peak of perfection due to the shop's own maturing rooms. This is much more than a cheese shop, though – there is an extensive range of charcuterie, oils, vinegars, and over 40 varieties of olive on offer.

Picnic Fayre Delicatessen

The Old Forge, Cley-next-the-Sea, Norfolk NR25 7AP T: 01263 740587
🚚 delivery service

There are some quirky items available at Picnic Fayre – lavender focaccia bread and perry vinegar to name just two. The accent is on East Anglian produce, with Norfolk free-range bacon and Norfolk fruit wines heading the list.

The Dedham Gourmet

High Street, Dedham, Colchester, Essex CO7 6HA T: 01206 323623
w: www.dedham-gourmet.co.uk

Though they specialize in artisan British cheeses, of which there are 40 or 50 to choose from, there is still plenty of regional East Anglian fare here, with local jams, honeys and fruit juices all well represented.

H Gunton

81–83 Crouch Street, Colchester, Essex CO3 3EZ   T: 01206 572200
w: www.guntons.co.uk

A deli with a mind-boggling array of cheeses – over 100 different types. Alongside the British farmhouse cheeses, continental cheeses are well represented. There is also an interesting selection of cooked meats, such as home-cooked hams, ox tongue, kassler and parma ham.

The Food Company

London Road, Marks Tey, Colchester, Essex CO6 1ED   T: 01206 214000

The Food Company is a huge shrine to quality food, encompassing an artisan bakery with a great range of breads, including unusual European varieties and sourdoughs, a butchery offering meats direct from small farms, and a fishmonger who sources fish daily from Billingsgate and Lowestoft. There is an extensive deli section and greengrocers, and upstairs you'll find a 70-seat brasserie and panini bar. There's so much going on, and with regular wine tastings and cookery demonstrations, you could really make a day out of a visit to the Food Company.

La Hogue Farm Shop and Delicatessen

La Hogue Farm Foods, Chippenham, Ely, Cambridgeshire CB7 5PZ   T: 01638 751128
w: www.lahogue.co.uk
⬤ farm shop

An enormous array of home-produced and local produce – fruit, vegetables and salads, free-range meats, farmhouse cheeses, and game (in season), all sourced from the farm and Sussex estates. The farm kitchen produces some really good breads, cakes and pastries and ready meals, and the farm shop has an off-licence, selling wines and local ales. La Hogue was awarded the 2003–2004 Newmarket Business of the Year award.

super hero

THE HARDINGHAM FAMILY, of Alder Carr Farm, Needham Market (see below)

This farm shop is committed to environmentally sensitive farming, leaving many areas wild and using biological pest control (introducing birds and insects to keep pests under control); as a result the farm is teeming with wildlife and is even a haven for the endangered otter. Alder Carr has an equally sensitive attitude to the foods sold in the shop. Home-grown fruits and vegetables are available and the farm shop is also brimming with locally produced and organic food. Their own fruit is used to make unique ice-cream, containing nothing but fruit, cream and sugar, with imaginative flavours such as rhubarb and ginger. Even the imported produce they stock is fairly traded – the family is keen to support small-scale farmers in other countries, too. Alder Carr even runs a farmers' market on site, with 25 stalls selling local foods including unpasteurized Jersey cream, free-range pork, game and organic meat, fruits, vegetables, juices and herbs.

EAST ANGLIA   IPSWICH

Alder Carr Farm

super hero

Needham Market, Ipswich, Suffolk IP6 8LX   T: 01449 720820
w: www.aldercarrfarm.co.uk
🠗 farm shop   🠗 farmers' markets

Committed to environmentally sensitive farming, Alder Carr Farm Shop sells a good selection of their own and locally produced products. See the Super Hero box, above, for more information.

EAST ANGLIA   IPSWICH

Fruits of Suffolk

Mill House, Stone Street, Crowfield, Ipswich, Suffolk IP6 9SZ   T: 01449 760397
🠗 farmers' markets

Hand-made preserves and chutneys, using local ingredients, are made in small batches, which has a significant effect on the flavour – they are cooked for less time, and so remain tastier. Some unusual jams are available – greengage, damson and Victoria plum, along with apple chutney and spicy plum chutney. Old-fashioned lemon curd is also available, made from fresh lemons, pure butter and free-range eggs. Available from Woodbridge, Needham (Alder Carr), South Lopham and Tivetshall farmers' markets.

The Manningtree Delicatessen

21 The High Street, Manningtree, Essex CO11 1AG   T: 01206 395071

🚚 delivery service   ✉ mail order

Simon of The Manningtree Deli is passionate about good food, and is keen to stock local produce – he tends to know all his suppliers very well and has local wines, Suffolk bacon, and fresh fish from Lowestoft, with live lobsters to choose from. The choice of cheeses is impressive – around 120 different types, of which about three-quarters are British. The Manningtree Delicatessen now has a mobile deli – a unique, handmade traditional vehicle taking Italian delicacies to all the nearby villages.

Hoo Hing

Commercial Centre, Freshwater Road, Chadwell Heath, Romford, Essex RM8 1RX
T: 020 8548 3636   W: www.hoohing.com

✉ mail order

As far as Eastern ingredients go, if it's not available at Hoo Hing, then it probably doesn't exist!

Chisnalls Delicatessen

3 Market Walk, Saffron Walden, Essex CB10 1JZ   T: 01799 528239

The shopping experience at Chisnalls is described as 'interactive' – lots of customer tastings, and advice and help from the staff. All the usual deli items here, with a really good choice of farmhouse cheeses.

Jules and Sharpie

Broadway Hall, Verdons Lane, Stradbroke, Suffolk IP21 5NN   T: 01379 384364
W: www.julesandsharpie.com

✉ mail order

Award-winning, hand-made hot pepper jellies that are ideal as accompaniments to hot or cold meats, or in sandwiches. There are seven varieties, all with chillies in them, including several savoury fruit flavours, their classic hot pepper jelly and an extremely hot version. Jules and Sharpie started the business making the jellies in their own kitchens, and even though they now work from a purpose-equipped unit, they still do everything by hand themselves. The jellies have recently won a clutch of medals at the Great Taste Awards.

Swayfen Herb Farm

Swayfen House, Rose and Crown Road, Swavesey, Cambridgeshire CB4 5RB
T: 01954 267111   w: www.swayfen.co.uk
✉ mail order

Home-grown, unsprayed herbs form the basis for many of the products here. Extra-virgin olive oil, traditional vinegars and fresh herbs are combined for a flavourful range of condiments and dressings. Swayfen Herb Farm was the proud recipient of eight Great Taste Awards in 2003.

Didlington Manor

Didlington, nr Thetford, Norfolk IP26 5AT   T: 01842 878673
✉ mail order

Unpasteurized single-crop honey, from hives placed in some of the Royal Parks of London and Sandringham, where bees gather nectar from aboretums rich in unusual tree varieties.

Thorpeness Village Store

Peace Place, Thorpeness, Suffolk IP16 4PL   T: 01728 454464
🚚 delivery service

Thorpeness Village Store is run with a commitment to locally produced, high-quality food, and to maintaining a sense of community in the village. Among the produce the owner stocks are her own home-grown vegetables, local cheeses and bread baked in the village. She also does a free delivery round for those customers unable to get to the shop.

Tastebuds

The Street, Earl Soham, Woodbridge, Suffolk IP13 7RT   T: 01728 685557
W: www.tastebudsfood.com

The foods available at Tastebuds are entirely British in origin, from
East Anglia wherever possible, and Lucie Walker, the owner, makes
great 'takeaway' foods from local produce – Suffolk ham and hickory-
cured pork from locally reared pigs, fish cakes made from fish caught
at Lowestoft, and organic, locally grown fruits and vegetables.
There's local game available, and even bottled beer from the brewery
next door. There is now a coffee garden with gazebo.

Chatsworth Farm Shop

Pilsley, Bakewell, Derbyshire DE4 1UF   T: 01246 583392   W: www.chatsworth.org
⬇ farm shop

A wonderful selection of home-made or locally produced foods,
including beef and lamb from the estate's farms, and venison from
the park. The farm shop also runs seasonal events, such as the
apple day in October, which showcases English apple varieties, and
the Summer Food Fair, where suppliers meet the customers to talk
about their produce.

The Original Farmers' Market Shop

3 Market Street, Bakewell, Derbyshire DE45 1HG   T: 01629 815814
⬇ farm shop

Many people love to shop at farmers' markets but find that the
markets are not frequent enough. The Original Farmers Market Shop
in Bakewell seeks to be a permanent farmers' market, with all the
stock coming from small-scale producers within a 35-mile radius.
Rare-breed free-range pork, local game, home-baked breads and
locally smoked meats and fish are all available – the range is huge.

Farmshop Home Delivery

Shackerdale Farm, Car Colston, Bingham, Nottinghamshire NG13 8JG
T: 01949 829006   W: www.farmshop.net
🚚 delivery service

Farmshop Home Delivery is a great new idea for busy families, offering a huge range of local produce, delivered to your doorstep. There's plenty to choose from – meat from local farms, both organic and conventional, artisan cheeses, locally grown fruit and vegetables at the peak of freshness, bread and cakes, even ready-made meals created using local produce. The producers are carefully chosen – all have to demonstrate environmentally sensitive production. This really is a one-stop-shop for local foods, and you needn't even leave the house! Delivery is available throughout Nottinghamshire and Leicestershire.

The Granary

Hungerford, Craven Arms, Shropshire SY7 9HG T: 01584 841027
W: www.corvedale.com

A great place to find the best produce from Shropshire, Herefordshire and Worcestershire, The Granary offers Neal's Yard Creamery, Lightwood and Anstey's cheeses (see page 67), Maynard's bacon, Corvedale lamb and chutneys, jams, beer and fruit gins. There is a tearoom on site.

Taste of the Country

Countrywide Stores, Worcester Road, Evesham, Worcestershire WR11 4QR
T: 01386 760386 W: www.tasteofthecountry.co.uk
➼ farm shop

Taste of the Country take traceable food to a whole new level – in each of the three stores you'll find a 'Food Fact File' – a weighty tome giving you detailed information about each of the shop's suppliers, including their location, production practices and a company history, giving customers the chance to make an informed buying decision. Local sourcing is the key to this company, with producers of the best local foods chosen to give customers a great range, from meat and fish, cheese, butter and eggs, to fruit and vegetables, single varietal apple juices, breads and condiments. Taste of the Country is a wonderful one-stop shop for those who really care where their food comes from. There are two further shops in Ledbury and Long Compton (page 124).

Ceci Paolo

21 High Street, Ledbury, Herefordshire HR8 1DS   T: 01531 632976
w: www.cecipaolo.com

A deli for the adventurous home cook, the owner, Pat Harrison, aims to stock the best ingredients for serious cooks. Mediterranean, oriental and Australian delectables sit next to home-made dips and purées, regional cheeses and locally grown salads and herbs.

Taste of the Country

Countrywide Stores, Hazle Park, Dymock Road, Ledbury, Herefordshire HR8 2JQ
T: 01531 635600

For details, see under the Evesham branch (see page 123).

Taste of the Country

50 Main Street, Long Compton, Warwickshire   T: 01608 684993
w: www.tasteofthecountry.co.uk
🥄 **farm shop**

For details, see under the Evesham branch (see page 123).

The Chocolate Gourmet

16 Castle Street, Ludlow, Shropshire SY8 1AT   T: 01584 879332   w: www.chocmail.co.uk
✉ **mail order**

Alongside all the delicious truffles and filled chocolates, The Chocolate Gourmet has a great range of couverture chocolate, with many single-origin, 'grand cru' bars from Valrhona, Michel Cluizel and El Rey. These are fantastic very-high-cocoa-content chocolates, made with the very best beans.

Deli on the Square

4 Church Street, Ludlow, Shropshire SY8 1AP   T: 01584 877353
w: www.justmustard.com

In the centre of Ludlow, the legendary 'foodie's' paradise, is this deli selling great local produce, including fresh foods such as free-range ham on the bone, organic smoked salmon and unpasteurized cheeses. A subsidiary company, Just Mustard, is part of the deli, allowing the owner, Tracey Colley, to indulge her love of mustard – a huge selection is available, from the well known to the esoteric, including Tracey's own mustard – Shropshire Lad Beer Mustard.

Special Edition Continental Chocolate

Willingham Hall, Market Rasen, Lincolnshire LN8 3RH   T: 01673 844073 OR
0800 316 0834   E: willingham.rasen@virgin.net
✉ mail order

Good-quality couverture chocolate can be found here, with dark chocolate at 70% cocoa solids and white chocolate with 30% cocoa solids. Special Edition are particularly interesting for their unusual hand-made chocolates; the double-cream truffles recently won a Great Taste Award and there are all kinds of unusual combinations to try, such as dark chocolate with chilli or cranberry and nutmeg. For those with nut allergies, this chocolate shop is paradise – nothing contains nuts. Available from the shop or by mail order.

The Cheese Shop

6 Flying Horse Walk, Nottingham NG1 2HN   T: 0115 941 9114

With a range of over 200 cheeses, The Cheese Shop specializes in British farmhouse cheese, mainly unpasteurized, with ewes'- and goats'-milk cheeses well represented. Lots of local deli goods can be found here, too, along with Italian specialities. Tasting of the cheeses and other foods is encouraged.

Kim's Cakes

39 Shanklin Drive, Weddington, Nuneaton, Warwickshire CV10 0BA   T: 02476 351421
E: colin.a.bickley@btinternet.com
🛒 farmers' markets ✉ farm gate sales

A one-woman cottage industry, Kim makes a staggering range of 38 different cakes, jams and pickles, almost all organic. Using ingredients procured as locally as possible, with fruit she has picked herself, she also makes jams and chutneys. Everything is laboriously made by hand and when she arrives at her farmers' market stalls, the cakes and scones are so fresh that they are often still warm. Find Kim at Stratford, Warwick, Rugby and Kenilworth farmers' markets, or call her to place an order.

Plantation Cottage Herbs

1 Plantation Cottage, Bricklehampton, Pershore, Worcestershire WR10 3HL
T: 01386 861507 w: www.plantation-cottage.com
🔖 farmers' markets

Locally grown apples and home-grown, pesticide-free herbs are the foundations of the traditional 'drip-bag' process fruit jellies sold here. The jellies range from the traditional mint or quince, to the unusual jalapeño pepper. All made in small batches, and available from lots of farmers' markets, including Worcester, Stratford-upon-Avon, Mosley, Cheltenham, Tewkesbury, Broadway and Winchcombe. Plantation Cottage are winners of the Waitrose Small Food Producer award.

A Country Kitchen

Owd Barn, Ede Crost Street, Ross on Wye, Herefordshire HR9 7BZ T: 01989 565751
🔖 farmers' markets

Eileen Brunnarius has been devoting her time to resurrecting a selection of British dishes that have either been forgotten or corrupted due to commercial 'progress'. First on the list are traditional, old-fashioned pies – Mrs Mac's Gloster Old Spot, and Hereford Beef Luncheon pies. Mrs Mac's pies are classic pork pies, made using a 19th century recipe, with only the belly and shoulder meat of rare-breed Gloster Old Spot pork from a local farm (Bower Farm, see page 95). The meat benefits from a simple but perfectly balanced seasoning of just salt, white pepper and sage – no other additives at all. The beef pie is made with the same attention to detail, using rare-breed Hereford beef from a nearby farm. Other traditional dishes are available, including puddings, with the range growing all the time. Find Eileen at a number of local farmer's markets – call to find out where.

Lincolnshire Organics

Holme Hall, Scunthorpe, Lincolnshire DN16 3RE   T: 01724 844466
w: www.lincolnshireorganics.co.uk
➜ farm shop

The Jackson family at Lincolnshire Organics rear or grow their
own organic pork, chicken, eggs and vegetables, dry-cure their own
bacon, make their own cakes, and fill their café with home-made
meals. It's a miracle they find time to source the local Red Lincoln
beef (hung for a full three weeks), local Lincoln lamb, artisan
cheeses and plethora of local produce that graces the shelves
of their farm shop. Lincolnshire Organics is a treasure trove of
thoughtfully produced food.

Meg Rivers

Blackwell Business Park, Blackwell, Shipston-on-Stour, Warwickshire CV36 4PE
T: 01608 682858   w: www.megrivers.com
✉ mail order

Cakes like your grandmother used to make (if you were very lucky!).
Julian Day says their cakes are 'nothing grand or exotic' – but he
simply makes the best traditional cakes you have ever tasted,
through his attention to detail and the quality of his ingredients.
Favourites include ginger cake (with stem ginger) and festival cake –
a riot of fruits and nuts. All available mail order, or you can join the
Cake Club – an annual subscription fee gets you a monthly delicious
surprise through the post.

Greenfields Farm Shop

Station Road, Donnington, Telford, Shropshire TF2 8JY   T: 01952 677345
➜ farm shop 🛒 box scheme

A farm shop filled with local produce – home-produced fruit and
vegetables, local cheese, local beef (hung for three weeks), cakes,
dry-cured bacon and even wild boar.

Berrow Honey

The Berrow, Martley, Worcester WR6 6PQ   T: 01886 821237
w: www.theberrow.co.uk/honey

⬤ **farm shop**   ✉ **mail order**

Honey from the old native British Black bee, gathering nectar from
wild flowers and heather. Available mail order, or from several local
farmers' markets, including Teme Valley – call for details.

Granthams of Alderley Edge

68 Heyes Lane, Alderley Edge, Cheshire SK9 7LB   T: 01625 583286
E: mrmikegrantham@aol.com

This traditional family grocer's has developed into a great deli.
Alongside the fresh fruit and vegetables are local dry-cured bacon,
150 different kinds of cheese, home-cooked hams and locally reared
chicken. Customers are welcome to taste many of the products.

Lucy's Specialist Grocers

Church Street, Ambleside, Cumbria LA22 0BU   T: 01539 432399
w: www.lucysofambleside.co.uk

Lucy Nicholson is a tireless crusader for good food, and her
specialist grocery store in Cumbria is a shrine to artisan foods.
Not content to showcase the finest producers from Cumbria and
around the world, she has also been busy resurrecting traditional
old Cumbrian recipes, such as the Cumberland Dream Cake that
she discovered in an 18th century cook book. The theme continues
in Lucy's restaurant and bar/bistro, making Church Street in
Ambleside a gourmet's paradise.

Cartmel Sticky Toffee Pudding Co. Ltd

Cartmel Village Shop, The Square, Cartmel, Cumbria LA11 6QB   T: 01539 536201
w: www.stickytoffeepudding.co.uk

⬤ **shop**   ✉ **mail order**

The home of gooey, home-made comfort food! Available from the shop, by mail order or from Fortnum & Mason and some branches of Waitrose.

1657 Chocolate House

54 Branthwaite Brow, Kendal, Cumbria LA9 4TX   T: 01539 740702
w: www.thechocolatehouse.co.uk

A chocolate shop and restaurant, filled with hand-made chocolates.

Low Sizergh Barn Farm Shop

Low Sizergh Farm, Sizergh, Kendal, Cumbria LA8 8AE   T: 01539 560426
w: www.low-sizergh-barn.co.uk
⬇ farm shop

Low Sizergh Farm is an organic, family-run dairy farm, with its own farm shop and café. The focus is on local and regional foods, from small-scale producers. There is a big range of British farmhouse cheese, including an organic Lancashire made with the farm's own milk, home-grown organic vegetables, local meat and game, home-produced free-range eggs and traditional Cumbrian baking. The staff know the stories behind the produce, as they personally know many of the producers. The tearooms overlook the milking parlour, so diners can see the cows being milked, and there is also a farm trail. A one-stop-shop, with plenty more besides.

Country Fare

Dale Foot, Mallerstang, Kirkby Stephen, Cumbria CA17 4JT   T: 01768 371173
E: countryfareuk@aol.com
🛒 farmers' markets

Country Fare won two Great Taste Awards in 2002, most notably for their pickled damsons – local damsons, pickled in vinegar, spices and brown sugar, according to an old recipe. The small staff of farmers' wives and daughters at Country Fare make a vast range of cakes, from fruit cakes, gingerbread and parkin to flapjacks and tray bakes – they simply make whatever they like to eat themselves. There are even gluten-free cakes and some suitable for diabetics. Country Fare recently won gold and bronze medals in the 2004 Great Taste Awards. Find the produce at Kendal, Orton, Carlisle, Brough farmers' markets.

Seasoned Pioneers

Unit 101 Summers Road, Brunswick Business Park, Liverpool L3 4BJ
T: 0800 068 2348   W: www.seasonedpioneers.co.uk
✉ **mail order**

Whatever kind of spice you need, Seasoned Pioneers will have it, often in organic form. The house blends are revered by many food writers for their authenticity.

deFINE Food and Wine

Chester Road, Sandiway, nr Northwich, Cheshire CW8 2NH   T: 01606 882101
E: office@definefoodandwine.com

'If it's good, and it's British, we'll stock it!' the owner of deFINE, Jon Campbell told me. The range of products, such as the British artisan cheeses, comes from sources as local as possible, with Jon demanding that the small producers he buys from exhibit 'good production practices'.

Huntley's

Whalley Road, Samlesbury, nr Preston, Lancashire PR5 0UN   T: 07960 451522
⬦ **farm shop**

Huntley's are famed for their ice cream – an astonishing 80 flavours or so, made with milk and cream from the farm's own dairy herd, and often home-grown fruit. There's plenty more at this farm shop, too – a 96-seat restaurant, with traditional, home-cooked foods, a big cheese counter devoted to Lancashire farmhouse cheeses, and plenty of home-reared meat – wild boar, rare-breed pork and Aberdeen Angus beef.

Godfrey C Williams & Son

9–11 The Square, Corner House, Sandbach, Cheshire CW11 1AP   T: 01270 762817
E: godfreycwilliams@supanet.com

Mr Williams has been busy experimenting with a local cheesemaker, and between them they have come up with blue Cheshire, which is a rare find. Other goodies include home-cured bacon, locally baked bread and the coffee beans that are roasted on the premises. Provenance is a priority – Mr Williams states that 'we like to know the whole story behind a food before we stock it'.

The Hollies Farm Shop

Forest Road, Little Budworth, nr Tarporley, Cheshire CW6 9ES   T: 01829 760414
E: holliesfarmshop@aol.com
👜 farm shop

Every October, the Cowap family hold a food festival at their farm shop, inviting their suppliers (often small-scale, regional producers) to come along and speak to the customers about the produce. The emphasis is on artisan producers, 'anything that's a little bit different', and customers are encouraged to taste the foods. Fruit and vegetables grown on the family farm are always available, freshly picked, and Edward Cowap says the joy of this is that with the changing seasons there is always something new being harvested.

Demel's Sri Lankan Chutneys

Cross Lane, Ulverston, Cumbria LA12 9DQ   T: 01229 580580
W: www.demels.co.uk
✉ mail order

Chutneys and pickles made to traditional Sri Lankan recipes that have been handed down through the generations of this family.

The Chocolate Society

Clay Pit Lane, Roecliffe, nr Boroughbridge, North Yorkshire YO51 9LS   T: 01423 322230
W: www.chocolate.co.uk
✉ mail order

Hand-made truffles, Valrhona bars, and organic, single-bean bars. This is the home of chocolate obsession! See also the London branch, page 113.

Campbell Lindley's

49 Cold Bath Road, Harrogate, North Yorkshire HG2 0NL   T: 01423 564270
w: www.campbelllindleys.co.uk

Martin Lindley of Campbell Lindley's says that Harrogate citizens are
very loyal to Yorkshire produce, and so his shop is filled with foods
from small-scale, regional producers. He and his partner spent three
years researching the local produce available and the fruit of their
labours is now visible on the shelves of the shop, which also includes
single estate olive oils and other hard-to-find continental foods.

The Rocky Valley Deli

19 Grove Promenade, Ilkley, West Yorkshire LS29 8AF   T: 01943 607681
w: www.rockyvalleydeli.co.uk

The aim of Sarah and Simon Lawson is to make shopping a happy
experience, rather than a chore, and the staff at Rocky Valley are all
enthusiastic and knowledgeable about the produce on the shelves.
Yorkshire and Cumbrian goods are well represented here, all coming
from small-scale, passionate producers. Discussion and tasting is a
big part of the experience of shopping at Rocky Valley.

Rosebud Preserves

Rosebud Farm, Healey, Masham, North Yorkshire HG4 4LH   T: 01765 689174
  farm shop   mail order

A great selection of jams, jellies and chutneys, from the traditional,
like the Old Yorkshire chutney, to the innovative, such as the
rhubarb and orange jam. The staff at Rosebud Farm harvest wild
fruits from nearby to make their classic preserves, like the wild
Rowan and the crab-apple jellies.

New Barns Farm Shop

New Barns, Warkworth, Morpeth, Northumberland NE65 0TR   T: 01665 710035
  farm shop

There's so much to choose from at New Barns that you won't know
where to begin – home-reared rare-breed pork, home-cured bacon,

Hereford and Aberdeen Angus beef, and award winning terrines, sausages, pies and pates. Lots of local produce too – bread, cakes, ice cream – too much to list. There is also a restaurant on site, where you'll find home-cooked dishes made with home produced ingredients – of course!

The Honey Tree Organic Greengrocers and Good Food Store

68 Heaton Road, Heaton, Newcastle-upon-Tyne NE6 5HL   T: 0191 240 2589
www.thehoneytree.biz

The Honey Tree is packed with the best local produce, from Northumbrian meat and game, really fresh fruit and vegetables to dairy produce, bread and eggs. It's a one-stop organic shop for people who want their food to taste fantastic, and who also care about where that food comes from.

Garth Cottage Nursery

Newby Wiske, Northallerton, North Yorkshire DL7 9ET   T: 01609 777233
E: mail@garth-cottage.fsnet.co.uk
📇 farmers' markets

Over 340 different culinary herbs are grown at Garth Cottage Nursery, with a staggering range of 46 varieties of mint alone (including the chocolate mint, great sprinkled on hot chocolate!). Paul and Chris Turner are constantly increasing their collection of herbs, searching abroad for new varieties. All the herbs are grown without any pesticides. Cold-infused herb oils, vinegars, marinades and salad dressings are also available. The nursery is not open to the public – the produce is available from farmers' markets and food events in the north; call for details.

The Garden House

Anvil Square, Reeth, nr Richmond, North Yorkshire DL11 6TE   T: 01748 884188
W: www.gardenhousepottery.co.uk
🏠 shop ✉ mail order

Jane Davies specializes in traditional damson cheese, a regional speciality in North Yorkshire and Cumbria. Contrary to its name, this is not a dairy product but is more closely related to a preserve.

Made with just damsons and sugar, it is a very intensely fruity, set conserve, and can be eaten as a dessert, or as a 'tracklement' with meat and game. An added bonus is that the damson cheese comes in a lovely pottery container, made by Jane's husband. Jane won the prestigious Small Producers Award in conjunction with Waitrose in 2002, for 'excellence and innovation in food production'.

NORTH EAST   SEAHOUSES

Northumbrian Hamper

25b Main Street, Seahouses, Northumberland NE68 7RE   T: 01665 720999

This deli sells plenty of native Northumbrian produce but the real speciality is the kipper stotty – local kipper fillets in a soft bun.

NORTH EAST   STOCKTON-ON-TEES

Red Berry Foods at Station House Tea Rooms

Wynyard Woodland Park, Thorpe Thewles, Stockton-on-Tees, TS21 3JG
T: 07743 322631 OR 01740 630731   W: redberryfoods@hotmail.com
🚚 delivery service

Red Berry Foods take the freshest local produce, and create a cornucopia of fine foods, all firmly reflecting the season. From home-made bread, like the imaginative potato and red onion focaccia, to terrines packed with home-cured ham and even quiches made with pheasant eggs, new ideas and fresh flavours are the aim. Call Stephanie or Angus to request a menu, or make an order and arrange a delivery – whether you need a few items, or an entire dinner party catered for, they'll be happy to help. Alternatively, pop into the tea rooms they run for a sample of their fine foods.

NORTH EAST   TADCASTER

Organic Pantry

St Helen's Farm, Newton Kyme, Tadcaster, North Yorkshire LS24 9LY   T: 01937 531693
🚚 delivery service

A big selection of organic produce, including local fruit and veg, dairy produce and organic meat from local farms.

NORTH EAST   YORK

Henshelwood Deli

10 Newgate, York YO1 7LA   T: 01904 673877   W: www.delidivine.co.uk
✉ mail order

Lynn at Henshelwood's happily admits to being obsessed with food, and her commitment to packing her deli with the best produce won her great acclaim in the Observer Food Awards this year. She makes lots of the goodies on display herself, including her now famous Whitby crab pâté. You'll find plenty of rarities at Henshelwoods, from incredibly small-scale artisan cheeses, to delights like the rhubarb pickle with caramelized onion. If you can't make it up to York, then don't panic – it's all available by mail order.

The Chocolate Room

529 Lisburn Road, Belfast BT9 7GS   T: 028 9066 2110 AND AT 23 Queens Arcade, Belfast BT1 5FE   T: 028 9032 0446   W: www.thechocolateroom.com

People in Belfast who are serious about chocolate need to get themselves down to The Chocolate Room. Many of the chocolates are sourced direct from the makers, from Ireland, Belgium, France and England, and there are many brands that you will struggle to find elsewhere. With over 150 different types of chocolate and hot chocolate drinks made with the finest melted chocolate, not powder, this is heaven for chocoholics.

Feasts

39 Dublin Road, Belfast BT2 7HD   T: 028 9033 2787

Feasts has a great selection of charcuterie, but it specializes in Irish farmhouse cheeses – all the classic, award-winning Irish cheeses and those from small, less-well-known dairies can be found here. There is also a great range of home-made pasta and sauces.

The Olive Tree Company

353 Ormeau Road, Belfast BT7 3GL   T: 028 9064 8898
W: www.olivetreecompany.com

The aim of the Olive Tree Company is to stock foods that you won't find anywhere else – there is a great choice of olives, an ever-growing selection of artisan cheeses, oils and vinegars and some local produce.

The Belfry Deli and Café

4–5 Church Lane, Coleraine, Co. Londonderry BT52 1AG   T: 028 7034 2906 OR
0800 3280212 (FREEPHONE)   E: paul@thebelfrydeli.fsnet.co.uk

Plenty of Irish produce graces the shelves of this deli, accompanied by
English and continental delicacies. Local cheese, made a few miles
away, dry-cured bacon and hams, artisan Irish cheeses, and home-
made wheaten bread are all popular.

REPUBLIC OF IRELAND   GALWAY

McCambridges of Galway Ltd

38–39 Shop Street, Galway   T: 091 563470   W: www.mccambridges.com

McCambridges has great wines, own-baked breads and own-grown
soft fruit in season, alongside all the other deli foods stocked, but a
big attraction are the cheeses – over 100 at any one time, many of
which are from small-scale Irish dairies.

REPUBLIC OF IRELAND   NENAGH

Country Choice

25 Kenyon Street, Nenagh, Tipperary   T: 067 32596   W: www.countrychoice.ie

This is the sort of shop that gourmands dream about – packed full
of fantastic artisan Irish produce, with farmhouse cheeses ripened
in the maturing room on site and fresh produce from local farms and
gardens. There is also plenty of continental deli fare to choose from,
all of it out of the ordinary. The café at the back of the shop serves
home-made local foods like beef and Guinness pie and bacon and
cabbage, with great coffee, fruit crumbles, rich chocolate cakes or
home-made scones and jam for dessert.

REPUBLIC OF IRELAND   NEW ROSS

Farmer Direct

New Ross, Co. Wexford   T: 051 420816

At Farmer Direct they can tell you where all the produce comes from
– most of it is very local. Local vegetables arrive fresh each day, as
does the locally baked bread. Milk and butter, cheese, bacon and
meat, eggs, ice cream and fruit juices all come from the best local
producers.

super hero

JIM TYNAN, of The Kitchen and Food Hall, Portlaoise (below)

'Some people say we're nitpicking,' says Jim Tynan of The Kitchen. He's talking about the attention to detail when it comes to stocking the shop – every ingredient of every product is looked at and, if it falls short of the high standards employed here, the product is rejected. Irish artisan products are what The Kitchen is all about – cheese from small dairies, traditionally smoked salmon, classic Irish soda breads – everything is hand-made. Jim's motto is simple: quoting Oscar Wilde, he says, 'I have simple tastes – I only want the best.'

REPUBLIC OF IRELAND   OLDCASTLE

Aines Chocolates

Oliver Plunkett Street, Oldcastle, Co. Meath   T: 049 854 2769
w: www.aineschocolates.com
✉ **mail order**

The starting point of Aines is the best couverture chocolate, often a blend of varieties to get just the right balance. Everything is hand-made and only natural ingredients are used – fresh butter and cream. This attention to detail has paid off – Aines Chocolates won three Great Taste awards in 2004.

REPUBLIC OF IRELAND   PORTLAOISE

The Kitchen and Food Hall   super hero

Hynds Square, Portlaoise, Co. Laois   T: 0502 62061

Jim Tynan of The Kitchen and Food Hall prides himself on the high standards he sets for all the produce he stocks. See the Super Hero box, above, for more information.

REPUBLIC OF IRELAND   SLIGO

Tir na nOg

Grattan Street, Sligo   T: 071 91 62752

A treasure-trove of the best local produce, with fruit and vegetables, artisan cheeses, organic eggs and honey.

Isle of Colonsay Apiaries

Isle of Colonsay, Argyle PA61 7YR   T: 01951 200365   W: www.colonsay.org.uk

✉ **mail order**

Wildflower honey is difficult to produce in Britain – so much land here is taken up with commercial crops, such as rapeseed, and hedgerows and field margins have been eroded. Given a choice between wild flowers and commercial agricultural crops, a bee will head for the agricultural fields, as they generally contain more nectar. What makes Colonsay wildflower honey so unique is that the bees that make it have no choice – there are only flowers and herbs for them to collect from. While this means that they make less honey overall, it also means that the flavour of the honey they do produce has an unrivalled depth and complexity. It is completely different from honeys based on commercial crops and is available by mail order.

Plaisir du Chocolat

251–253 Canongate, Edinburgh EH8 8BQ ALSO AT 270 Canongate, Edinburgh, EH8 8HA
T: 0131 556 9524 (NO. 251–253); 0131 556 0112 (NO. 270)
W: www.plaisirduchocolat.co.uk

✉ **mail order**

A shrine to the cocoa bean, Plaisir du Chocolat offers hand-made chocolates and the best couverture money can buy.

Valvona & Crolla

19 Elm Row, Edinburgh EH7 4AA   T: 0131 556 6066   W: www.valvonacrolla.com

✉ **mail order**

Valvona & Crolla are renowned throughout the country, not just in Edinburgh, for their astonishing array of continental produce, all offered with a distinctive Italian flair.

Phoenix Community Stores

The Park, Findhorn Bay, Moray IV36 3TZ   T: 01309 690110
w: www.findhorn.org/store

This award-winning community-run shop has a great deli-style
section alongside the books and local crafts it sells. An organic
bakery on site provides fresh bread, made with local flour, and local
cheeses, vegetables and honey are available, as is organic smoked
salmon from the Western Isles.

Struan Apiaries

Burnside Lane, Conon Bridge, Ross-shire IV7 8EX   T: 01349 861427
✉ **mail order**

Struan Apiaries specialise in 'monofloral' honeys – the careful
positioning of the hives means that the bees harvest nectar from
only one type of flower at a time, creating the honey equivalent of
single estate olive oil, or vintage wine. Varieties available can include
raspberry, clover or heather.

Heart Buchanan

380 Byres Road, Glasgow G12 8AR   T: 0141 334 7626   w: www.heartbuchanan.co.uk

Heart Buchanan is a compact deli, but it is packed to the rafters
with gorgeous foods. Scottish artisan produce is showcased here –
you'll find smoked venison from Islay, wild Scottish chanterelles,
langoustines from Uist, and hand-made Scottish cheeses among
the many goodies. And if you're not sure quite how to make the
best of these ingredients, then let Fiona Buchanan and her team
help – you can pick up complete dishes painstakingly made in Heart
Buchanan's kitchens to take home for dinner. Whatever you need,
you'll find friendly help and a lively food-based discussion always
available at this deli – they simply love good food here, and never
tire of talking about it.

Gourmet's Lair

8 Union Street, Inverness IV1 1PL   т: 01463 225151   w: www.gourmetslair.co.uk

A delicatessen specializing in the unusual and surprising, Gourmet's Lair offers the luxurious, the original and the best; see the Super Hero box, below, for more information.

super hero

MAUREEN PRITCHARD, of Gourmet's Lair, Inverness (see above)

Maureen took over the Gourmet's Lair in late 2003, and has injected the legendary deli with her own passion for artisan foods. She has been busy searching Scotland for more producers of traditional foods, and has found many who, while working on a very small scale, are creating fantastic and unusual foods. Many of them belong to the Slow Food Movement. Amongst the delights to be found here are over 100 varieties of cheese, truffles, and the famous Charlie Barley's Stornoway Black Pudding. A key part of Maureen's ethos is to make shopping at the Gourmet's Lair great fun, so there is always plenty of lively discussion and the chance to taste and try.

Gillies Fine Foods

Inchrory Drive, Dingwall Business Park, Dingwall, Ross-shire N15 9HX   т: 01349 861100
w: www.gilliesfinefoods.co.uk

✉ **mail order**

All kinds of unusual condiments and the like – rowan jelly, lavender vinegar, cinnamon mustard, and Glenferlie, an own-recipe hot toddy, to name just a fraction of the range. Recently introduced is a lavender jelly for cheese, and a range of oatcakes, including one flavoured with lapsang souchong tea! Almost all the ingredients are either home-grown or locally produced and there is a purity about the flavours of the products that is in sharp contrast with much of the over-processed food available today. Available direct from the shop or by mail order.

The Treehouse

14 Baker Street, Aberystwyth, Ceredigion SY23 2BJ   T: 01970 615791
w: www.aber-treehouse.com

A great example of local produce staying local – Jane Burnham at
The Treehouse grows organic fruit and vegetables, which she stocks
in her organic shop, and uses in her organic restaurant. There is
also lots of local produce stocked alongside her own, and Jane can
happily and confidently tell customers the provenance of everything
in the shop.

Wendy Brandon Handmade Preserves

Felin Wen, Boncath, Pembrokeshire SA37 0JR   T: 01239 841568
w: www.wendybrandon.co.uk
shop   mail order

Although this is a very small company, the range of jams, jellies and
chutneys produced here currently stands at about 150 different
varieties. All are hand-made in small batches, and there is a happy
meeting of tradition and imagination – Victorian-sounding rose-petal
jelly and damson cheese are accompanied by Indian-inspired
chutneys and orange with molasses and rum marmalade. Fruit
vinegars and unusual jams (Warwickshire Drooper Yellow Plum jam!)
complete the range.

Popty Cara

Lawrenny, Pembrokeshire SA68 0PN   T: 01646 651690
w: www.poptycara.co.uk
farmers' markets   mail order

Popty Cara have won many Great Taste Awards for their hand-made
cakes, including bara brith (traditional fruit bread) made to a
200-year-old recipe. Local ingredients predominate, and all the
cakes are preservative free. Their own recipe black sticky ginger
cake recently won a silver medal at the Great Taste Awards.

super hero

JENNY AND TEIFI DAVIES, of Llwynhelyg Farm Shop, Llandysul (see below)

Recently awarded the honour of Best Farm Shop in Wales by the National Farmers Union, Llwynhelyg is a celebration of the freshest and most interesting produce that West Wales offers. Jenny and Teifi Davies are tireless campaigners for Welsh producers, and encourage customers to see the benefits of spending their money with local businesses. They have seen the far-reaching repercussions of local businesses closing – affecting not just the owners of that business, but the whole local network of firms, and are keen to support small producers. This attitude makes for a shop brimming with locally grown fruit and vegetables, meat reared on nearby farms, Welsh farmhouse cheese, milk, cream and butter, home-made chutneys, jams, cakes, pies … the list goes on and on. There is nothing in the shop that Jenny hasn't tasted – she can tell you everything about what's on the shelves, and her enthusiasm is infectious.

WALES   **LLANDYSUL**

Llwynhelyg Farm Shop

Sarnau, Llandysul, Ceredigion SA44 6QU T: 01239 811079
E: llwynhelygfarm@aol.com

A truly outstanding farm shop, Llwynhelyg offers the freshest and most interesting produce from West Wales; see the Super Hero box below, for more information. There is now a licensed café on site.

WALES   **LLANRWST**

Blas Ar Fwyd

Heol yr Orsaf, Llanrwst, Conwy, North Wales LL26 0BT T: 01492 640215
W: www.blasarfwyd.com

An award-winning Welsh deli with a real commitment to local and Welsh produce. Blas Ar Fwyd holds the widest range of Welsh cheeses and Welsh alcoholic drinks in the country, and much of the fresh produce is home-made.

Foxy's Deli

7 Royal Buildings, Penarth, Vale of Glamorgan CF64 3ED   T: 02920 251666
E: foxysiany@aol.com

Having fulfilled a long-held dream to run a deli, Foxy is busy gathering Welsh produce to fill the shelves; he strongly believes that the quality of the local produce is excellent and has some interesting Welsh cheeses and Glamorgan sausages available. There is now a licensed café on site.

This book has a clear bias towards traditional foodstuffs, foods made with time and thoughtfulness, with respect for old recipes and old methods and with respect for our heritage. The focus will be the same in this section, and I've listed makers of cider and perry, real ale, pure juices pressed from the fruits of the producer's own orchards, vineyards fighting for the recognition of English and Welsh wines and even fruit wine and mead producers.

I recall reading a less than complimentary remark about English wine in an edition of Robert Parker's *Wine Buyer's Guide*. Robert Parker is by far and away the most influential wine writer in the world. He said that our country was too far north and too wet and windy to be taken seriously as a wine-growing nation. Quite humorous he was about it. Sitting, writing this, during an unbelievably hot summer and beginning to think that maybe our climate is changing, I wonder if he is right – particularly when you consider somewhere like the Nyetimber Vineyard in Sussex (see page 159). Their sparkling wine has beaten the best Champagnes in the world in blind tasting competitions. We have a very good sparkling wine in Cornwall, too, from Camel Valley Vineyard

drinks

(see page 146). I think their Camel Valley Brut shows that our climate suits sparkling wine very well indeed, because it needs good acidity.

As to our ability to make other excellent beverages there is no doubt. But you'll notice there is something significant missing – whisky. The range of producers making whisky is now so big that I felt this was a book in itself, so sadly, I will have to leave whisky for another day. However, I did find someone whose knowledge of whisky is positively encyclopaedic so, if you'd like to explore the world of this drink, I can think of no better hands to leave you in than Mr Wright of the Wright Wine Company (see page 167). Mr Wright currently holds over 500 Scottish malts alone in his shop, so perhaps you'll see why I felt there was not space in these pages to do justice to this particular topic!

The producers featured all have one thing in common: they are struggling against the tide of modern production, and cheap imitations. And yet, featured here are artisans making honest, unadulterated drinks, using methods that allow the flavours to achieve their true potential. These producers embody so much of the history of these isles, so search out and taste some liquid heritage.

FOOD HEROES OF BRITAIN

Camel Valley Vineyard

Nanstallon, Bodmin, Cornwall PL30 5LG   T: 01208 77959   w: www.camelvalley.com
📬 **farm gate sales**   ✉ **mail order**

Dry white wine specialists, with a Champagne-style brut called
Cornwall, which has recently been winning awards, Camel Valley
also make a red wine that has the distinction of aging well. Wines
are available direct from the vineyard, where tours can be arranged.

K G Consultants

The Bailiff's Cottage, The Green, Compton Dando, Bristol BS39 4LE   T: 01761 490624
🛒 **farmers' markets**

Keith Goverd has the biggest collection of single-variety apple juices
in the world, with over 100 to choose from. He seeks out rare
varieties, some of which don't even have a name, and presses the
fruit to make pure juice. He also makes pear, plum and damson juice,
and cider, perry and damson vinegars. His ciders, juices and
vinegars are available from Bath, Bradford-on-Avon, Frome,
Thornbury, Warminster, Devizes and Westbury farmers' markets.

Haye Farm Scrumpy Cider

Haye Farm, St Veep, Lerryn, Lostwithiel, Cornwall PL22 0PB   T: 01208 872250
📬 **farm gate sales**

Using only windfall apples from Haye Farm's own orchard, Rita
Vincent makes unpasteurized, barrel-fermented traditional cider.
According to folklore, cider has been made on this farm since the
1200s.

Somerset Cider Brandy Company

Pass Vale Farm, Burrow Hill, Kingsbury Episcopi, Martock, Somerset TA12 5BU
T: 01460 240782   w: www.ciderbrandy.co.uk
🍷 **shop**   ✉ **mail order**

Traditional cider-makers, the Somerset Cider Brandy Company
have diversified into cider brandy and now offer three-, five- and
ten-year-old versions of their distilled cider. The cider is made

with vintage cider apples from the farm's own orchards and, once distilled, is aged in oak barrels. This is an artisan product in the best of Somerset cider-making traditions, using over 40 different varieties of apple. It's also an unusual product: the Somerset Cider Brandy Company were granted the first cider-distilling licence in recorded history.

Three Choirs Vineyards

Newent, Gloucestershire GL18 1LS   T: 01531 890223   w: www.threechoirs.com
farm gate sales

Three Choirs make wines made from a huge range of grape varieties, including a good selection of reds. This is considered a leading vineyard for its experimentation with new grape varieties. Tastings and tours are offered and wines are available to buy.

Tuckers Maltings

Teign Road, Newton Abbott, Devon TQ12 4AA   T: 01626 334734
w: www.tuckersmaltings.com
shop

Tuckers Maltings hold a beer festival every year in April, and they also have a shop selling over 200 different types of beers from small breweries. This is also the home to Teignworthy Brewery, a microbrewery producing four beers made with local barley. All are unpasteurized cask or bottle-conditioned brews.

Plymouth Gin

60 Southside Street, Plymouth, Devon PL1 2LQ   T: 01752 665292
w: www.plymouthgin.com
shop   mail order

Plymouth Gin is now believed to be the only traditionally made gin in the UK, in a dedicated distillery that was last modernized in 1855; the gin is still made using Victorian methods. A specialist distiller spends three months of each year selecting botanical ingredients to make the perfect balance of flavours and, as a result, the gin is much softer tasting than other gins. Sloe gin is also made, with wild sloes from Dartmoor, and damson gin is available. There is a cocktail lounge and café. The distillery is open to the public, or you can buy mail order, or from many supermarkets.

super hero

AVALON VINEYARD (Pennard Organic Wines), Shepton Mallet (see below)

Many different kinds of drinks are made at the Avalon Vineyard, from grape wines and fruit wines to cider and mead. The traditional fruit wines include some unusual varieties – particularly the Folly wine, made with vine leaves. All the wines are organic and vegetarian and made using traditional methods – the cider is made using an ancient hand-turned press, in which the apples are made into a 'cheese' with straw, the old way of stacking the fruit to press it, and this has been adapted to use with the grapes. Hugh Tripp, the cider- and winemaker, feels strongly that these old-fashioned methods are vital for the quality of the drinks – 'they keep all their individuality of flavour intact'. Admitting that England is not the kindest environment for grape-growing, Hugh nonetheless turns the problems into positives: 'Grapes grown in this country may appear disadvantaged by our climate. Indeed they do struggle, but this very difficulty can to be turned to advantage by the fact that the long season and the slow ripening actually produces grapes of better quality for wine-making.' Hugh also produces organic apple juice, elderberry wine, and a raspberry liqueur.

SOUTH WEST   SHEPTON MALLET

Avalon Vineyard (Pennard Organic Wines)

The Drove, East Pennard, Shepton Mallet, Somerset BA4 6UA   T: 01749 860393
w: www.pennardorganicwines.co.uk
shop   mail order

See the Super Hero box, above, for more information.

SOUTH WEST   SHERBORNE

Benson's Fruit Juices

Stones Farm, Sherborne, Gloucestershire GL54 3DH   T: 01451 844134
w: www.bensonsapplejuice.co.uk
farmers' markets   mail order

Using entirely English fruit, Benson's makes some interesting combinations of juices – apple and rhubarb, apple and mango, apple and cinnamon. Pear juice is also available. The key to the flavour lies in the fact that the juices are left unfiltered and Benson's say this leaves all the flavour intact. Buy mail order, or the juices are available at many local and London farmers' markets – call to find out where.

Bramley and Gage

4 Long Meadow, South Brent, Devon TQ10 9YT   T: 01364 73722
W: www.speciality-foods.com
✉ **mail order**

Fruit liqueurs are made here using whole fruit from the West Country
– damsons, greengages, blackberries and many more – simply
pressed and preserved with alcohol and sugar. Sloe and damson gin
are favourites and a recent addition to the range is a herb liqueur.

Hecks Farmhouse Cider

911 Middle Leigh, Street, Somerset BA16 0LB   T: 01458 442367
⬎ **farm shop**

A staggering 20 varieties of cider are made at Hecks, all from single
varieties of own-grown apple, and five varieties of perry. The cider is
made the traditional West Country way. 15 varieties of apple juice
are also available. The farm shop (also on site) is open all week.

Grays Farm Cider

Halstow, Tedburn St Mary, Devon EX6 6AN   T: 01647 61236
E: ben@graysdevoncider.co.uk
✉ **farm gate sales**

The Gray family have been in continuous production of cider for over
300 years, from the same Devon farm. Made today just as it has
always been made, the cider is a blend of apples from the Grays'
own orchard, pressed and fermented naturally on the farm and is
available direct from the farm, or from local farm shops.

Minchews Real Cyder and Perry

Rose Cottage, Aston Cross, Tewkesbury, Gloucestershire GL20 8HX   T: 07974 034331
W: www.minchews.co.uk

The list of awards that Minchews have won for their single-variety,
traditionally made ciders and perries is incredibly long – the produce
from this cider maker is very well respected in the industry. Find the
cider and perry at Orchard Hive and Vine (page 162).

FOOD HEROES OF BRITAIN

Sharpham Vineyard

Ashprington, Totnes, Devon TQ9 7UT   T: 01803 732203   W: www.sharpham.com

➜ **farm shop**

Sharpham Vineyard is part of the Sharpham Estate, which also specializes in cheesemaking (see the separate entry, page 62). Classic grape varieties are used here, including Cabernet Sauvignon, and, unusually, Merlot. Sharpham have received the English Red Wine of the Year award four times now, and have attracted a lot of attention from wine experts. There are two trails at the vineyard, allowing customers to see the vines at close quarters, and also walk along the banks of the River Dart, which runs through the vineyard, making for a great day out, especially when accompanied by a tasting session (of both wine and cheese) back at the winery.

Biddenden Vineyards and Cider Works

Little Whatmans, Gribble Bridge Lane, Biddenden, Kent TN27 8DF   T: 01580 291726
W: www.biddendenvineyards.com

▱ **farm gate sales**   ✉ **mail order**

Not just wines, but also fresh pressed apple juice and classic Kent cider (made using culinary apple varieties, not cider apples) are made at Biddenden. The wines include single-variety oaked whites, sparkling whites and a rosé made partly with Pinot Noir grapes. This is believed to be the oldest commercial vineyard in Kent and customers are welcome to take tours, either guided or self-guided, and can taste and buy the wines, juice and cider on site.

Neals Place Farm

Neals Place Road, Canterbury, Kent CT2 8HX   T: 01227 765632
E: kenro@onetel.net.uk

▱ **farmers' markets**   ▱ **farm gate sales**

Ken Jordan of Neals Place Farm won the Best Bottled Cider title at the CAMRA awards in 2002. Growing his own apples, he uses a single variety (Cox's), and adds absolutely nothing – no sugar, no water, no carbonates. A minimum of six months in the barrel produces a very dry, tasty cider. Apple juices are also available – six single varieties and some blends, including Cox's and ginger, and Bramley and honey – and also whole-fruit jams. All available

direct from the farm or from Epsom, Croydon, Egham and
Wokingham farmers' markets.

Ridgeview Wine Estate

Fragbarrow Lane, Ditchling Common, Sussex BN6 8TP   T: 01444 241441
w: www.ridgeview.co.uk

📨 **farm gate sales**

Sparkling wine specialists, Ridgeview makes wines in the
Champagne style, using exactly the same methods as the
traditional Champagne houses, and from the three traditional
Champagne grape varieties. In blind tastings, Ridgeview has, on
numerous occasions, beaten classic Champagnes such as Veuve
Clicquot. Tastings, tours and sales of the wines are all available at
the vineyard.

Denbies Wine Estate

London Road, Dorking, Surrey RH5 6AA   T: 01306 876616
w: www.denbiesvineyard.co.uk

📨 **farm gate sales**   ✉ **mail order**

This is the largest of the English vineyards, making wine with many
different grape varieties, including the famous Chardonnay (when
grown in England, Chardonnay grapes produce a 'greener',
aromatic wine, less heavy than those grown in warmer climates).
This vineyard is really geared up for visitors, with tours, tastings,
a cinema showing films about the winemaking and two restaurants,
one with a viewing gallery over the vineyard. The wine can be
bought from the vineyard, or by mail order.

Ringden Farm Apple Juice

London Road, Hurst Green, Etchingham, East Sussex TN19 7QY   T: 01580 879385
w: www.ringdenfarm.co.uk

🍴 **farm shop**

Traditional cloudy apple juice – just pressed, gently pasteurized, and
bottled. All the apples used are from the farm's own orchards, where
there are around 25 different apple varieties. Blended juices are also
on offer, including apple with rhubarb or elderflower. There is a shop
on site, where customers can see demonstrations of the juice being
pressed. The juice has won many Great Taste Awards.

food facts

ENGLISH AND WELSH WINES

Like the wine of any other country, there are good Welsh and English wines and there are less than good ones. Many people have never tasted wine from the UK and those that have done may have been unfortunate enough to taste one in the latter category, enforcing a widely held belief that wine from this country is a very poor relation to the produce from French or Italian vineyards. There is a vital difference between English and Welsh wine and British wine. English and Welsh wine must adhere to strict regulations; the grapes must have been grown and the wine made in this country. Wine labelled as British is almost certainly made from cheap, imported concentrate. When trying native wine, choose bottles that are labelled English or Welsh.

The majority of UK wines are whites; we are too far north to grow most black grape varieties, so only around 10% of the wines made here are red. The wines we produce offer a myriad of different taste experiences but a classic English wine will have a floral bouquet, a fresh taste and an acidic finish.

British vineyards have many hurdles to overcome when it comes to producing wine. As we are rarely blessed with long, hot and sunny summers, the growers have to harvest the grapes as late as possible, to maximize the sugar content, and this can be as late as November. This is fraught with peril – disease can strike, birds can destroy the crop, frost can ruin the grapes or wet weather can prevent picking. And yet these vineyards are producing world-class wines. In a recent blind tasting at *Wine* magazine, a sparkling white from Camel Valley vineyard in Cornwall outscored every French and Italian wine in the same category. It is high time we took wine made in this country more seriously. English Wine Producers, the body promoting the vineyards of England and Wales, is a treasure-trove of information and advice about buying native wines. Julia Trustram Eve, from English Wine Producers, gave us a great deal of advice in compiling our list of featured vineyards. Find out more on their website www.englishwineproducers.com

---

SOUTH EAST   FAREHAM

Suthwyk Ales

Offwell Farm, Southwick, Fareham, Hampshire PO17 6DX T: 023 9232 5252
w: www.suthwykales.com
farmers' markets

CAMRA-recognized Martin Bazeley grows barley in two fields on his farm. The fields are named Skew and Bloomfields and the two types of beer he makes with the barley are named after the fields. Numerous local businesses are involved in the production of Skew Ale and Bloomfields Bitter, including a company that malts the barley by hand, the old-fashioned way. New for 2004 was a new beer, Liberation, to celebrate D-Day. The beer is available by the bottle (bottle-conditioned) at several Hampshire farmers' markets (listed on the website), or by the pint at the Golden Lion in Southwick. Call Martin or see the website for more details of outlets.

SOUTH EAST   FAVERSHAM

Pawley Farm Traditional Kentish Cider

Painters Forstal, Faversham, Kent ME13 0EN   T: 01795 532043
🏠 farm gate sales

The Macey family have been cider-makers for over 250 years; the current representative, Derek Macey, has been doing it for 40 years. The ciders are made the traditional Kentish way, with culinary apples, not cider apples, and the cider is blended from any number of the eight varieties grown in the Maceys' orchard. The cider is matured for up to two years in oak casks, for a far fuller flavour. The Maceys also make apple juice in six or seven varieties. Find the produce at the Goods Station in Canterbury or at Rochester, Meopham or Graves End farmers' markets.

SOUTH EAST   HARTFIELD

Kent and Sussex Apple Juice and Cider Centre

Perryhill Orchard, Edenbridge Road, Hartfield, East Sussex TN7 4JJ   T: 01892 770595
🏪 farm shop

This is the hub for a group of farms producing traditional ciders and pressed apple juices in Sussex. Perryhill Orchard itself produces juices from eight varieties of apple, along with a clutch of single-variety ciders, and these and others can be tasted and bought at the farm shop on site at the orchard.

SOUTH EAST   HASLEMERE

Gospel Green Cyder

Gospel Green Cottage, Haslemere, West Sussex GU27 3BH   T: 01428 654120
🏠 farm gate sales   ✉ mail order

The Lane family take apples from their own and neighbouring orchards and make cider by the Champagne method, which produces a very different drink from traditional ciders. It has been described as 'very French' in style – dry, with a distinct apple flavour.

FOOD HEROES OF BRITAIN

Owlet Apple Juice

Owl House Fruit Farm, Lamberhurst, Kent TN3 8LY   T: 01892 890553

farmers' markets

Owl Farm produces award-winning unfiltered, cloudy fruit juices from fruit grown on the farm and in neighbouring orchards. Some single-variety apple juices are available, along with a few blends, pear juice, and some flavoured with raspberries or blueberries. Available from Tunbridge Wells farmers' market or from many farm shops in the south east – call to find your nearest outlet.

Breaky Bottom Vineyard

Rodmell, Lewes, East Sussex BN7 3EX   T: 01273 476427
w: www.breakybottom.co.uk

mail order

Peter Hall makes Loire-style wines and *méthode Champenoise* sparkling wines, predominantly with the Seyval Blanc grape. The still whites age well, maturing in the bottle for up to a decade, and are available lightly oaked or unoaked. Breaky Bottom has won gold, silver and bronze medals at the International Wine Challenge, beating many champagnes. The wines are available direct from the vineyard, or mail order.

Middle Farm

West Firle, Lewes, East Sussex BN8 6LJ   T: 01323 811411
w: www.middlefarm.com

farm shop

Middle Farm is home to the National Collection of Cider and Perry – and what a collection it is, with around 250 different ciders and perries available to taste and buy. These are farm ciders – made with just the fruit, and nothing else – from all over the country, many from producers who make very small quantities, so you are unlikely to find them anywhere else. Middle Farm produces its own drinks, too, with apple juices pressed fresh each day, and cider made the old-fashioned way. This is also a working farm, with a huge farm shop stocking their own organic beef, cheese made with the farm's Jersey milk, alongside a great range of British cheeses and lots of fresh local produce.

CIDER AND PERRY

Traditional cider makers have a very simple list of ingredients: apples. No added sugar or yeast, no preservatives, no flavour enhancers. On a traditional cider farm, the apples are picked by hand (the old trees don't suit mechanized picking) and milled into pulp. Pressing takes place in a cider 'cheese' – a stack of cloth envelopes containing the pulp, layered with oat straw or wooden slatted boards, up to 20 layers high. The pressing of this stack to extract the juice can take two days, before the juice is put into oak barrels without pasteurization. Fermentation will then take place, using only the wild yeasts already present in the apple skins, and maturing in the barrel can last six months or more.

The vast majority of old and traditional cider orchards have been grubbed up and destroyed to make way for more economical crops. Many native varieties of cider apple have been made extremely difficult to find or, in some cases, have disappeared altogether. Perry pear varieties have suffered to an even greater degree. Perry making has declined enormously – it is more difficult than cider making, and is a poor candidate for a profit generating product. Perry pear trees do not bear fruit for at least 30 years after planting, so many people would consider them obsolete in these days of 'fast food'. The survival of many old varieties of apples and pears hangs in the balance, but some of the producers listed are helping to conserve them, maintaining old orchards, and planting new ones, keeping this heritage alive.

SOUTH EAST   LONDON

Pitfield Brewery (The Beer Shop)

14 Pitfield Street, London N1 6EY   T: 020 7739 3701   W: www.pitfieldbeershop.co.uk
shop   **mail order**

The Pitfield Beer Shop is both a microbrewery and a beer shop. They produce their own range of 14 traditional ales, based on old recipes (one, Imperial Stout, comes from a 1792 recipe), none of which are filtered or pasteurized and all of which are cask- or bottle-conditioned. The shop has an incredible range of beers from all over the world – around 600 different kinds – available by mail order. Pitfield's own beer is available on tap in numerous London pubs – call to find out where.

The Porterhouse

21–22 Maiden Lane, Covent Garden, London WC2E 7NA T: 0207 836 9931
W: www.porterhousebrewco.com

This microbrewery is a branch of an Irish one. It makes six different
beers, including a traditional red ale and an oyster stout. For details,
see under the Dublin branch on page 170. There is another branch
in Bray (see page 169).

Bearsted Vineyard

Bearsted, Maidstone, Kent ME14 4NJ T: 01622 736974   W: www.bearstedwines.co.uk
✉ mail order

The Gibson family produce eight different varieties of wine, including
a red and a rosé. Mail order is available, but do visit if you are in the
area, or find the wines at Canterbury, Lenham, Twickenham and
Blackheath farmers' markets.

Chegworth Valley Juices

Water Lane Farm, Chegworth, Harrietsham, Maidstone, Kent ME17 1DE
T: 01622 859272 W: www.chegworthvalley.com
🛒 farmers' markets ✉ mail order

The juices made at Chegworth Valley are recent winners at the Great
Taste Awards. Most of the fruit used – lots of varieties of apples,
pears, and soft fruit – is grown on the farm, which has some organic
land, with more planned. The apple juices are available as single
varieties, blends, or mixed with strawberries, raspberries,
blackberries and even rhubarb, and have no additives. All are
available from Borough Market in London.

Lurgashall Winery

Dial Green, Lurgashall, nr Petworth, West Sussex GU28 9HA T: 01428 707292
W: www.lurgashall.co.uk
🛒 shop ✉ mail order

Lurgashall Winery specializes in English country fruit wines, based
on old recipes, using old-fashioned ingredients such as rose petals

and silver birch. Ingredients are sourced as locally as possible. Visitors can take a tour of the winery and visit the shop. Lurgashall is a member of the UK Vineyards Association.

Sedlescombe Organic Vineyard

Cripps Corner, nr Robertsbridge, East Sussex TN32 5SA T: 01580 830715 OR 0800 980 2884 W: www.englishorganicwine.co.uk AND www.rentavine.co.uk

shop mail order

A staggering array of English drinks is made here. Amongst the choice are red and white wines using Bacchus and Pinot Noir grapes, including, unusually for England, a full-bodied red. Fruit wines are also produced – apple, cherry and plum, traditional still cider, pear juice and even blackberry liqueur. All are organic and vegan. You can even rent your own vine and benefit from the wine that it produces.

Davenport Vineyards

Limney Farm, Castle Hill, Rotherfield, East Sussex TN6 3RR T: 01892 852380 W: www.davenportvineyards.co.uk

farm gate sales mail order

Davenport Vineyards have recently achieved full organic status. Will Davenport feels that growing organically produces the highest quality possible, and the two wines produced here – a dry white and a pinot noir-based champagne style – are aromatic, fresh and clean-tasting. No yeast is added in the wine-making process, so fermentation is achieved with the wild yeasts in the grape skins and this lends greater complexity to the wine itself. Wines are sold under the 'Limney' label. Recent awards include the Montague Trophy in the 2004 UK Vineyards Association 'Wine of the Year' competition.

Gran Stead's Ginger Wine

43 Old Fort Road, Shoreham-by-Sea, West Sussex BN43 5RL T: 01273 452644 W: www.gransteadsginger.co.uk

farmers' markets mail order

Made with a 150-year-old recipe, this ginger wine is made with pure ginger oil. A true cottage industry, Gran Stead's make wine in only five-gallon batches to ensure the balance of ingredients is perfect.

The ginger wine is available mail order or from many farmers' markets – call for details.

Wickham Vineyard

Botley Road, Shedfield, Southampton SO32 2HL   т: 01329 834042
w: www.wickhamvineyard.co.uk

🛒 **shop**

Award-winning dry whites, including single varietals and a lightly oaked version, are the speciality here, and Wickham vineyard wine has the distinction of being served both in the House of Commons and on the Ark Royal. There is a small shop on site, tours of the vineyard can be taken, and now there is also a restaurant, currently open for group bookings and functions.

English Wines Group plc

Small Hythe, Tenterden, Kent TN30 7NG   т: 01580 763033
w: www.englishwinesgroup.com

✉ **mail order**

Using unusual grape varieties has prompted this vineyard to call one of its ranges Curious Grape (the other range is called Chapel Down). The vineyard grows some of its own grapes and sources more from grape-growers around the country. Passionate about retaining the heritage of Kent as 'the garden of England', English Wines Group encourages farmers to develop vineyards. Tastings and tours are available at the vineyard.

Broughton Pastures Organic Fruit Wine

The Silk Mill, Brook Street, Tring, Herts HP23 5EF   т: 01442 823993
w: www.broughtonpastures.co.uk

✉ **mail order**

Broughton Pastures are the only organic fruit-wine specialists in the country, with four fair-trade drinks available. They have twice won Soil Association organic awards for their drinks, and have also received six medals at the 2004 National Fruit Wine Awards. Nine varieties are available, including blackberry, mead, and a *méthode Champenoise* elderflower sparkling wine. All the wines are available by mail order.

JON LEIGHTON, of Valley Vineyard, Twyford, (see below)

Unusually for an English vineyard, Jon Leighton at Valley Vineyard produces a Pinot Noir red wine – unusual, because this is a grape that is generally unwilling to grow this far north. Jon told friends and acquaintances some years ago that he was going to win a top British wine award for a red wine, and they all laughed – it was considered impossible – and yet in 1998 he did just that. In fact, Valley Vineyard has probably won more awards over the years than any other British vineyard. Classic French grapes are the order of the day here, with still reds and whites, and sparkling whites; this vineyard is constantly pushing the boundaries to see what varieties can be grown in this country. Jon is proud that he produces English wine recognized for its high quality – he says it is time that the British stopped being 'besotted by the idea that anything from abroad is better than the British version'. There is an off licence on site that sells the wines, and customers can take a tour of the vineyard. The wines are also available by mail order.

SOUTH EAST   TWYFORD

Valley Vineyard   super hero

Stanlake Park, Twyford, Berkshire, RG10 0BN   T: 0118 934 0176
w: www.valleyvineyards.co.uk
🛒 **shop** ✉ **mail order**

Award-winning wines including an unusual English Pinot Noir red wine. See the Super Hero box, above, for more information.

SOUTH EAST   WEST CHILTINGTON

Nyetimber Vineyard

Gay Street, West Chiltington, West Sussex RH20 2HH   T: 01798 813989
w: www.nyetimber-vineyard.com
✉ **mail order**

The winner of many, many awards, Nyetimber Vineyard produces Champagne-style sparkling wines, only ever vintage, using the Chardonnay and Pinot grape varieties. Nyetimber was served at numerous royal events during the Golden Jubilee. Available by mail order (the vineyard is not open to the public), or from outlets such as Fortnum & Mason and Berry Bros in London, and some branches of Waitrose.

food facts

REAL ALES

The definition of real ale is very simple – according to CAMRA (the Campaign for Real Ale), it is 'beer brewed from traditional ingredients, matured by secondary fermentation in the container from which it is dispensed and served without the use of extraneous carbon dioxide'. Real ale is effectively alive in the bottle or cask – still with active yeasts fermenting the liquid. It is not pasteurized, which kills off the live organisms, and so real ale can be compared to an unpasteurized artisan cheese. Britain is alive with a culture of small breweries making real ale in time-honoured fashion. These are people who are not interested in the uniform beers coming out of the large breweries; instead, they are making drinks, often in small quantities, that are imbued with a real sense of heritage and of place. We asked CAMRA which breweries were really exceptional – were winning awards, were really pushing the field of real ale forward, or that were particularly interesting in terms of the heritage of ale, and you'll find them here.

EAST ANGLIA   CAMBRIDGE

Chilford Hall Vineyard

Linton, Cambridge CB1 6LE   T: 01223 895600   W: www.chilfordhall.co.uk
⊠ farm gate sales

Simon Alper at Chilford Hall makes wines that range from 'fresh and bright' to 'full and rounded'. Some are made to go with specific foods (there is even advice on the website regarding which of the wines would suit Chinese and Vietnamese dishes) while others can be drunk very happily on their own. Their sparkling rosé has gained many accolades. All the wines can be tasted and bought at the vineyard.

EAST ANGLIA   DISS

The Old Chimneys Brewery

Church Road, Market Weston, Diss, Norfolk IP22 2NX   T: 01359 221013

Alan Thompson brews 19 different real ales, all either cask- or bottle-conditioned, and two ciders, from his Norfolk brewery. He happily admits to being obsessed with real ale but also stocks local wine and fruit juices. Available from the brewery on Friday afternoons and Saturday mornings.

Crones Cider

Fairview, Fersfield Road, Kenninghall, Norfolk NR16 2DP   T: 01379 687687

w: www.crones.co.uk

⊠ farm gate sales

Award-winning cider and juices (single-variety apple juices and
cherry juice) are made by Crones Cider. The cider is made with a
traditional stack press, from a mix of culinary and dessert apples, as
is customary in East Anglia. Both it and the fruit juices are available
direct from the premises (call first) or from many wholefood shops
and delis in the south east.

Woodforde's Norfolk Ales

Broadland Brewery, Woodbastwick, Norwich, Norfolk NR13 6SW   T: 01603 720353

w: www.woodfordes.co.uk

👑 shop ✉ mail order

Woodforde's are unique in having won the Supreme Champion Beer
at CAMRA's Great British Beer Festival twice for two different beers,
although this is only the tip of the iceberg when it comes to awards
won by this brewery. The heritage of real ale in Britain is alive and
well at this Norfolk brewery, which has CAMRA's philosophy of
educating the public in the merits of real ale at heart. The beers are
available at the three 'tied' pubs, which have Woodforde's beers on
tap (all in Norfolk): The Fur and Feather Inn, Woodbastwick, 01603
720003; The Billy Bluelight, 27 Hall Road, Norwich, 01603 623768;
and the Swan Inn, Ingham, 01692 581099.

Shawsgate Vineyard

Badingham Road, Framlingham, Woodbridge, Suffolk IP13 9HZ   T: 01728 724060

w: www.shawsgate.co.uk

👑 shop

Shawsgate Vineyard makes over ten different varieties of wine, using
predominantly the Bacchus grape variety, which produces delicate,
aromatic wines with a similarity to those from the Alsace region.
There is also a dry, still cider and an apple dessert wine. Leasing is
also available – rent a row of vines, have your own wine made for
you and personalize your labels – you can check the progress of
your grapes throughout the season and learn all about grape-
growing and winemaking.

Gwatkin Cider at Abbey Dore Farm Shop

Moorhampton Park Farm, Abbey-Dore, Herefordshire HR2 0AL   T: 01981 550258

⬥ **farm shop**

Award-winning cider from over a dozen old English apple varieties is made by Gwatkin's without added yeast or carbonates – nothing but fruit is used. All the apples are either from the farm's own orchard, or nearby local orchards. The farm also sells its own home-produced lamb and beef, local wine, beer and vegetables.

Jus

Glebe Farm, Aylton, Ledbury, Herefordshire HR8 2RQ   T: 01531 670121

▨ **farm gate sales** ✉ **mail order**

Traditional unfiltered juices from around 35 different apple and pear varieties, all left as single varieties, are made here. The fruit is all from Herefordshire, some coming from the farm's own orchards. The juices are available direct from the farm, but call first.

Orchard Hive and Vine

4 High Street, Leominster, Herefordshire HR6 8LZ   T: 01568 611232

w: www.orchard-hive-and-vine.co.uk

✉ **mail order**

Orchard Hive and Vine stocks a fantastic selection of juices, cider and perry from many artisan producers around the country. Bottled beers and wines, both local and overseas – from small-scale producers whose drinks are otherwise difficult to find – are also available.

Gregg's Pit Cider and Perry

Much Marcle, Herefordshire HR8 2NL   T: 01531 660687   w: www.greggs-pit.co.uk

Using windfall fruit from his own and a neighbouring orchard (all grown without artificial fertilizers or pesticides), James Marsden makes single-variety and blended perries and ciders. These drinks have won many awards, having been overall champion on seven occasions at the Big Apple Cider and Perry Trials; many people in the industry feel that Gregg's Pit traditionally made perry is simply one of the best in the country. Available from many local outlets including Ceci Paolo (page 124) and Orchard Hive and Vine (opposite).

Oliver's Cider and Perry   super hero

Stanksbridge, Ocle Pychard, Herefordshire HR1 3RE   T: 01432 820569
w: www.theolivers.org.uk

Tom Oliver makes a variety of award-winning ciders and perries. 2004 saw Oliver's scooping the prestigious Arthur Davis Cup for the best perry at the Royal Bath and West Show. See the Super Hero box, below, for more information.

super hero

TOM OLIVER, owner of Oliver's Cider and Perry, Ocle Pychard (see above)

Tom Oliver makes a myriad of different ciders and perries, searching out rare and old varieties of fruit, and making unadulterated drinks, tasting as they would have done generations ago. I asked him about his work: 'Cider and perry starts and finishes for me with the fruit. Growing on trees, especially perry pear trees, that are frequently planted by orchardists and enthusiasts who take the "long view" on life. Trees of 50 to 300 years old, whose size and canopy can only develop over many generations. These older trees frequently defy commercial exploitation and consequently build up an ecosystem of varied habitats for all manner of wildlife and insects while providing a fruit that is ideally suited to the craft cider- and perry-maker. Fruit that is free of chemicals, lower in nitrogen, falling when ripe onto a thicker grass sward to minimize bruising and providing an environment that is good for the heart and soul to work in.' Even the names of the apple and pear varieties Tom uses have a sense of history and myth about them – Foxwhelp, Ten Commandments and Cider Lady's Finger and perry pear varieties such as Stinking Bishop, Merrylegs and Painted Lady.

At the last count, Tom was offering eight different types of perry alone, with accompanying advice regarding the foods they work well with. There are perry varieties that go with fish, lamb, game and desserts – it's a very versatile drink. Call Tom to find out where to buy his cider and perry.

super hero

THE TALBOT AND THE TEME BREWERY, Worcester
(see opposite)

The Talbot is a unique establishment. It is the home of the Teme Brewery,
which brews three 'real' beers all year (This, That and T'other), with some
seasonal specialities at certain times of year. The owners of the Talbot, the Clift
family, are not content just to brew their own beers – they also grow their own
vegetables and herbs, make their own preserves, breads, black pudding and
raised pies, and forage around the fields and hedgerows to gather 'wild food'.
No processed food is bought into the pub and their menu reflects this – the
dishes have a real regional feel, with their firm belief that 'food should have an
identifiable character' clearly expressed. As if all this were not enough, they
even have a local produce market at the pub once a month. The Talbot is an
inspiration for those committed to buying local food.

MIDLANDS   PERSHORE

Avonbank

Pershore College of Horticulture, Avonbank, Pershore, Worcestershire WR10 3JP
T: 01386 551151
🛒 shop

Award-winning single-variety and blended perries and ciders, some
made using unusual varieties of apples and pears. Courses in cider
and perry making are run here.

MIDLANDS   STOURPORT-ON-SEVERN

Astley Vineyards

Astley, Stourport-on-Severn, Worcestershire DY13 0RU   T: 01299 822907
🛒 shop

Consistent award winners, Astley Vineyards make white wines
ranging from dry to medium dry and also a dessert wine. English
grape varieties are used; Jonty Daniels, the winemaker, believes that
'at their best, wines should reflect where they come from'. There is
a shop at the vineyard, where customers can taste and buy.

The Talbot at Knightwick

`super``hero`

Knightwick, Worcester WR6 5PH   T: 01886 821235   w: www.the-talbot.co.uk

The Talbot is the home of the Teme brewery as well as being a pub
with an amazing commitment to producing home-made food and
serving a menu of local specialities made with local produce. See
the Super Hero box, opposite, for more information.

Strawberry Bank Liqueurs

Crosthwaite, Cumbria LA8 8HX   T: 015395 68812   w: www.damsongin.com
🔲 **farmers' markets** ✉ **mail order**

Mike and Helen Walsh have their own damson orchard and, some
years ago, decided they wanted to make a drink that had a firm sense
of place. The result was damson beer, a double-fermented fruit beer,
which perfectly combines the fruit Cumbria is associated with and the
heritage of real ales in Britain. Next came damson gin, followed by
blackberry liqueur. New for 2004 are sloe gin, blackberry gin and
strawberry vodka. All the drinks are available from Penrith, Carlisle,
Kendal, Ulverston or Orton farmers' markets, by mail order, or from
local branches of ASDA and Boots.

Cowmire Hall Damson Gin

Cowmire Hall, Crosthwaite, Kendal, Cumbria LA8 8JJ   T: 015395 68200
w: www.cowmire.co.uk
🔲 **farmers' markets**

Damson gin is an old English drink, associated strongly with the
Lake District. Cumbria is rich in damson orchards and Cowmire Hall
are helping to conserve this piece of English heritage, using
damsons from their own orchards and from other local orchards to
make a traditional, additive-free drink. The gin is a hand-made
product, using old-fashioned methods, and is available from Kendal
and Orton farmers' markets, from various local outlets, including
Low Sizergh Barn (page 129), Fortnum & Mason in London, and our
own deli in Padstow.

Think Drink

PO Box 10, Sedbergh, Cumbria LA10 5GH   T: 015396 25148

farmers' markets

John Sheard gathers old varieties of British apples, mainly from
orchards within the Countryside Stewardship Scheme, and simply
presses them to make pure juice. He sells these juices at local
farmers' markets, including Carlisle, Orton and Kendal, where he
also sells a local real ale from a nearby microbrewery, Dent Brewery,
who make a cask-conditioned, live beer using spring water from
their own well.

Lanchester Fruit

Brockwell Farm, Lanchester, Co. Durham DH7 0TQ   T: 01207 528805
w: www.lanchesterfruit.co.uk

farm shop   farmers' markets

Lanchester Fruit takes a wide variety of English apples and presses
traditional juices – no additives, no blends (although some are
flavoured with rhubarb, elderflower or redcurrant), no pasteurizing,
and no filtering – just unadulterated juice. The farm also has plenty
of soft fruit and asparagus to pick in season. There is a farm shop in
the summer, and the juice is available at farm shops throughout the
country. There is also a tea room, and the farm shop has a wide
range of home-grown, unsprayed vegetables.

Leventhorpe Vineyard

Bullerthorpe Lane, Woodlesford, Leeds, West Yorkshire LS26 8AF   T: 0113 288 9088

farm gate sales

Leventhorpe is England's most northerly commercial vineyard,
producing mainly light, dry whites using classic French grapes. The
wines are available direct from the vineyard, which is a member of
the UK Vineyards Association.

PAUL THEAKSTON, of the Black Sheep Brewery plc, Wellgarth (see below)

The Black Sheep Brewery was founded by Paul Theakston, a fifth-generation member of the famous Theakston brewing family that has been resident in Masham for over 500 years. Paul was worried about the increasing levels of technology used in big brewing companies, and set up Black Sheep to get back to a simpler and more traditional way of producing cask-conditioned real ale. There is no modern technology used at Black Sheep, old-fashioned types of barley and hops are used, and some of the vessels used for the brewing are over 100 years old. Paul firmly believes that going back to basics in this way results in ales that have more body and flavour. At the 2004 Brewing Industry International Awards, Black Sheep won gold and bronze medals. Black Sheep ales are available from the cask in many pubs around the north east, and the bottled versions are available from supermarkets throughout the country.

NORTH EAST   RIPON

Black Sheep Brewery plc   super hero

Wellgarth, Masham, Ripon, North Yorkshire HG4 4EN   T: 01765 689227
w: www.blacksheepbrewery.com
✉ mail order

Paul Theakston brews traditional, award-winning cask-conditioned ale. See the Super Hero box, above, for more information.

NORTH EAST   SKIPTON

The Wright Wine Company

The Old Smithy, Raikes Road, Skipton, North Yorkshire BD23 1NP   T: 01756 700886
w: www.wineandwhisky.co.uk
✉ mail order

The Wright Wine Company are specialists in both wine and whisky. With over 1000 wines, and around 500 Scottish malts alone, this shop has been described as 'encyclopaedic'. Filled with the rare and unusual, these are drinks that you will find difficult to get elsewhere, with whisky from New Zealand and Japan and spirits and wines from the smallest producers around the world. The range of Irish whiskies is growing apace, too. The staff are enthusiastic and keen to pass on their expertise.

York Beer and Wine Shop

28 Sandringham Street, Fishergate, York YO10 4BA   T: 01904 647136
w: www.yorkbeerandwineshop.co.uk

A legendary shop selling the rare, the unusual and the obscure in beers, wines, ciders and cheese. Plenty of bottle-conditioned real ales, traditional ciders and perries, and wines from small vineyards that you are unlikely ever to see on a supermarket shelf. The cheeses they stock come from smaller dairies and artisan cheesemakers.

NORTHERN IRELAND BELFAST

The Vineyard Belfast Ltd

375–377 Ormeau Road, Belfast BT7 3GP   T: 028 9064 5774
w: www.vineyardbelfast.co.uk

Obscure and unusual alcoholic drinks are the speciality here, with over 200 different beers, 45 different vodkas, and liqueurs, wines and whiskies from little-known producers. Bottle-conditioned real ales, including ale from the Hilden Brewing Co. (see below and the Super Hero box, opposite) can be found here.

NORTHERN IRELAND KILKEEL

Whitewater Brewery

40 Tullyframe Road, Kilkeel, Co. Down BT34 4RZ   T: 028 417 69449

One of only two microbreweries in the whole of Northern Ireland, the 15 beers made here are real ales with a splash of imagination. The staples are a dark ale, and a session ale, with seasonal specials like the summer honey and ginger beer, and the winter beer with hedgerow fruits. Available from many pubs in Belfast (call for details), or from the brewery's own pub, the White Horse Inn, 47–51 Main Street, Saintfield, Co. Down, 028 9751 1143 or 028 9751 0417.

NORTHERN IRELAND LISBURN

The Hilden Brewing Co.

super hero

Hilden House, Hilden, Lisburn, Co. Antrim BT27 4TY   T: 028 9266 3863

A brewery making a great range of traditionally made real ales and offering brewery tours, with a restaurant on site, Hilden is well worth a visit. See the Super Hero box, opposite, for more information.

super hero

THE HILDEN BREWING CO., Lisburn (see opposite)

The Hilden Brewing Co. is a passionate campaigner for the return of real ale to Northern Ireland. The province is dominated by just two huge breweries, leaving little room for small independent breweries, and this has meant that, over the years, Northern Irish drinkers have lost their taste for real ale. To reverse this trend Hilden offers a great range of fantastic real ales, from stouts, to porters, to pale ales, all made traditionally without chemical additives. Visitors to the brewery can take a tour and taste the beer or settle down to a meal and a few pints in the restaurant on site.

REPUBLIC OF IRELAND   BRAY

The Porterhouse

Strand Road, Bray, Co. Wicklow   T: 01 286 0668   w: www.porterhousebrewco.com

This Irish microbrewery make six different beers, including a traditional red ale and an oyster stout. For details, see under the Dublin branch, opposite. There is another branch in London, see page 156.

REPUBLIC OF IRELAND   CORK

The Franciscan Well

14 North Mall, Cork, Co. Cork   T: 021 439 3434

A centre for real ale in Ireland, the Franciscan Well brew pub holds two beer festivals each year, with one focussing on and celebrating microbreweries. The pub is also home to five real ales, along with some seasonal specials, many of which have won awards for the brewery.

REPUBLIC OF IRELAND   DUBLIN

Messrs Maguire

1–2 Burgh Quay, Dublin 2   T: 01 670 5777

There is a growing number of brew pubs and microbreweries in Ireland, mainly concentrated in Dublin and Cork. Ireland has been dominated by big industrial breweries for many years, and it is good to see some smaller breweries springing up and making real ales.

Messrs Maguire is one where the beers that they make are only available in the pub itself, and the beers include a traditional Irish red ale and a wheat beer, among others.

The Porterhouse

16–18 Parliament Street, Dublin 2   T: 01 672 8087   w: www.porterhousebrewco.com

This Irish microbrewery makes six different beers, including a traditional red ale, but perhaps most interesting is its oyster stout. Ireland has a great tradition of eating oysters with stout and this ale, which has whole oysters added in the brewing process, combines the two perfectly. This creates a slightly sweet flavour, with a very smooth consistency. There are also branches in London and Bray (see pages 156 and 169).

The Biddy Early Brewery   super hero

Inagh, Ennis, Co. Clare   T: 065 683 6976   w: www.beb.ie

A brew pub with a deep commitment tor reviving the best of Ireland's beer-making traditions, Biddy Early brewery makes Ireland's only herb beer. See the Super Hero box, below, for more information.

super hero

NIALL GARVEY of the Biddy Early Brewery, Inagh (see above)

When the Biddy Early Brewery was first established in 1995, Ireland had only three breweries left, none of which were Irish owned and none making real ale. Niall Garvey started Biddy Early in an attempt to revive the tradition of real beer in Ireland, making, among other beers, Red Biddy, which is Ireland's only herb beer. Red Biddy is made with bog myrtle, a wild herb growing in the hills just next to the brewery, which was traditionally used instead of hops many generations ago. The beer is then clarified with carrigeen moss, a local seaweed: left unpasteurized and without preservatives, Red Biddy exemplifies the company ethos of using natural and local ingredients. Biddy Early makes a stout, a beer and a lager, with a few seasonal specials throughout the year; the defining characteristic of them all is a commitment to the heritage of brewing in Ireland.

Llewellyn's Orchard Produce

Quickpenny Road, Lusk, Dublin   T: 01 8431 650 OR 087 284 3879
E: pureapple@eircom.net
🛒 farmers' markets

A rarity in Ireland – traditional farmhouse cider. David Llewellyn's
cider is made with apples from his own orchard, which receive no
insecticide sprays. He makes single-variety and blended ciders,
all without additives. The ciders are fermented in the bottle, which
gives a slight natural sparkle. Pure apple juices are also available.
Find the drinks at Temple Bar Market in Dublin, and farmers'
markets in Wicklow.

Beers Scotland Ltd

Manor Farm, Stirling FK9 5QA   T: 01786 446224   W: www.beersofscotland.com
✉ mail order

Scotland has a thriving real ale and microbrewery industry and
CAMRA have bestowed many awards on some of the small
breweries of Scotland. Beers Scotland are passionate about these
real ales and offer many award-winners, including the 2002 winners
Dark Island and Red MacGregor from the Orkney Brewery, and
Bitter and Twisted from the Harviestoun Brewery. If the ale you are
after is not on the Beers Scotland website, call them – they'll do
their utmost to find it for you. There is now a good range of other
Scottish drinks, too.

Seidr Dai   super hero

Cardiff   T: 029 2075 8193   W: www.welshcider.co.uk

Fiona and Dave Matthews are busy trying to resurrect the Welsh
cider-making tradition. See the Super Hero box, page 172, for more
information.

super hero

FIONA AND DAVE MATTHEWS, of Seidr Dai, Cardiff (see page 171)

Cider-making has a long heritage in Wales, but the tradition all but died out around 40 years ago. Fiona and Dave Matthews are busy trying to resurrect it, finding and propagating old and rare Welsh apple trees from ancient orchards. While they make many single varietal ciders and perries, the Matthews also experiment with blends to find the best ways to use these rare varieties of fruit. A recent triumph was finding and using the incredibly rare Potato pear for perry. The ciders and perries have won numerous awards, and, while they are not available direct from the producers (the Matthews are not full-time cider-makers yet), they can be regularly found at the Boar's Head pub in Pontyclun, the Chapter Arts Centre in Cardiff and the Clytha Arms near Abergavenny.

WALES   CORWEN

The Natural Mead Company

Ty Brethyn Meadery, Maesmor Hall, Maerdy, Corwen, Conwy   T: 01490 460456
📧 **farm gate sales**

Many people think that mead, as it is made from honey, must be a very sweet drink. The Natural Mead Company are at pains to point out that they fully ferment their mead for at least four months and this results in an almost dry beverage – not at all sweet. As well as the plain version there are varieties flavoured with traditional British fruits – sloes, quince and blackberries. Available direct from Maesmor Hall (call first), or from local delis.

WALES   CRICKHOWELL

Gellirhyd Farm

Llangenny, nr Crickhowell, Powys NP8 1HF   T: 01873 810466
w: www.gellirhydfarm.co.uk
📧 **farmers' markets**

Colin and Daphne Gardiner produce around 40 different award-winning single-variety apple juices, made with organic apples grown on this farm in the Welsh hills. Most of the apple varieties are very unusual; in some cases, there is only one tree of a particular variety. Gellirhyd Farm now also produces organic shiitake mushrooms. Available from Usk farmers' market, or from local delis.

New Quay Honey Farm

`super hero`

Cross Inn, New Quay, Ceredigion SA44 6NN   T: 01545 560822
w: www.thehoneyfarm.co.uk
🥄 **farm shop**

The Cooper family at New Quay Honey Farm make honey wine, or
mead, an ancient drink that has strong links with Wales. See the
Super Hero box, below, for more information.

Bragdy Ceredigion Brewery

Unit 2, Wervil Grange Farm, Pentregat, Ceredigion SA44 6HW   T: 01545 561417 OR
01239 654888
✉ **mail order**

Bragdy is a real family business – Brian brews the beer, his wife
designs the (very artistic) labels and even their children are
occasionally roped in to help. The brewery grew out of Brian's
hobby of home-brewing, and now there are six beers, one of which
is organic, all of which are cask- or bottle-conditioned. The family
have always been strong advocates for 'real food', and now they
have turned to making real ale. Available by mail order direct from
the brewery, or find the beer on tap at the Ship Inn in Tresaith.

super hero

THE COOPER FAMILY, of New Quay Honey Farm, Ceredigion, (see above)

The Cooper family at New Quay Honey Farm are very careful where they place
their hives – dotted around the Pembrokeshire coast, the bees have access to
heather, wild flowers and borage. The Coopers then take the honey and allow it
to ferment at air temperature during the summer months, maturing the liquid in
oak barrels for several months. This simple process results in honey wine, or
mead, an ancient drink that has strong links with Wales – it has been made in
Wales since at least AD 600. Making the mead in such an uncomplicated way
allows the drink to retain 'a complex bouquet … the original flavour of the
honey comes through'. It is so easy, in these times of labour-saving devices
and 'added value' products to get carried away and lose the original nature of
a foodstuff. New Quay Honey Farm demonstrates that, sometimes, the old
ways are the best: 'if it ain't broke, don't fix it'.

CHAPTER

5

As an island nation, we are spoilt by the richness of seafood surrounding us just beyond our shores. The World Wildlife Fund says there are so many species local to our waters that we could happily eat a different type of fish every week of the year without eating the same type twice. How odd, then, that the fish we buy is dominated by only five types – cod, haddock, plaice, salmon and prawns – and most of these are from foreign seas. As has happened in almost every type of food supply, the specialists, the fishmongers, have been squeezed out and most of the produce offered to us is imported. This has caused some real problems. The wild stocks of those five popular types of fish are in a desperate state, our fishing industry is in decline and we are missing out on good-quality, locally caught fish, sold by people who really know their trade. For this section, I've tried to find

fish

fishmongers who understand the issues, who can offer you local produce and great variety and can answer all your questions.

Farmed fish, such as the ever-popular salmon, does help to ease the pressure on wild fish stocks, but brings its own problems: over-crowded cages, pollution, and escape of the farmed fish into the wild (where they can spread disease) being the key issues. Ultimately, farmed fish do not represent a perfect cure for over-fishing – farmed salmon and trout are fed fishmeal, made with smaller fish, which still depletes the oceans. We've listed some of the fish farms that are trying to tackle those issues and, in the process, are offering really good-quality fish. Fish is a contentious issue right now but, by extending the range you buy, trying new types and asking questions, you could help solve some of the problems and also find some very tasty fish on your plate.

FishWorks

6 Green Street, Bath, BA1 2JY   T: 01225 448707   W: www.fishworks.co.uk
shop   mail order

The FishWorks' venues feature a unique combination of a traditional fishmonger, a seafood café and cookery school, all under one roof, creating a distinct atmosphere and theatre in which to eat, purchase, or learn about the preparation of the freshest fish and seafood. FishWorks also run a home delivery service offering fresh fish prepared to individual requirements, delivered overnight from Cornwall to your door. There are also FishWorks branches in Bristol (see below), Christchurch (see page 178) and London (see page 187).

Club Chef Direct

Lakeside, Bridgewater Road, Barrow Gurney, Bristol BS48 3SJ   T: 01275 475252
W: www.chefclubdirect.co.uk
mail order

An amazing, ever-changing choice of fish. Look out for the sustainably caught fish – line-caught mackerel, creel-caught langoustines, hand-dived scallops and organically farmed salmon.

FishWorks

128 Whiteladies Road, Clifton, Bristol BS8 2RS   T: 0117 974 4433
W: www.fishworks.co.uk
shop   mail order

For details see under the Bath branch, above.

Barnacle Bill Direct

Harbour House, Unit 24, Northfields Industrial Estate, Northfields Lane, Brixham, Devon
T: 0800 970 5102   W: www.barnaclebilldirect.co.uk
mail order

Barnacle Bill Direct source the majority of their fish from the day boats landing at Brixham, and there is plenty of choice. At the top of their list of priorities is sustainability – Barnacle Bill made the news for suspending sales of sea bass when there was a possibility that the pair of trawlers catching it were linked with dolphin deaths, and now only sell line-caught bass.

Browse Seafoods

The Old Market House, The Quay, Brixham, Devon TQ5 8AW   T: 01803 882484

The only remaining fresh fish shop in Brixham, Browse Seafoods are crab specialists, and testament to the quality of their fish is the fact that many good London restaurants buy their crustacea from Browse. The shop is also filled with really fresh wet fish, all chosen from the day boats landing at Brixham.

Bude Shellfish

5 The Seres, Lansdown Road, Bude, Cornwall EX23 8BH   T: 01288 354727

Bude Shellfish is run by Cliff, an ex-fisherman, who buys his fish from Looe market, only ever from day boats. He selects the fish each morning from the fishermen, never buying from boats that have been out for more than a day. Next door, Cliff runs Scrummies, a seafood café.

Sarah's

The Steamer's House, Cadgwith Cove, Cornwall TR12 7LX   T: 01326 290539
🛒 shop

Fish doesn't get much more local than this – Sarah sells seafood caught by local fishermen in the waters around the Lizard Peninsula. A speciality is the fresh crab.

The Fish Stall

Mudeford Quay, Christchurch, Dorset BH23 4AB   T: 01425 275389

The fish on display at The Fish Stall is hand-picked from local day boats, with a good choice of fish from the less pressurized species. Hand-lined mackerel and wild sea bass are available in season. The Fish Stall is a member of the National Federation of Fishmongers.

food facts

WHICH KINDS OF FISH SHOULD I BUY?

Pollack and saithe are both similar to cod, but their stocks are under much less pressure. Herring, while once endangered, is well on the way to recovery, but people have not yet got back into the habit of buying and cooking herring, even though it is incredibly tasty and very good for you. Megrim sole, mackerel, john dory, wolf fish, weaver, black bream, trigger fish, flounder, dabs, the list goes on and on. It is still important to buy cod and haddock every once in a while – there needs to be a market for them when the stocks recover or the fishing industry will never get back on its feet. At present, most of the cod and prawns we buy come from Iceland and Norway; these countries are relatively successful at maintaining the stocks of these fish within safe limits, so it makes sense to buy from them. Don't boycott fish because of over-fishing worries. It could force the price down due to lack of demand, ending in more of each species being caught to pay fishermens' bills. Go for other species, but we must eat fish. It's an essential part of our diet, as research into the fatty acid omega, found in fish oil, has proved.

SOUTH WEST   CHRISTCHURCH

FishWorks

10 Church Street, Christchurch, Dorset BH23 1BW   T: 01202 487000
W: www.fishworks.co.uk
🛒 shop   ✉ mail order

For details see under the Bath branch (page 176).

SOUTH WEST   CURRY RIVEL

Brown and Forrest

The Smokery, Bowdens Farm, Hambridge, nr Curry Rivel, Somerset TA10 0BP
T: 01458 250875   W: www.smokedeel.co.uk
🛒 shop   ✉ mail order

Brown and Forrest smoke duck, trout, chicken, salmon, pork and even lamb – but it is for their smoked eels that they are really famous. The eels are caught in rivers in Wiltshire and Hampshire, and then smoked in old wood-fired smokers. While oak is used for all the other produce, beech and apple wood is used for eels, for a more delicate flavour. Available from the smokery shop, or by mail order and there is a restaurant on the premises.

The Dartmouth Smokehouse

FISH

Nelson Road, Dartmouth, Devon TQ6 9LA   T: 01803 833123
w: www.dartmouthsmokehouse.co.uk

🛒 **shop**   ✉ **mail order**

A traditional smokehouse, producing a wide variety of gourmet smoked food using blends of wood smoke (oak, hickory, apple wood and alder) and herbs. Fresh fish and West Country meats are used to produce delicious cured and smoked food including: smoked Cornish chicken, hickory-roasted salmon, smoked eel fillets and smoked cherry tomatoes.

Pengelly's

The Fish Market, The Quay, East Looe, Cornwall PL13 1DX   T: 01503 262246

These two fish shops are run by fifth-generation fishmongers. Angela, the owner, is the only woman buying direct from Looe market each morning, selecting only fish from day boats, and offering line-caught fish whenever she can get it. Conservation is a big issue for her – she only buys fish that has been caught sustainably. There is also a branch in Liskeard, see opposite.

The Duchy of Cornwall Oyster Farm

Port Navas, Falmouth, Cornwall TR11 5RJ   T: 01326 340210

🛒 **shop**

Both native and Pacific oysters are available here, along with mussels. If you are visiting, try to get there in the morning to buy the produce, as the staff are likely to be out in the boats fishing in the afternoons.

Falmouth Bay Oysters

The Docks, Falmouth, Cornwall TR11 4NR   T: 01326 316600
w: www.falmouthoysters.co.uk

✉ **mail order**

Wild native oysters are harvested by traditional sailing boats from October to March in the Marine Conservation area around Falmouth. Lobsters, crabs, cockles and all other shellfish are also available.

Fowey Fish

37 Fore Street, Fowey, Cornwall PL23 1AH   T: 01726 832422   w: www.foweyfish.com
✉ **mail order**

Fish only sourced from day boats landing at Looe or Fowey.

Pengelley's

2 The Arcade, Fore Street, Liskeard, Cornwall PL14 3JB   T: 01579 340777

For details, see under the East Looe branch, page 179.

Mevagissey Wet Fish

The West Quay, Mevagissey, Cornwall PL26 6QU   T: 01726 843839

Everything sold at this fish shop is from local waters, bought direct
from the day boats landing each morning at Mevagissey.

William's Kitchen

3 Fountain Street, Nailsworth, Gloucestershire GL6 0BL   T: 01453 832240

Billed as 'the antidote to supermarkets', William's Kitchen offers a
fish slab consisting of incredibly fresh fish from Cornwall, only from
day boats. Fruits and vegetables, meats and deli foods are all of the
best quality available.

The Pilchard Works/Cornish Fish Direct

Tolcarne, Newlyn, Cornwall TR18 5QH   T: 01736 332112
w: www.pilchardworks.co.uk AND www.cornishfish.co.uk
👑 **shop**   ✉ **mail order**

This is the only salt pilchard works in the UK, preserving and
packing the fish in the traditional manner – layered in barrels with
salt, and left for at least six weeks. An intensely flavoured food, salt
pilchard can be used in any dishes that call for anchovies. At the
pilchard works is a museum giving an insight into the history of this
food. Fresh Cornish fish is also available by mail order.

NIGEL AND JUDE EKINS, of Cornish Cuisine, Penryn (below)

Nigel and Jude Ekins are a father-and-son team who select some of the finest Cornish produce and smoke it traditionally using the draft method – the smoke is drawn gently across the food, ensuring the produce is not damaged by harsh high temperatures. The mackerel they use is caught locally by the ecologically sound method of hand-lining, and each fillet is hand-prepared for smoking. This old-fashioned method of smoking requires constant attention – smoked over a lengthy period of time, the kiln cannot be just left to its own devices because the temperature and smoke must remain consistent. This means that Nigel or Jude will often find themselves at the smokehouse at 2am, checking on the fish in the kiln.

A great range of local cheeses, often organic, also gets the smoking treatment, including a feta-style cheese – all ingredients are bought as close to home as possible. One of their smoked cheeses won the Supreme Award at the 2002 World Cheese Awards. The wood used can be apple, cherry or almond, which have a more delicate smoke than the oak usually used in smokeries, allowing the flavour of the fish, cheese or meat to shine through. Available mail order, or from the shop on site at the smokery.

SOUTH WEST   PENRYN

Cornish Cuisine

`super hero`

The Smokehouse, Islington Wharf, Penryn, Cornwall TR10 8AT   T: 01326 376244
w: www.smokedsalmon-ltd.com

🛒 **shop** ✉ **mail order**

Traditionally smoked fresh Cornish produce. Nigel and Jude Ekins offer a selection of fine smoked foods including mackerel and cheese. See the Super Hero box, above, for more information.

SOUTH WEST   PENRYN

Seabourne Fish

The Fish Shop, Unit T, Islington Wharf, Penryn, Cornwall TR10 8AT   T: 01326 378478
🚚 **delivery service**

David Seabourne goes to Newlyn market every morning to choose the fish he will stock in his shop, buying from day boats operating with good sustainable practices. Hand-lined mackerel, pollack and bass and hand-dived scallops are all on offer.

Frank Greenslade

Fish Market, New Quay Road, Poole, Dorset BH15 4AF T: 01202 672199

Lots of fish from local waters are sold at this shop, mainly from day boats landing at Bournemouth. Local scallops, lobster and oysters are the stars.

Quayside Fish Centre

The Harbourside, Porthleven, Cornwall TR13 9JU T: 01326 562008
w: www.quaysidefish.co.uk
✉ mail order

A great place for fresh, sustainably caught fish – everything is local and from day boats, or line caught.

The Cornish Smoked Fish Company

Charlestown, St Austell, Cornwall PL25 3NY T: 01726 72356
w: www.cornishsmokedfish.co.uk
🏪 shop ✉ mail order

Smoked traditionally with oak, the Cornish Smoked Fish Company offer a dizzying choice of produce, from trout and salmon to prawns and mussels, and even eel. The majority of the fish is from Cornish waters.

Wing of St Mawes

4 Warren Road, Indian Queens, St Columb, Cornwall TR9 6TL T: 01726 861666
w: www.cornish-seafood.co.uk
✉ mail order

The fishmongers at Wing are all happy to offer advice and suggestions and will prepare the fish according to the customer's requirements. All the fish is from Cornish day boats and the aim is for it to be delivered to you the day after it was caught (or customers can collect direct from the premises).

Martin's Seafresh

St Columb Business Centre, Barn Lane, St Columb Major, Cornwall TR9 6BU
T: 0800 027 2066   W: www.martins-seafresh.co.uk
✉ mail order

Plenty of fresh Cornish fish from a fishmonger's run by an ex-fisherman. Lobsters, oysters and mussels are specialities at Martin's Seafresh. Mail order only. Martin's Seafresh is a member of the National Federation of Fishmongers.

Matthew Stevens & Son

Back Road East, St Ives, Cornwall TR26 1NW   T: 01736 799392
W: www.mstevensandson.co.uk
✉ mail order

Wet fish and shellfish, landed at Newlyn, St Ives and Looe, mainly from day boats are sold here. There is sometimes hand-lined mackerel available, too.

Market Fish

Market Place, Sidmouth, Devon EX10 8AR   T: 01395 577342

Fish comes fresh each morning to Market Fish's stall from the day boats landing at Brixham and Exmouth. During the summer, fish comes straight off the boats landing at Sidmouth, bringing crabs and lobsters and some hand-lined fish. Market Fish is a member of the National Federation of Fishmongers.

Donnington Trout Farm

Upper Swell, nr Stow-on-the-Wold, Gloucestershire GL54 1EP   T: 01451 830873
🛶 farm shop

Brown trout and rainbow trout grown in pure spring-water ponds.

super hero

TONY FREE, owner of Purely Organic, Warminster (opposite)

One of the few trout farms in the UK that holds Soil Association organic accreditation, Purely Organic treats its rainbow trout very differently from most trout farms. The water the fish live in is exceptionally pure, having been underground for around 400 years, and it first passes through watercress beds, picking up tiny freshwater shrimps as it goes. These shrimps make up around 90% of the diet of the trout and they grow fit and healthy catching this live food. A big factor in their rearing is the space the fish have – they are stocked at one-third of the density of non-organic fish. Equally important is the lack of antibiotics in their diet. Tony Free, the owner of Purely Organic, told me that antibiotics can cause fish to take on 10–20% of their own weight in water. When they are cooked, this water evaporates and, if they have been reared in less than clean water, there can be an unpleasant earthy residue, affecting the flavour. Tony believes it is vital to respect the fish he rears and the environment he rears them in and says that the firm, well-flavoured fish he sells are worth this care and attention. There is a farm shop on site, where not only are the trout available, but also a wide range of local organic fruit and vegetables, local honey and all sorts of grocery items. The trout is also available from numerous local farmers' markets, or by mail order.

SOUTH WEST   TAUNTON

Phil Bowditch

7 Bath Place, Taunton, Somerset TA1 4ER   T: 01823 253500

✉ **mail order**

Phil Bowditch imports virtually no fish at all – the majority of what he sells comes from the day boats landing at Brixham, or from his own boat.

SOUTH WEST   TOTNES

The Ticklemore Fish Shop

10 Ticklemore Street, Totnes, Devon TQ9 5EJ   T: 01803 867805

The owner of the Ticklemore Fish Shop goes to Brixham fish market each morning, selecting fish from the day boats that land there. There is also home-reared trout available from the shop's own farm.

SOUTH WEST WARMINSTER

Mere Fish Farm

Ivymead Mere, Warminster, Wiltshire BA12 6EN T: 01747 860461

farm shop **delivery service**

Cold- or hot-smoked rainbow trout, using fish reared in pure spring water. Local deliveries.

SOUTH WEST WARMINSTER

Purely Organic

super hero

Deverill Trout Farm, Longbridge Deverill, Warminster, Wiltshire BA12 7DZ
T: 01985 841093 W: www.purelyorganic.co.uk

farm shop **farmers' markets** **mail order**

Well-flavoured, firm trout, reared to exceptionally high standards by Tony Free, are available from Purely Organic. See the Super Hero box, opposite, for more information.

SOUTH WEST WESTBURY-ON-SEVEN

Severn and Wye Smokery

Chaxhill, Westbury-on-Severn, Gloucestershire GL14 1QW T: 01452 760190
W: www.severnandwye.co.uk

shop **mail order**

Traditionally smoked wild salmon and also organically farmed salmon are available here. Smoked eel, trout and mackerel are also on offer, as well as line-caught, fresh wild sea bass.

SOUTH WEST WEYMOUTH

Hand Picked Shellfish Company

85 Fortune's Well, Portland, Dorset DT5 1LY T: 07968 176485
W: www.handpickedshellfish.com

farmers' markets

A fishmonger's run by fishermen, everything sold here has been caught by the staff. Alongside the hand-dived shellfish is a range of unusual wet fish, with species less pressurized by overfishing, such as gurnard. The fish is caught off Weymouth. Available from many London farmers' markets, and Weymouth, Bristol and Bath farmers' markets.

super hero

FREIA AND NIGEL SAYER, of N. Sayers Fish Merchants, Brighton (below)

When I spoke to Freia Sayer, one half of the husband and wife team running N. Sayers Fish Merchants in Brighton, they had a sign outside their shop with a list of fish they refuse to sell. N Sayers' is a rare fishmonger's indeed – it has put the fisheries' crisis before profits and stocks only those types of fish that are not under pressure from overfishing, a move inspired by increasing concern over the sustainability of the fishing industry. Shopping here, you'll find gurnard, saithe, pollack and a great range of local fish, all at the peak of freshness, but no monkfish or cod. Although this could have been a very dangerous move financially, they have found that their customers have supported them wholeheartedly and are reaping the benefits by trying out a whole range of different, delicious fish. Freia told me that their new policy was a 'leap of faith', but that 'it's really exciting how it's changing the direction of our business'. While Freia's husband, Nigel, sources the very best local fish, Freia is on hand to advise customers on how to cook some of the less familiar types.

SOUTH WEST   **WIMBORNE**

Bell's Fisheries

Rear of 1 High Street, Wimborne, Dorset BH21 5PS   T: 07850 093096
✉ **mail order**

Bell's Fisheries is a permanent fish stall rather than a shop, selling day-caught fish landed mainly at Brixham. There is plenty of fish from species less endangered than cod and Mr Bell will happily advise on cooking. Bell's Fisheries is a member of the National Federation of Fishmongers. Home-smoked salmon is available by mail order.

SOUTH EAST   **BRIGHTON**

N Sayers Fish Merchants   `super hero`

198 King's Road Arches, Brighton BN1 1NB   T: 01273 823488

Husband and wife team Freia and Nigel Sayer sell a whole range of local fish, none of which is under pressure from overfishing. See the Super Hero box, above, for more information.

The Fresh Food Company

The Orchard, 50 Wormholt Road, London W12 0LS   T: 020 8749 8778
w: www.freshfood.co.uk
✉ mail order

This pioneering company, established in 1989, select sustainably fished seafood from Cornwall and the south coast for nationwide home-delivery within 48 hours of the fish being landed at port. There is plenty of fish from inshore boats and, when available, fish from Marine Stewardship Council-approved fisheries, such as hand-lined mackerel, Thames herring and cockles from the Burry Inlet. Organic fruit, vegetables, meat and wild-harvested game are also on offer.

H Forman & Son

30a Marshgate Lane, London E15 2NH   T: 020 8221 3900   w: www.formanandfield.com
shop   ✉ mail order

Forman's is one of the oldest smokehouses in the country, smoking wild salmon to great critical acclaim.

FishWorks

6 Turnham Green Terrace, Chiswick, London W4 1QP89 ALSO AT 89 Marylebone High Street, London, W1U 4QW   T: 020 8994 0086 (CHISWICK); 020 7935 9796 (MARYLEBONE)
w: www.fishworks.co.uk
shop   ✉ mail order

The FishWorks' venues feature a unique combination of a traditional fishmonger, a seafood café and cookery school, all under one roof, creating a distinct atmosphere and theatre in which to eat, purchase, or learn about the preparation of the freshest fish and seafood. FishWorks also run a home delivery service offering fresh fish prepared to individual requirements, delivered overnight from Cornwall to your door. In addition to the two London branches, there are FishWorks branches in Bath, Bristol (page 176), and Christchurch (page 178).

Steve Hatt

88–90 Essex Road, Islington, London N1 8LU   T: 020 7226 3963

Steve Hatt is a committed campaigner for UK fishing rights and quality fish. The fish is always bought by Steve on quality, not price.

Hayman's Fisheries

21–23 Covered Market, Avenue One, Market Street, Oxford OX1 3DU   T: 01865 242827
W: www.haymansfisheries.co.uk

The majority of the fish at Hayman's comes from British waters, with a really wide range available. Fish straight from the day boats landing at Looe and Grimsby, shellfish from clean Scottish waters and hand-dived scallops are all available.

Botterell's

Seafarers, Harbour Road, Rye Harbour, Rye, East Sussex TN31 7TT   T: 01797 222875
🠖 **farmers' markets**

The Botterell family buy their fish direct from day boats landing at Rye, and always have a big selection of whatever is in season. Flat fish are the staples here, with crabs and lobster, scallops and samphire available in season. Everything is super-fresh – the fish on the Botterell's stall is always less than 24 hours old. Find the produce at local farmers' markets, including Rolvenden, Rye and Battle.

Whitstable Shellfish Company   **super hero**

Westmead Road, Whitstable, Kent, CT5 1LW   T: 01227 282375
W: www.whitstable-shellfish.co.uk
✉ **mail order**

Philip Guy harvests native oysters from Whitstable Bay. Only available from September until April, the oysters are a rare delicacy. See the Super Hero box, opposite, for more information.

super hero

Native oysters are difficult to find these days – they are notoriously tricky to farm, taking five years to grow to maturity, and are more vulnerable to disease than the more commonly farmed Pacific variety. Ask an oyster connoisseur which variety he'd rather eat and there will be no hesitation – he'll always say the native. Phillip Guy of the Whitstable Shellfish Company has his own boat, the Angelina, and harvests the oysters from the wild beds around Whitstable Bay. This is not as easy as it sounds; there used to be inshore beds of oysters, but these were almost wiped out by a fungus unwittingly spread when French and Dutch oysters were imported to help bolster the stock, and so Philip has to fish further out to sea, where the beds were not damaged. These oysters are in deeper water, in small pockets. Says Philip: 'Finding the small pockets of oysters is a task on its own, further off shore it is more exposed in the bad weather, so limiting the days available for fishing. A small boat will average about 200 oysters on a good 12-hour day.' Add to this the fact that native oysters are only available from September to April, and we are talking about a very special food. Given the less than consistent supplies of the natives, the Whitstable Shellfish Company also supply Pacific oysters, sent live from the west coast of Scotland. While Whitstable provides truly excellent native oysters, Pacific oysters are less happy growing there and Philip chooses to source his in Scotland, where the quality is outstanding. 'We have formed a very strong working partnership with some of the crofters in the Scottish Highlands who also cultivate Pacific oysters on the west coast. This high-quality Pacific oyster acts as an excellent all-year-round complement to the native. Our specialized sea-water holding tanks enable oysters from a remote area to reach otherwise unobtainable markets in prime condition and in turn allows the Whitstable Shellfish Company to sell a very high-quality Pacific oyster all year round.' This variety has a fresh, salty flavour with a hint of cucumber.

EAST ANGLIA   ALDEBURGH

Aldeburgh Fish Stall

Aldeburgh Seafront (opposite White Lion Hotel), Aldeburgh, Suffolk   T: 01728 452827

Dean Fryer runs a fish stall on Aldeburgh seafront seven days a week, selling only fish that has been caught in local waters with his own boats. The fish literally comes off the boat and onto the stall, and is so fresh, he says it's still jumping! Crabs and lobsters are a speciality.

food facts

DOES IT MATTER HOW THE FISH WAS CAUGHT?

In terms of sustaining the fisheries, yes, it does. The Marine Stewardship Council is busy encouraging fishermen to use sustainable methods to catch fish, and as a result, they accredit certain products from fisheries that have demonstrated that they are catching fish with the future of the stocks in mind – look out for them in supermarkets. Sustainable methods tend to include the old-fashioned ways – hand-lining, creeling, hand-diving for shellfish. These methods usually give better-quality fish – they cause the fish far less damage. Day boats, as opposed to the large factory freezer trawlers that go out for weeks at a time, can offer fresher fish – the fish is back in port the same day it was caught, and it is more sustainable, as the boats can only go so far out to sea, leaving large areas unfished, where stocks can recover. The thing to do is ask questions when you buy fish. You might not always get an answer, but the more people that ask, the more suppliers will want to be able to answer you. The best fishmongers are those that hand-pick fish from the markets or ports themselves every day. They know which boats they want to buy from and they have built up relationships with the fishermen; they will be able to tell you a lot more about the fish, and how and when it was caught.

For more information on the MSC and its accredited products, check out the website www.msc.org

---

EAST ANGLIA   **BRANCASTER STAITHE**

The Fish Shed

Brancaster Staithe, Norfolk PE31 8BY   T: 01485 210532

Fish from local day boats provides the mainstay of the produce at the Fish Shed and in season there are crabs and lobsters straight from the boats. Local game is also available in season.

EAST ANGLIA   **COLCHESTER**

Colchester Oyster Fishery Ltd

Pyefleet Quay, Mersea Island, Colchester, Essex CO5 8UN   T: 01206 384141
w: www.colchesteroysterfishery.com
🛒 **shop**   ✉ **mail order**

The native oysters on sale here are harvested from the famous fattening grounds around Mersea Island. The fishery also sells rock oysters, lobsters, clams and crabs, all at the height of freshness.

The Company Shed

129 Coast Road, West Mersea, Colchester, Essex CO5 8PA   T: 01206 382700
🛒 shop   ✉ mail order

Famous Colchester native oysters are available here between
September and April, harvested locally by the Hawarth family, now
in their sixth generation of oyster fishing.

Richard and Julie Davies

7 Garden Street, Cromer, Norfolk NR27 9HN   T: 01263 512727

Cromer is famous for its crabs, which are small and sweet, with a
distinctive flavour. The crabs and lobsters at the Davies' shop are
caught by the shop's own boat.

Cookies Crab Shop

The Green, Salthouse, Holt, Norfolk NR25 7AJ   T: 01263 740352   w: www.salthouse.org.uk

The crabs and lobsters at Cookies are all caught using the shop's
own boats in local waters. Available to take home fresh, or you can
eat them at Cookies' own restaurant.

W J Weston

5A Westgate Street, Blakeney, Holt, Norfolk NR25 7NQ   T: 01263 741112

William Weston is a fisherman himself and his shop in Blakeney is
filled with local delicacies such as lobster, crab, cockles and home-
potted shrimps. His wife Dawn makes all kinds of deli-style foods
with the fresh seafood – smoked salmon tortilla wraps, seafood
quiches and fish pâtés, and also runs the seafood café next door.

Crowe Fishmongers

3 Provisional Market, Gentleman's Walk, Norwich, Norfolk NR2 1ND   T: 01603 767411

A vast selection of fish is on offer at Crowe's stall, usually around
40 varieties, with plenty coming from day boats landing at Lowestoft.

FOOD HEROES OF BRITAIN

John's Fish Shop

5 East Street, Southwold, Suffolk IP18 6EH   T: 01502 724253
W: www.johns-fish-shop.co.uk

Owned and run by an ex-fisherman, John's is a fishmonger selling fish mainly from Southwold harbour and Lowestoft; John hand-picks the fish every morning.

Butley Orford Oysterage

Market Hill, Orford, Woodbridge, Suffolk IP12 2LH   T: 01394 450277
W: www.butleyorfordoysterage.co.uk

Most of the fish sold at Butley Orford are caught with the shop's own boats. Pacific oysters and wet fish are on offer, including cod, skate, brill and wild Irish salmon, along with traditionally smoked fish. There is also a restaurant.

Carley and Webb

52 The Thoroughfare, Woodbridge, Suffolk IP12 1AL   T: 01394 385650

A real find for foodies, Carley and Webb stocks great local fresh fish and all manner of locally produced foods, including farmhouse cakes and breads.

Stephenson's Fishmongers

205 Retail Market, Queen Victoria Road, Coventry CV1 3HT   T: 07974 140255
W: www.stephenson-fish.co.uk

Robert Stephenson has a firm policy when it comes to buying fish – he buys with sustainability in mind. This means he won't cater for the fashion in 'baby' fish – young fish that have not had a chance to reproduce. The fish is almost all British and always from day boats.

The Organic Smokehouse

Clunbury Hall, Clunbury, Craven Arms, Shropshire SY7 0HG   T: 01588 660206
w: www.organicsmokehouse.com

🐟 **farmers' markets** ✉ **mail order**

Organic salmon from the Shetlands and the Hebrides is dry-salted
and air-dried before being smoked for at least 24 hours over
naturally fallen Shropshire oak – a traditional method which won the
company a Soil Association award in 2003. Smoked organic butter,
Cheddar cheese, sea salt and ricotta cheese are also available.

Alfred Enderby

Fish Dock Road, Grimsby, Lincolnshire DN31 3NE   T: 01472 342984
w: www.alfredenderby.co.uk

✉ **mail order**

Famous for large undyed smoked haddock and cod fillets,
Enderby's buys its fish fresh off the quayside every morning and
smokes it the slow, traditional way overnight in 100-year-old brick
smokehouses. Their sides of smoked salmon are from fish sourced
direct from salmon farms in the Shetland Isles.

Grapevine

31 High Street, Kington, Herefordshire HR5 3BJ   T: 01544 231202

Organic fish is well represented here, with salmon from Orkney and
trout from Wales. Welsh crabs and lobsters are also available, along
with local organic fruit and vegetables, and local game in season.

Hawkshead Trout Farm

The Boat House, Ridding Wood, Hawkshead, Ambleside, Cumbria LA22 0QF
T: 01539 436541   w: www.organicfish.com

🏪 **shop**

Organic trout are reared in roomy conditions at Hawkshead, with
much lower stocking densities than conventional fish farms. No
chemicals or colourings are involved in their production. Organic
salmon from Orkney is also available from the shop or via mail order.

Bessy Beck Trout Farm

Newbiggin-on-Lune, Kirkby Stephen, Cumbria CA17 4LY   T: 01539 623303
E: bessybecktrout@aol.com

➤ **farm shop**   ✉ **mail order**

The trout at Bessy Beck are farmed non-intensively – the stocking densities are much lower than conventional fish farms and the fish are fed by hand. They are reared slowly, giving the flesh a flakier texture, with more flavour. The fish are available fresh from the farm shop or from Orton, Brough, Barnard Castle or Penrith farmers' markets.

Moore's Traditional Curers

Mill Road, Peel, Isle of Man, IM5 1TA   T: 01624 843622   W: www.manxkippers.com

✉ **mail order**

Moore's kippers are smoked for 12 hours using the old-fashioned draft method, above burning oak chips. They are the last traditional Manx kipper curer on the Isle of Man. The fish is undyed. Bacon is also smoked slowly (for up to a week). Smokery tours are available and Moore's is a member of the Manx Producers Organisation.

Southport Potted Shrimps

66 Station Road, Banks Village, Southport, Lancashire PR9 8BB   T: 01704 229266
W: www.pottedshrimps.co.uk

✉ **mail order**

James Peet manufactures potted brown shrimps to his own specially devised recipe. He tried traditional recipes first, from the times before refrigeration, but felt that the old recipes overpowered the shrimp flavour with their need for preserving ingredients. James's recipe is simpler – shrimps, butter, and a light shake of ground mace, salt and pepper – the flavour of the shrimp shines through. Southport Potted Shrimps belongs to the Shellfish Association of Great Britain.

The Cheshire Smokehouse

Vost Farm, Morley Green, Wilmslow, Cheshire SK9 5NU   T: 01625 548499
W: www.cheshiresmokehouse.co.uk

🏪 **shop**   ✉ **mail order**

The Ward family smoke all kinds of foods, from salmon and trout to bacon and ham and even nuts (the smoked cashews are fantastic). Old-fashioned methods are used – oak and beech chips, and an unhurried attitude. Fresh foods are also available – local fruit and veg and fresh bread made on the premises daily.

Robertson's Prime

Unit 1d Willowtree Industrial Estate, Alnwick, Northumberland NE66 2HA   T: 01665 604386

✉ mail order

Most of the fish at Robertson's Prime comes from day boats landing at nearby Amble, and some is line-caught. Ian Robertson hand-picks the fish for the shop each day as it comes into the port. Local game in season is also offered.

Lindisfarne Oysters

West House, Ross Farm, Belford, Northumberland NE70 7EN   T: 01668 213870

w: lindisfarneoysters.co.uk

▱ farm gate sales   ✉ mail order

There has been a long tradition of oyster beds around Lindisfarne but these declined some time in the 19th century. Chris Sutherland's father resurrected the beds a few years ago and now Chris and his wife Helen are continuing the tradition. The Pacific oysters they farm take three or four years to reach maturity before they are purified at the Sutherlands' own tanks at the farm. Available direct from the farm, from Swallow Fish in Seahouses (see their entry, page 196), or by mail order.

Ridley's Fish and Game

17 Watling Street, Corbridge, Northumberland NE45 5AH   T: 01434 632640

The fish at Ridley's is hand-chosen by the owner, David, from the local ports, direct from the fishermen. He only uses fish from day boats, ensuring freshness. Local game from nearby estates is also sold here – all bought direct from the shoots and prepared at the shop. There is also a branch in Hexham, see page 196.

FOOD HEROES OF BRITAIN

Bleikers Smokehouse

Unit 88 Glasshouses Mill, Glasshouses, Harrogate, North Yorkshire HG3 5QH   T: 01423 711411   W: www.bleikers.co.uk

✉ **mail order**

When it comes to smoking, at Bleikers they admit that nothing happens quickly. The salmon used are hand-fed fish from low-density farms in the Hebrides, and they are smoked very slowly in an old-fashioned smokery. Poultry, game, meat, cheese and vegetables are also smoked without using any colourings or artificial preservatives. Bleikers' produce has won a clutch of medals from the Great Taste Awards. They supply by mail order.

Ridley's Fish and Game

2 Battle Hill, Hexham, Northumberland NE46 1BB   T: 01434 603138

For details, see under the Corbridge branch on page 195.

Swallow Fish

2 South Street, Seahouses, Northumberland NE68 7RB   T: 01665 721052
W: www.swallowfish.co.uk

🛒 **shop**   ✉ **mail order**

The smokehouse at Swallow Fish dates from the 19th century, and the fish smoked in it are locally caught, undyed haddock and cod and wild salmon. Fresh local fish is also available. Everything is smoked slowly and gently for a traditional flavour. Swallow Fish is a member of the National Federation of Fishmongers.

Kilnsey Park

Kilnsey, nr Skipton, North Yorkshire BD23 5PS   T: 01756 752150
W: www.kilnseypark.co.uk

🌾 **farm shop**   🏠 **farmers' markets**   ✉ **mail order**

Kilnsey Park is blessed with a natural spring in the grounds and it is in this clean water that trout are reared. Lower than average stocking densities allow the fish plenty of room to grow and the attention to detail extends to hand feeding. Buy the fish whole or made into a variety of dishes – chowder, pâtés, terrines or fishcakes – from the farm shop, by mail order, or from many local farmers' markets. There is also a restaurant.

Bywell Fish and Game Smokery

South Acomb Farm, Bywell, Stocksfield, Northumberland NE43 7AQ   T: 01661 844084

≛ **farmers' markets** ✉ **mail order**

Locally caught cod and haddock, and pheasant and venison are smoked over oak, prepared using traditional curing methods and recipes. All the produce is undyed and prepared by hand. Dry-cure bacon is also available. Available by mail order and from Hexham farmers' market.

food facts

FARMED FISH

Fish farming has lowered the price of salmon, making what was once a luxury food available to most of us. Sometimes, however, the salmon can be disappointing – an artificially bright pink, with a flabby texture and bland flavour. Many people point the finger of blame for this at the conditions in which the fish are reared. As salmon grew in popularity, farmers endeavoured to produce greater quantities at a lower price. As a result, more fish are crammed into smaller spaces, fed high-protein foods to accelerate growth, and this food is often full of antibiotics to prevent the spread of disease in such crowded conditions. In some cases the fish have less than half a bathful of water each to swim in, so it's hardly surprising that they are not firm and muscular like their wild equivalents. Some fish farms are much better than others – those sited out to sea, where the fish swim against powerful currents, which in turn clean away the waste the farm produces, and organic farms, which, by regulation, give the fish more space and don't feed antibiotics or growth promoters.

Shellfish farming is different – the pollution is minimal, the fish live virtually as they would were they wild and for those concerned about sustainability issues farmed shellfish are a good choice. We've found some great producers, including those who farm the prized native oyster, notoriously difficult to farm, but well worth the effort.

Fortunes

22 Henrietta Street, Whitby, North Yorkshire YO22 4DW,   T: 01947 601659

🛒 **shop**

Fortunes is a long-established traditional smokehouse, producing good old-fashioned kippers. The fish are hung over beech and oak shavings and smoked for at least 16–18 hours, resulting in a rich, strong flavour.

Cross of York

3 & 4 Newgate Market, York YO1 2LA   T: 01904 627590

The majority of the fish here is landed at Scarborough or Whitby. Cross of York was a previous winner of the Best Fishmonger in Northern England award.

Morton's

9 Bayview Road, Ballycastle BT54 6BP   T: 028 2076 2348

Morton's have their own fishing boats, so the fish comes straight off the boat and into the shop – no middlemen, no delay.

Walter Ewing

124 Shankhill Road, Belfast BT13 2BD   T: 028 9032 5534

Wet fish and shellfish from local waters, chosen from day boats. Walter Ewing is justly famous for the freshness of his fish.

Cuan Sea Fisheries

Sketrick Island, Killinchy, Co. Down BT23 6QH   T: 028 9754 1461 w: www.cuanoysters.com

✉ **mail order**

Pacific and native oysters grown in the very clean waters of Strangford Lough, a designated Marine Nature Reserve.

super hero

THE CONNEMARA SMOKEHOUSE, Clifden, County Galway (see below)

The Connemara Smokehouse has won a prestigious Bridgestone Guide Award for its mouthwatering specialist products, namely, smoked salmon, tuna and gravadlax. Only natural ingredients are used – just fish, salt, sugar, honey, Irish whiskey and herbs – with no colourings or artificial additives. This smokehouse specializes in wild salmon, although organic salmon from Clare Island is also available. Smoked line-caught Irish tuna is a product unique to this smokehouse. All the fish is filleted by hand and traditionally dry-cured, followed by a long drying and smoking period over beechwood in an old-fashioned kiln that dates from 1946. The Connemara Smokehouse won three medals at the 2004 Great Taste awards.

REPUBLIC OF IRELAND   BALLYCONNEELY

The Connemara Smokehouse

Bunowen Pier, Ballyconneely, Clifden, Co. Galway   T: 095 23739 W: www.smokehouse.ie
✉ mail order

An award-winning smokehouse, specialising in wild smoked salmon. Unusual smoked line-caught Irish tuna is also available. See the Super Hero Box, above, for more details.

REPUBLIC OF IRELAND   CASTLETOWNSHEND

Woodcock Smokery

Castletownshend, Skibbereen, Co. Cork   T: 028 36232   E: sallybarnes@iolfree.ie
✉ mail order

Traditionally smoked wild salmon, haddock, mackerel, tuna and kippers. The Woodcock Smokery won two Great Taste awards in 2003

REPUBLIC OF IRELAND   COBH

Belvelly Smokehouse

Cobh, Co. Cork   T: 021 481 1089   W: www.frankhederman.com
🛒 farmers' markets ✉ mail order

In his old timber smokehouse Frank Hederman smokes wild and organic Irish salmon using the delicate smoke of beech wood. Using organic sea salt, he first dry-cures the fish and then, using exactly the right size of beech wood chips, slowly smokes the salmon – the size of the wood chips is vital in creating the correct density. Hot-smoked mackerel and eel are also available; check them out at Midleton and Douglas farmers' market, and Temple Bar Market in Dublin.

REPUBLIC OF IRELAND   CORK

K O'Connell Ltd Fish Emporium

Cork English Market, 13–20 Grand Parade Market, Cork City, Co. Cork
T: 021 427 6380   W: www.koconnelfish.com

The O'Connells select the fish for their stall themselves, buying only with freshness in mind. Everything on the stall is from Irish waters and can be bought whole, or they will fillet it while you watch.

REPUBLIC OF IRELAND   DUBLIN

Nicky's Plaice

Store F, West Pier, Howth, Dublin   T: 01 832 3557 OR 832 6195
W: www.nickysplaice.ie

Nicky and his son Martin have many, many years of experience as fishmongers, and buy their fish straight from the boats. They know which skippers bring in the best fish and that's who they buy from.

REPUBLIC OF IRELAND   DUNGARVAN

Helvick Seafood

Cross Bridge Street, Dungarvan, Co. Waterford   T: 058 43585

The fish at Helvick Seafood comes straight from the local boats every morning – day boats, so the fish is always very fresh. Lots of choice, including fresh prawns, and all the fish is local, never imported. Most are available either whole or filleted.

REPUBLIC OF IRELAND   DUN LOAGHAIRE

Caviston's Seafood

59 Glastule Road, Sandycove, Dun Loaghaire   T: 01 280 9120   W: www.cavistons.com

A shop renowned for the freshness of the fish on display, supplemented with a good choice of Irish artisan cheeses. There is also a restaurant.

McDonagh's Seafood House

22 Quay Street, Galway   T: 091 565001   W: www.mcdonaghs.net

This fishmonger's sells locally caught fish and the famous oysters from Clarinbridge. There is a seafood bar and a fish and chip bar.

Michael Kelly (Shellfish) Ltd

Aisling, Tyrone, Kilcolgan, Co. Galway   T: 091 796120   W: www.kellyoysters.com

✉ **mail order**

Legendary native oysters from the west coast of Ireland – believed by many to be the best-tasting oysters in the world – fished to order.

Kinsale Gourmet Store   **super hero**

Guardwell, Kinsale, Co. Cork   T: 021 477 4453

Martin Shanahan buys only the best quality fish from local day boats to sell at his shop and restaurant. See the Super Hero box, below, for more information.

super hero

MARTIN SHANAHAN, of the Kinsale Gourmet Store, Kinsale (above)

Kinsale Gourmet Store is a fish-lover's paradise. The restaurant on site serves only fish, no meat, and the same high standard of fish is available to take away from their fish counter. Everything comes from the local day boats landing at Kinsale Harbour and the range available at any given time is governed by seasonality. Martin Shanahan is a perfect example of a retailer working well with his suppliers. He's not content to buy fish from a wholesaler – by far the easiest option. Instead, he buys direct from the local fishermen and has worked hard with them, encouraging them to use good practices to raise the quality of the fish they bring in. Both parties are now reaping the benefits – Martin gets the best fish around and the fishermen know they have a guaranteed outlet for their produce.

Kinvara Smoked Salmon

Kinvara, Co. Galway   T: 091 637489   W: www.kinvarasmokedsalmon.com

✉ **mail order**

Kinvara is one of the few smokeries offering organic salmon. The fish are reared on farms 5 km off the west coast of Ireland and the strong sea currents there ensure the farms are clean and the fish are fit and healthy. The stocking density is around half of that in conventional salmon farms, so the fish have much more space to swim around. The smoking is conducted over traditional oak shavings for a classic flavour.

Burren Smokehouse

Lisdoonvarna, Co. Clare   T: 065 707 4432   W: www.burrensmokehouse.ie

✉ **mail order**

Much more than a smokehouse, Burren also offer hand-made Irish chocolates, artisan cheeses, pâtés, jams and chutneys. They remain most famous for their smoked fish – eel, mackerel, trout, and the organic salmon for which they won a Great Taste Award.

Ummera Smoked Products

Inchybridge, Timoleague, Co. Cork   T: 023 46644   W: www.ummera.com

✉ **mail order**

Wild salmon from the Cork coastline and organic farmed salmon from Clare Island are traditionally smoked using oak. The fish is delicately smoked, allowing the flavour of the fish to balance well with the smoke. Hot-smoked chicken, dry-cure smoked bacon and eel are also available and the smokery is accredited by the Organic Trust and the Slow Food Movement.

Ken Watmough

29 Thistle Street, Aberdeen AB10 1UY   T: 01224 640321   E: ken.watmough@virgin.net

Ken buys his fish fresh each morning at Aberdeen Market; he knows the schedules of landings and which skippers he wants to buy from. A really wide choice is on offer here.

FISH

Summer Isles Foods

Achiltibuie, Ross-shire IV26 2YR, T: 01854 622353 w: www.summerislesfoods.com
✉ mail order

The fish at Summer Isles Foods is smoked using oak shavings, which gives a slower burn that results in a sweeter flavour. Organic salmon is available and it is marinated in an unusual blend of rum, molasses, juniper and garlic before smoking.

The Hand-Made Fish Company

Bigton, Shetland ZE2 9JF T: 01950 422214 w: www.handmadefish.co.uk
✉ mail order

David Parham is keen to sell only sustainably sourced fish and often has line-caught fish available. Organic salmon is also on offer. He also smokes fish using an unusual selection of woods: alongside the regular oak he smokes with beech, plum wood, peat and olive wood.

Isle of Skye Seafood

Broadford Industrial Estate, Broadford, Isle of Skye IV49 9AP T: 01471 822135
w: www.skye-seafood.co.uk
✉ mail order

Fresh langoustines and lobster from the clean waters around Skye, and also traditionally smoked eel and monkfish.

Loch Fyne Oysters Ltd

Clachan, Clairndow, Argyll PA26 8BL T: 01499 600264 w: www.lochfyne.com
✉ mail order

Smoked salmon, haddock, eels and kippers, using fish from suppliers who operate sustainably, and organically if possible. Oysters come from the company's own beds, in the clean waters of Loch Fyne. Scottish beef, lamb and game are also available.

food facts

HOW CAN YOU TELL IF FISH IS TRULY FRESH?

Follow these simple clues, and you'll be able to tell at a glance how fresh the fish is:

- Are the eyes bright? Cloudy or sunken eyes indicate a fish well past its prime.
- Are the scales shiny and healthy looking? Reject fish with rough, dry or dull scales.
- Does the flesh feel firm? Soft or flabby flesh denotes a stale fish.
- Does the fish smell fresh, with the scent of the sea? Only old fish smells fishy.
- Are the gills a lustrous pink or red, moist and a delight to the eye, not at all faded or brown?
- Is the skin shiny and vivid, with colours such as orange spots on plaice or the turquoise green and blue lines on a mackerel, bright and cheerful?
- Are the fins clearly defined, not scraggy and broken?

SCOTLAND   CRAIL

The Lobster Store

34 Shoregate, Crail, Fife KY10 3SU   T: 01333 450476

Fantastically fresh lobsters and crabs from local waters sold from a stall.

SCOTLAND   DINGWALL

Keltic Seafayre

Unit 6, Strathpeffer Road Industrial Estate, Dingwall, Ross-shire IV15 9SP
T: 01349 864087
✉ mail order

Keltic Seafayre specialise in hand-dived scallops from the clean waters of Northern Scotland. This gentle method of fishing produces better quality scallops, as they are undamaged by harsh trawling. Wild mushrooms from the highlands are also available.

Eddie's Seafood Market

7, Roseneath Street, Edinburgh EH9 1JH T: 0131 229 4207

shop

Packed with both local and exotic fish, Eddie's Seafood Market specialises in shellfish, with lobsters and razor clams heading the list.

Crannog

Town Pier, Fort William, Inverness-shire PH33 7PT T: 01397 700072 (OR 01397 705589 FOR RESTAURANT) W: www.crannog.net

mail order

Conservation is a key issue for Crannog, and so the fish available is caught using sustainable methods. Hand-dived shellfish, including scallops, are available, simply because Crannog never sell dredged shellfish, due to the damaging effects this has on the seabed. There is plenty of wet fish on offer, caught in local waters by the shop's own boat, all of it at the peak of freshness – langoustines are a speciality. You can even take a boat trip to see the fishermen at work and the fish farms, and there is also a restaurant.

MacCallums of Troon

71 Holdsworth Street, Glasgow G3 8ED T: 0141 204 4456

Lots of locally caught prime fish, hand-dived scallops and razor clams, native oysters in season and, occasionally, line-caught mackerel.

Cowie's of Helmsdale

1 Shore Street, Helmsdale, Sutherland KW8 6JZ T: 01431 821329

This fishmonger's is run by Alexander Cowie, the husband of Fiona, who runs the Helmsdale Smokehouse next door (see separate entry, page 206). The fish sold here is at the pinnacle of freshness – the Cowies meet the boats as they come in and choose from the local fish that have just been caught – scallops, prawns, haddock, whiting, herring and lemon sole are just a few of the varieties on offer.

super hero

ANDY RACE FISH MERCHANTS, The Port of Mallaig (see opposite)

Andy Race has a great guiding principle when it comes to the fish he buys from the local west-coast fishermen. He simply asks himself, 'Would I want to eat this?' Only the fish that he answers 'yes' to get on to his counter. He believes firmly that the local waters are the cleanest around Britain and that is why most of the fish he stocks is caught locally.

Peat-smoking is a speciality of Andy's. The smoked salmon he offers is gently smoked for a full three days and many have marvelled at the depth of flavour and the firm, muscular texture this lengthy smoking gives the fish. His salmon has also received a great deal of acclaim in the national press.

SCOTLAND   HELMSDALE

The Helmsdale Smokehouse

1 Shore Street, Helmsdale, Sutherland KW8 6JZ   T: 01431 821370
🛒 **shop**

A source of pride for the Cowie family at the Helmsdale Smokehouse is their use of local raw ingredients. The salmon is from Orkney, the pork and chicken are from a nearby farm and the venison is from a local estate. Local mussels and cheese are also smoked. Oak from old whisky barrels is used in the smoker and nothing is rushed – the salmon takes three days to be ready.

SCOTLAND   LOCHCARNON

Salar Smokehouse Ltd

Lochcarnon, South Uist, Outer Hebrides HS8 5PD   T: 01870 610324   w: www.salar.co.uk
✉ **mail order**

Award-winning hot-smoked salmon that is succulent, with a firm, flaky texture from fish farmed on the site.

SCOTLAND   LOCHGILPHEAD

Cockles

11 Argyll Street, Lochgilphead, Argyll PA31 8LZ   T: 01546 606292
E: elizabeth.cockhill@btinternet.com

Elizabeth Cockhill, a member of the National Federation of Fishmongers, has all manner of local delicacies in her deli-cum-fish shop, such as local and British farmhouse cheeses, locally baked bread and bread-making flours – including the hard-to-find chestnut flour – oils and vinegars and many different varieties of olives. The speciality, though, is the fresh fish, particularly the local langoustines, caught by her husband.

SCOTLAND   LOCHEPORT

Hebridean Smokehouse Ltd

Clachan, Locheport, Isle of North Uist, Outer Hebrides HS6 5HD   T: 01876 580209
W: www.hebrideansmokehouse.com
✉ mail order

The key to the quality of the smoked fish at the Hebridean Smokehouse lies firstly in the way the salmon and seatrout are reared. Stocked at around a third the density of most commercial fish farms and reared without antibiotics, the fish here have much more space in which to swim, and they are placed in fast moving tidal water, so they grow strong and firm. The fish are hand-filleted, and allowed to cure for eight hours in dry sea salt, before they are smoked slowly and gently over traditional peat, which imparts a rich but mellow flavour. Available by mail order only.

SCOTLAND   PORT OF MALLAIG

Andy Race Fish Merchants   super hero

The Harbour, Port of Mallaig, Inverness-shire PH41 4PX   T: 01687 462626
W: www.andyrace.co.uk
🛒 shop   ✉ mail order

Salmon smoked slowly over peat is Andy Race's speciality. See the Super Hero box, opposite, for more information.

SCOTLAND   PORTREE

Anchor Seafoods

The Pier, Portree, Isle of Skye IV51 9DE   T: 01478 612414

Anchor Seafoods is a permanent fish stall, stocking only local fish from the clean west-coast waters. Langoustines are a speciality and scallops, haddock and Dublin Bay prawns are all popular. Local lobster is available in season. Everything comes from day boats. Open six days a week in summer, limited hours in winter.

Colfin Smokehouse

Portpatrick, Stranraer, Dumfries and Galloway DG9 9BN   T: 01776 820622
w: www.colfinsmokehouse.co.uk

🛒 **shop** ✉ **mail order**

The Colfin Smokehouse takes classic Scottish foods (salmon from
Shetland and Orkney, Ayrshire bacon and Galloway Cheddar) and
smoke it over the wood from old whisky casks.

Inverawe Smokehouse

Taynuilt, Argyll PA35 1HU   T: 01866 822446 or 01866 822777
w: www.smokedsalmon.co.uk

🛒 **shop** ✉ **mail order**

Undyed salmon and trout, smoked over oak for 48 hours in a
traditional brick smokehouse are available from Inverawe
Smokehouse.

Tobermory Fish Company

Baliscate, Tobermory, Mull PA75 6QA   T: 01688 302120   w: www.tobermoryfish.co.uk

✉ **mail order**

The Tobermory Fish Company specializes in produce from Mull.
Although the emphasis is on smoked fish (local trout, salmon and
mussels), hard-to-find wild, hand-dived scallops are also available.

Fish on the Quay

Aberaeron, Ceredigion SA46 0BU   T: 01545 570599

There is plenty of local shellfish available at Fish on the Quay,
caught using the shop's own boat. All the wet fish is from day boats
and there is sometimes line-caught local sea bass, along with local
cockles, lobster and crab.

Minola Smoked Products

Triley Mill, Abergavenny, Monmouthshire NP7 8DE   T: 01873 736900
w: www.minola-smokery.com

✉ mail order

Welsh whole and split oak logs are used to smoke a vast range of
produce at Minola, in five traditional smokehouses – trout, scallops,
mussels and Scottish salmon, game, chicken, lamb, beef, bacon,
cheese, even butter and vegetables. You can visit the mill and make
your own selection at the shop or buy by mail order.

Celtic Dawn

The Shellfish Bar, Upper House, Aberiddy, nr St Davids, Haverfordwest, Pembrokeshire
SA62 5AS   T: 01348 837732

The Phillipses have their own boat, fishing off the Pembrokeshire
coast for crabs and lobsters, which are available, very fresh, from
their shellfish bar. Dressed crabs and hand-picked crab meat are
also available.

New Quay Fresh Fish Shop

South John Street, New Quay, Ceredigion SA45 9NP   T: 01545 560800

New Quay Fish Shop is seasonal, opening from around Easter until
the autumn. There is plenty of fish to choose from, but the really
interesting fish is the hand-lined mackerel and the crabs and
lobsters that the owner, Winston, catches from his own boat.

Coakley-Greene

Stall 41c, The Market, Oxford Street, Swansea SA1 3PF   T: 01792 653416

Lots of local fish from day boats fishing off the Welsh coast. The
staff are enthusiastic and happy to advise on cooking.

Due to the wide variety of soil types and local climates in this country, the range of fruit and particularly vegetables that can be grown here is staggering and so it seems sad that, with such bounty available, we import so much; currently around 70% of the organic produce we buy has been grown abroad.

The list of fruit and vegetable producers in this book predominantly consists of organic growers, many of them accredited by the Soil Association or other organic bodies. Others, though not recognized by one of these bodies, grow to organic standards and others still keep their crop-spraying to the absolute bare minimum, using the safest pesticides they can find and then only when there is a real danger of losing an entire crop (some crops, such as apples, are notoriously difficult to grow without a little intervention). Why spray produce unless it is absolutely necessary? A great many people are concerned about the possible effects of pesticides on health and on the soil, and organic farming can be seen to have a whole range of benefits, hence the bias towards organic growers in these listings.

It is in the fruit and vegetable sector that buying locally is perhaps most pertinent. The problem of food miles – the distance that food travels between producer and consumer, particularly excessive for imported foods – is very

fruit and vegetables

easy to address for fruit and vegetables; there are few parts of the country where a reasonable range is not grown. The added benefit of buying from a local grower is that the produce will be very fresh – many of the growers listed here pick the vegetables on the day they are sold, and some even pick to order.

I'm not suggesting that we should never buy imported fruit and vegetables – with fruit, in particular, there are times of the year when the native fruit available is few and far between and life without bananas and oranges would be all the poorer. Finding a local farm shop, joining a box scheme or rummaging around your local farmers' market, however, can reveal a treasure-trove of the freshest, tastiest, most nutritious fruit and vegetables, grown close to where they are being sold by farmers whose key concern is quality, not price. Look out for the members of the Northern Ireland Greengrocers Association in Northern Ireland – this is a small group of greengrocers who are committed to buying local fruit and vegetables direct from local producers. The rural economy is boosted, food miles are reduced and, because the produce is never warehoused, it arrives on your plate at the peak of freshness. It is heartening to see retailers taking this approach.

Orswell Cottage Organic Garden

Stoke Rivers, Barnstaple, Devon EX32 7LW   T: 01598 710558

⊠ **farm gate sales**   ⊠ **box scheme**

Sue Lugg grows organic vegetables, trying to grow a selection of
varieties for each type of vegetable. Organic hens' and guinea fowl
eggs are also available, and organic lamb to order. Sue operates a
local box scheme and sells at Barnstaple Pannier Market. She is a
member of the Henry Doubleday Research Association.

Gold Hill Organic Farm

Childe Okeford, nr Blandford Forum, Dorset DT11 8HB   T: 01258 861413

⬇ **farm shop**

The maxim by which Sara and Andrew Cross farm is 'anything you
can grow in this country, we'll try to grow', and the selection of fruit
and vegetables is impressive, including aubergines, mange tout,
peppers and chillies. Organic beef from British White cattle is also
available, as are milk, cream, eggs and a full range of organic
groceries from the weekend farm shop or from Castle Cary market.

Elwell Fruit Farm

Waytown, Bridport, Dorset DT6 5LF   T: 01308 488283

⬚ **farmers' markets**   ⊠ **farm gate sales**

Elwell Fruit Farm grows five varieties of pear and around 20 varieties
of apple, from the familiar to the very rare. Bottled apple juice is
available, too. All the produce can be found at Bridport, Dorchester
(Poundbury), Sherborne and Blandford Forum farmers' markets, or
direct from the farm, but call first.

Arne Herbes

Limeburn Nurseries, Limeburn Hill, Chew Magna, Bristol BS40 8QW   T: 01275 333399
W: www.arneherbs.co.uk

⬇ **farm shop**   ⬚ **farmers' markets**

Anthony Lyman-Dixon is said to be a walking encyclopaedia when it
comes to herbs and the list of varieties he grows at Limeburn

Nurseries is incredibly long. From the well known to the exotic, the herbs are all grown without pesticides and can be bought direct from the nursery or at Bristol and Glastonbury farmers' markets.

SOUTH WEST   BRISTOL

Jekka's Herb Farm

Rose Cottage, Shellards Lane, Alveston, Bristol BS35 3SY   T: 01454 418878
w: www.jekkasherbfarm.com

✉ **mail order**

Plant and seed herbs from this award-winning organic grower are available by mail order. Jekka also runs four open days a year, and workshops, so you can learn about growing your own herb garden.

SOUTH WEST   BUCKFASTLEIGH

Riverford Farm Organic Vegetables

Wash Barn, Buckfastleigh, Devon TQ11 0LD   T: 01803 762720   w:www.riverford.co.uk

📦 **box scheme**

Award-winning organic growers, offering a great-value, weekly box scheme packed with flavoursome organic vegetables.

SOUTH WEST   CHELTENHAM

Slipstream Organics

34a Langdon Road, Leckhampton, Cheltenham, Gloucestershire GL53 7NZ   T: 01242 227273   w: www.slipstream-organics.co.uk

📦 **box scheme**

Slipstream Organics' double-award-winning organic box scheme delivers to Gloucester, Stroud, Cheltenham and outlying villages. There is plenty of choice, with six different box sizes available. The produce is sourced as locally as possible and freshness is key – the vegetables have often been picked less than 24 hours before delivery.

SOUTH WEST   CHIPPENHAM

V & P Collins

81–83 Devizes Road, Bromham, Chippenham, Wilts SN15 2DZ   T: 01380 850228 OR 07971 120601

🥕 **farmers' markets**

The Collins family produce a huge selection of vegetables on their 70 acres, from the usual basics like root vegetables and brassicas to the more unusual, such as the pink fir apple potato and white sprouting broccoli. Using an integrated management system, they encourage beneficial insects to control pests, only spraying when absolutely necessary. Find them at almost all the Wiltshire farmers' markets: call for details.

Westwood Farm

Rode Hill, Colerne, nr Chippenham, Wilts SN14 8AR   T: 01225 742854

farm shop   farmers' markets

Mrs Trotman and her husband grow a vast range of organic vegetables and fruit, including apples, plums and strawberries; they offer a great salad bag of oriental leaves. There is a farm shop on site, open on Fridays from 2–7pm and the Trotmans attend Bath farmers' market every Saturday, selling their produce to, as Mrs Trotman calls them, 'refugees from the supermarket'.

The Organic Farm Shop

Abbey Home Farm, Burford Road, Cirencester, Gloucestershire GL7 5HF
T: 01285 640441   W: www.theorganicfarmshop.co.uk

farm shop

Award-winning organic farm shop, selling incredibly fresh, home-produced vegetables and herbs (over 100 varieties throughout the season). The farm is committed to strengthening the link between consumer and producer and runs farm trailer rides. Free-range meat and all kinds of groceries are also available.

Linscombe Farm

Newbuildings, Sandford, Crediton, Devon EX17 4PS   T: 01363 84291
E: farmers@linscombe.fsnet.co.uk

farmers' markets   box scheme

Helen Case and Phil Thomas produce an awesome range of vegetables – around 300 varieties in season, which can include over 20 different types of potato. This ensures that their box scheme customers (who need to live within a five-mile radius of Linscombe Farm) never get bored with the same vegetables, and 'heritage' varieties are preserved. Linscombe Farm was highly commended in the Waitrose/Times Small Producers Award, and is a member of the

Henry Doubleday Research Association. Find the produce at
Crediton, Exeter, Exmouth and Plymouth farmers' markets.

Green Valley Foods at Longmeadow

Godmanstone, nr Dorchester, Dorset DT2 7AE   T: 01300 342164

⬇ **farm shop** ✉ **box scheme**

Home-produced organic vegetables and locally produced foods,
with an emphasis on organic are available from Green Valley Foods.
There is also a good range of wholefoods.

Peppers By Post

Sea Spring Farm, West Bexington, Dorchester, Dorset DT2 9DD   T: 01308 897892
w: www.peppersbypost.biz

✉ **mail order**

A fantastic range of peppers and chillies and even tomatillos are all
available by mail order.

Higher Crop

Pynes, Bridford, nr Exeter, Devon EX6 7JA   T: 01647 252470

✉ **farm gate sales**

Chris Towell has a fascination with old varieties of vegetables that
are no longer commercially grown. He has grown nine different
varieties of garlic and blue potatoes and is now experimenting with
growing a great variety of beans. Call him to arrange an order which
you can then collect from the farm.

Rod and Ben's Food from the Soil

Bickham Farm, Kenn, Exeter, Devon EX6 7XL   T: 01392 833833
w: www.rodandbens.com

✉ **mail order** ✉ **box scheme**

Rod and Ben grow a dazzling variety of organic fruit and vegetables
on their 106-acre farm. See the Super Hero box, page 216, for more
information.

super hero

ROD AND BEN'S FOOD FROM THE SOIL, Exeter (see page 215)

It is dizzying to look at the list of fruit and vegetable varieties that Rod and Ben grow on their 106-acre Devon farm – from aubergines to watercress, artichokes to sweetcorn and even, for a brief spell in September, melons – all organic. With the chance of chocolate-brown free-range eggs from the Maran hens and honey from the farm's own hives, a vegetable box from Rod and Ben's box scheme will always be full of surprises. What drives them to grow such a huge diversity of vegetable varieties? 'Our aim is to supply fresh home-grown vegetables for as much of the year as possible. Good quality, variety and value for money are our key principles. We try and source any bought-in produce locally and have established links with local growers in order to compensate for shortfalls in our own production.' If you're a customer of theirs, Rod and Ben aren't content to let you just take your fruit and veg and run – they want you to feel involved. They'd really like you to visit at least once a year to find out what's going on at the farm. 'We involve our customers in the box scheme through a regular newsletter, *Rod and Ben's Roundup*, and farm walks, strengthening the link between producer and consumer. Many of our customers have followed our story through organic conversion and feel a stronger association with the farm as a result, as well as having a better understanding of what is involved and the principles of organic farming.' Rod and Ben won the *Devon Life* Best Food Producer of the Year award, 2004.

SOUTH WEST   **GLASTONBURY**

West Bradley Orchards

West Bradley, nr Glastonbury, Somerset BA6 8LT   T: 01458 850227
E: westbradleyorchards@ukonline.co.uk
↙ **farm shop**   🛒 **farmers' markets**

Lots of varieties of apple and pear are grown here, many that you will have never heard of, since they are old varieties seldom grown now. Pick your own in season, or buy the fruit ready-picked at the farm shop or at Glastonbury farmers' market.

SOUTH WEST   **HOLSWORTHY**

Holsworthy Organics

Ceridwen, Old Rectory Lane, Pyworthy, Holsworthy, Devon EX22 6SW   T: 01409 254450
📭 **box scheme**

Despite being a small-scale producer, Holsworthy Organics, a duet of organic growers, won the Best Box Scheme Award at the 2002 Soil Association Organic Food Awards. A year-round box scheme, with produce that is almost all home-grown with occasional supplements of produce from other local organic growers, Holsworthy offer a great variety of fresh fruit and veg.

Merricks Organic Farm

Park Lane, Langport, Somerset TA10 0NF   T: 01458 252901
W: www.merricksorganicfarm.co.uk
⬇ farm shop   ✉ box scheme

Throughout the season, around 150 different varieties of fruit and vegetable are grown at Merricks Farm – anything it's possible to grow in this country, they'll have a go at. Nothing is ever imported or brought in from elsewhere. Alongside the vegetables, there are free-range hens' eggs and free-range geese and turkeys at Christmas. The fruit and vegetables are available through the box scheme; the meat is available at the farm shop on site.

Boddingtons Berries

The Ashes, Tregony Hill, Mevagissey, Cornwall PL26 6RQ   T: 01726 842346
W: www.boddingtonsberries.co.uk
⬇ farm shop

Boddingtons are strawberry specialists and grow all sorts of varieties. The Boddington family believe that the sea breezes blowing over the fields allow the fruit to ripen more slowly, increasing the sugar content and making for a deliciously sweet strawberry. PYO is available, along with home-made preserves.

Camphill Village Trust (Oaklands Park)

Newnham-on-Severn, Gloucestershire GL14 1EF   T: 01594 510365
E: cvtoaklandspark@hotmail.com
✉ box scheme

A biodynamic box scheme, with fruit and vegetables, and optional lamb and beef, all grown or reared at Oaklands Park.

Bosavern Farm

Bosavern, St Just, Penzance, Cornwall TR19 7RD   T: 01736 786739
E: joandguy@bosavern.fsnet.co.uk

➥ **farm shop**

Everything sold at Bosavern farm shop is home-grown or home-reared and for the meat a local butcher and abattoir are used. Organic vegetables, grass-fed Hereford beef, free-range pork and eggs are all available.

Guernsey Organic Growers

La Marcherie, Ruette Rabey, St Martins, Guernsey GY4 6DU   T: 01481 237547
W: www.cwgsy.net/business/guernseyorganics

🔲 **box scheme**

An organic box scheme covering the island of Guernsey, with most of the contents of the weekly boxes being home-grown. Guernsey Organic Growers run the only mixed organic nursery on Guernsey.

Coleshill Organics

59 Coleshill, Swindon, Wilts SN6 7PT   T: 01793 861070

➥ **farm shop**   🛒 **farmers' markets**   🔲 **box scheme**

Beautifully fresh, organic vegetables, delivered locally or buy them from Barnes farmers' market in London. Organic free-range eggs are also available.

Charlton Orchards

Charlton Road, Creech St Michael, Taunton, Somerset TA3 5PF   T: 01823 412959

➥ **farm shop**   🛒 **farmers' markets**

Charlton Orchards yield 32 different varieties of apple, including one thought to date back to Roman times. Tours of the orchards are available, during which visitors can taste the fruit, which also includes pears, plums, damsons, quince and soft fruit.

Duchy Home Farm Organic Vegetables

Broadfield Farm, Tetbury, Gloucestershire GL8 8SE   T: 01666 504287

farmers' markets   **box scheme**

An interesting selection of home-grown organic vegetables from the prestigious Duchy Estate. Find them at Tetbury, Cirencester and Stroud farmers' markets.

Bee Organic

Moothill Cross, Staverton, Totnes, Devon   T: 07817 467936

farmers' markets

Paul Hutchings likes to grow the less usual types of vegetable and has been known to grow up to 35 different types of tomato and ten kinds of chilli. He likes to grow 'heritage crops' – the varieties of fruit and vegetable that are in danger of dying out – and is also cultivating almonds and walnuts on his land. Find Bee Organic produce every week at Buckfastleigh farmers' market.

Cusgarne Organics

Cusgarne Wollas, nr Truro, Cornwall   TR4 8RL   T: 01872 865922

farm shop   **box scheme**

An organic farm that runs a fantastic-value vegetable box scheme, comprising almost entirely home-grown produce, with a good selection of unusual varieties of vegetables. Also available are organic eggs and home-produced Angus beef.

John Hurd's Organic Watercress

Stonewold, Hill Deverill, nr Warminster, Wilts BA12 7EF   T: 01985 840260
w: www.organicwatercress.co.uk

farm shop

Traditionally bunched watercress, grown to maturity for a strong, peppery taste. Available direct from the farm or from Waitrose.

The Bell and Birdtable

Runnington, Wellington, Somerset TA21 0QW   T: 01823 663080
w: www.bellandbirdtable.com
▷◁ **farm gate sales**

This tiny smallholding produces an amazing range of tomatoes –
49 varietes were grown here at the last count, none of which you'll
ever see on supermarket shelves. The varieties are chosen for
flavour; Anne McGrath, the grower, procures seeds from around the
world to grow unusual varieties. She also rears rare-breed pork
(Oxford Sandy & Blacks), which are slowly matured and range freely.

The Dorset Blueberry Company

352 Hampreston, Wimborne, Dorset BH21 7LX   T: 01202 579342
w: www.dorset-blueberry.com
▵ **farmers' markets** ✉ **mail order**

The acidic, well-draining soil of Dorset is perfect for growing
blueberries and the Dorset Blueberry Company have over 50 years
of experience in growing them. Not only can you buy the fruit fresh
direct from the farm or from the countless farmers' markets they
attend (see their website), but you can also buy blueberry pies,
sauce, juice and jam.

Hayles Fruit Farm

Winchcombe, Cheltenham, Gloucestershire GL54 5PB   T: 01242 602123
w: www.hayles-fruit-farm.co.uk
⬐ **farm shop**

Hayles Fruit Farm make pure juices from their fruit – in all, there are
11 apple varieties, nine plums, and two pears. Soft fruit is also
available and, unusually in this part of England, cob nuts. It's also
possible to pick your own and there is a tearoom at the farm.

Millets Farm Centre

Kingston Road, Frilford, nr Abingdon, Oxfordshire OX13 5HB   T: 01865 392200
w: www.milletsfarmcentre.com
⬐ **farm shop**

What started as a small PYO in an attempt at diversification in the 1970s has become a big farm centre with all sorts going on – a farm shop selling a variety of home-grown apples, pears, plums and vegetables, fresh fish and local meats, a restaurant, and a 'maize maze'. The idea is to bridge the gap between town and country – kids can go on trailer rides and see the crops and farm animals.

SOUTH EAST   AYLESBURY

The Sustainable Lifestyles Research Co-op Ltd

Pond Cottage East, Cuddington Road, Dinton, Aylesbury, Buckinghamshire HP18 0AD
T: 01296 747737   E: mike.george@euphony.net
farm shop (please phone first)

A co-operative of workers growing all kinds of fruit and vegetables using the permaculture method, a holistic form of agriculture. The speciality here is Victoria plums – there are 500 plum trees. Free-range chicken, eggs and lamb are available from the small on-site farm shop and the smallholding is run with an open policy – visitors are welcome. Accredited by the Organic Food Federation.

SOUTH EAST   BASINGSTOKE

Laverstoke Park Produce

Home Farm, Laverstoke, Whitchurch, Hampshire RG28 7NT   T: 01256 890900
box scheme

Laverstoke Park provides a year-round organic box scheme in the Winchester and Basingstoke areas, producing the widest possible range of vegetables and fruit. Meat and free-range eggs are also available and almost everything in the boxes is home-grown. There is an on-site butchers' shop. selling home-reared meat, organic chickens, organic geese and turkeys at Christmas, and home-grown organic fruit and vegetables. Laverstoke is currently in conversion to Biodynamic status.

SOUTH EAST   BILLINGSHURST

Costrong Fruit Farm

Plaistow Road, Kirdford, Billingshurst, West Sussex RH14 0LA   T: 01403 820622
E: costrong2000@yahoo.co.uk
farm shop   farmers' markets

Over 40 varieties of apple and pear are available here, many of them old British types. There is also a small apple and pear museum on site. All the produce is available from the farm shop or Chichester farmers' market.

FOOD HEROES OF BRITAIN

Perry Court Farm Shop

Garlinge Green, Canterbury, Kent CT4 5RU T: 01227 732001

➜ **farm shop**   🛒 **farmers' markets**   📦 **box scheme**

Lots of organic and biodynamic fruits and vegetables are available here – over 50 varieties at the last count. Home-grown cereals are milled into flour and there is also organic beef from a closed herd.

Sarsden Organics

Sarsden Estate Office, Sarsden, Chipping Norton, Oxfordshire OX7 6PW
T: 07977 445041   E: sarsdenorganics@btopenworld.com

🛒 **farmers' markets**   📦 **box scheme**

Rachel Siegfried works within a classic two-acre Victorian walled garden, growing a good range of vegetables, including some less well-known heritage varieties. Unusual lettuces, herbs and salads are a speciality. The produce is available through a box scheme but customers can choose what their box contains. The produce is also available from Wolvercote (Oxford) farmers' market.

Kingfisher Farm Shop

Guildford Road, Abinger Hammer, Dorking, Surrey RH5 6QX T: 01306 730703

➜ **farm shop**

This farm shop specializes in fresh watercress, grown without insecticides or fertilizers in natural spring water, and also stocks organic local produce – goats' and ewes' milk cheese, yoghurt, chickens and cakes.

Godshill Organics

Yard Parlour, Newport Road, Godshill, Isle of Wight PO38 3LY T: 01983 840723
E: godshill.organics@virgin.net

➜ **farm shop**   🛒 **farmers' markets**   📦 **box scheme**

There is a really extensive range of organic vegetables grown at Godshill Organics and everything in their box scheme and on their farmers' market stall is home-grown. Seasonality is important to Ruth, who runs the business – she strives to teach customers about the British seasons for food and will always tell you if she has had to buy something in.

Tendring Fruit Farm

Magham Down, Hailsham, East Sussex BN27 1QA T: 01323 841812 OR 01323 842116

⬥ **farm shop**

The farm shop at Tendring Fruit Farm offers so many different varieties of apple and pear that Tony Eales, the grower, couldn't remember exactly how many; he thought it was in the region of 27. He also grows plums. Such is the range that there are varieties cropping all the time, giving a year-round supply of fresh fruit.

food facts

BIODIVERSITY

Thank goodness for the Henry Doubleday Research Association. They maintain a seed library conserving the huge number of varieties of fruit and vegetables that have been grown in this country. Thousands of plant varieties have been lost in this country since the 1970s alone. The main problem is that agribusiness, in its drive for bigger and bigger yields, has focussed on varieties that can achieve those high yields, and so the number of varieties grown commercially has progressively narrowed – it is thought that around 30 plant types now feed the majority of the world's population. Along comes the EU, with its reams of regulations, and decides that every variety that is to be marketed must be registered, classified, tested and trialled, shown to be 'sufficiently uniform and stable', with 'satisfactory value for cultivation and use'. This testing can take around two years and cost over £2000 – an unrealistic sum of money for a small-scale producer more interested in flavour and diversity than high yields and price points. Some of the growers listed in this section have no time for these rather imperious regulations and, if you are lucky, you might find an enlightened farmer growing blue potatoes, purple carrots, orange beetroot, or tomatoes the size of a fingernail. Not only will those vegetables be maintaining genetic diversity in this country, they'll be grown specifically because they are tasty; they'll also make a real talking point at dinner. Find out more on the Henry Doubleday website www.hdra.org.uk

While not organic, the fruit is grown with the absolute minimum of spraying.

Sussex Saffron

Glebe Cottage, Hooe, East Sussex, TN33 9HD   T: 01424 846645
W: www.sussex-saffron.co.uk

✉ **mail order**

Sussex Saffron produce what is almost certainly the only commercially grown saffron in England. Saffron was widely produced in this country until around 200 years ago; Anthony Lee at Hooe is now single-handedly trying to resurrect the tradition, despite the fact that it's a laborious process, fraught with potential problems due to the delicacy of this crop. English saffron was renowned as the best in the world, so try some of Anthony's and see if this is still the case!

Home Cottage Farm

Bangors Road South, Iver, Buckinghamshire SL0 0BB   T: 01753 653064
W: www.homecottagefarm.co.uk

⬇ **farm shop**

Fifteen varieties of apple, two of pear and four of plum are grown here, along with summer and autumn raspberries and blackberries. Buy from the farm shop or pick your own in season.

Boathouse Organic Farm Shop

The Orchards, Uckfield Road, Clayhill, Lewes, East Sussex BN8 5RX   T: 01273 814188

⬇ **farm shop**

A farm shop boasting a huge range of home-grown organic vegetables, organic beef, lamb and mutton, pork and home-cured bacon, and local cheeses from organic dairies.

Blackmoor Apple Shop

Blackmoor Estate, Liss, Hampshire GU33 6BS   T: 01420 473782

⬇ **farm shop**

Twenty varieties of apple are grown at Blackmoor, with over 300 acres of orchard. Plums, quinces and strawberries are also grown and all the produce is available, in season, from the farm shop.

Cool Chile Co.

Unit 7, Buspace Studios, Conlan Street, London W10 5AP   T: 0870 902 1145
w: www.coolchile.co.uk

✉ mail order

Every kind of chilli you can imagine, along with some hard to find Mexican ingredients. Available by mail order, or from Borough or Portobello markets.

Mrs Tees Wild Mushrooms

Gorse Meadow, Sway Road, Lymington, Hampshire SO41 8LR   T: 01590 673354
w: www.wildmushrooms.co.uk

✉ mail order

Fresh wild mushrooms from the New Forest, available by mail order.

Warborne Organic Farm

Boldre, Lymington, Hampshire SO41 5QD   T: 01590 688488

↧ farm shop ✉ box scheme

Winner of the 2003 Best Box Scheme award from the Soil Association, Warborne Farm has an amazing range of vegetables and fruit – around 300 varieties in season. Staunch believers in eating locally and seasonally, the farmers at Warborne run a box scheme within a 30-mile radius and have a farm shop, open Thursday to Sunday.

The Hen on the Gate

Newick Lane, Mayfield, East Sussex TN20 6RE   T: 01435 874852

↧ farm shop ✉ box scheme

A farm shop and box scheme, offering fruit and vegetables, Sussex beef, lamb, pork, chickens and eggs – all organic and home produced.

Cross Lanes Fruit Farm

Mapledurham, Reading, Berkshire RG4 7UW   T: 0118 972 3167
W: www.crosslanesfruitfarm.co.uk

🠗 **farm shop** ✉ **mail order** 🖙 **farmers' markets**

There are a staggering 60 varieties of fruit grown at Cross Lanes, including 46 varieties of apple. The Franklin family are keen to re-introduce the old and unusual varieties of fruit and choose the most flavourful varieties. At the farm shop, customers can taste the fruit before they buy. Available from the farm shop in season (late August to Christmas), by mail order or at Reading, Henley, Beaconsfield, Newbury, Maidenhead and Wallingford farmers' markets.

SOUTH EAST   ROBERSTBRIDGE

Simply Wild

Scragoak Farm, Brightling Road, Robertsbridge, East Sussex TN32 5EY
T: 08456 586140   E: enquiries@simplywildorganics.co.uk

🠗 **farm shop** 🖙 **box scheme**

A large range of organic vegetables, with several varieties of each type of vegetable on offer, in order to encourage species diversity. Home-reared organic meat, poultry and eggs are also available.

SOUTH EAST   SEVENOAKS

Allens Farm

Allens Lane, Plaxtol, nr Sevenoaks, Kent TN15 0QZ   T: 01732 812215
W: www.allensfarm.co.uk

🖙 **farm gate sales**

Allens Farm is a traditional Kentish farm growing cherries, damsons and cobnuts, available from the farm (phone first). See the Super Hero box, opposite, for more information.

SOUTH EAST   SITTINGBOURNE

Thrognall Farm

Bull Lane, Newington, Sittingbourne, Kent ME9 7SJ   T: 01795 842220

🖙 **farmers' markets**

Joan Atwood of Thrognall Farm is always on the lookout for interesting things to grow. Among the huge list of fruit and vegetables she offers at local farmers' markets are cherries, chillies, tomatillos, globe artichokes and black cabbage. Although not registered organic, the produce is not sprayed with pesticides or herbicides and no artificial fertilizers are used. Call to find out which farmers' markets she attends.

Fruitwise

Winchester Street, Botley, Southampton, Hampshire SO30 2AA   T: 01489 796790
w: www.fruitwise.co.uk

🔸 farmers' markets

Dr and Mrs Hayes enthusiastically tend an orchard full of old English apple varieties (around 45 at the last count), varieties never seen in supermarkets. Vegetables are also grown in season, and home-made cider, and all the produce is available from local farmers' markets – call for details.

super hero

SAMANTHA PETTER, of Allens Farm, Plaxtol (opposite)

Allens is a traditional Kentish farm, growing cherries, damsons and cobnuts. Such is the scarcity of these crops – and of the traditional orchards that produce them because most have been grubbed up to make way for more commercial crops – that the farm has Countryside Stewardship status, to conserve the heritage of this area. So why do Samantha Petter and her family still grow these crops when, clearly, other crops would be far more profitable? 'Not for prestige or glamour, and certainly not for financial gain!' laughed Sam when I asked her, 'but because we feel a sense of responsibility towards preserving a unique but diminishing part of Kentish life, and because they taste fantastic....' Sam went on to tell me about the history behind the cobnut orchard she tends: 'Over 100 years ago, 2,700 Kentish Cobnut trees were planted in the Bourne Valley. This was at a time when nuts were prized as a delicious and nutritious crop ... now the Kentish Cobnut is scarcely known, swamped by foreign imports. But our ancient, gnarled trees still stand, still bearing plentiful harvests ... who could fail to be moved and impressed by the sense of history, by our great grandfathers' endeavours all those years ago? So we still continue to promote this wonderful fresh fruit, against all odds, to a small, but dedicated and passionate following.'

The cobnuts, cherries, plums, damsons and also home-reared lamb are all available direct from the farm, but call first before visiting.

FOOD HEROES OF BRITAIN

Brook Cottage Farm

Charney Bassett, Wantage, Oxfordshire OX12 0EN T: 01235 868492

🛒 **box scheme**

Brook Cottage Farm offers a year-round box scheme, with home-produced vegetables and fruit.

Waterperry Gardens

Waterperry, nr Wheatley, Oxfordshire OX33 1JZ T: 01844 339226
w: www.waterperrygardens.co.uk

🥄 **farm shop**

Apples are the speciality here, with over 50 varieties being grown, many of them rare and unusual. There are also pears, raspberries, plums and fresh herbs, and 16 single-variety apple juices. Everything sold is grown on the farm.

Waterland Organics

Willow Farm, Lode, Cambridge CB5 9HF T: 01223 812912
w: www.waterlandorganics.co.uk

🧺 **farmers' markets** 🛒 **box scheme**

A wonderful range of seasonal vegetables, available through a weekly box scheme or at Ely farmers' market. Everything is grown organically and the growers, Doreen and Paul Robinson, are committed to farming with minimal impact on the environment.

Lathcoats Farm

Beehive Lane, Galleywood, Chelmsford, Essex CM2 8LX T: 01245 266691
w: www.eapples.co.uk

🥄 **farm shop**

Lathcoats Farm operates an integrated farming system, which means that though they are not organic, a biological approach is taken – beneficial insects are encouraged to control pests and spraying is only undertaken when absolutely necessary. It's primarily a fruit farm; cherries and 40 varieties of apple are grown here, along with all kinds of soft fruits. The on-site farm shop stocks local produce – poultry, meat and dairy. You can even choose an apple tree and 'rent' it, which means you get all the apples from your tree at harvest time, and you can also pick your own.

EAST ANGLIA   CLACTON

Brooklynne Farm Shop

Chapel Road, Beaumont-cum-Moze, nr Clacton, Essex CO16 0AR   T: 01255 862184
🞂 **farm shop** 🞂 **farmers' markets**

A farm shop stocked with lots of home-grown produce – around three-quarters of the produce in the shop is grown on the farm. In season there is every vegetable you can imagine, some produce is organic, some conventionally grown. The shop is open every day except Monday or you can find Brooklynne produce at Long Melford, Sudbury, and Clacton Common farmers' markets.

EAST ANGLIA   COLCHESTER

Clay Barn Orchard

Fingringhoe, Colchester, Essex CO5 7AR   T: 01206 735405
🞂 **farm gate sales** 🞂 **mail order**

A rare quince orchard, offering the old-fashioned fruit by mail order. Quinces are notoriously vulnerable to bad weather and some years the harvest is very poor, so call for availability (season starts beginning of October).

EAST ANGLIA   COLCHESTER

Crapes Fruit Farm   super hero

Rectory Road, Aldham, Colchester, Essex CO6 3RR   T: 01206 212375
E: andrew.tann1@virgin.net
🞂 **farm gate sales** 🞂 **mail order**

An apple orchard with over 150 varieties; see the Super Hero box, page 230, for more information.

super hero

ANDREW TANN, of Crapes Fruit Farm, Colchester (see page 229)

You could be forgiven for assuming that Andrew Tann is somewhat obsessed with apples – he grows around 150 different types, although in some cases there is only one tree of a particular variety. In a time when we think of apples only in terms of the three or four varieties available in supermarkets, most of which seem to have been imported, it is refreshing to find someone so dedicated to preserving the rich diversity of apple types that has been so overlooked. Apples are notoriously difficult to grow without pesticides and, while Crapes is not organic, the farm operates a system of 'sympathetic management' – no organophosphates, no preserving chemicals, no wax or other dressings to improve the appearance of the apple skins. Andrew Tann is pleased to report a recent renewed public interest in the more unusual varieties of apples – perhaps more of us are becoming concerned about the loss of such tasty fruits. Even though Crapes Fruit Farm has such an enormous range of apple varieties it is by no means exhaustive and Andrew says that there is a small but increasing band of fellow apple fans who enjoying seeking out the rare and unusual. If you are searching for a particular type that Andrew does not grow, he'll still be able to help you out – 'any enquiry is welcomed – if I cannot help, then it is usually possible to direct an avid apple hunter to another possible source'. The apples are available from the orchard direct, or by mail order, but only to individuals – Andrew does not wholesale.

EAST ANGLIA   EPPING

Ashlyns Organic Farm Shop

Epping Road, North Weald, Epping, Essex CM16 6RZ T: 01992 225146 (SHOP) OR 01992 523038 (BOX SCHEME) W: www.ashlyns.co.uk
➔ farm shop 🖾 box scheme

Ashlyns Farm produces over 30 different varieties of vegetables, and free-range eggs from Black Rock hens, all organic. There is also a small herd of Lincoln Red beef cattle. A driving aim behind the farm is to create a stronger link between customers and the source of their food, so open days are regularly held. Ashlyns Farm is accredited by the Countryside Stewardship Scheme.

Clive Houlder, Mushroom Man

98 West Street, North Creake, Fakenham, Norfolk NR21 9LH   T: 01328 738610
E: mushroomman@ntlworld.com

✉ mail order

Clive Houlder is expert at seeking out the wild mushrooms of East Anglia.

Park Fruit Farm

Pork Lane, Great Holland, nr Frinton-on-Sea, Essex CO13 0ES   T: 01255 674621
w: www.parkfruitfarm.co.uk

⬦ farm shop

There is plenty of choice at Park Fruit Farm – 39 varieties of apple, four varieties of pear, with raspberries, wet walnuts, honey, blackberries and vegetables, all grown at the farm.

Gourmet Mushrooms

Morants Farm, Colchester Road, Great Bromley, Essex CO7 7TN   T: 01206 231660
w: www.springfieldmushrooms.co.uk

🛒 farmers' markets

Over 20 different varieties of mushroom, all grown organically. are available from Notting Hill, Islington, Pimlico, and Stoke Newington farmers' markets. Gourmet Mushrooms is accredited by the Organic Food Federation.

Hollow Trees Farm Shop

Semer, Ipswich, Suffolk IP7 6HX   T: 01449 741247   w: www.hollowtrees.co.uk

⬦ farm shop

A recent winner of the National Farmers' Union Best Farm Shop award, Hollow Trees stocks home-grown fruit and vegetables, and home-reared meat, alongside produce from other small-scale producers, including beer, honey and cream.

Laurel Farm Herbs

Main Road, Kelsale, Suffolk, IP17 2RG T: 01728 668223 W: www.laurelfarmherbs.co.uk

🛒 shop

Chris Seagon grows an astonishing range of herbs at Laurel Farm – including 45 different varieties of thyme. They are all grown without heat, which means that the range is subject to seasonality. No pesticides are used, they are grown in peat-free compost, and Chris will even grow some of the more unusual herbs to order.

Abbey Farm Organics

Flitcham, King's Lynn, Norfolk PE31 6BT T: 01485 609094 E: flitcham@eidosnet.co.uk

🧺 farmers' markets 📦 box scheme

Offering a choice of set or 'à la carte' weekly boxes, Abbey Farm offers an ever-expanding range of organic vegetables. Delivered within 24 hours of harvest, the vegetables are at the peak of freshness. You can also find Abbey Farm vegetables at local farmers' markets – call for details – and King's Lynn Friday market.

Plumbe and Maufe

The Parsonage, Burnham Thorpe, King's Lynn, Norfolk PE31 8HW T: 01328 738311
E: nina@creeke.demon.co.uk

🛒 farm shop

Over 30 varieties of unusual plums and gages are grown here, most of them no longer commercially grown. Available from the on-site farm shop, but please call first.

Barker Organics

The Walled Garden, Wolterton Hall, Wolterton, Norwich, Norfolk NR11 7LY
T: 01263 768966

📦 box scheme

The Walled Garden at Wolterton dates back to the 18th century. Within it, David Barker grows between 30 and 40 different crops, from carrots to aubergines and peppers, all biodynamically. Available through the box scheme David runs.

food facts

WHAT'S IN SEASON?

Ever bought strawberries in January and been disappointed when they tasted of almost nothing? Seasonality is a key aspect of getting the maximum flavour in food and that's especially true for fruit and vegetables. The growers we have featured all offer you great-tasting produce – but only when it is in season. Some may extend their growing seasons slightly or grow varieties not normally associated with these shores, such as peppers and aubergines, with the use of sheltering poly-tunnels (one grower in Wales can sometimes offer peaches!) but, in general, the seasons rule. This means flavoursome strawberries in the summer, not at Christmas – but crisp and sweet native apples in December. Local asparagus, peppery watercress and buttery new potatoes in the spring and early summer; richly flavoured blackberries, plums and courgettes in the autumn and sweet-tasting, comforting parsnips and leeks as the winter arrives all give a great sense of time and place. Accepting and understanding seasonality can re-awaken the sense of anticipation as a favourite food comes into season to be eaten at the peak of perfection.

EAST ANGLIA   NORWICH

Stable Organics

The Stables, Gresham, Norwich, Norfolk NR11 8RW   T: 01263 577468

⊨ farm gate sales

Organic produce grown in an old walled garden – everything sold is grown on site and includes vegetables, soft and top fruit and salads. The aim is to provide 'a bit of everything'. The produce is picked to order, so it will be incredibly fresh! Available direct from the farm, but call first.

EAST ANGLIA   SAFFRON WALDEN

Audley End Organic Kitchen Garden

Saffron Walden, Essex CB11 4JF   T: 01799 522842 OR 01799 522148

⏷ farm shop

The Henry Doubleday Research Association, for which Audley End Organic Kitchen Garden is a display garden, is committed to both organic gardening and maintaining the biodiversity of plant species in the UK. At Audley End the walled garden produces many heritage varieties of fruits and vegetables, all grown organically, and they are available to buy from the shop on site.

High House Fruit Farm

Sudbourne, Woodbridge, Suffolk IP12 2BL   T: 01394 450263 OR 01394 450378
w: www.high-house.co.uk

⬤ **farm shop**

High House Fruit Farm has a wide choice of apples, from the well known to the more unusual, along with loganberries, blackberries, gooseberries, currants, asparagus, cherries and plums. Even apricots are planned for the future! Single-variety apple juices are also available. Only produce grown on the farm is available in the farm shop. PYO is also on offer.

Field 2 Kitchen

Dobbies Garden Centre, Mancetter Road, Atherstone, Warwickshire CV9 1RF
T: 01827 715511

For details, see under the Wolverhampton branch on page 239.

New Farm Organics

Soulby Lane, Wrangle, Boston, Lincolnshire PE22 9BT   T: 01205 870500
w: www.newfarmorganics.com

✉ **farm gate sales**

Mrs Edwards grows a varied selection of organic fruits and vegetables, available direct from the farm, usually harvested that day for total freshness.

Trinity Farm

Awsworth Lane, Cossall, Notts NG16 2RZ   T: 0115 944 2545   w: www.trinityfarm.co.uk

⬤ **farm shop**   ▦ **box scheme**

Specializing in vegetable varieties you won't find in the supermarket, Trinity Farm produces 30 types of lettuce and 12 types of tomato in season, along with all manner of exciting fruit and vegetables. The farm shop stocks the home-grown vegetables picked on the day of sale and there is also a weekly box scheme. Organic fish is also available, as are pork and home-cured bacon and free-range eggs.

Ryton Organic Gardens

Ryton-on-Dunsmore, Coventry CV8 3LG   T: 02476 303517
w: www.hdra.org.uk/ryton.htm
shop   box scheme

The Henry Doubleday Research Association is committed to both organic gardening and maintaining the biodiversity of plant species in the UK. At Ryton there are acres of demonstration gardens, with a kitchen garden and an 'unusual vegetable' garden. You can buy the fabulous produce from the gardens in the shop, have a meal in the restaurant, visit the Vegetable Kingdom Museum and even sign up to the box scheme and get a weekly delivery.

Hampton Farm Shop

Pershore Road, Evesham, Worcestershire WR11 6LT   T: 01386 41540
w: www.hamptonfarmshop.co.uk
farm shop

Seventeen varieties of plum are grown here, plus damsons. Ian Lovall, the grower, is passionate about these fruits and grows many rare and unusual varieties. The farm shop also stocks apples from a nearby farm and locally grown vegetables.

Court Farm and Leisure

Tillington, Hereford HR4 8LG   T: 01432 760271   E: courtfarm@onetel.net.uk
farm shop

Soft fruit of every description is grown here, including blueberries, plums, blackberries, raspberries, cherries and redcurrants and PYO is available.

super hero

THE STANIER FAMILY, of Dragon Orchard, Ledbury (see below)

English orchards, with their profusion of native apple, plum and pear varieties, are becoming more and more rare. They just don't pay – apples are cheaper from abroad – so many farmers simply cannot afford to keep their orchards; they need the land for more profitable crops. The Stanier family at Dragon Orchard faced a stark choice – stop growing apples altogether or find some way of making money from them. They came up with a novel idea – crop-sharing. For an annual fee, a family can become part of Dragon Orchard, visiting four times a year to see what is going on at the farm (and, depending on the season, this can include wassailing, blossom time, harvesting or cider-making). At the end of each season they will receive a share of the orchard's bounty – boxes of apples of numerous varieties, pears, bottled juice, cider and jams. It is a great way to explore the life cycle of a working orchard and you will be saving a traditional English orchard from being grubbed up and lost forever. Ann Stanier won the Country Living Enterprising Rural Women award this year

MIDLANDS   HOPTON WAFERS

Augernik Fruit Farm

Hopton Wafers, Shropshire DY14 0HH   T: 07968 231631

🛒 **farmers' markets**

Claire and Bill at Augernik Fruit Farm have been growing organically for 15 years, producing an amazing range of fruit from their orchards – three types of cherry, nine varieties of plums, 22 of apples plus pears, greengages, apricots, gooseberries and autumn raspberries. Fresh cobnuts, filberts, chestnuts and walnuts are also available. Find Claire and Bill at farmers' markets in Stourbridge, Moseley, Ludlow, Halesowen and Birmingham.

MIDLANDS   LEDBURY

Dragon Orchard

Dragon House, Putley, Ledbury, Herefordshire HR8 2RG   T: 01531 670071
w: www.dragonorchard.co.uk

A traditional English apple orchard that regained profitability by an innovative crop-sharing scheme, in which families pay an annual fee in exchange for visits and a share of the orchard's produce (see the Super Hero box, above, for more information).

SoilMates

PO Box 67, Ross-on-Wye, Herefordshire HR9 5ZA T: 01989 767444
w: www.soilmates.com

farm gate sales mail order

A specialist chilli-grower; see the Super Hero box, page 238, for
more information.

Five Acres

Ford, nr Shrewsbury, Shropshire SY5 9LL T: 01743 850832 w: www.organicapples.co.uk

farm gate sales

Ian Mason has over 100 different apple varieties in his orchards and
around 15 varieties of plum. All are grown organically, with pests
controlled by the 200 hens that range around the orchard, who also
provide eggs. The fruit and eggs are available from the farm gate,
but call first.

Hopwood Organic Farm

Bickenhill Lane, Catherine de Barnes, Solihull, West Mids B92 0DE T: 0121 711 7787
w: www.hopwoodorganic.co.uk

farm shop box scheme

Hopwood won a fistful of awards at the 2003 Soil Association
Organic Food Awards. Their produce, which includes peppers,
spinach and aubergines alongside the regular basic vegetables, is
available from the farm shop on site, which also stocks other organic
produce from nearby farms, or through the weekly box scheme.

Walsgrove Farm

Egdon, Spetchley, Worcestershire WR7 4QL T: 01905 345371 w: www.walsgrove.co.uk

farm shop

Over 60 varieties of apple and 18 of plum are available at Walsgrove
Farm. Conservation of heritage varieties is the driving force behind
this fruit farm, although varieties are also chosen with flavour in
mind. The farm is not organic but natural insect predators are used
to control pests as far as possible.

super hero

RICHARD HUIJING, of SoilMates, Ross-on-Wye (see page 237)

Richard Huijing is a man obsessed by chillies – he must be, since he grows over 400 varieties. He started growing them because he was disappointed by the lack of choice in supermarkets – it often comes down to just red or green, which is a poor representation of the variety that is actually available. Indeed, Richard grows brown chillies, white ones, purple ones … They come in a range of strengths, from the reasonably mild to the downright dangerous – for hard-core fans only! He has followed this with what he terms an 'heirloom' collection of tomatoes, currently running at about 160 varieties – 'all built around the criteria of exceptional taste, texture and intriguing appearance'. These two specializations are accompanied by other interesting fruit and vegetables that would be almost impossible to find elsewhere. While he sells to many professional chefs, he also offers the produce to 'adventurous cooks' direct from the smallholding or occasionally by mail order. Call for more information.

MIDLANDS   ST MARGARETS

Fern Verrow Vegetables

Fern Verrow, St Margarets, Herefordshire HR2 0QF   T: 01981 510288
E: fernverrow@btopenworld.com
🚜 **farm gate sales** 🛒 **farmers' markets**

Biodynamic fruit and vegetables with a great selection of basics and some more unusual varieties. Rare-breed pork, chickens, ducks, geese, turkeys (at Christmas) and free-range eggs are also available. Find the produce at Borough Market or at the farm itself.

MIDLANDS   WOLVERHAMPTON

Essington Fruit Farm

Bognop Road, Essington, Wolverhampton, Staffs WV11 2BA   T: 01902 735724
W: www.essingtonfarm.co.uk
🥄 **farm shop**

Soft fruit comes in every form imaginable at Essington – even blueberries. The varieties grown are carefully selected for maximum flavour and PYO is available, as well as a tearoom.

Field 2 Kitchen

Gailey Garden Centre, Watling Street, Gailey, Staffs ST19 5PP   T: 01902 798585
w: www.field2kitchen.co.uk

◡ **farm shop**

Home-grown and local produce are picked fresh each day to go into
the farm shop here. There is a big choice of varieties, some of which
are organic. There is also a branch in Atherstone (see page 234).

Howbarrow Organic Farm

Cartmel, Grange-over-Sands, Cumbria LA11 7SS   T: 01539 536330
w: www.howbarroworganic.demon.co.uk

◡ **farm shop**   ◪ **box scheme**

Howbarrow Farm is part of the Soil Association's Open Farm
Network so it is open to visitors who would like to see how an
organic farm operates. The farm is run with great commitment to
sustainability and conservation – old stone walls are being repaired
and ancient hedgerows restored. There are plenty of organic
vegetables available from the farm shop, along with rare-breed meat
that has been reared slowly for maximum flavour. Howbarrow was
voted Organic Farm Shop of the Year in 2002, and are one of the
few certified organic bed and breakfasts in the country.

Eddisbury Fruit Farm

Yeld Lane, Kelsall, Cheshire CW6 0TE   T: 01829 759157   w: www.eddisbury.co.uk

◡ **farm shop**   ▭ **farmers' markets**

Twenty-six varieties of apple grown here provide the basis for the
farm shop; they are made into pressed juices and, unusually this far
north, cider. Pears, soft fruit and vegetables complete the range.

Dawson Fold Farm

Lythe, Kendal, Cumbria LA8 8DE   T: 01539 568248

◡ **farm shop**

Home-grown, pesticide-free damsons, plums and vegetables.

super hero

GROWING WITH NATURE, Pilling (see below)

Growing With Nature is a co-operative of a handful of organic growers in Lancashire, offering a really big range of vegetables throughout the season. Most of the produce sold is home-grown and the company takes pride in its ability to deliver everything incredibly fresh – for example, salad crops are sent out within 24 hours of harvesting. Recipes and newsletters are included in the weekly boxes. Growing With Nature's box scheme has been operating for 12 years and was one of the first to be set up in Britain – a great example of organic growers collaborating to provide a really good service.

NORTH WEST   KENDAL

Flodder Hall

Lythe, Kendal, Cumbria LA8 8DG   T: 01539 568261 OR 01539 552005
🡇 **farm shop**

The Lythe valley is famous for damsons and for three weeks of the year, starting at the end of August, you can buy them from the temporary farm shop at Flodder Hall.

NORTH WEST   PILLING

Growing With Nature

Bradshaw Lane Nursery, Pilling, Lancashire PR3 6AX   T: 01253 790046
📦 **box scheme**

Growing With Nature is a co-operative of a handful of organic growers in Lancashire, offering a really big range of vegetables throughout the season. See the Super Hero box, above, for more information.

NORTH WEST   THURSTASTON

Church Farm Organics

Church Farm, Church Lane, Thurstaston, Wirral CH61 0HW   T: 0151 648 7838
w: www.churchfarm.org.uk
🡇 **farm shop**

Church Farm Organics are past winners of the Best Farm Shop award at the Soil Association Organic Food Awards and they offer a fantastic range of organic fruit and vegetables, all home-grown. Asparagus and strawberries are seasonal specialities, and Church Farm run a variety of seasonal events, such as the Haunted Hay Ride at Hallowe'en. Church Farm were voted Best Farm Shop for 2004.

NORTH EAST   BARNARD CASTLE

Bluebell Organics

Forcett Hall Walled Garden, Forcett, Richmond, North Yorkshire DL11 7SB
T: 01325 718841   E: katrina@bluebell30.fsbusiness.co.uk
🛒 farmers' markets 📦 box scheme

Bluebell Organics offer a good range of fresh fruit and vegetables, with many really unusual varieties. See the Super Hero box, page 242, for more information.

NORTH EAST   BARNARD CASTLE

Eggleston Hall

Eggleston, Barnard Castle, Co. Durham DL12 0AG   T: 01833 650553
W: www.egglestonhall.co.uk
🛒 shop

Eggleston Hall has a five-acre old walled kitchen garden, producing organic vegetables and herbs. These can be bought at the shop on site, where you will also find some great local produce – lamb and venison, cheese, home-baked goods and gourmet ready-cooked meals. There is also a bistro on site.

NORTH EAST   BEDLINGTON

North East Organic Growers Ltd

West Sleekburn Farm, Bomarsund, Bedlington, Northumberland NE22 7AD
T: 01670 821070   W: www.neog.co.uk
📦 box scheme

A workers' co-operative, growing and sourcing organically grown fruits and vegetables, as locally as possible. There is a big range of vegetable varieties, from the basic to the unusual, such as chard, sugar snap peas and kohlrabi. This is sold via a weekly box scheme, delivering between Durham and Alnwick.

super hero

BLUEBELL ORGANICS, of Barnard Castle (see page 241)

The Forcett Hall Walled Garden offers many delights. Yes, you'll find great Soil
Association accredited organic potatoes, carrots, cabbages and all the basics.
But you'll also find fruit and vegetables you may well have never seen before –
tomatillos (a cross between a plum and a tomato), stripy beetroot, exotic Chinese
vegetables – all in a riot of colour and shape. Katrina Palmer and her husband
Steve Barker like to search out unusual varieties no longer commercially grown
and in danger of dying out because they don't suit intensive growing methods.
They have found that customers at their farmers' market stalls are happy and
willing to try the less well-known varieties of vegetables she grows 'as long as I
explain what it is and how to cook it!' and are amazed at the diversity of flavours
and textures. Also on offer are home-made soups, pickles, preserves and
marmalade, utilizing some of the unusual ingredients; for example, marrow and
garlic, or pumpkin and chilli soup. The aim of Bluebell Organics is far more
simple, however, than all this may suggest – 'the thinking behind Bluebell
Organics is quite simply to provide people with good, healthy, fresh food'. Find
the produce at Richmond, Brough, Stanhope, Barnard Castle, Hexham and Orton
farmers' markets, or join Bluebell Organics' box scheme.

NORTH EAST   CORNHILL-UPON-TWEED

Carroll's Heritage Potatoes

Tiptoe Farm, Cornhill-on-Tweed, Northumberland TD12 4XD   T: 01890 883060
w: www.heritage-potatoes.co.uk

✉ **mail order**

The potatoes grown by the Carroll's are unlike any you've seen before
– these are spuds with a firm sense of history; varieties that have,
until now, been in danger of disappearing. Coming in a dazzling
range of flavours, textures and colours (even blue and black), and
with evocative names such as Highland Burgundy Red and Dunbar
Rover, these rare vegetables will renew your enthusiasm for cooking
with potatoes, and will be a real talking point at dinner.

NORTH EAST   DRIFFIELD

Barmston Organics

Elm Tree Farm, Barmston, Driffield, East Yorkshire YO25 8PQ   T: 01262 468128

🏠 **farmers' markets**   📦 **box scheme**

The Hunt family grow their own wheat, have it milled at a local watermill and then sell the flour through their box scheme – and it has proved very popular with their customers. The box scheme also contains great vegetables and lamb, reared on home-grown feed. Find the produce at Driffield farmers' market, too.

NORTH EAST   EBCHESTER

The Herb Patch

Brockwell House, Newlands, Ebchester, Co. Durham DH8 9JA   T: 01207 562099
W: www.herbpatch.fsnet.co.uk
⬐ **farm shop** ⬒ **farmers' markets**

Over 100 varieties of home-grown herbs, grown without chemicals in peat-free compost. The farm shop also stocks plenty of local produce, from Northumberland cheese to organic vegetables, and the herbs can also be found at Hexham, Barnard Castle and Tynemouth farmers' markets.

NORTH EAST   LEEDS

Swillington Organic Farm

Coach Road, Swillington, nr Leeds, West Yorkshire LS26 8QA
T: 0113 286 9129 OR 07974 826876
⬐ **farm shop** ⬒ **farmers' markets**

Jo Cartwright specializes in unusual kinds of vegetables – she says there are plenty of people around growing cabbages so she tries to go for more interesting varieties. The vegetables are harvested on the day of sale from the old walled garden that Jo farms; free-range organic eggs, rare-breed pork, organic lamb and chicken, all home-produced, are also available. Buy the produce direct from the farm (phone first), from Leeds, Wakefield or Otley farmers' markets.

NORTH EAST   PONTEFRACT

Brickyard Farm Shop

Badsworth, nr Pontefract, West Yorkshire WF9 1AX   T: 01977 617327
E: brickyardorganics@yahoo.co.uk
⬐ **farm shop** ⬔ **box scheme**

Over 40 different varieties of organic fruit and vegetables are grown here, all picked fresh every day. The farmshop is open on Saturday only.

super hero

GOOSEMOOR ORGANICS, of Wetherby (see below)

It would be difficult to find a box scheme run on more environmentally sound principles than those at Goosemoor Organics. Absolutely every aspect of their business has been considered. Despite taking back its packaging from customers, the company only produces one bag of rubbish every week. LPG vans (better ecologically than petrol) are used for deliveries, the electricity supply is from sustainable hydro-electrics, and local businesses are used (and paid on time) to ensure small producers are not under financial strain and can focus on organic growing. There is even a two-acre nature reserve on Goosemoor's land. But what about the vegetables? Goosemoor Organics grow an interesting selection of squashes and some unusual chilli peppers, salad leaves and potatoes, including the pink fir apple, great for salads but usually hard to find. A good range of other fresh vegetables from nearby organic farms supplements their own produce, along with over 2000 vegetarian, vegan and fair trade grocery items.

NORTH EAST WAKEFIELD

E Oldroyd and Sons Ltd

Ashfield House, Main Street, Carlton, Wakefield, West Yorkshire WF3 3RW
T: 0113 282 2245
🛏 **farm gate sales**

Traditional 'Champagne' rhubarb from the famous 'Wakefield triangle' rhubarb-producing area.

NORTH EAST WETHERBY

Goosemoor Organics

Warfield Lane, Cowthorpe, Wetherby, West Yorkshire LS22 5EU   T: 01423 358887
w: www.goosemoor.info
🛒 **box scheme**

Goosemoor Organics have given thought to the environmental impact of every aspect of their business, from packaging to power-use, and their organic produce is available in a box scheme. See the Super Hero box, above, for more information.

Four Seasons

38–40 Gilnahirk Road, Belfast BT5 7DG   T: 028 9079 2701

If you're looking for super-fresh, locally grown fruit and veg, then Four Seasons can provide it. Buying direct from the growers, food miles are minimal, the local economy benefits, and there is very little time-lag between the grower harvesting and the customers eating the produce. Four Seasons belong to the Northern Ireland Greengrocers Association.

Michel's Fresh Fruit & Veg

435 Ormeau Road, Belfast BT7 3DW   T: 028 9064 2804   E: mjgroggin01@hotmail.com

A big selection of locally grown produce in season, bought direct from the growers. The fruit and vegetables offered at Michel's have not been warehoused, as they generally are at supermarkets, which means they arrive on your plate much fresher. There are seven varieties of potato to choose from and even fresh herbs. Michel's belong to the Northern Ireland Greengrocers Association.

Organic Doorstep

125 Strabane Road, Castlederg, Co. Tyrone BT81 7JD   T: 028 8167 9989
W: www.organicdoorstep.net
🛒 **box scheme**

This box scheme delivers within the Belfast area and almost everything in the boxes is grown in Northern Ireland. Organic Doorstep operates a flexible scheme, delivering home-grown vegetables and home-produced milk and yoghurt, along with bread and eggs. You choose what you want in the box and deliveries can be made two or three times a week. Everything is organic.

Sperrin's Organic Wholefoods

24 Gorse Road, Claudy, Co. Londonderry BT47 4HY   T: 028 7133 8462
🛒 **box scheme**

None of the produce in the weekly boxes sent out by Sperrin's is imported – everything is home-grown, from the essential basics like potatoes, carrots and onions to the unusual fennel and Jerusalem artichokes through to fresh strawberries and raspberries in the summer. Great value and totally fresh – the produce is often harvested only a few hours before delivery.

Helen's Bay Organic Gardens

Coastguard Avenue, Helen's Bay, Co. Down   T: 028 9185 3122
w: www.helensbayorganicgardens.com
box scheme

Organic and biodynamic vegetables fill the boxes for local delivery at Helen's Bay Farm, all home-grown or sourced as locally as possible, with a little imported fruit when necessary. Locally baked organic bread and local organic eggs are also on offer.

Kelly's

116 Long Stone Street, Lisburn, Co. Antrim BT28 1TR   T: 028 9266 3371

As a member of the Northern Ireland Greengrocers Association, Kelly's are committed to buying direct from the local growers, ensuring that the produce is as fresh as possible and hasn't travelled halfway across the world before it lands in your shopping bag.

Home Grown

66b East Street, Newtownards, Co. Down BT23 7DD   T: 028 9181 8318

Margaret Whyte comes from a farming background and she knows a good vegetable when she sees one. She buys the fresh produce for her shop direct from the growers around Northern Ireland – many are within two or three miles of the shop. You really can't get fresher than this – they are on the shelves in the shop less than 24 hours after harvesting. Home Grown belongs to the Northern Ireland Greengrocers Association.

Brooklodge Nursery

The Old Monastery, Ballyglunin, Co. Galway   T: 093 41456
farm gate sales box scheme

Brooklodge Nursery grows a wide range of fruit, herbs and vegetables, only selling what they themselves grow – they never buy produce in. Available through a weekly box scheme or direct from the farm.

Caroline's Home Grown Veg

Parkmore, Templemartin, Bandon, Co. Cork   T: 021 7330178

🍴 **farmers' markets**

A great range of chemical-free vegetables, from salads to field vegetables, aubergines and courgettes. Find Caroline at the Cornmarket Street market in Cork on Saturdays or Macroom farmers' market on Tuesdays.

Peppermint Farm & Garden

Toughraheen, Bantry, Co. Cork   T: 028 31869   W: www.peppermintfarm.com

📨 **farm gate sales**   ✉ **mail order**

Around 100 different varieties of organic herbs, sold as growing potted herbs, are available mail order, direct from the farm, or from Bantry and Schull farmers' markets. Peppermint Farm is accredited by the Organic Trust.

The Apple Farm

Moorstown, Cahir, Co. Tipperary   T: 052 41459   W: www.theapplefarm.com

🛒 **farm shop**   🍴 **farmers' markets**   ✉ **mail order**

While not actually certified, this fruit farm is run on principles pretty close to organic. There are ten varieties of apple to choose from here and single-variety juices too. The farm even makes jams and jellies with the fruit. Find the produce at Cahir farmers' market.

The Garden

English Market, Cork   T: 021 4272368

During the summer and autumn this market stall is packed with dewy-fresh organic vegetables and fruit sourced direct from organic growers around Cork. The winter and spring seasons call for imported produce but this is still organic.

super hero

THOMAS BECHT, of Donegal Organic Farm Produce, Glenties (see below)

Thomas Becht, the farmer at Donegal Organic, is a mine of information about organic and biodynamic farming; he can tell you all kinds of facts and history regarding chemical-free farming and easily convinces you that it all makes a great deal of sense. Donegal Organic Farm Produce is run on biodynamic principles and so it is a mixed farm, offering everything from fruit and vegetables, milk and dairy products, to meat and poultry, all grown and reared without pesticides or commercial fertilizers. Asked how this mode of farming affects the flavour of the food, Thomas felt that all the produce, from the meat to the vegetables, benefited from being allowed to grow at its own pace – not forced with artificial stimulants – and that the flavour is more intense as a result. Given also that he selects breeds and varieties specifically for flavour, the produce has a head start already. Passionate about good-quality food and equally passionate about sustainable production, Thomas takes a holistic approach to farming – not only are homeopathic remedies used for the livestock, they are also used for the soil, to maintain natural fertility. Donegal is famed for the good quality of its soil and Thomas Becht intends to keep it that way. The produce is available from the farm shop on site or is delivered locally through a weekly box scheme.

REPUBLIC OF IRELAND   GLENTIES

Donegal Organic Farm Produce   super hero

Doorian, Glenties, Co. Donegal   T: 074 95 51286   w: www.esatclear.ie/~tbecht
⬇ **farm shop** ⮿ **box scheme**

Donegal Organic Farm Produce is a mixed farm run on biodynamic lines to produce organic fruit and vegetables, milk, dairy products, meat and poultry. See the Super Hero box, above, for more information.

REPUBLIC OF IRELAND   KILPEDDER

Marc Michel

Tinna Park, Kilpedder, Co. Wicklow   T: 01 2011 882
⬇ **farm shop**

Open Tuesday to Saturday, this farm shop sells wonderfully fresh, home-grown, organic vegetables. Marc Michel is accredited by the Organic Trust. There is now a café/restaurant on site.

Ballinroan

Kiltegan, Co. Wicklow   T: 059 64 73278

⬇ **farm shop**   🥬 **box scheme**

Penny and Udo Lange grow 'anything you can grow on a mountain top in Wicklow'. This includes all kinds of basics, and some more unusual items, such as pak choi and sugarloaf lettuce. All the vegetables are biodynamically grown and are available through the box scheme that the Langes run. As well as the box scheme and farm shop they also sell at local markets.

Briarneuk Nursery

Braidwood, Carluke, Lanarkshire ML8 5NG   T: 01555 860279

🍅 **farmers' markets**

Briarneuk Nursery specializes in tomatoes, with several different sorts grown here, from cherry tomatoes and cocktail tomatoes to full-size varieties. They arrive at the farmers' market having been picked only the day before – they are fresher and picked when more ripe than most of the tomatoes you'll find at supermarkets. Their flavour remains sweet, as they are never put into cold stores.

Pillars of Hercules Organic Farm

Falkland, Fife KY15 7AD   T: 01337 857749   W: www.pillars.co.uk

⬇ **farm shop**

Bruce Bennett of Pillars of Hercules aims to offer his customers a one-stop shop, with great local fresh produce – from fruit and vegetables, dairy produce and bread, to meat, all accredited to Soil Association standards. There is also a café.

Glendale Salads

19 Upper Fasach, Glendale, Isle of Skye IV55 8WP   T: 01470 511349

🥬 **box scheme**   ✉ **mail order**

Really unusual salad leaves and herbs are grown at Glendale – 250 different varieties throughout the season, every kind of shape, colour and flavour imaginable.

Huntly Herbs

Whitestones of Tillathrowie, Gartly, Huntly, Aberdeenshire AB54 4SB   T: 01466 720247
E: huntlyherbs@hotmail.com

🡒 **farmers' markets** ⇌ **farm gate sales**

About 150 different varieties of herbs are grown here, although some are seasonal and not always available. 12 varieties of specialist potatoes are available, such as the unusual pink fir apple, Edzel Blue and Arran variety, along with jams, chutneys and preserves.

Croft Organics

Skellarts Croft, Daviot, Inverurie, Aberdeenshire AB51 0JL   T: 01467 681717
W: www.croft-organics.co.uk

🡒 **farm shop** ⇌ **box scheme**

Croft Organics grow both basic fruit and vegetables and the more unusual – such as blueberries. Fresh herbs and free-range eggs are also available. A recipe sheet is supplied with the vegetable boxes, just in case you're not sure how to cook the more unusual items.

Lenshaw Organics

Upper Lenshaw Farm, Rothienorman, Inverurie, Aberdeenshire AB51 8XU
T: 01464 871243

⇌ **farm gate sales** ⇌ **box scheme**

The box scheme operated from Upper Lenshaw Farm is 100% organic and 100% home-produced.

The Really Garlicky Company

Craggie Farm, Craggie, Nairn IV12 5HY   T: 01667 452193   W: www.reallygarlicky.co.uk

✉ **mail order**

The Really Garlicky Co. produce the large-cloved Porcelain garlic, which packs a powerful garlicky flavour, and is closely related to wild garlic. Available by the bulb, or in a variety of foods made at Craggie Farm – garlic cream cheese, garlic relish, or buttery garlic bread.

Earthshare Ltd

65 Society Street, Nairn IV12 4NL   T: 01667 452879   W: www.earthshare.co.uk
 box scheme

Earthshare is a Community Supported Agriculture scheme
established in 1994, growing vegetables and soft fruit for up to 200
local families. People commit to the scheme for a year at a time and
in return they receive their share of all that is harvested in the form
of a weekly box. The boxes include all kinds of seasonal vegetables:
root crops like carrots, parsnips, beetroot and kohlrabi in the winter,
and courgettes, beans, tomatoes and Chinese greens in the
summer. All produce is grown by organic methods. Subscribers are
encouraged to become involved at the farm and receive a discount
off the cost of their box if they commit to carry out three workshifts
per year. Call Pam Bochel for more details.

Burnarrachie

Bridge of Muchalls, Stonehaven, Kincardineshire AB39 3RU   T: 01569 730195
farm gate sales **box scheme**

Long before organics or biodynamics were as well known as they
are now, John and Maggie Fraser were growing winter vegetables.
A huge range is available, far too many to list, and they are always
picked to order. Call with your order first and it will be ready when
you arrive. Organic beef is also available.

Ty Mawr Organics

Greathouse Farm, Penpergwm, Abergavenny, Monmouthshire NP7 9UY
T: 01873 840247   E: www.ty-mawr-organic-veg.com
farmers' markets   **farm gate sales (please phone first)**

Organic vegetables, cut fresh to order at the farm gate, or from Usk,
Cardiff, Abergavenny, Brecon, Cowbridge or Penarth farmers'
markets.

super hero

SANDRA STORR, of Savages, Gwynedd (see opposite)

Sandra Storr grows some interesting fruit and vegetables on her mountainside smallholding – all the basics, along with pak choi, mizuna, blueberries and raspberries. She operates a box scheme, giving local residents the benefit of super-fresh produce that has clocked up almost no food miles. Her shop also stocks her produce, plus plenty of locally produced deli foods, such as pâtés, jams and preserves, cheeses and fair-trade coffees and teas. A new and exciting development is the addition of a vegetarian café during the day, which opens as a bistro in the evening. Both menus are packed with local and organic produce.

WALES   ABERYSTWYTH

Nantclyd Organics

Nantclyd Farm, Llanilar, Aberystwyth, Ceredigion SY23 4SL   T: 01974 241543
⊫ farm gate sales

Nantclyd Farm won the top award in the 2002 Soil Association Organic Food Awards for their strawberries, judged in a blind tasting by a panel of experts. The farm also has Poll Dorset lamb, which lamb in autumn, and free-range eggs, all certified by the Soil Association. All the produce is available from the farm direct or from local shops, including the Tree House in Aberystwyth (see page 141).

WALES   ANGLESEY

Porthamel Organic Farm

Porthamel, Llanedwen, Llanfair PG, Anglesey LL61 6PJ T: 01248 430355
E: porthamelfarm@virgin.net
⊫ farm gate sales

Seasonal vegetables are the mainstay here, with some fruit, and organic, free-range hens' eggs. Call before visiting or to arrange to place an order for collection.

Savages

21c High Street, Bethesda, Gwynedd, LL57 3AF   T: 01248 605191
w: www.astorr.freeserve.co.uk/savageshome.htm
box scheme

An exceptional deli and grocery shop, filled with local and home-grown produce, and with a café/bistro on site. See the Super Hero Box, opposite, for more details.

The Fruit Garden

Groesfaen Road, Peterston-super-Ely, Cardiff, South Glamorgan CF5 6NE
T: 01446 760358
farm shop   farmers' markets

Specialist soft fruit growers, offering 18 varieties of strawberry, who are continually experimenting with varieties to achieve the best flavour. They also make their fruit into ice cream. PYO is on offer, as is a range of specialist vegetables such as chillies and borlotti beans. An extended farm shop is planned – this will feature the best of Welsh artisan produce.

Glyn Fach Farm

Pontyates, Llanelli, Carmarthenshire SA15 5TG T: 01269 861290
w: www.glynfachfarm.co.uk
Farm gates sales

This smallholding offers a wonderful range of fresh produce, including free-range eggs, which can be bought direct from the farm gate. They also supply local restaurants. Call to arrange order and see the Super Hero box, page 254, for more information.

super hero

JEFF AND JEAN PEACE, of Glyn Fach Farm, Llanelli (see page 253)

Members of the Wholesome Food Association, Jeff and Jean Peace are truly adventurous small-scale growers. Jean admitted to me that they'll have a go at growing anything, even having had some success with peaches, lemons and oranges – with the only artificial encouragement being a polytunnel. The range of fruit and vegetables offered from this smallholding is staggering – far too many to list – and is supplemented with free-range hens' and ducks' eggs, all sold from the farm gate (the Peaces firmly believe in keeping 'food miles' to a minimum). With so much produce growing in her own garden, Jean Peace cannot even remember the last time she visited a supermarket! The Peaces have a committed and loyal following of customers enjoying the ultimate freshness of produce picked on the day it is sold – call Jeff or Jean if you'd like to join them.

WALES   MONMOUTH

Carrob Growers

Llangunville, Llanrothal, Monmouth NP25 5QL   T: 01600 714529

▨ **farm gate sales**   🍴 **farmers' markets**

Carrob Growers produce berries you may have never heard of – such as sunberries and jostaberries. Unusual fruit is the norm here, and there is a great range available in season, picked to order to collect from the farm gate and also at Usk farmers' market.

WALES   NEWPORT

Berryhill Fruit Farm

Coedkernew, Newport, Gwent NP1 9UD   T: 01633 680938

🍴 **farm shop**

Twelve varieties of apple, many of them rare, with pears, plums, gooseberries, some unusual berries, raspberries and vegetables, all home-grown. The farm shop also stocks local free-range eggs, jams, chutneys and pickles, and Welsh beef and lamb.

Cwm Harry Land Trust

Lower Cwm Harry, Tregynon, Newtown, Powys SY16 3ES   T: 01686 650231
w: www.cwmharrylandtrust.org.uk

Cwm Harry Land Trust is a Community Supported Agriculture
Scheme. Similar to a vegetable box scheme, local growers produce
vegetables without chemicals and then offer a share of the harvest
to local consumers. Paying a subscription fee means that you get
regular deliveries of fresh vegetables and in a good year your share
of the harvest can be considerable. It's a great way to feel part of the
community, to reduce food miles and to be more involved with the
production of the food you eat. Call to find out how to join.

Llangybi Organics

Mur Crusto, Llangybi, Pwllheli, Gwynedd LL53 6LX   T: 01766 819109
w: www.llangybi-organics.co.uk
🏠 box scheme

A small-scale box scheme but with an enormous range of produce –
last season, around 50 different varieties of fruit and vegetables
were grown, including apples and plums from the orchard on the
farm. Call to find out if you can become part of the box scheme.

Spring Meadow Farm

Caerfarchell, St Davids, Pembrokeshire SA62 6XG   T: 01437 721800
🛒 farm shop   🏪 farmers' markets

Spring Meadow Farm produces a fantastic range of vegetables –
up to 60 different crops throughout the season. There are all the
everyday favourites and then some of the more unusual varieties –
fennel, celeriac, pattypan, yellow courgettes and sugar snap peas.
Available from the farm shop on site (May 1st to Christmas) or from
Fishguard and Haverfordwest farmers' markets.

Game meats are beginning to grow in popularity, having once suffered from a poor image – they used to be thought of as either very expensive, for special occasions only, or as a food of inconsistent quality, bought from slightly shady characters. Some people associate game with meat that has been hung for so long that it has an incredibly strong flavour and a very potent aroma. These days, however, you can buy really fresh, good-quality game at reasonable prices, from suppliers who adhere to strict regulations. The meat is versatile and can be used for both traditional dishes and modern recipes and ways of cooking. Some of the suppliers I feature are members of the National Game Dealers Association (NGDA) or the Guild of Q Butchers, both of whom have stringent codes of practice.

The merits of wild game as opposed to farmed, especially with venison, is always a hotly contested topic. Farmed game offers an assurance of consistency and there is some superb venison and wild boar available now, from animals that have been reared on high-quality, home-produced feed and slaughtered at just the right age to produce tender and tasty meat. Equally, there are many who swear that wild venison is preferable – they say the texture is better, that it reacts better to traditional hanging and has a more authentic flavour. Wild

game

venison often has a stronger, 'gamier' taste, while farmed will often be milder, with a less robust texture.

The key to buying game is to know what to look for, to be aware of the shooting seasons and to buy from suppliers who can tell you exactly where their stock came from. The good news is that many gamekeepers on shooting estates (where most of the game you'll find in the shops will have come from) are raising standards constantly. The NGDA says that two-thirds of gamekeepers in this country have specially designed game larders and a third have chillers, to keep the meat in perfect condition before it is collected by the game dealer. Many have had professional training in food hygiene and this number is rising all the time. More and more members of the Guild of Q Butchers are becoming licensed game dealers, so they are able to give you more information about the provenance of the game and how to store and cook it. Most of the suppliers listed in this section source the game they sell direct from shoots – they have a higher level of quality control and usually receive the game before it has been processed. This makes it far easier to see how old the bird or animal is and if it has been damaged by poor shooting, and allows them to choose the best. If you've always been nervous about trying game at home, now is a great time to give it a go.

Framptons of Bridport

Market House, East Street, Bridport, Dorset DT6 3LF ALSO AT, 9e Westbay, Westbay,
Bridport, Dorset DT6 4EW   T: 01308 422995 (EAST STREET); 01308 423124 (WESTBAY)
w: www.framptonsofbridport.co.uk

The game at this butcher's comes from local shoots around Dorset
and can include wild duck, pigeon, hare, snipe or teal as well as the
more usual pheasant and venison. Local organic pork and poultry
are specialities.

Somerset Organics

Gilcombe Farm Shop, Gilcombe Farm, Bruton, Somerset, BA10 0QE   T: 01749 813710
w: www.somersetorganics.co.uk

⬦ **farm shop** 🗺 **farmers' markets** ✉ **mail order**

Somerset Organics produce and sell organic beef, pork, lamb and
chicken on their 300-acre farm as well as stocking all local game,
including rabbbit, hare, venison and wild boar. They also produce
the highest quality ready-meals, pies, pasties and soups from the
farm kitchen.

Deer Force 10

Mardlewood House, Higher Combe, Buckfastleigh, Devon TQ11 0JD   T: 01364 644420

One of the very few producers of certified organic venison, Deer
Force 10 allow their deer to live as naturally as possible, with low
stocking rates giving them plenty of space to roam, with access to
woodland. The deer are shot on site, virtually eliminating stress, and
are then hung for a week to ten days. The venison is available from
Riverford Farm Shop (see pages 106 and 107).

L & C Game

Court Farm, Buckland Newton, Dorset DT2 7BT   T: 01300 345271
E: landcgame@sturminsternewton.fsnet.co.uk

⬦ **farm shop** 🗺 **farmers' markets** 🚚 **delivery service**

Local game from small Dorset shoots and various different kinds of
wild venison. The venison is hung to order and butchered on site

and home-made sausages, cold-smoked and cured game are
available. There is a farm shop on Saturdays.

Palmers of Tavistock

50 Brook Street, Tavistock, Devon PL19 0BJ, T: 01822 612000
w: www.palmers-tavistock.com

✉ **mail order**

Devon is rich in wild game and Palmers make the most of it, offering
plenty of choice in season. Locally sourced beef, pork and lamb is
also available.

Gary Dutton Butchers

25 Molesworth Street, Wadebridge, Cornwall PL27 7DH T: 01208 812866

Lots of local game is offered at Dutton's in season. Collected fresh
from local shoots, there is pheasant, partridge, duck, woodcock and
teal, and wild venison. All arrive at the shop unprepared so that
Gary can gauge the condition easily. He'll even prepare and dress
game that customers bring in themselves.

The Thoroughly Wild Meat Co. Ltd

Bratton House, Bratton Seymour, Wincanton, Somerset BA9 8DA T: 01963 824788
E: sales@thoroughlywildmeat.co.uk

🏪 **farmers' markets**

Andrew Moore is fanatical about meat, and his company, The
Thoroughly Wild Meat Co., markets an exciting range of game
products. His business has one aim – to produce quality game that
is particularly attractive to consumers not used to wild meat. The
birds are chilled and plucked quickly to produce a top-quality finish,
and with careful hanging the meat develops great flavour. The
Thoroughly Wild Meat Co. then go one stage further, producing
smoked breast of pheasant, stuffed fillets wrapped in bacon and
gourmet sausages. Andrew also sources speciality meats from local
producers for his clients – he can be found at most Somerset
farmers' markets throughout the game season.

Barrow Boar

Fosters Farm, South Barrow, Yeovil, Somerset BA22 7LN   T: 01963 440315
w: www.barrowboar.co.uk

✉ **mail order**

Barrow Boar rears free-range wild boar and creates an interesting range of foods from them, including salami and prosciutto. Even the liver is available for making an unusual pâté. The farm also produces Hebridean lamb and Aberdeen Angus beef, and all kinds of game from local estates is available.

Manydown Farmshop

Scrapps Hill Farm, Worting Road, Basingstoke, Hampshire RG23 8PU   T: 01256 460068

⏷ **farm shop**

In season there is a fantastic range of game available at this farm shop – pheasant, partridge and hare to name a few, all shot on the farm's own land. The shop also stocks home-reared, free-range chicken, Aberdeen Angus beef and Large Black pork.

Manor Farm Game

96 Berkeley Avenue, Chesham, Buckinghamshire HP5 2RS   T: 07778 706179 or 01494 774975   w: www.manorfarmgame.co.uk

🛒 **farmers' markets**   🚚 **delivery service**   ✉ **mail order**

Game specialists, offering a big selection of game, including venison, sourced from Manor Farm's own shoot as well as other local shoots and estates. The game is available in the feather, oven-ready, jointed into breast, steak and stewing packs or processed into a wide range of sausages, burgers and pies.

George Arthur Ltd

70 Guildford Road, Lightwater, Surrey GU18 5SD   T: 01276 472191
w: www.georgearthur.com

Dry-cured bacon and free-range pork from Norfolk are two of the specialities at this butcher's shop and a full range of local game is also available in season.

Randalls Butchers

113 Wandsworth Bridge Road, Fulham, London SW6 2TE   T: 020 7736 3426

Randalls offers some seriously good organic meat and also some hand-picked game from shoots not far outside London.

Hamblings

2 Moneyhill Parade, Rickmansworth, Herts WD3 2BQ   T: 01923 772557

Hamblings is a combination of butcher's and delicatessen, with a range of free-range meats always available, and local pheasant, partridge and venison.

Ashbee & Son

100 High Street, Rye, East Sussex TN31 7JN   T: 01797 223303
W: www.rye-tourism.co.uk

Local pheasant, grouse, duck, pigeon and rabbit are among the specialities at this traditional butcher's shop.

Castleman's Farm

Green Common Lane, Woburn Common, Buckinghamshire HP10 0LH   T: 07900 886459
≛ farmers' markets ⊨ farm gate sales

The Rayner family run their own shoot at Castleman's Farm, using pheasants and partridges that they have reared themselves. Other game shot on their land is also available – wild venison, duck and rabbit. Free-range poultry, including chickens and guineafowl, and turkeys and geese at Christmas, are also on offer, along with unpasteurized milk and cream from the farm's Guernsey herd. Available direct from the farm (call first) or from Marlow and Beaconsfield farmers' markets.

Brampton Wild Boar

Blue Tile Farm, Lock's Road, Brampton, Beccles, Suffolk NR34 8DX   T: 01502 575246

🛒 **farmers' markets**   ✉ **mail order**

The wild boar reared at Blue Tile Farm are pure-bred animals, from a stock brought over from the Polish/German border, and they have even been DNA-tested to verify their purity. Reared outdoors, the boar are fed a diet without artificial additives or GM foods and reared slowly to 12 months of age before slaughter. Steaks and roasting joints are available, along with parma-style ham, pancetta, patés and a hot-smoked haunch that is glazed with the farm's own damson jam. Find all the produce at Hatfield, St Albans, Waltham Abbey and Halesworth farmers' markets or buy it mail order, by arrangement.

Harvey's Pure Meat

63 Grove Road, Norwich, Norfolk NR1 3RL   T: 01603 621908   w: www.puremeat.org.uk

Alongside all the local organic meats, Harvey's also offer plenty of fresh local game, all from Norfolk. The game comes from nearby shoots, collected personally from the gamekeepers. All varieties of venison are available – red, fallow, roe and muntjack – and all are prepared and hung on the premises. Partridge, pheasant, woodcock and some wild fowl are also available. Harvey's are accredited by the Organic Food Federation.

K B Stannard & Sons

8 High Street, Saxmundham, Suffolk IP17 1DD   T: 01728 602081

A good old-fashioned butcher's, selling local meats and a good range of local game. There is now an extensive cheese selection (50–60 types at any one time), and rare local Red Poll beef.

Wild Meat Company

Low Road, Sweffling, Saxmundham, Suffolk IP17 2BU   T: 01728 663211
w: www.wildmeat.co.uk

🛒 **farmers' markets**   ✉ **mail order**

The quality control process at the Wild Meat Company is so stringent that they estimate they reject around a third of the game that they receive from local shoots. All of the game offered is from Suffolk and includes the harder to find varieties, such as woodpigeon, wild duck and woodcock. Wild venison is also available. Call to find out which farmers' markets the Wild Meat Company attends or buy mail order. Wholesale supply available.

C E Brown

Southlawns, Main Street, Shudy Camps, Cambridgeshire CB1 6RA T: 01799 584461

✉ **farm gate sales**

Colin Brown knows which gamekeepers look after the game well before and after local shoots and they are the keepers he buys from. His stock is always very fresh because he collects the game either on the day of the shoot or the day after and prepares it all himself. Wild venison, hare, rabbit, pheasant, partridge and mallard are all local and he also has grouse from Yorkshire.

Brown's of Stilton

4 Church Street, Stilton, Cambridgeshire PE7 3RF T: 01733 242486
W: www.browns-finefoods.co.uk

✉ **mail order**

Most of the game at Brown's is locally sourced and includes pheasant, venison, rabbit and wild boar.

Bradshaw Bros Ltd

Bleak House Farm, Ironstone Road. Chase Terrace, Burntwood, Staffordshire WS7 1YL
T: 01543 279437

This traditional butcher is a licensed game dealer, including wholesale, and stocks wild game, predominantly game birds, from a local shoot. Richard Crisp, the manager, says the key to getting good-quality game is to always buy from a trusted source – he never sources game from dealers he does not know. Speciality meats include local Hereford beef and Gloucester Old Spot pork.

super hero

RACHEL GODWIN AND JEANETTE EDGAR, of Alternative Meats, Weston-under-Redcastle (see below)

Quality control can often be an issue with wild game. How can you tell if a game bird will be young and tender? Just how old was that wild rabbit when it was shot? Rachel and Jeanette at Alternative Meats are fanatical about quality. Every item of game that they stock has been rigorously checked and anything that is questionable will be rejected. Buying from the same gamekeepers enables them to build a rapport – the keepers know what Rachel and Jeanette want and won't try to fob them off with something of dubious quality. Wild boar can also be tricky. Less scrupulous dealers will sometimes try to pass off old male pork as wild boar. Rachel and Jeanette can't be fooled – they insist on DNA testing the meat.

Though it is difficult to offer watertight guarantees with wild game – by its very nature there is a degree of the unknown about birds and animals shot in the wild – Alternative Meats really do put in the effort to offer as much reassurance as possible and the honesty and openness of their approach is a real treat in an industry that has often suffered from an unwelcome air of 'muck and magic'.

MIDLANDS   SHREWSBURY

Alternative Meats   super hero

Hough Farm, Weston-under-Redcastle, Shrewsbury, Shropshire SY4 5LR
T: 01948 840130   W: www.alternativemeats.co.uk
✉ **mail order**

A great range of wild game, including rabbit, hare, venison, and all the game birds, from trustworthy sources. Quality control is rigorous, down to DNA testing to ensure that the wild boar is just that and not regular pork! Free-range duck is also available, as is free-range goose at Christmas. See the Super Hero box, above, for more information.

Sillfield Farm

super hero

Endmoor, Kendal, Cumbria LA8 0HZ   T: 01539 567609
w: www.sillfield.co.uk

📇 **farmers' markets** ✉ **mail order**

Peter Gott of Sillfield Farm rears free-range, rare-breed pigs and
wild boar and makes dry-cured bacon as well as pancetta and other
interesting preserved meats. See the Super Hero box, page 266, for
more information.

The Housekeeper's Store at Tatton Park

Tatton Park, Knutsford, Cheshire WA16 6QN   T: 01625 534424
w: www.tattonpark.org.uk

Find award-winning hot-smoked venison at Tatton Park. Marinated
in juniper berries, the venison haunch is smoked over oak and the
meat is then ready to eat, needing no more cooking. The venison
comes from Tatton Park's own deer, which are culled at 18 months
to produce a mildly flavoured meat without the strong gamey taste
often associated with venison. The shop also sells a selection of
home-cured hams, bacon and gammon, as well as cheeses and
deli goods, all from British small-scale producers.

Lords of Middleton

18 Old Hall Street, Middleton, Manchester M24 1AN   T: 0161 643 4160
w: www.lordsofmiddleton.co.uk

✉ **mail order**

Wild Scottish venison is available at Lord's and in season there is a
wide range of British game. Scotch beef hung for a minimum of
three weeks, Highland lamb and free-range pork are all available.

super hero

PETER GOTT, of Sillfield Farm, Kendal (see page 265)

Peter Gott rears pigs and wild boar free-range on his Cumbrian farm but he's not just content to keep one type of each. Middle White, Berkshire and Gloucester Old Spot pigs rub shoulders with Russian, German, French and Polish wild boar and from these animals he makes all manner of unusual meats – prosciutto, pancetta and air-dried fillets of boar, and Bath chaps, Cumberland Speck and brawn – alongside the more well-known dry-cured bacon. With old-fashioned husbandry and natural feeds, the animals produce old-fashioned meat – dense, firm and intensely flavoured. The secret, says Peter, lies in two factors. Firstly, the animals live almost exactly as they would in the wild – rooting around in woodland – and so are fit and healthy. Just as important is the age of the animals at slaughter – the wild boar are never less than 18 months, which gives a mature, rich flavour. Peter has tried many different breeds in the search for the tastiest. Some unscrupulous suppliers sell pork from ageing pigs as wild boar, passing off the pungent meat as its wild counterpart, but there really is no comparison – Peter Gott's is the real thing, reared with immense care and attention, and the flavour testifies to this. The meats are available by mail order, or find them at Liverpool, Manchester and Carlisle farmers' markets or Borough Market in London SE1.

NORTH WEST   NORTHWICH

Arley Wild Boar

Moss Cottage, New Road, Crowley, Northwich, Cheshire CW9 6NY   T: 01565 777326
farmers' markets

Free-range wild boar, slowly matured for a full-flavoured meat. The boar are given a GM-free feed to supplement the root crops they forage for. The meat is hung for ten days after slaughter at a local abattoir and is available from Eddisbury, Nantwich, Ashton-under-Lyme and Birkenhead farmers' markets. A member of the British Wild Boar Association. Wild rabbit is also available.

J B Cockburn & Sons

12 Market Place, Bedale, North Yorkshire DL8 1EQ   T: 01677 422126

The game here comes from one of nine local estates and the Cockburns collect straight from the shoots, ensuring only the best is on offer to their customers. Wild boar is also available, and organic Highland beef from the butcher's own farm, local organic Swaledale lamb and free-range Berkshire pork are all popular.

Teesdale Game & Poultry

Durham Indoor Market, Market Square, Durham DH1 3NJ   T: 0191 375 0664 (MARKET)
OR 01833 637153 (MAIL ORDER)   E: teesdalegame@aol.com
✉ mail order

Game birds, including the hard to find teal and woodcock, wild rabbit and hare, and venison are supplied by Teesdale. The owners, Stephen and Alison Morrell, know where everything comes from (estates around Northumberland and Cumbria) and can supply recipe sheets to help those unfamiliar with some of the more unusual produce.

Hutchinsons

Main Street, Ripley, Harrogate, North Yorkshire, HG3 3AX   T: 01423 770110

The game at Hutchinsons is sourced directly from local gamekeepers and includes wild rabbits, venison, pigeon, pheasant and duck. Other specialities include Aberdeen Angus beef and Nidderdale lamb

C & G Starkey

8 Wolsey Parade, Sherburn-in-Elmet, Leeds LS25 6BQ   T: 01977 682696
W: www.c-gstarkey.co.uk
🚚 delivery service ✉ mail order

Plenty of game sourced from Yorkshire, a really wide selection, including hard to find teal and snipe, is available from this shop.

Yorkshire Game

Station Road Industrial Park, Brompton-on-Swale, Richmond, North Yorkshire DL10 7SN
T: 01748 810212   W: www.yorkshiregame.co.uk

✉ **mail order**

Yorkshire Game and their sister company, Weatherall Foods (www.blackface.co.uk) are passionate about sympathetic game management and high quality standards, so their sourcing of game is extremely careful. The range is extensive and game sausages are also available.

Wensleydale Wild Boar

Goose Park, Thornton Steward, Ripon, North Yorkshire HG4 4BB   T: 01677 460239

⇌ **farm gate sales** ✉ **mail order**

European wild boar are reared free-range in paddocks. Slowly matured, the boar are not slaughtered until they are about 18 months old, for a dark and gamey meat, and there are many different cuts to choose from. Available direct from the farm or by mail order. A member of the British Wild Boar Association.

Coffey's Butchers

380 Lisburn Road, Belfast BT9 6GL   T: 028 9066 6292   W: www.coffeysbutchers.co.uk

✉ **mail order**

Coffey's sell meat reared on their own and neighbouring farms but they are also game specialists. The game is collected direct from the estates where it is shot and has to pass a tough inspection before it is allowed on to the counter. It arrives at the shop in furred or feathered form and is processed on site. Wild venison, pheasant, woodpigeon, rabbit, hare and guineafowl are all available in season.

Finnebrogue Venison Company

20 Finnebrogue Road, Downpatrick BT30 9AB   T: 028 4461 7525

⇌ **farm gate sales**

The focus of the Finnebrogue Venison Company is to produce venison that is as tender as possible and so the farmed red deer are all under 15 months old when slaughtered. This results in a much milder meat than wild venison, without the strong gamey flavour.

Molloys of Donnybrook

Donnybrook Road, Dublin 4   T: 01 269 1678

A classic game merchant/fishmonger's. The fish is from local waters, almost always day caught, and the game includes wild venison, pheasant, pigeon, duck and rabbit, all from local shoots.

Highland Wild Boar

Millcraig Mill, Alness, Ross-shire IV17 0YA   T: 01349 883734

🔜 **farmers' markets**

The wild boar at Millcraig Mill have plenty of space in which to roam and eat additive-free feed. They do not go to the local abattoir until they are at least a year old, allowing the meat to develop flavour and texture. There are plenty of cuts available, and also sausages, burgers, bacon, ham and gammon, and the meat is dark and full-flavoured. Find the produce at Dingwall and Inverness farmers' markets, where you'll also be able to try the cooked sausages.

Fletchers   super hero

Reediehill Farm, Auchtermuchty, Fife KY14 7HS   T: 01337 828369
w: www.fletcherscotland.co.uk

🔻 **farm shop** 🔜 **farmers' markets**

The Fletchers are fervant campaigners for venison and have been producing it successfully for the last 30 years. See the Super Hero box, page 270, for more information.

D J MacDougall

Canal Side, Fort Augustus, Inverness-shire PH32 4AU   T: 01320 366214

A full range of local game is offered here, including wild venison. MacDougall is also the only butcher in the UK to hold a Q Guild Diamond award for its haggis.

super hero

NICHOLA AND JOHN FLETCHER, of Fletchers, Auchtermuchty
(see page 269)

Nichola and John Fletcher have spent the last 30 years producing venison and understand that 'happy deer are healthy and unstressed, and will produce the best meat'. The deer are shot in the fields and so never have the stress of a trip to the abattoir; it's all over in an instant. This lack of stress is very important in venison production – a stressed deer will produce tainted meat. The carcasses are then hand-skinned, prepared by a skilled butcher and hung for up to three weeks. This, says Nichola Fletcher, 'gives superb flavour and tenderness, but without that bitter or musty taste which some people regard as a gamey taste, but which is in fact just poor handling.'

The Fletchers were nominated for a coveted Slow Food Award for their attention to detail, their long hanging of the meat and their insistence on the highest standards – practices that allow meat to develop good texture and flavour. Nichola is a fervent campaigner for venison as she believes it to be the perfect meat – low in fat and cholesterol, high in the healthy fatty acids found in oily fish – and she is a mine of information regarding handling and cooking venison.

SCOTLAND   GLASGOW

Robertson Jeen

34 New Kirk Road, Bearsden, Glasgow G61 3SL   T: 0141 942 0154

Ian Jeen prides himself on his locally reared beef but he also offers a great selection of wild game. Fresh local grouse, woodcock and pheasant are on offer, alongside quail and quails' eggs, wild hare and rabbit. The venison stocked is wild, which Ian believes has a cleaner flavour than its farmed counterpart.

SCOTLAND   HUNTLY

Forbes Raeburn & Sons

7 Bogie Street, Huntly, Aberdeenshire AB54 8DX   T: 01466 792818

The butchers at Forbes Raeburn feel that wild venison is preferable to farmed – they say it hangs better and is a firmer, more robust meat – and so they only stock the wild variety, from local red deer. Other local game is also available – pheasant, wild duck and partridge. Everything is prepared on site.

Hilton Wild Boar

Johnston's Butchers, 46 High Street, Newburgh, Fife KY14 6AQ   T: 01337 842867
w: www.hiltonwildboar.co.uk

farmers' markets   mail order

The wild boar at Hilton Farm are free-ranging, living in small family
groups. Slowly reared to a year old or more, the meat is very
different from commercial pork – dark and well marbled. Sausages –
including some flavoured with prune and claret or honey and
mustard – haunches, loin and dry-cured bacon are all available and
the butchers at Hilton are experimenting with salami and air-dried
hams. All this is available from the shop or from Perth, Edinburgh,
Glasgow, Stirling, Cupar and Kirkaldy farmers' markets.

The Galloway Smokehouse

Carsluith, Newton Stewart, Wigtownshire DG8 7DN   T: 01671 820354
w: www.gallowaysmokehouse.co.uk

shop   mail order

The wild venison and other game arrive at the Galloway Smokehouse
from local shoots still in their furred and feathered condition. This
allows Allan Watson to check them over for age and quality – he
never accepts anything that has already been plucked or skinned.
The game and venison is available fresh, or there is smoked venison.
This is brined in a secret mixture and then smoked for four days over
oak chips from old port or whisky barrels.

Old Knockelly Smokehouse

The Stableyard, Drumlanrig Castle, Thornhill, Dumfries DG3 4AG   T: 01848 331611
w: www.oksmoke.co.uk

shop   mail order

The Old Knockelly Smokehouse uses the old-fashioned natural draft
method to smoke the produce, which takes much longer than more
modern techniques, but which results in more delicate flavours. The
produce is sourced locally: pigeon, trout, salmon, duck, pheasant
and venison. The venison is also transformed into ham, taking a
month to be ready for eating – long curing, smoking and air-drying
times are required to achieve the perfect texture and best flavour.
The principle aim here is quality, not quantity.

food facts

GAME: TIPS AND HINTS

Venison, like beef, benefits from hanging for up to two weeks; it can be cooked in the same ways as beef and is best eaten slightly rare. Unlike beef, venison is very low in fat. Red deer makes the strongest flavoured venison and is the type you will be most likely to find in butchers' shops.

Wild rabbit is generally considered to be tastier than its farmed counterpart but it is important to choose a young rabbit, aged between three and four months, or the meat may be tough with too strong a flavour. If you are planning to buy a whole unprepared rabbit, look for one with soft, easily torn ears, as this indicates a younger animal.

When buying wild pigeon, look for a good round, plump breast, which denotes a younger bird.

October and November is the time when partridges are considered to have the best flavour, although their shooting season lasts between September and February. Partridges fall into two types, the English Greyleg and French Redleg. Greylegs are generally wild and have a stronger and gamier flavour than the red, which are more often farmed. A simple roast is the best way to serve the Greylegs, while Redlegs are better served in casseroles and pot roasts.

A young pheasant will roast very well but if you have any doubt about the age of the bird it would be prudent to marinate it and/or use it in a casserole or similar dish. Hen birds are smaller, have less fat and are more tender than cocks.

If you'd like to learn more about buying and handling game, the Game Conservancy Trust is a mine of information, as is its publication, *The Game & Fish Cookbook*. See page 384 for contact details.

WALES   **ANGLESEY**

Owen Roberts & Son

Corwas, Amlwch, Anglesey LL68 9ET   T: 01407 830277
W: www.owenrobertsandson.com
✉ **mail order**

Much of the game offered at this traditional butcher's shop is local and wild boar is also available at Christmas. Meat from local farms within a 15-mile radius of the shop is also available.

GAME

The Welsh Venison Centre

Middlewood Farm, Bwlch, nr Brecon, Powys LD3 7HQ   T: 01874 730929
w: www.welshvenison.com
⟿ **farm shop** ✉ **mail order**

The red deer at the Welsh Venison Centre are farmed as naturally as possible, with an additive-free diet. Slaughtered locally, the deer are hung and butchered on site. Visitors to the farm shop can see the deer grazing in the hills.

Much of the food we eat is produced 'to a price'. This means that the price has been decided first and the produce reared or grown to meet this price. As a nation we demand cheap food and, inevitably, short cuts are taken in production to cut costs, in order to keep the price down. One of the casualties will be time, after all, time is money, and this is particularly true in meat production.

Often a modern intensive farm will choose hybrid breeds of animals that have been developed to carry more meat and to grow quickly. They are given concentrated feed to bulk them up more quickly so that they reach slaughtering age earlier. Often animals are transported around the country, from farm to farm, to abattoir, to packing centre. Hanging the meat to develop flavour and texture would be a costly delay and so often it is butchered and sold immediately. We are getting cheap meat but I wonder what the real price is? It is now widely agreed that the BSE crisis occurred because cattle were fed to cattle to save money. There were also suggestions that the recent outbreak of foot-and-mouth disease began and was made worse due to cost-saving activities taking precedence over sensible animal husbandry.

meat

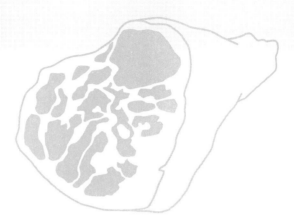

The meat producers I have listed here do things differently. Many rear their animals organically, offering assurances regarding the feed and welfare of the livestock. Many feed their animals on home-grown feed, with the lamb and beef being predominantly grass-fed. The animals won't be kept in cramped conditions, causing stress and disease; they'll range freely. The biggest difference of all, though, is how, when and where these farmers slaughter their livestock. Allowed to mature slowly, the animals go to slaughter much later than their intensively reared counterparts and they will be taken to a local abattoir to reduce the stress of travelling to a minimum (an animal stressed at the point of slaughter leads to inferior meat). Though most beef producers are forced to slaughter their animals before they are 30 months old (a rule imposed to try to control BSE), some of the farmers featured have government permission to slaughter at up to 42 months, as their farming methods make BSE so unlikely as to be virtually no risk. You'll almost certainly find that the meat these farmers produce will have a richness of flavour and a firmness and density of texture that will have people of a certain age crying delightedly 'this is how meat used to taste'.

Moorland Farm Shop

Axbridge, Somerset BS26 2BA   T: 01934 733341   E: moorlandfarm@btinternet.com

↲ **farm shop**   ☷ **farmers' markets**

Aberdeen Angus beef, from a closed herd, is grass-fed all year. Hung for three to four weeks, the beef is a rich ruby colour and is sold fresh, not frozen.

Norwood Farm

Bath Road, Norton St Philip, nr Bath, Somerset BA2 7LP   T: 01373 834356 (OFFICE HOURS) OR 01373 834856 (AFTER HOURS)   W: www.norwoodfarm.co.uk

↲ **farm shop**

Among the organically reared, rare-breed meats available here are no fewer than 12 different breeds of lamb, alongside rare-breed beef and pork. The farm shop also stocks home-grown organic vegetables and local Somerset cheeses.

The Real Meat Company

7 Hayes Place, Bear Flat, Bath BA2 4QW   T: 01225 335139   W: www.realmeat.co.uk

A traditional butcher's selling drug-free, welfare-friendly meat that comes from breeds chosen for their flavour and slow-growing nature. This shop was the winner of the 2002 *BBC Good Food Magazine* Best Sausage in Britain award. See the Super Hero box, page 367, for more information about The Real Meat Company.

Westleaze Farm

Whitesheet Hill, Beaminster, Dorset DT8 3SF   T: 01308 861408 OR 07814 390613

☷ **farmers' markets**

Geoff and Jayne Neal are passionate about mutton, and are busy encouraging all their customers to try this tasty old-fashioned meat. Their Poll Dorset and Cheviot lambs are reared on a hill farm, giving the meat a great texture, and are grass fed on chemical-free pasture for a traditional flavour. Lamb and hogget are available, and all are hung properly before sale. Geoff and Jayne are happy to advise on cooking, and also make mutton sausages, which are available to try at their stall at Beaminster, Lyme Regis and Poundbury farmers' markets.

Adeys Farm Organic Meats

Adeys Farm, Breadstone, Berkeley, Gloucestershire GL13 9HF   T: 01453 511218
E: cwilson@adeysfarm.fsnet.co.uk

🡒 **farmers' markets** ✉ **farm gate sales** ✉ **mail order**

Adeys is a treasure-trove of rare-breed meat, including Gloucester Old Spot pork, Suffolk lamb, Hereford and Aberdeen Angus beef, all reared outdoors, only being brought in during bad weather. Dry-cured bacon is also on offer. The meat is available from Cheltenham, Stroud and Thornbury farmers' markets as well as from the farm and by mail order.

The Real Meat Company

10 Silver Street, Bradford-on-Avon, Wiltshire BA15 1JY   T: 01225 309385
W: www.realmeat.co.uk

The owners of this butcher's shop are chefs by trade and add a different element to the welfare-friendly, chemical-free meats available here. Combining both butchery and chefs' skills, they make salami and all manner of charcuterie and can provide all the ingredients for a dinner party meal, from the meat to the accompaniments. The staff are very enthusiastic and full of information about their products. See the Super Hero box, page 367, for more information about The Real Meat Company.

Becklands Farm

Whitchurch Canonicorum, Bridport, Dorset DT6 6RG   T: 01297 560298
E: becklandsorganicfarm@btopenworld.com

🡒 **farm shop** ✉ **mail order**

Francis and Hilary Joyce of Becklands Farm produce Red Devon beef, geese, free-range eggs, farm-made preserves and some seasonal fruit and vegetables, all accredited by the Soil Association. They have a small farm shop on the farm and also sell mail order. Guided farm walks are regularly organised – call to find out when.

Denhay Farms Ltd

Broadoak, Bridport, Dorset DT6 5NP   T: 01308 458963   W: www.denhay.co.uk
✉ **mail order**

Great-Taste-Award-winning air-dried ham, dry-cured bacon and gammon and Cheddar cheeses, all hand-made at the farm.

Wyld Meadow Lamb

Wyld Meadow Farm, Monkton Wyld, nr Bridport, Dorset DT6 6DD   T: 01297 678318
🛒 **farmers' markets** ✉ **farm gate sales** ✉ **mail order**

Slowly reared Poll Dorset lamb, grass-fed all year without concentrates, is butchered on site at Wyld Meadow Farm and hung for ten days for a mature flavour. Available from many Dorset, Devon and Somerset farmers' markets – call for details or to arrange an order by mail or to collect from the farm. Home-reared beef is also available.

J C Burdge

Fenswood Farm, Says Lane, Langford, nr Bristol, North Somerset BS40 5DZ
T: 01934 852639
✉ **farm gate sales**

Traditional British breeds form the basis of the meat produced on Fenswood Farm, all organically. The Burdges operate a customer list, which Mrs Burdge works her way through whenever one of their livestock is sent to the abattoir. Call to get on the list.

Bill the Butcher

11 High Street, Bruton, Somerset BA10 0AB   T: 01749 812388

Accredited by the Rare Breeds Survival Trust, Bill the Butcher stocks native and rare breeds of meat from local smallholdings. Breeds can include Gloucester beef, Norfolk Horn lamb and British Lop pork.

Brewhamfield Organic Dairy Farm

North Brewham, Bruton, Somerset BA10 0QQ   T: 01749 850108 OR 01749 850469

✉ farm gate sales ✉ mail order

Beef from an unusual Aberdeen Angus and Jersey cross, reared according to organic principles, although not certified. The animals go to a local abattoir to reduce stress and the meat is then hung for three weeks before being butchered to order. There is also delicious pork to order from rare-breed British Lop pigs, the old pig of the West Country, and organic Jersey milk is also available.

The Real Meat Company

21 London Road, Calne, Wiltshire SN11 0AA   T: 01249 812362   W: www.realmeat.co.uk

The very enthusiastic husband and wife team at this butcher's sells only welfare-friendly, drug-free meat from the Real Meat Company, specializing in own-recipe faggots, parma ham and salamis, all made without artificial preservatives. See the Super Hero box, page 367, for more information about The Real Meat Company.

Wild Beef

Hillhead Farm, Chagford, Devon TQ13 8DY   T: 01647 433433

🚜 farmers' markets 🚚 delivery service

Rare- and native-breed cattle graze on traditional pasture (rather than commercially sown grasses) at Hillhead Farm. Welsh Blacks, North, South and Red Devons and Herefords come in all shapes and sizes but all are hung for four weeks to produce flavourful beef. Find them at farmers' markets and at Borough Market in London's SE1.

Old Castle Farm

Buckland St Mary, Chard, Somerset TA20 3JZ   T: 01460 234453
W: www.oldcastlefarm.co.uk

🚜 farmers' markets

Accredited by RSPCA Freedom Foods, the pork at Old Castle Farm comes from pedigree Saddleback pigs, reared in a straw-based yard system, with plenty of room to move around. GM-free feed is used, and homeopathy in cases of sickness. All the regular meat joints are available, along with home-made sausages. Find the produce at Crewkerne, Wincanton and Chard farmers' markets.

Swaddles Green Organic Farm

Chard, Somerset TA20 3JR T: 0845 456 1768 w: www.swaddles.co.uk

✉ mail order

A one-stop online shop for everything organic, from meat, fish and dairy to vegetables and prepared meals.

Hill End Farm

Brinkworth, Chippenham, Wiltshire SN15 5AZ T: 01666 510261

🚚 delivery service

The Welfare-friendly veal here comes from Hereford/Friesian cross cattle. Hill End Farm operates a closed herd, which means that all the cattle are born on the farm, and the calves have plenty of space to roam around their straw-bedded barn. With natural feed, milk and silage, the meat is rose veal not the white veal associated with the continental veal crate system. Call to find out about the delivery round and availability.

Langley Chase Organic Farm

Kington Langley, Chippenham, Wilts SN15 5PW T: 01249 750095

w: www.langleychase.co.uk

⊨ farm gate sales ✉ mail order

Buy Langley Chase organic lamb, hogget and mutton (from a breed native to the Isle of Man) at the farm gate by appointment or mail order and see the Super Hero box, opposite, for more information.

Marshfield Organic Farm

Field Farm, Ayford Lane, Marshfield, nr Chippenham, Wiltshire SN14 8AB

T: 01225 891397 w: www.marshfieldorganicfarm.co.uk

▱ farmers' markets

Traditional-breed animals are reared here – Hereford and Angus beef, and Poll Dorset and Jacob lamb. The herb-rich, organic pasture that the animals graze on contains traditional grasses, and the farmers here believe that this gives the meat particularly fine flavour, which is developed further by proper hanging on the bone. Home-made sausages are a speciality, and organic eggs are also available. Find the produce at Bath, Chippenham and Bristol farmers' markets.

Sandridge Farmhouse Bacon

Sandridge Farm, Bromham, nr Chippenham, Wiltshire SN15 2JL   T: 01380 850304
w: www.sandridgefarmhousebacon.co.uk

 farm shop   farmers' markets   mail order

Traditional bacon curers, Sandridge offers bacon and ham cured using some interesting regional recipes. Sausages and charcuterie, including prosciutto, are also available and all the meat used is raised on the farm.

super hero

JANE KALLAWAY, of Langley Chase Organic Farm, Chippenham (see opposite)

Jane Kallaway breeds organic Manx Loaghtan lamb, an ancient type of sheep native to the Isle of Man. This is a primitive breed, unlikely to be found on bigger commercial farms as they take far too long to reach maturity – in Jane's case, her lambs are 18 months old before they go to slaughter. Why does she wait so long for the Manx Loaghtans when other breeds are ready much sooner? Jane told me: 'I believe that good food should add to the quality of life. I care passionately about how livestock is reared, produced and processed. My aim is to produce the finest organic lamb and mutton. The flock are bred and reared on the farm to Soil Association organic standards with total traceability of each animal. They are also registered with the Rare Breeds Survival Trust. Our ewes are allowed to mature slowly, producing their first lambs when they are two years old. We should nurture all our old breeds to ensure their survival and to provide the public with variety and quality of taste. I totally believe in producing food which is the antithesis of fast food – pure, healthy – the natural way – with a natural breed.' Jane won first prize in the 2003 Soil Association awards in the lamb category.

Owls Barn

Derritt Lane, Sopley, Christchurch, Dorset BH23 7AZ   T: 01425 672239
w: www.owlsbarn.com

✦ farm shop

Poll Dorset and Llanwenog lamb and Hereford beef from a closed
herd are all organically certified and reared on the farm.

Chesterton Farm Shop

off Chesterton Lane, Cirencester, Gloucestershire GL7 6JP   T: 01285 642160

✦ farm shop   ✉ mail order

There is a big range of traditional and rare-breed meat at this farm
shop, all from local farms, and they also offer their own cured and
smoked bacon.

The Butts Farm Shop

The Butts Farm, South Cerney, Cirencester, Gloucestershire GL7 5QE   T: 01285 862224
w: www.thebuttsfarmshop.com

✦ farm shop   ✉ mail order

There is always a good choice of home-reared, rare-breed meats,
including sausages and home-cured bacon, at this shop, all reared
extensively and slowly for old-fashioned flavour. A good range of
local vegetables is also on offer.

Smallicombe Farm

Northleigh, Colyton, Devon EX24 6BU   T: 01404 831310   w: www.smallicombe.com

📷 farmers' markets   📷 farm gate sales   ✉ mail order

Beef from Ruby Devon and Dexter cattle, grass-fed all year and
hung for three weeks, Dorset Down lamb and Berkshire and British
Lop pigs (made into bacon and award-winning sausages) are all
reared slowly for full flavour. Ian and Maggie Todd from Smallicombe
Farm attend many local farmers' markets – call to find out where or
to arrange an order to collect from the farm. Smallicombe Farm is a

member of the British Pig Association. Bed and breakfast is available at the farm, with meals made from home-reared or home-grown produce.

Hazelbury Partners

Hazelbury Manor, Box, Corsham, Wiltshire SN13 8HX   T: 01225 812088

🛒 **farmers' markets**

Many rare breeds of all kinds of livestock are reared organically at Hazelbury Manor, including the native Wiltshire Horn lamb, Saddleback pork and Welsh Black beef. Free-range hens' and ducks' eggs are also available. Produce from Hazelbury Manor is available from the farmers' market in Bath.

Pipers Farm

Cullompton, Devon EX15 1SD   T: 01392 881380   W: www.pipersfarm.com

🏠 **farm gate sales** ✉ **mail order**

Pipers Farm is the hub of a network of small Devon farms, all producing high quality meats. Traditional breeds are reared, including Devon Red Ruby beef, and the Grieg family at Pipers Farm control every aspect of the rearing, from their own formulation feed to the choice of one small local abattoir. The farm also has a shop in Exeter, see below.

West Hembury Farm

Askerswell, Dorchester, Dorset DT2 9EN   T: 01308 485289   W: www.westhembury.com

🏠 **farm gate sales**

Buy organic rare-breed meat (from White Park beef) and organic hens' eggs here. The beef is hung for three weeks for a traditional flavour.

Pipers Farm

27 Magdalen Road, Exeter, Devon EX2 4TA   T: 01392 274504   W: www.pipersfarm.com

For details, see under the Cullompton entry, above.

Churchtown Farm

Lanteglos, Fowey, Cornwall PL23 1NH   T: 01726 870375

⊨ farm gate sales

Churchtown Farm is a coastal National Trust farm, rearing organic
lamb and beef from traditional breeds on herb- and clover-rich
pasture. They are previous winners of the prestigious Best Beef and
Best Lamb awards at the Soil Association Organic Food Awards.
Available direct from the farm (phone first).

Richard Kittow & Sons

1–3 South Street, Fowey, Cornwall PL23 1AR   T: 01726 832639

Richard Kittow won't source much of his produce from outside
Cornwall, so most of the meat comes from local farms. There is a
good selection of extensively reared, rare-breed meat and he breeds
Hereford beef on his own farm and has his own slaughterhouse.
Also available is home-cured bacon and unusual items such as
brawn and Hog's Pudding, a Cornish version of black pudding.

Lagan Farm Meats at Milton Park Garden Centre

Park Farm, Shaftesbury Road, Gillingham, Dorset SP8 5JG   T: 01747 822169
E: laganfarms@rarebreeds.freeserve.co.uk

↙ farm shop ⊨ farm gate sales

Meat from slowly matured, rare-breed cattle and pigs, including the
unusual Irish Moiled beef and British Lop pork. The animals have
traditional feed, free from additives, and the beef is hung for four
weeks. Wild venison, shot on the farm, is also available, as is mutton
ham and smoked mutton and free-range eggs from rare-breed hens.

Ham Street Farm Produce

Baltonsborough, nr Glastonbury, Somerset BA6 8QB   T: 01458 850508

≝ farmers' markets

Free-range pork, bacon, sausages, gammon and faggots from
Tamworth and Middle White pigs that are fed without artificial
additives are the speciality of Ham Street Farm. The pigs are slowly

matured to up to a year old, giving a fuller flavoured meat. Call to
find out which farmers' markets they attend.

Wallace's of Hemyock

Hill Farm, Hemyock, Devon EX15 3UZ   T: 01823 680307
W: www.welcometowallaces.co.uk
🐖 **farm shop** ✉ **mail order**

Grass-fed Highland beef and bison and also venison, outdoor-
reared pork and dry-cured bacon, are all reared slowly and naturally
by Wallace's. There is also a restaurant at the farm.

Gittisham Herd at Combe Estate

Beech Walk, Gittisham, Honiton, Devon EX14 3AB   T: 01404 45576
W: www.reddevonbeef.co.uk
🛒 **farmers' markets** ✉ **mail order**

Traditional Ruby Red Devon cattle are reared 'slowly and gently' at
Combe Estate, grass-fed all year on conservation grazing. The beef
is hung for three weeks and is well marbled, tender and tasty.
Available from Ottery St Mary, Seaton and Exeter farmers' markets.

The Country Butcher

Main Road, Huntley, Gloucester GL19 3DZ   T: 01452 831023
W: www.countrybutcher.co.uk

The Country Butcher is RBST accredited, with all kinds of rare-
breed meat from local farmers whom the butcher personally knows.

Fowlescombe Farm

Ugborough, Ivybridge, Devon PL21 0HW   T: 01548 821000   W: www.fowlescombe.com
✉ **farm gate sales** ✉ **mail order**

The rare-breed pedigree Manx Loaghtan, Shetland, Jacob and
Hebridean sheep at Fowlescombe are not slaughtered until they are
at least a year old; the meat is lean, with a slightly gamey flavour.
Pedigree Aberdeen Angus beef is also available. Barbara Barker
runs a customer list and can also do mail order by arrangement.

Fountain Violet Farm

Mount Ridley Road, Kingswear, Devon TQ6 0DA T: 01803 752363
E: ed@fvfarm.freeserve.co.uk

✉ **mail order** ▨ **box scheme**

A box scheme with a difference – Fountain Violet Farm's boxes contain a variety of cuts of their pure-breed South Devon beef, born and reared on the farm, grass-fed with home-grown supplements. Each 8kg box will contain 'a bit of everything'.

Pitney Farm Shop

Glebe Farm, Pitney, Langport, Somerset TA10 9AP T: 01458 253002
E: robwalrond@wagonhouse.freeserve.co.uk

⬥ **farm shop**

A great environmentally aware, community-minded farm shop, Pitney Farm does lots of organic goodies, such as vegetables, eggs, beef, lamb and pork, all home-produced, and foods from other very local producers – milk, ice cream and honey. Shoppers arriving by bike or on foot even get a discount.

Philip Warren & Son

1 Westgate Street, Launceston, Cornwall PL15 7AB T: 01566 772089 OR
01566 777211 W: www.philipwarrenbutchers.co.uk

This butcher's shop has some really interesting produce, including a selection of rare-breed meat. They also stock local game in season.

Cornish Country Meats

Treverbyn Mill, St Neot, Liskeard, Cornwall PL14 6HG T: 01579 320303
W: www.cornishcountrymeats.co.uk

▭ **farmers' markets** 🚚 **delivery service**

Traditionally reared beef and lamb and free-range pork all graze on unsprayed fields. Venison – from a closed herd of pure Hungarian deer – and wild boar are also available. The Barrow family offer home-made pies, including wild boar pasties! Call to find out which farmers' markets they attend or to discuss their local delivery service.

Bill and Sue Osborne

2 Orchard Cottages, Lydney Park Estate, Lydney, Gloucestershire GL15 6BU
T: 01594 841970 OR 07958 920430   E: castlemears2@hotmail.com
📨 farm gate sales

Dexter beef, Manx Loaghtan and Ryeland lamb and Berkshire pork,
and free-range Bronze turkeys at Christmas, are all reared with high
attention to welfare by the Osbornes. Although not registered
organic, the animals have an additive-free diet and are treated
homeopathically when ill. The Osbornes have a customer list and
they phone around when there is meat ready to be bought – quality,
not quantity, is the key here, so meat is not always available.

Heritage Prime

Shedbush Farm, Muddyford Lane, nr Lyme Regis, Dorset DT6 6DR   T: 01297 489304
W: www.HeritagePrime.co.uk
📨 farm gate sales

Shedbush Farm is a mixed, biodynamic farm producing beef, lamb
and pork from the oldest British breeds. The animals graze
fertilizer-free pasture and are born, raised and finished according
to biodynamic principles and slaughtered locally and humanely.
Ian and Denise Bell, the farmers, run a 'larder list' of customers
whom they call when meat is available, so they can stock up their
freezers – phone Denise for details.

Thornham Farm Shop

Great Thornham Farm, Trowbridge Road, Seend, Melksham, Wiltshire SN12 6PN
T: 01380 828295
🥄 farm shop

The Hawkins, a husband and wife team, rear traditional breed
animals – Gloucester Old Spot pigs and Aberdeen Angus beef cattle
– to produce meat with an old-fashioned flavour. There is also lamb
from a neighbour's farm, and local venison. Food miles are kept to a
minimum, with the animals taken to a very local abattoir.

Hindon Organic Farm

Exmoor Organic Hill Farm Produce, nr Minehead, Exmoor, Somerset TA24 8SH
T: 01643 705244   w: www.hindonfarm.co.uk

🛒 **farmers' markets** 📫 **farm gate sales** ✉ **mail order**

Hindon Farm offers slowly reared organic meats from traditional
breeds – Gloucester Old Spot pork, Aberdeen Angus beef and hill
farm lamb. Dry-cured bacon, gammon, ham and sausages, all
accredited to Soil Association standards, are available by mail order
and from West Somerset farmers' markets as well as at the farm gate.
Hindon Farm won the Producer of the Year Award at the 2003
Soil Association Awards.

East Hill Pride

High Street, Newton Poppleford, Devon EX10 0ED   T: 01395 567848
🥄 **farm shop**

Home-produced beef, which is hung for a month, pork and
Wiltshire-cure bacon are available from this traditional farm. The
animals are fed only home-grown feed, giving complete traceability.

Dartmoor Happy Hogs

Moorland Farm Shop, Whiddon Down, Okehampton, Devon EX20 2QL   T: 01647 231666
🥄 **farm shop**

Tamworth, Saddleback and Gloucester Old Spot pigs are all reared
at Moorland Farm, producing pork, ham, bacon and a range of
around 20 different award-winning sausages. The pigs are free-
range and slowly reared to maturity.

Eversfield Manor

Bratton Clovelly, Okehampton, Devon EX20 4JF   T: 01837 871400
w: www.eversfieldmanor.co.uk

The Aberdeen Angus cattle and Romney Marsh sheep at Eversfield
Manor graze rich organic pasture – they are not fed concentrates,
and this natural diet, along with proper hanging to allow the meat to

mature on the bone, results in great flavour. There is also wild venison and game, shot on the estate, and locally produced pork and free-range chicken. All the meat is available by mail order.

Eweleaze Farm

c/o The Cartshed, Church Lane, Osmington, Dorset DT3 6EW   T: 01305 833690
E: peter@eweleaze.co.uk
farm gate sales

The Aberdeen Angus beef, matured on the bone for three weeks before sale, and Poll Dorset lamb, matured for ten days, available from The Cartshed, have been slowly reared to Soil Association standards. Peter Broatch, the farmer, firmly believes that the flavour in meat comes from the fat and that the fat on organic meat, with its higher level of polyunsaturates, tastes better than its conventional counterpart. Also available are organic eggs from hens free to range amongst the trees and hedgerows of the farm.

Ian Lentern

1 Chapel Street, Penzance, Cornwall TR18 4AJ ALSO AT Old Bridge, Newlyn, Cornwall
T: 01736 363061 (PENZANCE); 01736 362760 (NEWLYN)   W: www.lenterns.com
mail order

Ian Lentern is committed to stocking only local meat in his shop. The shop is filled with meat from farms where animal welfare is a high priority, and a local speciality is also featured – Hog's Pudding, the Cornish version of black pudding.

The Well Hung Meat Co.

Carswell Farm, Holbeton, Plymouth, Devon PL8 1HH   T: 01752 830494
W: www.wellhungmeat.com
mail order

The organic lamb from The Well Hung Meat Co. was the 2001 and 2002 award winner for Best Lamb at the Soil Association Organic Food Awards. Hung for nine days after slaughter, the meat is tender and well flavoured. Organic beef and chicken are also available.

FOOD HEROES OF BRITAIN

The Real Meat Company

14 Bournemouth Road, Lower Parkstone, Poole, Dorset BH14 0ES   T: 01202 747972
w: www.realmeat.co.uk

Humanely reared meat without growth promoters or antibiotics, from slow-growing, traditional breeds of animal. There are 23 different types of sausage available, including the South African boerewors. See the Super Hero box, page 367, for more information about The Real Meat Company.

Clive Downs Butchers

High Street, Porlock, Somerset TA24 8PT   T: 01643 862667   w: www.clivedowns.co.uk

Dry-cured bacon, free-range veal, wild Exmoor venison and Exmoor lamb are the specialities here, all locally sourced.

Primrose Herd

Primrose Cottage, Busveal, Redruth, Cornwall TR16 5HF   T: 01209 821408
 farmers' markets farm gate sales

Sally Lugg rears Gloucester Old Spot and Large Black rare-breed pigs, allowing them to grow slowly on GM-free feed, ranging freely outdoors. A Taste of the West award winner, her pork and bacon have a great old-fashioned flavour and can be found at many Cornish farmers' markets, including Truro, Lostwithiel and Redruth, or call Sally to collect direct from the farm.

Crooked End Farm

Ruardean, Forest of Dean, Gloucestershire GL17 9XF   T: 01594 544482
 farm shop

All the produce on display at Crooked End Farm shop is either produced on the farm itself or comes from neighbouring farms. This can include organic fruit and vegetables, free-range eggs, cider and perry from the orchard, rare-breed beef and lamb and free-range pork – all the animals are fed on locally produced feed. All produce is accredited by the Soil Association.

Brown Cow Organics

Perridge Farm, Pilton, Shepton Mallet, Somerset BA4 4EW   T: 01749 890298
W: www.browncoworganics.co.uk
🚚 delivery service

An award-winning organic farm producing rare Guernsey beef. The beef is hung traditionally for four weeks, and has twice won in the Organic Food Awards. The meat is delivered fresh within 24 hours of being cut – no shrink-wrap or vacuum packing is used at Brown Cow Organics. Organically bred rare-breed pork and organic chickens from nearby farms are also available, along with home-grown vegetables and home-produced yoghurts.

John Thorner's Ltd

Bridge Farm Shop, Pyle, Shepton Mallet, Somerset BA4 6TA   T: 01749 830138
E: johnthorner@btopenworld.com
🚚 delivery service

Local beef from the Mendips, free-range pork and venison from the Balmoral estate in the stalking season. John Thorner has four shops in central Somerset; call to find your nearest store. A delivery service is also available within a 20-mile radius.

Haymans Butchers

6 Church Street, Sidmouth, Devon EX10 8LY   T: 01395 512877
W: www.haymansbutchers.co.uk

The current Mr Hayman running this butcher's is the fourth generation of his family to do so, and it was for the ox-tongue prepared to his grandmother's recipe that he received a recent Q Guild award. A real family affair, the beef stocked here comes from the butcher's cousin and, for those concerned about food miles, the meat has a round trip of only 16 miles from farm to butcher's.

food facts

PORK, BACON AND SAUSAGES

Nowhere does the battle between small-scale, thoughtful rearing of animals and mass production rage more fiercely than with pigs. Few people can tolerate the idea of such intelligent animals spending their lives in cramped conditions. It's a sad fact that over 40% of the pork we eat is intensively reared, imported meat. Why won't we pay a bit more and look after our own farmers? Maybe then we could reverse the fact that 40% of farms sold in the last year went to non-farmers. The producers listed here believe that pigs should be as free ranging as possible and allowed to grow slowly, because this creates the tastiest meat. Often they will be native-breed pigs, which produce better roasting joints because they have a good fat covering which, in addition to tasting so good, leads to great crackling. For the same reason they also make the best sausages and bacon.

SOUTH WEST   STROUD

Allen Hale Butchers

New House, Friday Street, Painswick, nr Stroud, Gloucestershire GL6 6QJ
T: 01452 813613

Allen Hale is a butcher who feels that food has been largely 'messed around too much – especially meat'. Such is his concern about the way conventional meat is produced, he stocks only welfare-friendly meat from the Real Meat Company (see the Super Hero box, page 367, for more information). This meat comes from slow-growing breeds of animals chosen for their flavour and reared traditionally without growth promoters or antibiotics.

SOUTH WEST   STURMINSTER NEWTON

Star Farm

Hazelbury Bryan, nr Sturminster Newton, Dorset DT10 2EG   T: 01258 817285
⬦ farm shop

Organic home-reared, rare-breed meat is available at this newly opened farm shop – Aberdeen Angus beef, Oxford Sandy & Black pork, dry-cured bacon and sausages and Poll Dorset and Llanwenog lamb.

Eastbrook Farms Organic Meat

Bishopstone, Swindon, Wiltshire SN6 8PL   T: 01793 790340
W: www.helenbrowningorganics.co.uk
✉ mail order

Eastbrook Farm was one of the pioneers of organic meat and is still revered for the high standards of animal welfare that are maintained there. A full range is available, including veal and poultry.

Lyng Court Organic Meat

West Lyng, Taunton, Somerset TA3 5AP   T: 01823 490510
🥩 farm gate sales

Lyng Court Farm produces lamb and beef from Norman breeds on the Somerset levels. The breeds were chosen because the grazing here is so similar to that in the animals' native Normandy. Reared naturally on grass and home-grown barley, the meat is available direct from the farm but please call first.

Pampered Pigs Pantry

2 The Green, Tolpuddle, Dorchester, Dorset DT2 7EX   T: 01305 848107
W: www.pampered-pigs.co.uk
🥓 farm shop 🥩 farmers' markets

Kevin and Amanda Crocker are part of the Countryside Stewardship Scheme and see conservation as a priority. The farm produces British White cross beef and traditional breeds of pork that are allowed to range freely in family groups. There is a small shop on site and the Crockers also attend numerous local farmers' markets.

Nancarrow Organic Farm

Marazanvose, Truro, Cornwall TR4 9DQ   T: 01872 540343
🥩 farmers' markets 🥩 farm gate sales 🚚 delivery service

Grazing on clover-rich pasture, the South Devon cattle at Nancarrow Farm produce organic beef. The slaughterhouse and butcher are next door, so full traceability is offered. Find the beef at Truro, Falmouth and Lostwithiel farmers' markets.

super hero

At the Cranborne Estate in Dorset, Judith and Giles Blatchford are determined that native pig breeds, such as Tamworth, Gloucester Old Spot and the Large Black, will not be replaced entirely with intensively reared pigs that are a cross-breed specifically designed to grow fast, lean and big. The pork they produce at Cranborne Farms is from a range of rare-breed pigs and these animals are reared in the woodlands around the farm (a pig's natural habitat), rooting around for much of their diet, which is topped up with farm-grown produce. The resulting rich, dark, densely flavoured meat is not the only benefit of this. The Blatchfords are helping to sustain the rare breeds and they are also encouraging the hobby of keeping rare-breed pigs by selling the best of the piglets to other rare-breed pig enthusiasts – 'We aim to create a market and underpin it with prices that make the hobby of rare-breed pig-keeping affordable.'
The pork products are available from the farm shop at Cranborne Estate.

SOUTH WEST   UMBERLEIGH

Country Ways

High Bickington, Umberleigh, Devon EX17 9BJ   T: 01769 560503
w: www.country-ways.net
✉ **farm gate sales**

The rare-breed pork at Country Ways is usually a mixture of Gloucester Old Spot, Berkshire and Tamworth, from pigs reared free-range on GM-free feed. Bacon, gammon and joints are available and, occasionally, Dexter beef. This is a small farm, so produce is not always available – phone to find out.

SOUTH WEST   UMBERLEIGH

Higher Hacknell Farm

Burrington, Umberleigh, Devon EX37 9LX   T: 01769 560909   w: www.higherhacknell.co.uk
✉ **mail order**

Higher Hacknell Farm produces organic beef, lamb and pork and they supply good free-range chicken from a nearby farm. Previously voted Producer of the Year at the Soil Association Organic Food Awards, the meat is available by mail order.

Boyton Farm

Boyton, Warminster, Wilts BA12 0SS   T: 01985 850208 OR 01985 850371
w: www.boytonfarm.co.uk

🡫 farm shop   ☰ farmers' markets   ✉ mail order

Caroline at Boyton Farm breeds the rare Tamworth pig – not
surprising, given that her mother-in-law was a founder member of
the Rare Breeds Survival Trust. Caroline's is the largest and oldest
herd in the country. The pigs are all born and reared on the farm,
fed with home-grown feed and slowly matured. Boyton Farm is now
also producing Sussex and Hereford beef, lamb, and venison and
pheasant.

Cranborne Farms Traditional Meats   `super` hero

Pound Farm, Cranborne, Wimborne, Dorset BH21 5RN   T: 01725 517168
w: www.cranborne.co.uk/farm

🡫 farm shop   ✉ mail order

Cranborne Farm rare-breed pigs are reared in the woodlands around
the farm to produce rich-tasting dark meat. See the Super Hero
box, opposite, for more information.

Vowley Farm   `super` hero

Bicknoll Lane, Wootton Bassett, Wiltshire SN4 8QR   T: 01793 852115
w: www.vowleyfarm.co.uk

☰ farmers' markets

See the Super Hero Box, page 296, for more information on this
welfare-conscious farm.

Burscombe Cliff Farm

Egerton, nr Ashford, Kent TN27 9BB   T: 01233 756468

☰ farmers' markets

Home-produced organic pork, beef and lamb, available at Wye,
Lenham, Faversham and Dulwich farmers' markets. The beef is
native Sussex beef, hung for at least two weeks, and there is cured,
smoked bacon, ham and gammon available.

super hero

VOWLEY FARM, Wootton Bassett, Wiltshire (see page 295)

Although the animals at Vowley Farm are destined for the plate, many would say that they still live a charmed life under the care of Lorraine and Mark Stanton. Animal welfare is of prime concern here, and this ethos, as we have seen again and again, results in a quality of meat that industrial-scale producers can never hope to achieve. The animals are all of old and traditional breeds: British White cattle, Gloucester Old Spot pigs, Norfolk Black turkeys, and a new addition to the farm, Ixworth chickens. Norfolk Horn lamb comes from a neighbouring organic farm. The beef is dark, well-marbled, and with a hint of sweetness, the lamb is rich yet not too fatty: all the meat benefits from the animals having been allowed to mature gently at their own pace. Such is the level of care at this farm, Lorraine undertakes all the butchery herself – she has such respect for her livestock, that she feels it her duty to be involved in every process, to make the very best of the meat. Find Lorraine at Wootton Bassett, Devizes, Cricklade, Calne, Marlborough and Swindon farmers' markets..

Little Omenden Sussex Beef

Little Omenden Farm, Smarden, Ashford, Kent TN27 8QP T: 01580 291272
W: www.easisites.co.uk/littleomendensussexbeef
⊨ **farm gate sales**

Sussex beef is a new venture for this Countryside Stewardship farm. Disillusioned with rearing beef for supermarkets, David Harrison has turned to a native breed and is slowly rearing the cattle on a natural diet of grass and rolled oats. Call him for more details about buying the beef.

Wealden Farmers Network

Homestead Farm, Darwell Hill, Netherfield, nr Battle, East Sussex TN33 9QL
T: 01424 838252 E: joamos2000@hotmail.com
↳ **farm shop**

Wealden Farmers Network is a co-operative of four farms, one of which is registered organic, while the others farm organically without being registered. The emphasis is on breeds of animal native to the area, so the rare Sussex beef is a speciality. Traditional-breed pork and lamb is also available. All the livestock is reared extensively, all are born on the farm, allowed to live in family groups, and go to a local abattoir to eliminate stress. The animals are fed entirely on grass or home-grown feed. The meat is available from the farm shop but call first.

Eastwoods of Berkhamsted

15 Gravel Path, Berkhamsted, Hertfordshire HP4 2EF   T: 01442 865012
w: www.eastwoodsofberkhamstead.co.uk

✉ mail order

Winner of the Q Guild's Top Shop award in 2001, and many times winner at the Soil Association Organic Food Awards, Eastwoods stock a great range of free-range and organic meats, with an emphasis on animal welfare.

Dennis of Bexley

Maplehurst Close, Bexley Park, Kent DA2 7WX   T: 01322 522126
w: www.dennisofbexley.co.uk

Winner of Best Butcher's Shop in Britain in 1995, Dennis of Bexley also won the European Fresh Food Championship in Utrecht, Holland in 2000, and their turkey and ham pie won a Good Housekeeping Award in 2002. They offer locally produced meat and a good range of game – local pheasant, rabbit and wild venison are available in season.

J M Walman Family Butchers

1 Station Road, Launton, Bicester, Oxfordshire OX26 5DS   T: 01869 252619

John Walman stocks plenty of slowly and naturally reared rare-breed meats, including the unusual British Lop pork – the rarest breed of pig in this country. The meat is labelled with the breed and details of its provenance and John Walman finds people travel from neighbouring counties to buy the produce.

food facts

TRACEABILITY

How much do you know about the sources of the food you eat? Who grew or reared it, and where has it been on the way to your plate? Food, and particularly meat and livestock, seem to be trucked endlessly around the country before reaching the shop shelves. The food industry has changed so much over the last half century or so, and we now have little sense of connection with the producers of our food. Buying meat direct from a good producer, or from a really good butcher, is different. They'll tell you as much as you want to know – where the animal was reared and slaughtered, what it was fed, its age, how long it was hung for. Many of the meat producers we feature run closed herds, so almost every animal they have was born on the farm. This old-fashioned style of husbandry means that you can feel confident that, yes, you do know where your food comes from, and this is welcome reassurance in this time of endless food scares.

SOUTH EAST   BLACKBOYS

Pounsley Hill Produce

Pounsley Hill Cottage, Pounsley, Blackboys, East Sussex TN22 5HT   T: 01825 830377
w: www.pounsleyhillproduce.co.uk
✉ **farm gate sales**

David and Angela Lewis run a smallholding specializing in free-range pork and lamb. Although not certified as organic, the farm is free from chemicals; the lambs eat nothing but grass and hay and the pigs are fed on home-grown corn and grains. David and Angela sell direct to the public and have an open-door policy – they are happy for visitors to see how the smallholding is run.

SOUTH EAST   BRIZE NORTON

Foxbury Farm

Burford Road, Brize Norton, Oxfordshire OX18 3NX   T: 01993 844141
w: www.foxburyfarm.co.uk
➥ **farm shop**

Home-reared, rare-breed meat (Hereford beef, lamb, and Gloucester Old Spot pork), all extensively reared, is supplemented at the farm shop with locally grown fruit and vegetables and locally made cakes.

W J Castle

11 High Street, Burford, Oxfordshire OX18 4RG   T: 01993 822113

Free-range chicken, Cotswold lamb and Gloucester Old Spot pork are the main stars at Castle's but everything they stock is fully traceable meat from local farms.

Chandler & Dunn Ltd

The Laurels, Lower Goldstone, Ash, Canterbury, Kent CT3 2DY   T: 01304 812262
W: www.chandleranddunn.co.uk
🥄 **farm shop**

Well-marbled beef from rare Sussex cattle, hung for three weeks, as well as home-reared lamb and locally produced pork is available from the farm shop.

The Real Meat Company

9 Gordon Road, Carshalton Beeches, Surrey SM5 3RG   T: 0208 395 8946
W: www.realmeat.co.uk

All the meat at Don Wenham's butcher's shop is welfare-friendly and extensively reared, supplied by farmers he knows he can trust – he has visited most of the farms. The beef stocked here is hung for around five weeks for a tender, traditional meat. See the Super Hero box, page 367, for more information about The Real Meat Company.

Sladden Farm

Alkham Valley, nr Dover, Kent CT15 7BX   T: 01304 825188
🏪 **farmers' markets** 🥄 **farm shop**

Di Smith, the owner of the Moomin herd of pedigree, prize-winning Dexter cattle, specializes in the production of Dexter beef. The calves are single suckled, then reared and slowly finished on the herb-rich ancient chalk downland around Dover. The fine-grained, mature and marbled beef is hung for three weeks. Also available is free-range rare-breed pork and lamb, home-made sausages and burgers, dry-cured bacon and ham.

food facts

LAMB

It's odd that we import so much lamb from New Zealand, transporting it halfway across the world, when Britain produces an impressive array of different types of tasty lamb, from the small, gamey-flavoured native breeds to the delicacy of the more modern types of lamb. I have nothing against New Zealand lamb but there is so much to choose from in the UK and Ireland. Welsh saltmarsh lamb is delicately flavoured by the salty Sparta grasses, washed by the tide twice a day, that the sheep graze on. Or try heather-fed lamb from Northumbria or lamb from upland farms, with its richer flavour and muscular texture. There are many different breeds of lamb to try – Castlemilk Moorit, Manx Loaghtan, Wensleydale and Soay will all have subtle differences in flavour and texture and you generally need to seek out small-scale producers to find these.

You can even choose the maturity of lamb. Many of the producers listed, instead of offering only spring lamb, which has the mildest of flavours, will offer the more flavoursome hogget, which is year-old lamb or older. Some even offer mutton, which can be from up to five-year-old sheep; however, this will not be the tough, rather pungent meat some people associate with the term, but a more robust, intensely flavoured version of the younger lamb.

SOUTH EAST   EAST HORSLEY

F Conisbee & Son

Park Corner, Ockham Road South, East Horsley, Surrey KT24 6RZ T: 01483 282073

The Conisbee family are butchers who like to know exactly where all their meat has come from and how it has been reared. 'From conception to consumption,' they can tell their customers everything about the produce in their shop. The family rear their own beef and seasonal turkeys; almost everything else comes from local farms – Neil Conisbee goes to the farms himself to select the animals.

SOUTH EAST   EPSOM

Kenneth J Eve

9 Corner House Parade, Epsom Road, Ewell, Epsom, Surrey KT17 1NX
T: 020 8393 3043 W: www.kjeve.co.uk

One of the specialities at this butcher's shop is the free-range Devon chicken, reared traditionally without antibiotics, hormones or growth promoters. Norfolk free-range pork is also popular and Eve's recently won a Guild of Q Butchers gold award for their Leeky Lamb in 2003.

A. J. Barkaway Ltd

20 Ospringe Street, Faversham, Kent ME13 8TL ALSO AT 6 West Street, Faversham, Kent ME13 7JE   T: 01795 532040 (OSPRINGE STREET); 01795 532026 (WEST STREET)

A member of the Q Guild of Butchers, Chris Barkaway is the fourth generation of his family to be running this award-winning traditional butcher's. Chris sources from trusted local farms, hand-picking the meat himself. There's plenty to choose from – free-range pork and chicken, local game, beef hung for around three weeks for a good old-fashioned flavour, and free-range Bronze turkeys at Christmas. Try the sausages here – Chris has been Kent Supreme Sausage Maker three time in a row, and his pies have won Q Guild gold medals.

Tablehurst Farm

Forest Row, East Sussex RH18 5DP   T: 01342 823173   E: tablehurst_farm@talk21.com
⬤ farm shop

Biodynamic and organic meats from many different rare breeds, all from closed herds, are butchered on site. An amazing 25 different types of sausage are produced here and seasonal home-grown vegetables and organic eggs are also available.

C H Wakeling Ltd

41 Farncombe Street, Godalming, Surrey GU7 3LH   T: 01483 417557
w: www.wakelings.co.uk
✉ mail order

A Q Guild member, Wakeling's source as much meat as possible from local farmers. Local Aberdeen Angus beef and free-range and rare-breed (Saddleback) pork, reared on chemical-free pasture without hormones or GM food. They also have Soil Association accredited organic veal and free-range chicken, and game in season. Wakeling's won a five-star Good Housekeeping Award in October 2002 for their home-cooked smoked ham on the bone.

Gabriel Machin

7 Market Place, Henley-on-Thames, Oxfordshire RG9 2AA   T: 01491 574377
w: www.gabrielmachin.co.uk

Classified as a butcher, Gabriel Machin offers much more than the
local Chiltern lamb, free-range local pork and Scottish beef he
stocks. There is a traditional smokehouse on the premises, used to
smoke Scottish salmon and eel from Loch Neagh, and there is a
vast cheese selection – some are local, most are from the UK, with
a few continental varieties too.

Shiprods Farm

Bashurst Hill, Slinfold, West Sussex RH13 0PD   T: 01403 790485
w: www.shiprods.co.uk

🍴 **farmers' markets** ▨ **farm gate sales**

Grass-fed Aberdeen Angus beef, hung for four weeks and butchered
on site and also lamb and mutton are available from this farm. Buy it
at eight local farmers' markets or direct from the farm, but call first.

The Swan Inn

Craven Road, Lower Green, Inkpen, Hungerford, Berkshire RG17 9DX
T: 01488 668326   w: www.theswaninn-organics.co.uk

🡇 **farm shop**

The Swan Inn is a must for those with a passion for organics.
The farm shop sells organic beef reared by the owner himself, and
organic lamb and pork from nearby farms. Chickens, fruit and
vegetables and dairy produce – again, all organic and all local.
The restaurant and pub follow with this theme – all the wines and
Champagnes served are organic, as are many of the beers.

The Isle of Wight Bacon Company

Moor Farm, Godshill, Isle of Wight PO38 3JG   T: 01983 840210
w: www.isleofwightbacon.co.uk

🍴 **farmers' markets** ✉ **mail order**

The free-range pigs at Moor Farm are reared on an additive-free diet, with humane husbandry. All cuts of pork, sausages and dry-cured bacon and ham are available.

Piggybank Farm

Hollybank, Lenham Heath Road, Sandway, Lenham, Kent ME17 2NB   T: 01622 859776
W: www.piggybank-farm.co.uk

farm gate sales **delivery service**

The Tamworth and Middle White pigs at Piggybank Farm have three acres of woodland to forage and roam in. They don't have their teeth or tails clipped and are fed on locally produced nuts. Allowed to mature to six months old, the meat is richly flavoured. Piggybank Farm will do a rare-breed hog roast for your event.

Kingsland Edwardian Butchers

140 Portobello Road, London W11 2DZ   T: 020 7727 6067

Everything at this butcher's is free-range or organic – Jacob lamb and rare-breed pork, salt-marsh lamb and Aberdeen Angus beef from Scotland, free-range chickens and free-range Bronze turkeys at Christmas.

C Lidgate

110 Holland Park Avenue, London W11 4UA   T: 020 7727 8243

Organic and/or free-range meats, some from the prestigious Gatcombe and Highgrove royal estates.

M Moen & Sons

24 The Pavement, London SW4 0JA   T: 020 7622 1624   W: www.moen.co.uk

The butchers and Moen's source meat direct from the farms, allowing them to hand pick the best that each farm offers. The meat is predominantly organic or free range, and game in season is also available.

G G Sparkes

24 Old Dover Road, Blackheath, London SE3 7BT   T: 020 8355 8597
w: www.ggsparkesorganicbutchers.com

🚚 **delivery service**

A traditional butcher's specializing in organic meats, including veal.

Stenton Family Butchers

55 Aldensley Road, Hammersmith, London W6 9PL   T: 020 8748 6121

Mr Stenton is keen to buy the meat he stocks direct from the farms and most of the farms he buys from are organic. Believing that Britain produces the best food in the world, supporting small-scale farmers is a priority for him; none of the meat in the shop is imported. A speciality is organic Welsh Black beef.

Fullers Organic Farm Shop

Manor Farm, Beachampton, Milton Keynes, Buckinghamshire MK19 6DT
T: 01908 269868   E: fullersorganics@farmline.com

🌱 **farm shop**

The Fullers are passionate about rare and native breeds and their farm shop is filled with rare-breed pork, beef, lamb and poultry (including duck and quail), all reared and butchered on site.

Head Fine Foods

135 Kingston Road, New Malden, Surrey KT3 3NX   T: 020 8942 0582

Roland Head only stocks meat from the Real Meat Company (see the Super Hero box, page 367), because he believes it is 'the best meat on the market – it addresses all the concerns the public have about meat farming'. Dry-cured bacon and home-baked pies are his specialities.

Little Warren Farm

Fletching Common, Newick, East Sussex BN8 4JH   T: 01825 722545
📭 **farm gate sales**

Organic, humanely reared veal: the calves stay with their mothers and are free-range. The cows are Jersey, so the calves have a rich Jersey milk diet, contributing to the meat's flavour. Available direct or from C H Wakeling Ltd in Godalming (see page 301).

Sussexway Meat

Home Farm, Tilgate Forest Lodge, Pease Pottage, West Sussex RH11 9AF
T: 01342 834940   W: www.sussexwaymeat.com
✉ **mail order**

Sussexway Meat is a co-operative of organic farmers, producing meat from native breeds such as Sussex and Hereford cattle, and Dorset, Suffolk and Lleyn sheep. Grass-fed all year, the animals graze amongst river meadows, wetlands and heathlands. Tamworth pork, bacon and hams are also available.

Lower Thorne Farm

Smarden Road, Pluckley, Kent TN27 0RF   T: 01233 840493
📭 **farm gate sales** ✉ **mail order**

Organic British White beef, Wiltshire Horn lamb and pork from rare-breed Tamworth pigs are joined by free-range organic chickens and turkeys at Christmas.

Ranger Organics

Holmes Oak Farm, Collins End, Goring Heath, Reading, Berkshire RG8 7RJ
T: 01491 682568
🛒 **farmers' markets**

The beef from Ranger Organics, which was commended at the 2002 Soil Association Organic Food Awards, can be from a variety of different breeds, including Aberdeen Angus, Hereford, Devon and Sussex. Theresa Whittle cuts the steaks to customers' requirements in front of them at her farmers' market stalls, ensuring they get exactly what they want. Salt beef and home-made sausages are also available – find Theresa at Notting Hill Gate farmers' market on Saturdays, and closer to home at local farmers' markets – call to find out where she'll be, or check out the Thames Valley Farmers' Market website: www.tvfm.co.uk.

SOUTH EAST   READING

Whitings Butchers

20 Coldicutt Street, Caversham, Reading RG4 8DU   T: 01189 472048

A butcher who cares passionately about animal welfare and good husbandry, Martin Howarth takes all the meat for his shop from the Real Meat Company (see the Super Hero box, page 367, for more information). Martin has visited most of the farms the meat comes from and is totally confident in his sources.

SOUTH EAST   READING

Wysipig

Ellis's Hill Farm, Sindlesham Road, Arborfield, Reading RG2 9JG   T: 0118 976 2221
w: www.wysipig.com

🡇 farm shop ✉ mail order

The rare-breed pigs at Ellis's Hill Farm are reared in family groups, with plenty of access to woodlands, a pig's natural habitat. Slowly matured, without routine antibiotics or growth promoters, the meat – from Saddlebacks, Large Blacks, Middle Whites, Gloucester Old Spots, Tamworths and Berkshires – is dark and intensely flavoured.

SOUTH EAST   RUDGWICK

Rudgwick Organic Beef & Veal

Canfields Farm, Lynwick Street, Rudgwick, West Sussex RH12 3DL   T: 01403 822219
w: www.rudgwickorganic.co.uk

🡄 farm gate sales

Organic Aberdeen Angus/Blonde crossed beef from a closed herd and welfare-friendly, free-range veal, reared naturally with their mothers, are available direct from this farm.

SOUTH EAST   SLOUGH

Ashgood Farm

Stanwell Road, Horton, Slough, Berkshire SL3 9PA   T: 01753 682063

🡇 farm shop

Ashgood Farm is a small farm shop selling home-produced Aberdeen Angus and Shorthorn cross beef, and rare-breed pork. Sausages are made on the premises and are all additive-free with a high meat content.

Fuglemere Rare Breeds

48 Northcroft, Slough, Berkshire SL2 1HR   T: 01753 642029

🗞 farmers' markets ✉ mail order

Rare-breed lamb from a variety of breeds, from the small, gamey-flavoured native types such as the Portland and the White Faced Woodland, is offered alongside traditional Portland mutton in season. All the sheep are reared on grass and home-grown barley and are hung for around a week. Longhorn beef, well marbled and hung for three weeks, is also available. Find the produce at Beaconsfield and Henley farmers' markets.

Osney Lodge Farm

Byers Lane, South Godstone, Surrey RH9 8JH   T: 01342 892216
w: www.britmeat.com

🍴 farm shop 🗞 farmers' markets ✉ mail order

The farm shop at Osney Lodge Farm acts as a permanent farmers' market, with locally produced meat, dairy, vegetables and fruit from small-scale producers. The speciality is the pedigree Sussex beef, reared on the farm itself. Slowly reared, grass-fed and hung for three weeks, this is a mature, well-marbled meat.

Uptons of Bassett

351 Winchester Road, Bassett, Southampton, Hampshire SO16 7DJ   T: 023 8039 3959

Uptons won a clutch of 2002 Great Taste Awards – for dry-cured bacon (made to the present owner's great grandfather's 1901 recipe), for air-dried ham (which can take up to a year to be ready) and for pâtés. This year, Uptons roast beef also won an award. The pork used is free-range, from a Surrey farm, and other locally produced meat is available. Game is also a strong part of the business and comes from just two local estates, where it is collected personally by the butcher.

Dairy Barn Farm Shop

North Houghton, Stockbridge, Hampshire SO20 6LF   T: 01264 811405
E: dairybarnshop@aol.com

farm shop   **mail order**

Rare-breed meat, including Dexter and Belted Galloway beef,
Saddleback pork and Manx Loaghtan and Portland lamb, is farmed
on unfertilized, herb-rich pasture and available from the farm shop
or mail order.

A G Millers

152 Waldegrave Road, Teddington, Middlesex TW11 8NA   T: 020 8977 2753
W: www.agmillers.com

All the meat at Miller's comes from the Real Meat Company (see the
Super Hero box, page 367, for more information), so the butchers
here are confident that the beef comes from farms that have never
had a reported case of BSE, and from animals that have been
reared without routine antibiotics or growth promoters.

M Newitt & Sons

10 High Street, Thame, Oxfordshire OX9 2BZ   T: 01844 212103   W: www.newitt.co.uk

Newitt's were named Britain's Best Butcher in 2002 and also
scooped 23 medals out of a possible 24 at the International Meat
Awards at Utrecht in 2003. The meat they sell is sourced direct from
farms personally visited by the Newitt family.

Evans & Paget

Stark House Farm, Goose Hill, Headley, Thatcham, Berkshire RG19 8AR
T: 01635 268205

farmers' markets   **farm gate sales**

Grazing on unsprayed fields, the Hereford cattle at Stark House
Farm mature slowly. The meat is matured well on the bone before
traditional butchering. Saddleback pork is also produced on the
farm, from a free-range herd. Find Evans & Paget at Andover,
Basingstoke, Newbury and Winchester farmers' markets.

The Real Meat Company

4 Mill Walk, Wheathamstead, Hertfordshire AL4 8DT   T: 01582 834656
w: www.realmeat.co.uk

Selling only welfare-friendly, drug-free meat from the Real Meat
Company, this traditional butcher's will cut all the meat according
to customers' requirements. A full range of meats is available here:
free-range chicken, pork, beef and lamb are all produced without
routine antibiotics or hormones. See the Super Hero box, page 367,
for more information about The Real Meat Company.

J Wickens Family Butchers

Castle Street, Winchelsea Town, East Sussex TN36 4HU   T: 01797 226287

The speciality at Wickens is Sussex beef, sourced from just one
local farm – a fine-grained, well-marbled and sweet-tasting meat.

Hepburns of Mountnessing

269 Roman Road, Mountnessing, Brentwood, Essex CM15 0UH   T: 01277 353289

A Q Guild award-winner, Hepburn's maple-cured bacon (a unique
recipe) won at the 2002 Smithfield Awards. Some interesting meats
are available here – beef reared on the butcher's own farm, local
pork and award-winning smoked gammon.

Longwood Farm

Tuddenham, Bury St Edmunds, Suffolk IP28 6TB   T: 01638 717120
E: longwoodorganics@hotmail.com
⬥ farm shop

Longwood Farm has been organic for 12 years and produces
organic South Devon beef, Saddleback pork, lamb and free-range
chickens, all allowed to grow slowly at a natural pace. Open on
Wednesdays, Fridays and Saturdays, the on-site farm shop also
stocks local organic vegetables, locally baked organic bread, a huge
range of organic groceries, and organic turkeys and geese at
Christmas.

Better Beef

Fenton House, Conington, Cambridge CB3 8LN   T: 01954 267615
W: www.betterbeef.co.uk

🏠 **farm gate sales**

The Burgesses rear the very rare Gloucester beef, hanging the mature, marbled meat for a full four weeks before sale. Fed on grass and home-produced hay, the cattle are allowed to mature at their own pace before being taken to a local abattoir. Meat is not always available – phone to check first. Better Beef is a member of the Gloucester Cattle Association.

P & S Cruickshank

10 South Street, Comberton, Cambridge CB3 7DZ   T: 01223 262212

One of the largest selections of rare-breed meats in the country, including some difficult to find breeds such as Castlemilk Moorit lamb and Gloucester beef can be found at Cruickshank's.

Buntings Butchers

18 Church Street, Coggeshall, Essex CO6 1TU   T: 01376 561233

A traditional butcher's with a selection of rare-breed meat from mainly local farms, including Jacob lamb, Gloucester beef and Gloucester Old Spot pork. There is another branch in Maldon (see page 312).

Weylands Farm

Stoke by Nayland, Colchester, Essex CO6 4SR   T: 01206 337283
E: fweylands@aol.com

🏠 **farm gate sales**

Pork from the rare Large Black Suffolk pigs, slow-reared for an intensely flavoured meat, is available from Weylands Farm; call for details.

Ash Farm Organics

Ash Farm, Stone Lane, Bintree, Dereham, Norfolk NR20 5NA   T: 01362 683228
W: www.ashfarmorganics.co.uk

⟶ **farm shop**

Saddleback cross pork and bacon, beef, lamb and chicken are all organically reared on home-grown feed. The farm also holds occasional open days with trailer rides so that customers can see the animals and see how the farm works.

The Sausage Shop

45 Bull Street, Holt, Norfolk NR25 6HP   T: 01263 7122255

The Sausage Shop stocks the extensive range of meats supplied by Tavern Tasty Meats of North Walsham – see page 312 for details.

Monach Farms

The Green, Hilton, Huntingdon, Cambridgeshire PE28 9NB   T: 01480 830426
W: www.monachfarm.co.uk

⟚ **farm gate sales**

Old-fashioned traditional husbandry and slow-growing rare breeds produce great eating qualities in the meat from Monach Farms. Dexter and Highland beef, Shetland lamb and mutton and even pure-bred goat meat are available direct from the farm. There is also a farmshop in Langenhoe (see page 312).

Baylham House Rare Breeds Farm

Mill Lane, Baylham, nr Ipswich, Suffolk IP6 8LG   T: 01473 830264
W: www.baylham-house-farm.co.uk

⟚ **farm gate sales**

Traditionally reared, rare-breed lamb from a variety of breeds – Castlemilk Moorit, Grey-Faced Dartmoor, Herdwick and Norfolk Horn to mention just a few. The lambs are reared on additive-free feed and grass. Mutton and Large Black pork and bacon are also available. Call to get on to the customer list.

Monach Farm

Butterfly Lodge, Smithfields, Mersea Road, Langenhoe, Essex CO5 7LG
T: 07951 703909
⬦ **farm shop**

For details, see under Monach Farms (Huntington) on page 311.

Buntings Butchers

89 High Street, Maldon, Essex CM9 5EP   T: 01621 853271

This is the sister branch to Buntings in Coggeshall (see page 310),
which specializes in organic meats. Beef, lamb and pork, along with
free-range organic poultry, is available.

Tavern Tasty Meats

The Farm Shop, The Street, Swafield, North Walsham, Norfolk NR28 0PG
T: 01692 405444   W: www.taverntasty.co.uk
⬦ **farm shop** ⬛ **farmers' markets**

A really wide range of rare-breed meats is all either home-reared or
from small-scale local producers. All the meats are extensively and
traditionally reared and you can find them at farmers' markets in
Norfolk as well as at the farm shop. There is also an outlet, The
Sausage Shop, in Holt (see page 311).

Emmett's Store

Peasenhall, Saxmundham, Suffolk IP17 2HJ   T: 01728 660250
E: emmettsham@aol.com

This fine food store has an array of interesting produce, from olives
through fresh vegetables to chocolates, but the real star is their
sweet pickled ham and bacon. Locally produced pork is pickled in
molasses and beer and then traditionally smoked; it has a Royal
Warrant from the late Queen Mother as an endorsement.

Red Poll Beef

Botany Farm, Farnham, Saxmundham, Suffolk IP17 1QZ   T: 01728 688166
E: redpolls@btinternet.com

≛ **farmers' markets** ⊠ **farm gate sales**

Botany Farm is currently in conversion to organic status and specializes exclusively in indigenous Red Poll beef – a breed renowned for finely grained, moist meat. It is available direct from the farm or from Felixstowe, Royston, Newmarket, Shelford and Woodbridge farmers' markets.

Steeple Wick Farming Company

Steeple Wick Farm, Stansgate Road, Steeple, Essex CM0 7LQ   T: 01621 773368
E: steeplewickfarm@aol.com

⊠ **farm gate sales**

A great selection of rare breeds is reared on this farm, grazing on conservation land. The farm has an open policy – visitors are welcome to see the animals. The meat is only available directly from the farm.

Five Winds Farm Smokehouse and Butchery

The Station, Melton, Woodbridge, Suffolk IP12 1LS   T: 01394 461481
W: www.fivewindsfarm.com

⊯ **farm shop**

Five Winds Farm has recently won an award for its bacon cured in Guinness and black treacle. The bacon comes from local free-range pork. Smoked Suffolk ham and black sweet pickled ham are also available, along with smoked free-range chicken, local fish and a full range of game.

Barkers

West Farm, Ruckley, nr Acton Burnell, Shropshire SY5 7HR   T: 01694 731318

≛ **farmers' markets** ⊠ **farm gate sales**

Sue Barker rears rare-breed Large Black pigs using old-fashioned husbandry – no teeth or nail clipping, no castration, a natural organic diet and access to pasture all year. She then makes sausages using traditional skins, and dry-cured bacon. Lamb comes from the primitive North Ronaldsay breed, producing a gamey meat, and beef is Dexter, a mature, well-marbled meat.

Picks Organic Farm Shop

The Cottage, Hamilton Grounds, King Street, Barkby Thorpe, Leicestershire LE7 3QF
T: 0116 269 3548

🖒 **farm shop**

Slowly matured Dexter beef, Gloucester Old Spot pork, lamb, chicken, Aylesbury ducks, guineafowl and turkeys at Christmas are all organic, all home-produced at Picks. The farm shop also stocks local organic vegetables and dairy produce, and has an on-site tea shop.

M Finn Butchers

17 Stanton Road, Great Barr, Birmingham B43 5QT   T: 0121 357 5780

✉ **mail order**

Vaughan Meers of M Finn is keen to stock extensively reared, chemical-free meat and offers free-range chickens, wild boar and properly hung beef and lamb, all from local farms. Staffordshire Black dry-cured bacon is a speciality.

F C Phipps

Osborne House, Mareham-Le-Fen, Boston, Lincolnshire PE22 7RW   T: 01507 568235
w: www.britainsbestbutcher.co.uk

✉ **mail order**

F C Phipps offers a good choice of rare-breed meats and poultry, including the famous Lincoln Red beef. Lincolnshire Chine (cured shoulder ham stuffed with parsley) is also available.

S & A Rossiter

247 Maryvale Road, Bournville, West Midlands B30 1PN   T: 0121 458 1598

A real find for anyone passionate about organics, Rossiter's stock locally produced organic meat from farms personally known to the butcher, and also cheese, eggs, bread, including locally made organic Italian specialities, fish, including organic trout and salmon, and home-made sausages and charcuterie.

A Johnson & Son

1 Hadley Street, Yoxall, Burton-on-Trent, Staffordshire DE13 8NB   T: 01543 472235
E: yoxallbutcher@aol.com

John Bailey is passionate about his work and stocks some really interesting meats, including great rare-breed beef, pork and lamb and even seaweed-fed lamb from Scotland. Because John uses mainly local farmers and his own slaughterhouse, the meat is fully traceable. John was voted Butcher of the Year in 2002 by the RBST. The shop also stocks around 40 different British farmhouse cheeses, and has a good deli section.

Lower Hurst Farm

Hartington, nr Buxton, Derbyshire SK17 0HJ   T: 01298 84900
W: www.lowerhurstfarm.co.uk
✉ farm gate sales   ✉ mail order

Organic Hereford beef is allowed to grow slowly at Lower Hurst Farm and is hung for three weeks after slaughter. Every piece of meat is supplied to the customer with an ID pack, guaranteeing full traceability. Organic lamb is also available.

Aubrey Allen Ltd

Curriers Close, Canley, Coventry CV4 8AW   T: 02476 422222
W: www.aubreyallen.co.uk
🛒 shop   ✉ mail order

A very well established butchers, now being run by the third generation of the same family that founded the business. Specialities include Aberdeen beef, matured on the bone for three weeks, award-winning sausages made only with free-range pork, free-range, corn-fed chickens, and a full range of game.

Berkswell Traditional Farmstead Meats

The Farm Shop, Larges Farm, Back Lane, Meriden, nr Coventry, Warwickshire CV7 7LD
T: 01676 522409

🠖 **farm shop**

All kinds of rare-breed meat are available here, butchered to order.
The staff know where everything has come from and will happily
explain all the details to customers. Dry-cured bacon, sausages
and burgers are also available, all made on the premises.

D W Wall & Son

Corvedale Road, Craven Arms, Shropshire SY7 9NL   T: 01588 672308
w: www.wallsbutchers.co.uk

With over 90% of their meat being rare breed, Wall & Son really are
specialists. They offer a fantastic selection of breeds, including the
very difficult to find Irish Moiled beef, hung for a month for a mature
flavour. Most of the meat is from nearby farms, including the free-
range chicken. There is also a branch in Ludlow (see page 322).

Checketts of Ombersley

Ombersley, Droitwich, Worcestershire WR9 0EW   T: 01905 620284
w: www.checketts.co.uk

The Checketts have been in the butchery business for over 100
years and have won many awards for their products. The emphasis
here is on meat sourced from local farmers with whom they have
built lasting relationships. Game is also available in season and can
include pheasant, partridge, wild duck, hare and rabbit.

Detton Beef and Lamb

Detton Hall Farm, Little Detton, Cleobury Mortimer, Kidderminster, Worcestershire
DY14 8LW   T: 01299 270173   w: www.detton.co.uk

🠖 **farmers' markets**   🠖 **farm gate sales**   ✉ **mail order**

Grass-fed beef from steers only (no bull beef, which is sometimes
considered to have a tainted flavour), is reared extensively on this
traditional family farm. Hung for three weeks, the beef is mature but

lean. Lamb is also available, direct from the farm, by mail order or from Bewdley, Kidderminster, Bromsgrove and Stourbridge farmers' markets. Detton is a member of Heart of England Fine Foods.

Chantry Farm Shop

Kings Newton Lane, Kings Newton, Derbyshire DE73 1DD   T: 01332 865698

🢗 **farm shop**

Although not certified organic, most of the rare-breed meat sold here is sourced through the RBST or comes from the farm itself. Beef is hung for over three weeks to enhance the traditional flavour.

Routledge's Butchers

182 Nuncargate Road, Kirkby-in-Ashfield, Nottinghamshire NG17 9EA
T: 01623 753267   W: www.routledges-butchers.co.uk

Beef from local farms at Routledge's is well marbled and from rare breeds such as Hereford. The butcher uses rare-breed pork (Gloucester Old Spot) for his home-made, dry-cured bacon. There is also an outlet in Nottingham (see page 323)

Meynell Langley Farm Shop

Meynell Langley, Kirk Langley, Derbyshire DE6 4NT   T: 01332 824815

🢗 **farm shop**

Organic Welsh Black beef, Cheviot lamb and chickens are produced on the farm for sale in the farm shop. All the breeds are chosen specifically for their slow-growing nature and good flavour. Organic pork from a neighbouring farm is also available, and organic turkeys and geese are available to order at Christmas.

John Miles Traditional Breeds Butcher

21 The Homend, Ledbury, Herefordshire HR8 1BN   T: 01531 632744
W: www.johnmiles.co.uk

John Miles is happy to tell you exactly where each cut of meat in his shop came from – almost all from local farms, most within 10 miles. A huge range of traditional-breed meat is available.

Heards of Wigston

69 Long Street, Wigston, Leicester LE18 2AJ   T: 0116 288 0444

Heards source their meat direct from local farms and will happily arrange for customers to visit the farms to see the animals in situ. The meat is free-range and drug-free, some certified organic and some from rare or traditional breeds, such as the Gloucester Old Spot pigs.

Quenby Hall Organic Foods

nr Hungarton, Leicester LE7 9JF   T: 0116 259 5224   w: www.quenbybeef.co.uk
farm gate sales

English Longhorn cattle are a rare breed associated with the East Midlands since the 18th century. Freddie de Lisle rears them outside on grass all year round and the beef is then hung on the bone for three weeks. A variety of vacuum-packed cuts, from a minimum quantity of 10kg upwards, is available direct from the farm, but phone first.

The Real Meat Company

8 Allandale Road, Stoneygate, Leicester LE2 2DA   T: 0116 270 3396
w: www.realmeat.co.uk

The butcher here has been in the business for 40 years and made the decision to stock only Real Meat Company meat because he was so concerned about standards in the majority of meat production. He firmly believes that good husbandry and attention to welfare issues makes for better meat and is proud of the meat he sells. See the Super Hero box, page 367, for more information about The Real Meat Company.

Michael F Wood

51 Hartopp Road, Leicester LE2 1WG   T: 0116 270 5194   w: www.mfwood.co.uk

There is plenty of organic meat to choose from here, from small local producers whom the butcher has personally visited to inspect. Beef traditionally hung for three weeks and dry-cured bacon are a couple of the specialities.

Curtis of Lincoln

Long Leys Road, Lincoln LN1 1DX   T: 01522 527212

✉ **mail order**

A long-established Lincolnshire butcher, Curtis is famous for the regional speciality, Lincolnshire Chine, a cured shoulder ham stuffed with parsley.

Elite Meats

89 Bailgate, Lincoln LN1 3AR   T: 01522 523500

Plenty of locally produced meats are available here, including the native Lincoln Red beef. Hung for three weeks, this beef is slowly reared on grass all year. Organic pork, free-range, corn-fed chicken and lamb all come from nearby farms.

Henclose Farm Organic Produce

Henclose Farm, Little Dewchurch, Hereford HR2 6PP   T: 01432 840826

☞ **farm gate sales**

Registered organic for 23 years, Henclose Farm produces Jacob cross lamb, Gloucester Old Spot/Berkshire cross pork, bacon and sausages, kid meat, and goats' milk, and free-range eggs, all organic. This is a very small farm, and produce is not always available, so phone first to check.

Home Farm Organics

Home Farm, Woodhouse Lane, Nanpantan, Loughborough, Leicestershire LE11 3YG
T: 01509 237064   W: www.growingconcern.co.uk

⬇ **farm shop** 🏠 **farmers' markets**

A family-run farm shop, selling meat only from their own land. Lots of rare-breed meat here, all fully traceable, properly hung and matured. The on-site café/restaurant, Beth's Kitchen, serves food from the farm. Find the produce at Stratford-upon-Avon, Leicester, Hinckley and Loughborough farmers' markets.

food facts

ORGANIC MEAT

It is relevant to mention the organic movement in relation to meat production. Respect for animal welfare is a crucial factor in the production of safe, good-quality meat and in the prevention of the spread of disastrous diseases such as BSE and foot-and-mouth disease. Compassion in World Farming, a UK-based operation campaigning to end factory farming, say that the Soil Association's regulations in meat production are the most stringent, and the highest in terms of animal welfare in the UK. Feed must be free from animal byproducts, antibiotics and growth promoters. The animals must have access to fields (themselves unsprayed with chemicals) and be able to express their natural behaviour. Travelling to abattoirs is kept to a minimum. Farms are encouraged to be diverse, with mixed species, which is better for the environment, and organically raised animals must be kept separate from those reared conventionally.

Equally, biodynamic farms are producing great meat. A biodynamic farm is an organic one taken a little further and run entirely holistically – it will be a mixed farm, where balance and harmony with nature is strived for. Closed herds are a key feature of biodynamics and this means every animal is totally traceable, often back through several generations. On a biodynamic farm planting and harvesting are conducted according to a strict calendar and the farm is treated as a self-contained organism with any inputs kept to an absolute minimum. Many of the producers we list are Soil Association or Demeter (biodynamic) accredited and many more, though not accredited, farm to the Soil Association's standards.

MIDLANDS   **LOUGHBOROUGH**

Manor Farm

77 Main Street, Long Whatton, Loughborough, Leicestershire LE12 5DF
T: 01509 646413   w: www.manororganicfarm.co.uk
⤖ farm shop ᙏ box scheme

Organic vegetables are cut freshly every morning for the farm shop at Manor Farm; home-reared Longhorn beef, Lleyn lamb (both entirely grass-fed), alongside pork from a neighbouring farm are all on offer. Manor Farm operates a box scheme in Loughborough. New for 2004 was an on-farm bakery, using wheat grown on the farm.

MEAT

Stephen Morris Butchers

26–27 High Street, Loughborough, Leicestershire LE11 2PZ   T: 01509 215260

Stephen Morris specializes in organic and biodynamic meats, mainly sourced from one local biodynamic farm, where the meat is hand-picked by the butcher. The meat is all traditionally reared for an old-fashioned flavour.

Lakings of Louth

33 Eastgate, Louth, Lincolnshire LN11 9NB   T: 01507 603186

Lakings is a traditional butcher's that specializes in local meat; signs tell the customer exactly where each piece of meat has come from. They also stock a full range of local game in season.

Orleton Farm Shop

Overton Farm, Orleton, nr Ludlow, Shropshire SY8 4HZ   T: 01568 780750
W: www.orletonfarmshop.co.uk
⬇ **farm shop**

Winner of the National Farmer's Union Great British Food Award, Orleton Farm Shop sells its own organic Aberdeen Angus beef, lamb and poultry. Also available are vegetables and fruit from nearby farms.

G & R Tudge

The Bury, Richards Castle, Ludlow, Shropshire SY8 4EL   T: 01584 831227
W: www.tudge-meats.co.uk
🚍 **farmers' markets**

The Tudge family rear rare-breed Tamworth and Berkshire pigs, freely ranging in small family groups. The pigs are reared on GM-, antibiotic- and growth-promoter-free feed. Dry-cured bacon and ham are available as well as joints. Free-range chicken from slowly growing breeds is also on offer; all the produce can be found at Hereford, Ludlow, Leominster, Malvern and Abergavenny farmers' markets.

D W Wall & Son

14 High Street, Ludlow, Shropshire SY8 1BS   T: 01584 872060

For details, see under the Craven Arms branch on page 316.

Malvern Country Meals

37 Church Street, Malvern, Worcestershire WR14 2AA   T: 01684 568498

✉ **mail order**

Rare-breed and free-range meats from local farms and award-winning sausages are on offer at the shop or by mail order.

Corvedale Organic Lamb

Corve House, Rowe Lane, Stanton Long, Much Wenlock, Shropshire TF13 6LR
T: 01746 712539   W: www.corvedale.com

🚚 **delivery service**

Paul Mantle rears the large Suffolk sheep, a breed you are unlikely to find in supermarkets as they do not fit within the size restrictions supermarkets impose. The lambs graze parkland rich in herbs, wild garlic and wild grasses and Paul feels this benefits the flavour of the meat. Available through a delivery round in Ludlow – call for details.

Wenlock Edge Farm

Longville-in-the-Dale, Much Wenlock, Shropshire TF13 6DU   T: 01694 771203
W: www.wenlockedgefarm.com

🥄 **farm shop**

Customers at Wenlock Edge can watch the home-reared pork being transformed into dry-cured bacon or sausages while they shop at the farm. There is a good range of charcuterie, including prosciutto, salami and air-dried ham. Home-reared lamb and beef from a neighbouring farm are also available.

MEAT

Routledge's Butchers

195 Main Street, Newthorp, Nottingham NG16 2DL
T: 01773 712188   w: www.routledges-butchers.co.uk

Beef from local farms at Routledge's is well marbled and from
rare breeds such as Hereford. The butcher uses rare-breed pork
(Gloucester Old Spot) for his home-made, dry-cured bacon. There
is also an outlet at Kirkby-in-Ashfield (see page 317).

Northfield Farm

Whissendine Lane, Cold Overton, nr Oakham, Rutland LE15 7QF   T: 01664 474271
w: www.northfieldfarm.com
🠖 **farm shop** ✉ **mail order**

Fantastic rare- and traditional-breed meats, including home-reared
Dexter beef. The staff will happily tell you the breed, age and diet of
any of the meat they have on offer. As well as the shop and mail
order Northfield Farm sells at Borough Market, London SE1.

Huntsham Farm – Pedigree Meats

Goodrich, Ross-on-Wye, Herefordshire HR9 6JN   T: 01600 890296
w; www.huntsham.com
✉ **mail order**

Properly hung meat from Middle White pigs, Ryeland lamb and
Longhorn beef, all chosen for their taste and texture.

G N F & G A Browning

Feldon Forest Farm, Frankton, Rugby, Warwickshire CV23 9PD,   T: 01926 632246
w: www.feldon-forest-farm.co.uk
🠖 **farm gate sales (by appointment)**

All kinds of organic goodies are available here, the speciality being
rare-breed meats from Shetland cattle and Castlemilk Moorit sheep.
Organic strawberries, other fruit and various vegetables are also
available in season, along with eggs, wool and sheepskins, and the
very rare Shetland beef.

Ted's Meat, the Traditional Taste of Shropshire

Hungerhill Farm, Sherrifhales, nr Shifnal, Shropshire TF11 8SA   T: 01952 461146
W: www.tedsbeef.co.uk

⬂ **farm shop**

Rare-breed and native meats – from Aberdeen Angus, Longhorn and
Hereford cattle, free-range Large Black pigs and local lamb – are all
reared for an old-fashioned flavour and texture. Hand-made
sausages and dry-cured bacon are also available. All produce is
available from the farm shop or home delivery can be arranged.

Curradine Angus

Church Farm, Shrawley, Worcestershire WR6 6TS   T: 01905 620283
W: www.farmhouseflora.com

⬂ **farm shop**

Pure-bred Aberdeen Angus beef from cattle born on the farm and
grass-fed all year is hung for at least two weeks and so has a
traditional, well-marbled texture. Ready meals are also available.

Maynards Farm Bacon   super hero

Hough Farm, Weston-under-Redcastle, Shrewsbury, Shropshire SY4 5LR
T: 01948 840252   W: www.maynardsfarm.co.uk

✉ **mail order**

An ever-increasing range of at least ten varieties of bacon cured to
traditional regional recipes is available here. See the Super Hero
box, opposite, for more information.

Hockerton Grange Farm Shop

Hockerton Grange, Hockerton, nr Southwell, Nottinghamshire NG25 0PJ
T: 01636 816472

⬂ **farm shop** ✉ **mail order**

Locally produced rare-breed meats, such as native Lincoln Red
beef, Gloucester Old Spot, Large Black and Tamworth pork, and
South Down, Ryeland, Soay and Hebridean lamb, are all sourced
from nearby farms that pay particular attention to animal welfare.

super hero

ROB AND FIONA CUNNINGHAM, of Maynards Farm Bacon, Shrewsbury
(see opposite)

Rob Cunningham has a fascination with bacon; to him, it is not just the ubiquitous essential for a cooked breakfast – it is the expression of a 17th-century craft and an evocation of a region. Dry-curing the local free-range pork into bacon is not a simple task at Maynards. There are any number of cures to choose from, from the Welsh Black recipe, strong and hearty, to the local Shropshire Mild, with spices and coriander. The current range stands at around ten regional curing recipes but Rob and his wife, Fiona, are searching for more and have added a variety of smoked bacons and hams to their selection. Starting with good local pork and continuing with such attention to detail (it takes about a month to transform pork into bacon using the traditional cures) results in bacon that is a far cry from the floppy, watery specimens we are more likely to come across from factory farming. Maynards' bacon does not sizzle with excess moisture in the pan. 'The sound it makes is more like a contented murmur,' states Rob.

MIDLANDS   **STANFORD BRIDGE**

Happy Meats

Bank House Farm, Stanford Bridge, Worcestershire WR6 6RU   T: 01886 812485
w: www.happymeats.co.uk

🍖 **farm shop**   🏷 **farmers' markets**   ✉ **mail order**

Traditional tasty meat as it used to be is reared on this farm where animal welfare comes first. Rare-breed pork, lamb and beef from this small, sustainable Teme Valley farm is all free-range, fed on locally produced food with no additives, growth promoters, antibiotics or GM ingredients. The animals are old, traditional rare breeds, so they take longer to mature but the taste is well worth the wait. Most of the pork is Gloucester Old Spot and the beef Long Horn and Dexter. There is also grass-fed hogget and mutton, home-dry-cured bacon and sausages with none of the usual preservatives or colouring. In season there is wild venison, pheasant and partridge and non-farmed fish, which is smoked in a traditional oak smokehouse.

food facts

BEEF AND VEAL

The beef we often see is bright red, wet-looking meat with little evidence of fat. When you buy from some of our listed producers, you might be surprised by the dark colour of the meat, the marbling of fat running through the cut and the closely grained texture. This is meat that has been properly hung for three or four weeks, vital for the development of flavour and for a tender cooked meat, from breeds chosen specifically for their eating qualities and decent fat cover. It is fat that keeps all meat moist in cooking and adds immeasurably to the flavour; even if you choose not to eat it, it is so important that it is allowed to remain on the meat for cooking. Breeds such as the Lincoln Red, White Park, Hereford and Red Poll can all provide fantastic-quality beef.

Many of our producers insist that their beef is entirely grass-fed, so the animals graze on rich, fresh pasture for most of the year, with hay or silage for the winter months, not concentrated feed. Grass-fed beef will not only taste better, but it is better for you, with higher levels of the healthier polyunsaturated fatty acids than the unhealthier, saturated kind. It also contains a substance called conjugated linoleic acid, which enables our bodies to break down fatty acids more efficiently.

We also feature a couple of producers who rear veal in a welfare-friendly fashion, allowing us to enjoy this delicacy with a clearer conscience. The method known as *veaux de lait élevé sous la mère*, allows the calf to stay with its mother, free-range, suckling her rich milk until it's weaned. The producers are adamant that this results in a far higher quality of meat. As with all the meat producers in this book, beef farmers rearing with great respect for their livestock, and an unhurried attitude, are producing great results.

NORTH WEST   APPLEBY-IN-WESTMORLAND

Barwise Aberdeen Angus

Barwise Hall, Hoff, Appleby-in-Westmorland, Cumbria CA16 6TD   T: 01768 353430
E: barwise@btinternet.com
🚚 **delivery service** ✉ **mail order**

Pedigree Aberdeen Angus beef, grass-fed and traditionally reared and hung for three weeks to mature on the bone. Available in boxes of mixed cuts or as single joints – phone for details.

Bromley Green Farm

Ormside, Appleby-in-Westmorland, Cumbria CA16 6EJ   T: 01768 353327

🔲 farmers' markets 🔲 farm gate sales

Norma Thompson rears Aberdeen Angus cattle, which are grass-fed in summer and have hay and silage grown on the farm in winter. A local slaughterhouse and butcher are used and, after hanging, the meat is available direct from the farm or at any one of the seven local farmers' markets Norma attends – call for details.

Border County Foods

The Old Vicarage, Crosby-on-Eden, Carlisle, Cumbria CA6 4QZ   T: 01228 573500
w: www.cumberland-sausage.net

🔲 farmers' markets 🔲 mail order

Traditional Cumberland sausage, made with home-reared, rare-breed pork – Gloucester Old Spot, Tamworth, Saddleback ... the list goes on! The pigs are reared extensively, outside whenever weather allows. Dry-cured bacon is available and 'real' black pudding. Austen, the sausage-maker, is a vigorous campaigner for a relaxation in the laws governing the making of black pudding. Currently, makers are forced to use dried blood, usually from abroad. Austen uses fresh and told me that it makes a huge difference to the quality of the pudding. All the products are available at many farmers' markets in the north of England or by mail order.

Hallsford Farm Produce

Hethersgill, Carlisle, Cumbria CA6 6JD   T: 01288 577329   w: www.hallsford.co.uk

🔲 farmers' markets 🔲 mail order

Well-marbled and mature shorthorn beef, rare-breed Llanwenog and Herdwick lamb and rare-breed pork from two upland family farms north of Hadrian's Wall in Cumbria, reared extensively and finished largely on grass and clover. The animals are slaughtered locally and butchered on site. Available by mail order or from Carlisle farmers' market.

Whiteholme Farm

Roweltown, Carlisle, Cumbria CA6 6LJ   T: 01697 748058   W: www.whiteholmefarm.co.uk
✉ **farm gate sales** 🚚 **delivery service** ✉ **mail order**

Black Faced lamb, Saddleback pork, free-range poultry and
Galloway Blue-Grey beef are all reared slowly and organically at
Whiteholme. All the butchery is carried out on the farm, which has
Countryside Stewardship status and belongs to Cumbria Organics –
the Perkin family are dedicated to sustainable farming and
conservation. All the meat, as well as local organic vegetables,
is available direct from the farm or through the local delivery round.

Keer Falls Forest Farm

Arkholme, Carnforth, Lancashire LA6 1AP   T: 01524 221019   W: www.keerfalls.co.uk
✉ **farm gate sales** 🚚 **delivery service**

Keer Falls Farm is an organic farm where attention to the welfare of
the livestock is paramount. White Faced Woodland lamb, Aberdeen
Angus beef, free-range mallard ducks and a choice of organic herbs
are all available through farm gate sales, or a local delivery round.

The Manx Loaghtan Marketing Co-operative Ltd

Ballaloaghtan, Kerrowkeil Road, Grenaby, Isle of Man IM9 3BB   T: 07624 492850
W: www.manxloaghtan.com
✉ **mail order**

Slow-maturing, primitive breed Manx Loaghtan lamb is slow-growing
(slaughtered at around 18 months, compared to around four to six
for other breeds) and the finely grained meat has a gamey flavour,
with less fat and cholesterol than conventional lamb.

Aireys Farm Shop

RBST
Rare Breeds Survival Trust

Snowdrop Villa, Ayside, Grange-over-Sands, Cumbria LA11 6JE   T: 01539 531237
🛒 **farm shop**

Although conventional meat is sold here, the specialities are home-
reared, rare-breed meats – Angus and Hereford beef, reared by the

owner, and Gloucester Old Spot, Middle White and Saddleback pork, reared on a nearby farm.

Savin Hill Farm

Savin Hill, Lyth Valley, Kendal, Cumbria LA8 8DJ   T: 01539 568410
w: www.savin-hill.co.uk
≈ farmers' markets ✉ mail order

Beef from pure-bred British White cattle and pork from pure Middle White pigs, ranging free at the farm throughout the summer months and bedded on straw, housed in purpose-built buildings during the wetter, colder season. The animals are fed a GM-free diet and no artificial fertilizers are used on the land. Find the produce at specialist food events nationally and regional farmers' markets. Check the website for details.

Yew Tree Farm

Rosthwaite, Borrowdale, Keswick, Cumbria CA12 5XB   T: 01768 777675
w: www.borrowdaleherdwick.co.uk
⬇ farm shop ✉ mail order

Slowly growing Herdwick lamb is the speciality of Yew Tree Farm. This is a breed native to Cumbria, not ready for eating until it is at least a year old (conventional lamb is often eaten at three months). Reared all year on the fells, it has a gamey flavour, and looks like venison. There is an on-site tearoom selling meals made with the lamb.

Kitridding Farm Shop

Lupton, nr Kirkby Lonsdale, Cumbria LA6 2QA   T: 01539 567484
E: christine@kitridding.co.uk
⬇ farm shop

Really local produce is available at this farm shop; most of the foods stocked are from within a five-mile radius. The ethos of the Lambert family is to encourage customers to rediscover traditional, local foods, and Kitridding Farm produces its own beef, and Swaledale lamb, home-made sausages and home-cured bacon.

Lune Valley

Nether Hall, Kirkby Lonsdale, Cumbria LA6 2EW   T: 01524 273193
w: www.rearednaturally.co.uk

✉ **mail order**

A wide choice of meat cuts from extensively reared livestock – beef, lamb and free-range pork. The Kelly family use a local abattoir and all the meat is traceable.

Mansergh Hall Farm

Mansergh Hall, Kirkby Lonsdale, Lancashire LA6 2EN   T: 01524 271397
w: www.manserghhall.co.uk

🖢 **farm shop** ✉ **mail order**

This farm shop sells home-reared lamb and Aberdeen Angus beef, grass-fed on clover-rich pasture all year and hung properly after slaughter. Jim Hadwin, the farmer, bases his business on honesty with his customers – he'll tell you exactly how the animals have been reared.

Farmer Sharp

Pennington Lane, Lindal-in-Furness, Cumbria LA12 0LA   T: 01229 588299
w: www.farmersharp.co.uk

🏪 **farmers' markets** ✉ **mail order**

Farmer Sharp is a co-operative of Cumbrian farmers producing the native Herdwick lamb. The sheep are reared on the fells and have an unusual gamey flavour and a closely textured meat. Air-dried Heldwick mutton is a speciality, and Cumbrian Galloway beef and rose veal are available. In addition to mail order, meat can be bought at Borough Market, London SE1.

Richard Woodall

Lane End, Waberthwaite, nr Millom, Cumbria LA19 5YJ   T: 01229 717237 OR
01229 717386   w: www.richardwoodall.co.uk

✉ **mail order**

Legendary air-dried Cumbrian ham, Cumberland sausages, pancetta and bacon, all made from pigs reared on the farm, which focusses particularly on animal welfare.

Brookshaws of Nantwich

8–10 Hospital Street, Nantwich, Cheshire CW5 5RJ   T: 01270 625302
w: www.brookshaws.co.uk

Aberdeen Angus beef, hung for three weeks, Gloucester Old Spot pork and saltmarsh lamb from Wales are some of the treats available at Brookshaws, as well as a good choice of local game.

Greystone House

Stainton, Penrith, Cumbria CA11 OEF   T: 01768 866952
⌣ farm shop

Marjorie Dawson enthusiastically runs this award-winning farm shop, stocking home-reared Galloway beef and lamb, home-grown organic vegetables and home-made cakes. There is also a café upstairs. Open every day.

The Old Smokehouse & Truffles Chocolates

Brougham Hall, Brougham, Penrith, Cumbria CA10 2DE   T: 01768 867772
w: www.the-old-smokehouse.co.uk
⌣ farmers' markets ⌣ shop

The Old Smokehouse, one of the smallest smokehouses in the country, recently changed hands, but the new owner, Richard Muirhead, is busy upholding the Old Smokehouse's tradition of winning Great Taste Awards, including a gold medal this year for the Fellman sausage. A wonderful range of foods is smoked here, from local lamb and venison to a variety of cheeses and salmon from the Shetland Isles. Hand-made chocolates are also on offer.

FOOD HEROES OF BRITAIN

Slacks of Cumbria

Newlands Farm, Raisbeck, Orton, Penrith, Cumbria CA10 3SG   T: 01539 624667
E: slacks@fsbdial.co.uk

✉ **mail order**

Slacks produce very old-fashioned dry-cured bacon, produced from locally sourced pigs, which are fed on whey to enhance the flavour. The pigs are antibiotic- and growth-promoter-free. The bacon is cured and then air-dried in a four-week process, giving an intense flavour and no nasty white residue in the pan.

Stoneyhead Pork

Stoneyhead Hall Farm, Sunbiggin, Orton, Penrith, Cumbria CA10 3SQ   T: 01539 624456

▭ **farmers' markets**

Pork from a wide selection of breeds – Gloucester Old Spot, Large Black and Saddleback – all reared in deep-bedded straw yards, slowly, for a mature-flavoured meat. Dry-cured bacon, gammon and Cumberland sausage are specialities. Find the pork at Orton, Kendal and Ulverston farmers' markets.

Jack Scaife

Stansfield Road, Waterfoot, Rossendale, Lancashire BB4 7LR   T: 0870 112 6881
W: www.jackscaife.co.uk

✉ **mail order**

Traditional, dry-cured bacon, ham and black pudding made using free-range pork from traditional British breeds, have made Jack Scaife a winner at previous Great Taste Awards.

Steve Brooks Butcher

25 High Street, Sandbach, Cheshire CW11 1AH   T: 01270 766657
W: www.qualitycuts.co.uk

✉ **mail order**

Most of the produce at Steve Brooks comes from local farms and there is plenty of local game to choose from in season, including wild rabbit, quail, guineafowl, hare, and wild Scottish venison.

Steadman's

2 Finkle Street, Sedbergh, Cumbria LA10 5BZ · T: 01539 620431
w: www.steadmans-butchers.co.uk

Almost everything on sale at Steadman's has originated within
Cumbria, including the local Dales quality lamb, beef and pork.
There is also a good range of locally shot game in season.
Steadman's are holders of an award for Best Dry-cured Bacon in the
North West.

Broughs of Birkdale

20 Liverpool Road, Birkdale, Southport, Merseyside PR8 4AY · T: 01704 567073
w: www.broughs.com

✉ **mail order**

A traditional butcher, offering Scotch beef, local pork and chicken.
Dry-cured bacon is produced using traditional salt beds and finished
with honey and brown sugar, and this product is not only a Q Guild
of Butchers award winner but also won a Good Housekeeping
award. There are also branches at Formby and Ormskirk.

R F Burrows & Sons

Old Post Office, Bunbury, nr Tarporely, Cheshire CW6 9QR · T: 01829 260342

Local pheasant, wild duck and Scottish wild venison are available at
Burrows, alongside traditional meats.

Rock Midstead Organic Farm Shop

Alnwick, Northumberland NE66 2TH · T: 01665 579225 · w: www.rockmidstead.co.uk

⬇ **farm shop**

Organic meat from animals reared in small family groups and fed on
home-grown feed. Rare and native breeds (Dorset lamb, Aberdeen
Angus beef and Tamworth pork) have been chosen here, producing
meat with an old-fashioned flavour. Organic chickens and eggs are
also available, as well as Christmas turkeys.

R Carter & Son Butcher

Front Street, Bamburgh, Northumberland NE69 7BW   T: 01668 214344

This butcher's shop is famous for its traditional Scotch pies and sausage rolls, all made the old-fashioned way.

Westholme Farm Meats

Westholme Farm, Marwood, Barnard Castle, Co. Durham DL12 8QP   T: 01833 638443

farmers' markets   **delivery service**

Lesley and Martin Bell specialize in beef, which is fed on home-grown cereals and grass and then hung traditionally after slaughter. The beef is reared for a lean meat, with light fat cover. The Bells attend many north east farmers' markets and run a delivery round – call for details.

R G Foreman & Son

13 Woolmarket, Berwick-upon-Tweed, Northumberland TD15 1DH   T: 01289 304442
W: www.borderbutcher.co.uk

For details, see under the Eyemouth branch on page 351. There are also branches in Coldstream and Norham-on-Tweed (see pages 350 and 338).

Piperfield Pork

The Dovecote, Lowick, Berwick-upon-Tweed, Northumberland TD15 2QE
T: 01289 388543   E: grahampeterhead@yahoo.com

farmers' markets   **mail order**

Pork, sausages, dry-cured bacon, gammon, chorizo and traditional air-dried ham from Middle White and Saddleback pigs can be found at this farm. The pigs are reared free-range in small family groups in grassy paddocks, without growth promoters or antibiotics – Piperfield has increased the national herds of Middle White and Saddleback pigs by 10% in the last year and has become an important factor in the conservation of these rare-breed pigs. Piperfield won the Champion Traditional Breed Sausage award at the 2001 National Festival of Meat for their Middle White sausages, and silver and gold medals at the 2004 Great Taste Awards. All their products are available by mail order from Berwick, Edinburgh and Newcastle farmers' markets, or delicatessens in Scotland and the North East.

Well Hung and Tender

Baldersbury Hill Farm, Berwick-upon-Tweed, Northumberland TD15 1UY
T: 01289 386216   W: www.wellhungandtender.com
▆ farmers' markets ▆ farm gate sales ✉ mail order

Pure-bred Aberdeen Angus beef is available fresh or frozen from Baldersbury Hill Farm. All the cattle are born and reared on the farm, so total traceability is guaranteed. The meat is matured on the bone for a minimum of three weeks to allow the flavour to develop fully. The meat is available from the farm direct or from many local farmers' markets – call for details.

F Simpson & Son

The Croft, Cockfield, Bishop Auckland, Co. Durham DL13 5AA   T: 01388 718264

Third-generation traditional butchers, Simpson's sell a range of beef from native breeds and lamb from their own farm. Traditional-breed pork from local farms is available, with home-made black pudding and home-baked breads and pies.

Rose Cottage Foods

Rose Cottage, Garton-on-the-Wolds, Driffield, East Yorkshire YO25 3ET
T: 01377 257700
▆ farmers' markets ▆ farm gate sales

Traditional breeds such as Aberdeen Angus beef and Gloucester Old Spot pork provide the basis for the meats offered at Rose Cottage. Dry-cured bacon, sausages and pies are all traditionally made without the fillers and additives commonly found in these products and the steaks and pork cuts have the mature flavour of slowly reared animals, free from hormones and antibiotics. Local game is often available, direct from local shoots, as is a great range of home-baked pies. Find the produce at Pickering, Driffield and Thirsk farmers' markets.

super hero

LISHMANS OF ILKLEY (see opposite)

An award-winning Q-Guild butcher, Lishman's have won the Champion of Champions award from the *Meat Trades Journal* for their sausages. The secret, says David Lishman, lies in the pork used – 'We produce our own rare-breed pigs (Saddlebacks and British Lops), the pigs which were common 40 years ago. They mature slower, and put down more fat than their modern-day counterparts, overall producing a far higher quality.' The same attention to detail is given to all the meat stocked – David has strong views on modern conventional farming techniques: 'In recent years the pursuit of healthy, lean meat, coupled with the farmers' commercial interest in producing livestock more quickly and economically, has reduced the eating quality of modern farmed animals to the tasteless, often dry texture that is common today.' David sources meat farmed the old-fashioned way; it is this, he states, that produces the three factors that give meat good eating qualities – 'succulence, tenderness and flavour, enhanced by the presence of fat, both on the surface and marbled throughout the flesh itself'.

NORTH EAST   **EASINGWOLD**

Thornhill Farm

Thirsk Road, Easingwold, Yorkshire YO61 3ND   T: 01347 823827
E: pennyhodgson@ouvip.com

🛒 **farm gate sales** 🛍 **farmers' markets** ✉ **mail order**

Penny Hodgson rears Dexter cattle the old-fashioned way – fed on grass and home-produced haylage, on chemical-free pasture, and allowed to mature until at least 24 months. They are slaughtered and expertly butchered locally, and then hung for a full three weeks, the result being richly flavoured, well marbled beef. Available from the farm gate (please phone first), or from Easingwold market.

NORTH EAST   **HEXHAM**

Northumbrian Quality Meats

Monkridge Hill Farm, West Woodburn, Hexham, Northumberland NE48 2TU
T: 01434 270184   W: www.northumbrian-organic-meat.co.uk

🛍 **farmers' markets** ✉ **mail order**

Home-produced organic and rare-breed meats, including heather- and clover-fed Black Faced lamb, hill-bred Aberdeen Angus beef, organic chicken and free-range pork, can all be bought from Northumbrian Quality Meats at farmers' markets or by mail order.

NORTH EAST ILKLEY

Lishmans of Ilkley

RBST Rare Breeds Survival Trust GUILD Q super hero

25 Leeds Road, Ilkley, West Yorkshire LS29 8DP T: 01943 609436

Award-winning sausages are one of the attractions at Lishmans, made with the pork from the Saddleback pigs reared by the butcher himself. Other rare-breed meats are available. See the Super Hero box, opposite, for more information.

NORTH EAST LARTINGTON

Lartington Lamb

Low Crag Farm, Lartington, Co. Durham DL12 9DJ T: 01833 628427
W: www.lartingtonlamb.com
farm gate sales **mail order**

Seasonal lamb, outside all year, grazing on unsprayed pasture. The lambs are allowed to grow at their own pace and the ewes are not forced to lamb early to give spring lamb. This means the first of the season's lamb is not available until August at the earliest but it is worth the wait. Visitors to the farm, which is part of the Countryside Stewardship Scheme, are welcome.

NORTH EAST LEYBURN

Happy Piggy Pork

Manor Grange Farm, Low Lane, Carperby, Leyburn, North Yorkshire DL8 4DP
T: 01969 663399
delivery service

Rare-breed pork, including Tamworth and Gloucester Old Spot, slowly matured, and reared free-range on a healthy diet of fruit and vegetables, is available locally by home delivery from Happy Piggy Pork – call for details.

Capri Lodge

Morpeth, Northumberland NE61 3BX   T: 01670 511467
E: caprilodge2003@yahoo.co.uk

🛒 **farmers' markets**   🚚 **delivery service**

Believe it or not, goat is actually the meat that is eaten more than
any other in the world – but we Western Europeans have yet to
become familiar with it. Muriel Brown rears both dairy and meat
goats and says that the meat is leaner than lamb, doesn't shrink
as much when cooked, is lower in cholesterol – but is just as tasty.
Joints and sausages, milk and yoghurt are available, and she also
makes unpasteurized cheese from the milk. Find Muriel at
Newcastle and Tynemouth farmers' markets or phone to see if she
can deliver.

George Payne Butchers

27 Princes Road, Brunton Park, Gosforth, Newcastle-upon-Tyne NE3 5TT
T: 0191 236 2992

Lots of rare-breed meats from Northumberland farms are on offer
here, all reared without additives, non-intensively. White Park and
Dexter beef, Wensleydale lamb and Middle White pork are all
popular.

R G Foreman & Son

8 Castle Street, Norham, Norham-on-Tweed, Northumberland TD15 2LQ
T: 01289 382260   W: www.borderbutcher.co.uk

For details, see under the Eyemouth branch on page 347. There are
also branches in Berwick-upon-Tweed and Coldstream (see pages
331 and 346).

Langthornes Buffalo Produce

Crawford Grange, Brompton, Northallerton, North Yorkshire DL6 2PD   T: 01609 776937

🛒 **farmers' markets**   🏠 **farm gate sales**

The water buffalo at Crawford Grange are grass-fed all year, producing tasty, low-cholesterol meat. Their milk is used to make a range of cheeses, including the classic buffalo mozzarella (the cheeses are made by local dairies). Farmed venison, free-range goats' meat, free-range wild boar, and rose veal (with a much higher attention to welfare than white veal) are all available, too. Find the meat at Otley, Richmond, Darlington and Wetherby farmers' markets (call for details) or direct from the farm on Wednesdays and Thursdays.

Highside Butchers

Main Street, Kirkby Malzeard, Ripon, North Yorkshire HG4 3RS   T: 01765 658423
E: highsidebutcherskm@hotmail.com

This traditional butcher's offers good, locally produced meat – when I contacted them there was rump steak available that had been hung for six weeks. Free-range Bronze turkeys are available at Christmas and free-range chickens are available all year.

Oxford Sandy & Black Pigs

Burgate Farm, Harwood Dale, Scarborough, North Yorkshire YO13 0DS
T: 01723 870333
🖂 **farm gate sales**

Katrina Cook started rearing her own pigs because she was disappointed with the pork she was able to buy from supermarkets. The Oxford Sandy & Blacks she rears are free-range and matured for longer than most commercial pigs. She has a customer list, ringing people when meat is available – phone her to get on the list.

The Real Meat Company

950 Ecclesall Road, Sheffield S11 8TR   T: 0114 266 1197   w: www.realmeat.co.uk

Specializing in butchery to order – customers bring their recipes in and the staff cut the meat to specific requirements – all the meat here is from the Real Meat Company, guaranteed drug-free and welfare-friendly. Dry-cured bacon and ham are specialities. See the Super Hero box, page 367, for more information about The Real Meat Company.

Larberry Pastures

Longnewton, Stockton-on-Tees, Cleveland TS21 1BN   T: 01642 583823
E: larberry@farmersweekly.net

farmers' markets   ⨝ farm gate sales

Home-produced organic beef and free-range eggs, locally reared organic pork, dry-cured bacon, ham and sausages and lamb can be bought at Larberry, and also available are organic fruit and vegetables, local baking, chutneys and preserves, with a good selection of wheat- and gluten-free foods.

Blacker Hall Farm Shop

Branch Road, Calder Grove, Wakefield, Yorkshire WF4 3DN   T: 01924 267202
W: www.blackerhall.com

⤵ farm shop

Home-reared meat is the mainstay of Blacker Hall Farm Shop – beef, hung on the bone for four weeks for a tender, rich flavour, lamb and pork. Everything about the rearing of these animals is geared towards exceptional eating quality, and the Garthwaite family are also expert butchers, making the very best of the meat at every stage. The farm shop houses its own bakery, too, with a wide selection of home-baked, hand-made pies.

Bowlees Farm Shop

Wolsingham, Weardale, Co. Durham DL13 3JF   T: 01388 528305
W: www.bowleesorganicfarm.com

⤵ farm shop

Bowlees Farm was the first Soil Association accredited farm in County Durham and is now a haven for all kinds of wildlife, due to the sensitive methods of farming employed. Rare-breed pork is produced, truly free-range – Large Blacks, Gloucester Old Spots and Saddlebacks. Grey Blue Galloway beef is also available, along with Suffolk-Lleyn cross lamb. The produce is also available from The Honey Tree in Heaton.

A Flanigan & Son

1 Scotch Street, Armagh BT61 7BY T: 028 3752 2805

Much of the meat sold here comes from the Flanigans' own farm, where they specialize in beef and lamb. Other meats are sourced from local farms and dry-cured bacon and ham is available.

Wysner Meats and Restaurant

16–18 Anne Street, Ballycastle, Co Antrim T: 028 2076 2372

A key product at Wysner's is their own-recipe black pudding – a distinctive flavour and something of a legend in Ballycastle.

Ballylagan Organic Farm

12 Ballylagan Road, Straid, Ballyclare, Co. Antrim BT39 9NF T: 028 9332 2867
w: www.ballylagan.com
farm shop

Ballylagan produces beef, lamb, pork and poultry, reared almost exclusively on grass and grain grown on the farm. A wide range of fruit and vegetables is available throughout the year, with as much as possible being home-grown. A comprehensive selection of organic groceries is also sold by the shop.

David Burns Butchers

112 Abbey Street, Bangor BT20 4JB T: 028 9127 0073

Plenty of traditionally reared, locally sourced meat, including some organic, and beef from the butcher's own herd, can be bought at David Burns.

Owen McMahon

3 Atlantic Avenue, Belfast BT15 2HN T: 028 9074 3535 w: www.owenmcmahon.com

McMahon's have won the accolade of producing the best pork sausage in Belfast and, come the summer, they offer all manner of imaginative barbecue meats – everything is produced in Ireland, nothing is imported. Part of the shop is given over to a fish section, where you can find locally caught fresh fish.

O'Kane Meats

69 Main Street, Claudy, Co. Londonderry BT47 4HR   T: 028 7133 8944
w: www.okanemeats.com

This multi-award-winning butcher's shop specializes in sausages, having won the Champion Beef Sausage award from the Northern Ireland Master Butcher's Association in 2002. Local beef is available, hung for a minimum of three weeks for a mature flavour.

Pheasants' Hill Farm Shop

3 Bridge Street, Link, Comber, Co. Down BT23 5AT   T: 028 9187 8470
w: www.pheasantshill.com
⬇ farm shop

Rare-breed pork, including dry-cured bacon and ham, and locally produced Dexter beef, Soay lamb, organic Aberdeen Angus beef and organic chickens and turkeys. Local dairy produce and organic fruit and vegetables and, at Christmas, free-range geese are also available. There is also a shop in Downpatrick (see below).

Pheasants' Hill Farm Shop

37 Killyleagh Road, Downpatrick, Co. Down BT30 9BL   T: 028 4483 8707 OR
028 4461 7246   w: www.pheasantshill.com
⬇ farm shop

For details, see under the Comber branch, above.

Arkhill Farm

25 Drumcroone Road, Garvagh, Co. Londonderry   T: 028 2955 7920
E: arkfarmministry@aol.com
▨ farm gate sales ▨ box scheme

Organic lamb and rare-breed chicken, Saddleback pork and free-range hens' and ducks' eggs are all available, all organic, either direct

from the farm or through the local box scheme – call for details.
Home-grown, organic vegetables are also available.

Norman Hunter & Son

53–55 Main Street, Limavady, Londonderry BT49 0EP T: 028 7776 2665

A traditional butcher's shop, selling only Northern Irish produce,
mainly from local farms. The emphasis is on 'chemical-free' produce
and specialities include home-cooked meats, including roast beef
and hams, dry-cured bacon and, in the deli section, Irish cheeses.

John R Dowey & Son

20 High Street, Lurgan, Co. Armagh BT66 8AW T: 028 3832 2547 E: jrdowey@aol.com

Local meats, Irish cheeses, salads and deli goods and home-made
pies can be obtained from this Elite Guild of Butchers member.
There is also great local beef, hung well for a fuller flavour.

McKees Butchers

26 & 78 Main Street, Maghera, Co. Londonderry BT46 5AY T: 028 7964 2559

McKees are famous not just for their great quality, properly
butchered local meats but also for their home-baked pies – the two
shops also boast deli and bakery sections.

Moss Brook Farm

6 Durnascallon Lane, Magherafelt, Londonderry BT45 5LZ T: 028 7963 3454
E: mossbrookbaconboys@utvinternet.com
🍖 farmers' markets ▨ farm gate sales

Dry-cured bacon is a speciality that has become hard to find in
Ireland but Moss Brook farm is happily restoring the tradition, curing
the bacon to its own sweet recipe. Ten different varieties of sausage
and cured gammon on the bone are also made from the meat of the
farm's own pigs. Available from St Georges Market in Belfast,
Dungannon farmers' market, or direct from the farm, but call first.
Moss Brook Farm have won a Bridgestone Good Food Award for
three years running.

McCartney's

56–58 High Street, Moira, Co. Down BT67 0LQ   T: 028 9261 1422

Award-winning sausages, of which over 30 varieties are made on the premises from local meats.

Mr Eatwells

16 Campsie Road, Omagh, Co. Tyrone BT79 0AG   T: 028 8224 1104

Sausages and home-made pies are the speciality for Mr Eatwells and the roast beef is very popular. Traditional butchery skills are an important part of the Elite Guild of Butchers, and they are well demonstrated here.

T Knox & Sons

38b West Street, Portadown, Co. Armagh BT62 3JQ   T: 028 3835 3713

This is a butcher's and deli combined, with lots of locally produced, traditionally prepared meat (the beef is hung for three weeks). There are also home-cooked pies and 'dishes to go'; Knox is a previous winner of Deli of the Year.

J E Toms & Sons

46 The Promenade, Portstewart, Co. Londonderry BT55 7AE   T: 028 7083 2869

Another butcher from the Elite Guild of Butchers, with a commitment to locally sourced meats and traditional butchery skills; the speciality here is imaginative barbecue meat.

Michael Hickey

Gortrua, New Inn, Cashel, Co. Tipperary   T: 062 72223
farm gate sales

Tipperary is legendary for beef production and Michael Hickey produces benchmark organic grass-fed Aberdeen Angus beef, as he has for the last 24 years. Buy direct from the farm.

James Whelan Butchers

Oakville Shopping Centre, Clonmel, Co. Tipperary   T: 052 22927
w: www.jameswhelanbutchers.com
⌂ **shop**

The Whelan family have many years of experience in producing their famed dry-aged beef, which has a unique nutty, buttery flavour. There is also plenty of other traditionally-produced meat, including traditional corned beef.

On The Pigs Back

The English Market, Cork   T: 021 427 0232   w: www.onthepigsback.ie

Home-made terrines, such as pork and plum, and pâtés, like the legendary chicken liver pâté with garlic and brandy, are what On The Pigs Back are famous for, all made with local free-range pork, free-range eggs and organic venison. Their market stall also has artisan Irish and continental cheeses, locally cured meats, continental specialities like foie gras and dried mushrooms and breads from Arbutus breads (see page 43).

O'Toole's Butchers

138 Terenure Road North, Dublin 6W   T: 01 490 5457   E: otoolebutchers@eircom.net

Danny O'Toole is renowned for his selection of Irish-reared organic meats; the beef is from a local farm and hung for three weeks and there is also organic free-range chicken and pork. A second shop can be found in Dun Loaghaire (see below).

O'Toole's Butchers

1b Glasthule Road, Sandycove, Dun Loaghaire   T: 01 284 1125

For details, see under the Dublin branch, above.

John David Power

57 Main Street, Dungarvan, Co. Waterford   T: 058 42339

A traditional butcher's widely believed to make some of the best dry-cured bacon in Ireland, Power's is a member of the Associated Craft Butchers of Ireland.

Tormey's Butchers

Galway Shopping Centre, Galway   T: 091 564067

These three butcher's shops (the others are in Mullingar and Tullamore, see below and page 348) are run by the Tormey brothers and the beef they sell is slowly reared on the family's own farm. Pork, lamb and poultry come from other local producers.

Continental Sausages

Fossa, Killarney, Co. Kerry   T: 064 33069
✉ **mail order**

An interesting range of sausages and charcuterie, all made with high-quality Irish meats.

McGrath's Butchers

Main Street, Lismore, Co. Waterford   T: 058 54350

The key to the quality of the meat at McGrath's is the fact that the majority of it is home-reared and slaughtered in the shop's own abattoir – giving McGrath's control of the whole process and guaranteeing traceability. McGrath's is a member of the Associated Craft Butchers of Southern Ireland.

Tormey's Butchers

Harbour Place, Mullingar, West Meath   T: 044 45433

For details, see under the Galway branch, above. There is also a branch in Tullamore (see page 348).

McGeogh's Butchers

Lake Road, Oughterard, Co. Galway   T: 091 552351

Find a good choice of locally sourced, traditionally reared meat, with the main attraction being the old-fashioned air-dried lamb, for which McGeogh's won a gold medal at the 2003 awards at Utrecht. McGeogh's is a member of the Associated Craft Butchers of Ireland.

Caherbeg Free Range Pork

Caherbeg, Rosscarbery, Co. Cork   T: 023 48474   W: www.caherbegfreerangepork.ie
🍴 **farmers' markets**   ✉ **farm gate sales**

The Saddleback and Tamworth pigs at Caherbeg are reared slowly and with great regard for animal welfare. A full choice of pork cuts, bacon, ham and sausages is available and also Aberdeen Angus beef. Caherberg won gold and silver medals at the 2004 Great Taste Awards. Buy the produce direct from the farm or at Clonakilty market every week.

Gubbeen Smokehouse

Schull, Co. Cork   T: 028 27824   W: www.gubbeen.com
🍴 **farmers' markets**

Fingal Ferguson takes the meat of the pigs his father rears (fed on organic grain and whey for a sweet-tasting meat) and creates all kinds of charcuterie. Salami, bacon and ham are all available but it is perhaps for the bacon that he is best known – produced with no artificial preservatives, a long, slow process of hanging, curing, smoking and air-drying creates a really tasty product, a million miles from the commercial bacon you'll find in supermarkets. Find the produce at Cork English Market, and Midleton, Bantry, Skibbereen and Clonakilty farmers' markets and delicatessens.

super hero

FRANK KRAWCZYK, of Krawczyk's West Cork Salamis, Schull (see below)

Frank Krawczyk takes the finest free-range or organic Irish pork and creates a range of eight salamis and a pancetta, all made by hand. He is also working on the recipe for a dry-cured smoked ham but the attention to detail this demands means that it is taking, quite literally, years because Frank is not yet satisfied that he has got the recipe perfect. Having won two Great Taste Awards and an award for 'pioneering work and constant innovation in the area of salamis', and having been named as Artisan Producer of the Year by the legendary food writers John and Sally McKenna, he is still determined to remain a small-scale producer, in control of everything. Find Frank's charcuterie at Clonakilty, Bantry, Limerick and Cork City farmers' markets, and Dun Loaghaire Peoples' Park Market from September to July.

REPUBLIC OF IRELAND | SCHULL

Krawczyk's West Cork Salamis

`super hero`

Derreenatra, Schull, Co. Cork   T: 028 28 579
🍽 **farmers' markets**

An award-winning producer of salamis, Frank Krawczyk, a member of Slow Food International, believes in attention to detail. See the Super Hero box, above, for more information.

REPUBLIC OF IRELAND | TULLAMORE

Tormey's Butchers

Bridge Street, Tullamore, Co. Offaly   T: 0506 21426

For details, see under the Galway branch on page 346. There is also a branch in Mullingar (see page 346).

SCOTLAND | ABERFELDY

Aberfeldy Butchers

12 Bank Street, Aberfeldy, Perthshire PH15 2BB   T: 01887 820310
✉ **mail order**

Traditional butchers offering Aberdeen Angus beef, hung for four weeks, highland lamb and local cheeses. There is also a good choice of game, including venison from Balmoral, which is a cross between wild and farmed – the gamekeepers there intervene only in harsh weather, to supplement the deer's natural food. Game birds are also available from local estates, including duck and all kinds of pigeon. All the meat is available mail order.

Lurgan Farm

Camserney, by Aberfeldy, Perthshire PH15 2JQ   T: 01887 829303
w: www.lurganfarmshop.co.uk

🚜 farmers' markets   ✉ mail order

Classic Scottish meats – Aberdeen Angus beef, Highland beef and heather-fed Black Faced lamb and wild venison – are available direct from the farm, by mail order, or from Perth farmers' market.

Speyside Organics

Knockanrioch, Knockando, Aberlour, Moray AB38 7SG   T: 01340 810484
w: www.speysideorganics.com

🚜 farmers' markets   🚚 delivery service   ✉ mail order

Traceability can be guaranteed as every piece of meat sold at Speyside Organics comes from animals born, reared and finished on the farm. Limosin, Shorthorn, Hereford and Highland beef are all grass-fed and allowed to mature fully before slaughter. Carcasses are then hung for a minimum of three weeks. Cheviot lamb is also available, as is mutton, and for 2004 a new range of smoked meat was added to the repertoire, winning Speyside Organics a Great Taste Award. Speyside Organics sell at Aberdeen and Inverness farmers' markets and also at the farm and by mail order.

Jamesfield Organic Farm

Abernethy, Perthshire KY14 6EW   T: 01738 850498   w: www.jamesfieldfarm.co.uk

🛒 farm shop   ✉ mail order

Organic Aberdeen Angus beef, Black Faced lamb and free-range pork from the farm's own land, and free-range chickens from a neighbouring farm, can be bought from Jamesfield Farm. New in 2004 were a visitors' centre and restaurant.

Ardalanish Farm

Bunessen, Isle of Mull PA67 6DR T: 01681 700265 W: www.ardalanishfarm.co.uk

✉ **farm gate sales** 🚚 **delivery service**

Highland beef and Hebridean lamb and mutton are all fed on home-grown feed and accredited by the Soil Association. The animals are slowly reared at their own pace. The meat is available direct from the farm, through local delivery or from Loch Fyne: www.lochfyne.com.

Ramsay of Carluke Ltd

Wellriggs, 22 Mountstewart Street, Carluke, South Lanarkshire ML8 5ED
T: 01555 772277 W: www.ramsayofcarluke.co.uk

✉ **mail order**

Ramsay's award-winning traditional Ayrshire bacon, dry-cured to an 1857 recipe, was named as 'the best bacon in Scotland' by the *BBC Good Food Magazine*.

R G Foreman & Son

▽**RBST**
Rare Breeds Survival Trust

68 High Street, Coldstream, Berwickshire TD12 4DG T: 01890 883881
W: www.borderbutcher.co.uk

For details, see under the Eyemouth branch, opposite. There are also branches in Berwick-upon-Tweed and Norham-on-Tweed (see pages 334 and 338).

Findlays of Portobello

116 Portobello High Street, Edinburgh EH15 1AL T: 0131 669 2783
W: www.haggisonline.co.uk

✉ **mail order**

Among the Scottish meat and poultry at Findlays are the home-made haggis, made to a traditional recipe using local ingredients. So good are they that they have been voted winners of the Scottish Haggis Championship by the Scottish Federation of Master Butchers.

R G Foreman & Son

4 Chapel Street, Eyemouth, Berwickshire TD14 5HF T: 01890 750209
w: www.borderbutcher.co.uk

Lots of rare-breed meats, all from farms within a 30-mile radius.
David Foreman, the owner, personally visits the farms, choosing
each individual animal. Welfare standards are always high. Breeds
include Dexter, Longhorn and Belted Galloway beef, Oxford Sandy
& Black, and Middle White pork. Free-range, organic, corn-fed
chicken is also available. There are branches of Foreman's in
Coldstream (see opposite), Berwick-upon-Tweed (see page 334)
and Norham-on-Tweed (see page 338).

Macbeths

11 Tollbooth Street, Forres, Moray IV36 1PH T: 01309 672254 w: www.macbeths.com
✉ mail order

A variety of properly hung and butchered beef is available at
Macbeths, from Aberdeen Angus, Highland and Shorthorn cattle.
Heather-fed lamb, local game and dry-cured bacon are also on offer.

Orkney Organic Meat

New Holland, Holm, Orkney KW17 2SA T: 01856 781345
w: www.orkneyorganicmeat.co.uk
✉ farm gate sales ✉ mail order

Organic Aberdeen Angus beef and heather-fed lamb are produced
at Orkney Organic, one of the first farms on the Orkney Islands to
go into organic conversion. See the Super Hero box, page 352, for
more information.

super hero

ORKNEY ORGANIC MEAT, Holm (see page 351)

The farm at Orkney Organic Meat was one of the first commercial farms to go into organic conversion on Orkney and Tony and Elizabeth Bown are proud that their farming system 'works with nature and is sustainable 21st-century farming'. Not content just to follow Soil Association guidelines, they have researched the effect of the balance of minerals in the soil on the eating qualities of the meat reared on it and have come up with some pretty interesting results – 'We have learned that a correct balance of minerals in the soil is vital for adequate nutrition of the animal, and how the animal is fed relates directly to how the meat tastes.' The Bowns constantly monitor their soil, sending it off to labs for analysis to achieve this perfect balance. The meat produced is Aberdeen Angus beef and heather-fed lamb, both organic. The taste is only one benefit of this kind of farming, says Elizabeth: 'In the summer our animals graze our organic pastures and in the winter we feed home-grown organic grass silage, grass juice and seaweed meal. This diet promotes good health in the animal and produces meat which is beneficial to human health also – our way of farming produces meat that is higher in beneficial essential nutrients such as omega-3 polyunsaturated fatty acids, vitamin E and beta-carotene.'

SCOTLAND   LERWICK

Globe Butchers

49–53 Commercial Road, Lerwick, Shetland ZE1 0NJ   T: 01595 692819
W: www.globebutchers.co.uk
✉ mail order

A traditional family butcher's selling uniquely flavoured Shetland lamb, Orkney beef and Shetland specialities including 'Reestit Mutton' – cured and air-dried Shetland lamb, very specific to these islands.

SCOTLAND   LOCHGILPHEAD

Ormsary Farm

by Lochgilphead, Argyll PA31 8PE   T: 01880 770700
✉ farm gate sales   ✉ mail order

Slowly reared, properly matured Shorthorn and Highland beef, from the Ormsary prize-winning fold of Highland cattle, plus venison from the island of Jura and lamb from the hills of Ormsary Farm, are all butchered and packed ready to use or freeze.

Saulmore Farm Shop

Connel, by Oban, Argyll PA37 1PU   T: 01631 710247   w: www.saulmore.com
👝 **farm shop** ✉ **mail order**

Highland cattle and Black Faced lambs graze coastal pasture at
Saulmore Farm and the resulting meat has a unique salty flavour,
similar to that of Welsh saltmarsh lamb. Also available are wild boar
and venison.

Pentland Hills Produce

Boghall Farm, Biggar Road, Hillend, Edinburgh EH10 7DX,   T: 0131 445 3383
w: www.pentland-hills-produce.co.uk
🛒 **farmers' markets** ✉ **mail order**

A group of farmers in the heather-covered Pentland Hills have joined
forces to create Pentland Hills Produce, offering sweet-flavoured,
heather-fed lamb and beef. Some of the meat is organic while some
is from traditional breeds, such as the Scottish Blackface lamb.
Available by mail order or from the Edinburgh farmers' market.

Brig Highland Beef

Gateside Home Farm, Bridge of Earn, Perth PH2 8QR   T: 01738 813571
E: hamish@dunkirkpark.freeserve.co.uk
👝 **farm shop** 🛒 **farmers' markets**

Beef from Highland cattle, slowly matured and slaughtered just
before reaching 30 months. The cattle are grass-fed, with their diet
supplemented with home-grown forage in winter. The farm is
accredited by RSPCA Freedom Foods. There is a café on site, with
dishes made from local produce.

J & M Stewart

Langraw Farm, St Andrews, Fife KY16 8NR   T: 01334 473061
🛒 **farmers' markets**

Highland beef is the speciality at Langraw Farm and John Stewart,
who is a member of Scottish Quality Meats Farm Assurance, feeds
his cattle on home-grown feed, sends them to a local slaughter

house and hangs the meat on the bone for at least three weeks for a traditional flavour. John's farm is accredited by RSPCA Freedom Foods. Find him at Kirkcaldy, St Andrews and Cupar farmers' markets.

Daren Farm

Cym Yoy, Monmouthshire NP7 7NR   T: 01873 890712

🛒 **farmers' markets**

Biodynamic Welsh Black beef, slowly matured and hung for at least two weeks, White Faced Woodland, Tor Wenn and Tor Ddu rare-breed lamb and British Lop pork are all available from Usk, Abergavenny, Monmouth and Chepstow farmers' markets.

New House Farm

Bryngwyn, Rhosgoch, Builth Wells, Powys LD2 3JT   T: 01497 851671
W: www.new-house-farm.co.uk

🛒 **farm gate sales**

New House Farm is a hill farm and the lamb that Sue and John levers produce here is lean and tasty. They also rear Highland cattle and all the animals are fed nothing but grass, silage and grains. The meat is available direct from the farm but call first. The levers also do B&B and evening meals, all with their own produce.

Penmincae Welsh Black Beef & Lamb

Gellynen Lodge, Penmincae Farm, Cwmbach, Builth Wells, Powys LD2 3RP
T: 01982 551242   E: welshblackbeef@fsmail.net

🛒 **farmers' markets**   🛒 **farm gate sales**

Organic, grass-fed Welsh Black cattle grow slowly and produce a uniquely flavoured, well-marbled beef. Total traceability is ensured – every animal is born on the farm, none is bought in and a small local abattoir is used. The meat is available at Brecon, Llandrindod Wells and Rhayader farmers' markets or you can call to make an arrangement to buy directly from the farm.

Pigs Folly

Irfon Valley Mill, Garth, Builth Wells, Powys LD4 4AS   T: 01591 620572
w: www.pigsfolly.co.uk

🌱 **farm shop** 🛒 **farmers' markets**

A good selection of rare-breed meats, including Dexter and
Aberdeen Angus beef, Tamworth pork and native Beulah
Speckleface lamb. All the meat is extensively reared and Dave Lang,
the owner, is happy to state that only his own meat is used in the
on-site restaurant. 70 varieties of sausage and dry-cured bacon are
available. Find the produce at the farm shop, or from Brecon,
Llandrindod Wells or Rhayader farmers' markets.

J T Morgan

44–46 Central Market, Cardiff CF10 2AU   T: 02920 388434 OR 02920 341247

✉ **mail order**

A fantastic selection of Welsh produce – Black Gold beef and
saltmarsh lamb heading the list. Free-range poultry and pork is
available, along with a range of rare-breed meats.

Albert Rees

Arfryn, Uplands, Carmarthen, Carmarthenshire SA32 8DX   T: 01267 237687
w: www.carmarthenham.co.uk

🛒 **farmers' markets** ✉ **mail order**

Traditional Carmarthen ham, cured to an old recipe, and then air-
dried to maturity. Available by mail order, or from Carmarthen,
Pembroke Dock, and Cardigan markets.

John James

Fferm Tyllwyd, Felingwm-Uchaf, Carmarthen SA32 7QE   T: 01267 290537

📭 **farm gate sales**

Organic Welsh Black beef, hung for three weeks after slaughter, is
available in a 'farmhouse box' – a mixed box containing a good
variety of cuts. Fillets and ribs are available separately.

Edwards of Conwy

18 High Street, Conwy, North Wales LL32 8DE   T: 01492 592443
w: www.edwardsofconwy.co.uk

✉ **mail order**

The famous Harlech saltmarsh lamb is available here, along with
plenty of meat from local farms, all traditionally reared and
butchered. Edwards have won awards at European level and were
voted the best shop in the Wales True Taste 2003 Awards.

Bumpylane Rare Breeds

Shortlands, Druidston, Haverfordwest, Pembrokeshire SA62 3NE   T: 01437 781234
w: www.bumpylane.co.uk

🛒 **farmers' markets** 🚚 **delivery service** ✉ **mail order**

Organic lamb and beef from the rare breeds of sheep and cattle
born and reared on this coastal farm. These traditional breeds, bred
for their flavour, include White Faced Woodland, Grey-Faced
Dartmoor, Llanwenog and Kerry Hill sheep, together with Longhorn
and White Park cattle. Pam and David sell their organic meat at
Haverfordwest and Fishguard farmers' markets. Freezer-ready packs
of lamb and beef are also available by mail order, with free delivery
in Pembrokeshire.

Knock Farm Organics

Knock Farm, Clarbeston Road, Haverfordwest, Pembrokeshire SA63 4SL
T: 01437 731342

🚚 **delivery service**

Knock Farm produces organic beef, pork and Llanwenog lamb,
and organic free-range eggs. The pork is also made into dry-cured
bacon and ham. All the produce is available through a delivery
round that encompasses Cardiff, Bristol and Cheltenham – phone
for more details.

Welsh Hook Meat Centre

Woodfield, Withybush Road, Haverfordwest, Pembrokeshire SA62 4BW
T: 01437 768876   W: www.welsh-organic-meat.co.uk
⬇ farm shop ✉ mail order

The Welsh Hook Meat Centre has won awards many times at the
Soil Association Organic Food Awards. The farm shop sells home-
reared beef and lamb and other meat from local organic farms.
Rare-breed and native meats are well represented, including Welsh
Black and Dexter beef. The centre is a member of the Humane
Slaughter Association.

Julia Coviello

Gelli Gwenyn, Silian, Lampeter, Ceredigion SA48 8AU   T: 01570 423545
E: Julia@coviello.co.uk
🚚 delivery service

A rare opportunity to experience the taste of very young, pure-bred
Vendéen lamb, reared on their dams' milk, grazing the wild herb/
grass and clover pastures of west Wales. The Vendéen breed has
been chosen for its exceptional flavour and early maturity. As a pure
meat breed, it is ready for slaughter from the age of ten weeks.
All lambs are from a scrapie-tested flock, providing the fullest
traceability. The lambs go to a small local abattoir, where carcasses
are hung for two weeks and butchered to individual requirements.
Julia has delivery rounds in London and Hampshire; call to see if
she can deliver to you.

The May Organic Farms

Panteg, Cellan, Lampeter, Carmarthenshire SA48 8HN   T: 01570 423080
www: themay.co.uk
✉ farm gate sales ✉ mail order

The Mays have a commitment to indigenous breeds of animal and
rear Highland beef, and Welsh Mountain lamb, all organically.
Members of the Beef Assurance Scheme, the Mays are allowed
to take their cattle past the 30-month slaughter rule, which can
produce a much more traditionally flavoured, mature meat. The
Mays are also members of the Humane Slaughter Association and
Slow Food International and their meat is available direct from the
farm or by mail order.

FOOD HEROES OF BRITAIN

Graig Farm Organics

Dolau, Llandrindod Wells, Powys LD1 5TL   T: 01597 851655   w: www.graigfarm.co.uk

🠋 **farm shop**   ✉ **mail order**

A previous winner of the Organic Retailer of the Year award from the Soil Association, Graig Farm has a good range of organic meats, most of which are reared on the farm itself, supplemented by meat from the Graig Farm Producer Group of organic farms in Wales and the borders. Organic fish, baby food, dairy, fruit and vegetables, bakery and dry goods are available.

Cambrian Organics

super hero

Horeb, Llandysul, Ceredigion SA44 3JG   T: 01559 363151
w: www.cambrianorganics.com

✉ **mail order**   🛒 **farmers' markets**

Cambrian Organics is a co-operative of small-scale Welsh farmers, committed to environmental awareness, producing organic, native-Welsh-breed lamb. See the Super Hero box, opposite, for more information.

Beef Direct Ltd and Lamb Direct Ltd

Plas Coedana, Llanerch y Medd, Anglesey LL71 8AA   T: 01248 470387
w: www.beefdirect.net

🛒 **farmers' markets**   ✉ **farm gate sales**

This is the outlet for two family farms in Anglesey, one registered organic, the other not, although neither farm uses any pesticides. The cattle are all Welsh Black, the sheep are the Welsh Mountain breed, and there is now outdoor-reared pork, too.

Edward Hamer

Plynlimon House, Llanidloes, Powys SY18 6EF   T: 01686 412209
w: www.edwardhamer.co.uk

✉ **mail order**

This traditional Welsh butcher offers a full selection of Welsh meat, including Welsh Black beef.

super hero

CAMBRIAN ORGANICS, Llandysul (see opposite)

Cambrian Organics is a co-operative of small-scale Welsh farmers selling organic meat, often from native Welsh breeds, such as Welsh Black beef and Welsh Mountain lamb. All the farmers share the same ethics of conservation and environmental awareness, and all the meat is fully traceable back to the farm it was reared on. Customers can visit the farms online and find out about organic farming, and the mail order phone line is always staffed by one of the farmers. Lamb is a speciality of the group, and the farmers all have strong views on the rearing of them – these farmers view the fashion for early spring lamb with deep suspicion. One of the leaders of Cambrian Organics told me: 'Nature has provided our sheep with a way of timing the birth of their lambs. Ovulation in ewes is triggered by the shortening days in autumn so that the lambs are born to coincide with the growth of spring grass. Here in Wales our mountain lambs are being *born* at Easter, not being eaten! Spring lamb for Easter is not for us at Cambrian Organics, as we believe in natural feeding and raising our stock on grass. The wilder and more varied the grasses, and the higher up the mountain, the better, for this is what gives them their unique taste. Our lambs are born in spring, and are ready for the table from late summer onwards.' The flavour is well worth the wait! After Christmas, store lambs from the mountains are finished on lower land. These hoggets as they are known still retain the unique flavour, but being older require more careful, and slower cooking to be appreciated fully. The lamb, beef, pork and chicken from the co-operative are available mail order or from local farmers' markets.

Rose Park Organic Farm

Llanteg, Pembrokeshire SA67 8QJ T: 01834 831111

🐄 **farm shop** ✉ **mail order**

Rose Park Farm operates an open policy, with farm walks available, so that visitors can see how the lambs are reared. A mixture of breeds, the lambs are reared organically with animal welfare as a priority. Hung for a week after slaughter, the lambs are butchered on site at the farm shop. Organic beef is also available, hung for three weeks. Only home-produced foods are stocked in the farm shop – nothing is brought in.

Maestroyddyn Organics

Maestroyddyn Fach, Harford, Llanwrda, Carmarthenshire SA19 8DU   T: 01558 650774
E: sjwallis@lineone.net
⛩ **farm gate sales**

Beef from Hereford cattle and lamb from Portland and Llanwenog sheep is available direct from the farm. The beef has been slowly reared and properly hung for full flavour and the animals go to a local slaughterhouse, minimizing stress and food miles.

N S James & Son

RBST
Rare Breeds Survival Trust

Crown Square, Raglan, Monmouthshire NP15 2EB   T: 01291 690675

Much of the meat sold here is extensively reared rare breeds from local farms. The butcher has his own abattoir and so everything is traceable, including the Longhorn beef from the country's largest herd of this rare breed.

Eynon's of St Clears Ltd

Deganwy, Pentre Road, St Clears, Carmarthenshire SA33 4LR   T: 0800 731 5816
W: www.eynons.co.uk
✉ **mail order**

Three times winner of the *Meat Trades Journal* Wales No.1 Butcher award, Eynon's specialize in Welsh Black beef and saltmarsh lamb from local farms. Phone for a price list and mail order details.

Penrhiw Farm Organic Meats

Trelewis, Treharris, Mid Glamorgan CF46 6TA   T: 01443 412949
E: penrhiw.farm@virgin.net
🛒 **farmers' markets**   ⛩ **farm gate sales**

From their dedicated cold room, Celia and John Thomas sell their organic Aberdeen Angus beef and South Welsh Mountain lamb to a growing band of loyal customers. All the cuts are available and it is Celia's mission to educate her customers regarding cooking the less popular cuts; the properly hung meat is so tasty, her customers even clamour for the brisket. Home-made burgers and sausages, traditionally made with all meat, with no rusk added, are also popular. Buy direct from the farm or find Celia at Usk or Cardiff farmers' markets.

Pentre Pigs

Pentre House, Leighton, Welshpool, Powys SY21 8HL   T: 01938 553430
w: www.pentrepigs.co.uk
✉ **farm gate sales (by appointment)** 🚚 **delivery service** ✉ **mail order**

Slowly reared, traditional and rare-breed pigs – Tamworth, Berkshire and even the unusual Kune Kune breed – enjoy GM-free feed and plenty of fruit and veg and range totally freely at Pentre Pigs. Most pork cuts are available as well as dry-cured bacon, gammon, sausages and offal. New customers buying half a pig even get a free cookery book.

CHAPTER

9

Many of the producers and suppliers in this chapter also offer other types of meat and, equally, many of those listed in the meat chapter sell poultry. I have chosen producers for this section for whom poultry is a speciality, who have won awards for their poultry or who simply excel at rearing poultry. Individual entries describe the complete range offered by the supplier or producer.

Chicken is our favourite meat and we consume, quite literally, millions of chickens every year. This hasn't always been the case – not so long ago, chicken was very much a luxury food and goose, guineafowl, duck and game birds would have been eaten as frequently. Most of the chicken we buy now will have been reared in factory, or battery, conditions but there are plenty of alternatives to this – farms slowly rearing plump and active free-range birds, often corn-fed to produce a rich colour and flavour. I've listed producers who offer a range of poultry, all of which will be very different from intensively reared birds. Reared without antibiotics, which force the pace of growth, these birds will have no added water, which renders the meat soft and flabby, and will in many cases have been dry-plucked, allowing for a properly crisp skin

poultry

when cooked. Properly free-range birds will be fit and healthy, having had an active life and so the meat will be dense and firm.

As with every other kind of meat, the eating qualities of poultry are enhanced by good husbandry, and there really is no substitute for time. The producers we feature allow their chickens to grow for much longer than factory broiler birds, in many cases for over twice the length of time, and the flavour reflects this. This goes for all the different types of poultry reared on the farms listed in these pages – the goose, duck and turkey producers featured here don't rush their birds along, but wait until they have slowly developed a full flavour and good texture. Many of them are also using old-fashioned breeds like the Norfolk Black turkey, or the Cornish Red chicken. These breeds may not yield the greatest quantity of the breast meat so slavishly sought by large scale commercial producers, but they often offer a more intensely flavoured meat. There is, of course a price to pay for these labour-intensive rearing practices, a good free-range bird will cost more than a factory-reared one, but it really is worth it.

The Meat Joint

Hillsborough House, Loxhore, Barnstaple, Devon EX31 4SU   T: 01271 850335
E: themeat.joint@care4free.net

🛒 **farmers' markets** 🖼 **farm gate sales**

All kinds of traditional meats are reared at The Meat Joint – Aberdeen Angus beef, hung for up to four weeks for a mature flavour, Large White pork and Poll Dorset lamb – and all are reared slowly to allow the flavour to develop. But it is with the chicken reared here that the differences between extensively reared organic meat and its conventional counterpart are most marked. The free-range chickens are allowed to grow for twice as long as conventional birds and they are partly grass-fed, giving their flesh a lovely golden yellow hue, and the flavour is of an intensity that factory farming can never achieve. Available direct from the farm (phone first) or from Barnstaple, Wrafton, Ilfracombe, Bratton Fleming, and Combe Martin farmers' markets.

Bath Organic Farms

6 Brookside House, High Street, Weston, Bath BA1 4BY   T: 01225 421507
W: www.bathorganicfarms.com

🥄 **farm shop** 🛒 **farmers' markets** ✉ **mail order**

All kinds of locally produced organic meat is available here, including lamb and mutton from the farm's own flock. A speciality is the free-range organic chicken, slowly reared for flavour, and there is also organic turkey and, unusually, organic guineafowl.

Home Farm Shop

Tarrant Gunville, Blandford Forum, Dorset DT11 8JW   T: 01258 830083
E: rod@rbelbin.fsnet.co.uk

🥄 **farm shop**

Free-range Aylesbury ducks, free-range chickens, quails' eggs and free-range hens' eggs, all home-produced. Also available are home-made sausages, beef and pork from the farm and local lamb and cheeses from nearby suppliers. There is also a tea room.

Wixon Farm

Chulmleigh, Devon EX18 7DS   T: 01769 580438

🔹 **farmers' markets**   🔹 **farm gate sales**

The organic chickens at Wixon Farm are reared entirely free-range.
Their diet does not encourage unrealistic growth, so the birds develop
great texture and flavour and the grass in their diet gives the flesh a
lovely yellow colour. Organic Aberdeen Angus beef is also available,
direct from the farm (phone first), or from Devon farmers' markets.

Ark Chicken

Roosters of Babylon, Babylon Lane, Silverton, nr Exeter, Devon EX5 4DT
T: 01392 860430   W: www.arkchicken.co.uk

🔹 **farmers' markets**   🔹 **mail order**

Free-range chickens and guineafowl are reared in small flocks,
housed in moveable arks, giving the birds access to continually fresh
pasture. The birds are slow-growing breeds, allowed to mature fully,
and are processed and hand-finished on site. Available from many
Devon farmers' markets, including Totnes, Tiverton, Wellington,
Crediton, Cullompton, Exmouth and Honiton, Taunton farmers'
market in Somerset, and by mail order.

South Torfrey Farm

Golant, Fowey, Cornwall PL23 1LA   T: 01726 833126   E: stf7@onetel.com

🔹 **farm gate sales**

Organic geese and turkeys are available from South Torfrey
(Christmas only), Longhorn beef and organic eggs, and organic
chickens from a neighbouring farm.

Providence Farm

Crosspark Cross, Holsworthy, Devon EX22 6JW   T: 01409 254421
W: www.providencefarm.co.uk

🔹 **farm shop**   🔹 **mail order**

Free-range organic pigs are slowly reared at Providence Farm, with
the resulting meat winning a Soil Association Organic Food Award

for Best Pork several years running. Free-range and organic chicken, duck, goose and guineafowl and traditional-breed lamb and beef are also available and you can find all this at the Tavistock Pannier Market every Friday, as well as at the farm, or buy mail order.

Exmoor Organic

Higher Riscombe Farm, nr Minehead, Somerset TA24 7JY   т: 01643 831184
w: www.exmoor-organic.co.uk

📧 **farm gate sales** 📧 **mail order**

Exmoor Organic are specialist producers of organic free-range ducks and organic Christmas geese. In 2002 the ducks won Best Poultry in the Organic Food Awards and a bronze Taste of the West award. As exclusive supplier to Duchy Originals of Christmas geese, Exmoor Organic ensures traceability and the highest standards, with all produce being reared and processed at Higher Riscombe Farm, high in the hills of Exmoor National Park. The organic duck won a gold Taste of the West medal in 2004.

Somerset Farm Direct

Bittescombe Manor, Upton, Wiveliscombe, Taunton, Somerset TA4 2DA
т: 01398 371387   w: www.somersetfarmdirect.co.uk

📧 **mail order**

Free-range chickens and Aylesbury ducks are reared naturally here, without additives or antibiotics. Local Exmoor lamb and mutton are also available, hung on the bone for three weeks.

Withyslade Farm

Tisbury Row, Tisbury, Wiltshire SP3 6RZ   т: 01747 871155   е: geese@withyslade.co.uk

📧 **farm gate sales**

The geese arrive at Withyslade Farm as day-old chicks, and then they are reared slowly on a diet of grass and home-grown wheat. They are killed at the farm to reduce stress, and then hung and dry plucked for a traditional flavour. Call to make an order for Christmas.

super hero

RICHARD GUY, of The Real Meat Company, Warminster (see below)

Of the millions of chickens eaten every year in the UK and Ireland, most will be breeds specifically selected to produce as much breast meat as possible. These breeds have been manipulated with this in mind, and one little-known effect of this causes immeasurable distress to the birds – their legs are not strong enough to support their unnaturally large breasts and, as a result, they suffer from deformities and broken legs and often cannot stand up for more than 15 minutes. Richard Guy wants no part of this cruelty and feels that such birds cannot be part of a good, healthy diet. Instead, he rears breeds of bird that have not been modified for such mercenary reasons and they can be seen on the farm, ranging freely and happily, growing fit and healthy. Their diet is free from antibiotics and growth promoters; they are fed by hand and they are killed by hand. Of course, this breed does not grow and fatten quickly like the intensively reared birds; the benefit of this is, when slaughtered at twice the age of factory-reared counterparts, Richard's chickens will have developed a flavour and texture almost certainly lacking in those from the battery hen house.

The attention to detail doesn't stop there – after slaughter, the birds are allowed to mature before being sold, allowing the flavour to develop further. Richard Guy believes that 'eating meat is a privilege, not a right' and he extends his welfare-based farming practices to the production of pork, beef and lamb, too. The farms used to supply meat to the Real Meat Company are trusted sources, monitored constantly – animals are reared to extremely tight regulations and the farmers who produce the beef have never had a case of BSE. See the meat chapter for addresses of Real Meat Company shops around the country, many of which buy their meat exclusively from Richard.

SOUTH WEST   WARMINSTER

The Real Meat Company   super hero

Warminster, Wiltshire BA12 0HR   T: 01985 840562   w: www.realmeat.co.uk

The headquarters of The Real Meat Company, which has franchises and approved stockists throughout the country. Richard Guy, one of the founders of the company, believes that 'eating meat is a privilege, not a right' and farms supplying the company are trusted sources, adhering to strict regulations. See the Super Hero box, above, for more information.

super hero

PETER AND JULIET KINDERSLEY, of Sheepdrove Organic Farm, Lambourn
(see page 370)

Sheepdrove Farm is part of the Organic Farm Network run by the Soil
Association (an 'open farm' scheme whereby the public can see how organic
farming works) and Peter and Juliet Kindersley are happy to let people visit
and see the farm as it functions. And what a glowing recommendation of the
Soil Association it is – the Kindersleys' mission is 'a farm that is self-
sustaining, protects the environment, and is able to invest in its people and
future, producing great food'. The farm teems with wildlife and is home to the
Barn Owl Conservation Network. The livestock breeds are all carefully chosen
to suit the extensive farming and to produce the tastiest meat. While all types
of meat are available (beef, lamb and pork), it is with the chickens that the
effects of high-welfare farming are the most obvious. The free-range chickens
are traditional outdoor breeds, producing a bird that is well muscled, growing
slowly on a diet of home-produced grain. The birds are well looked after –
an animal behaviourist is consulted to make sure the birds are all happy and
healthy; when it is time (at over twice the age of factory-farmed birds), they
are slaughtered on site to minimize stress. For the farmers at Sheepdrove, the
level of care their livestock receives is well worth the effort – 'We are inspired
by support from our customers, who enjoy a direct link to the source of their
meat and poultry and can visit the farm at any time. They can see our aim is to
have the highest animal welfare standard, a diverse habitat, and a sustainable
production system.'

Dunning Quality Geese

Goose Slade Farm, East Coker, Yeovil, Somerset BA22 9JY   T: 01935 863735
E: dunning@gooseslade.fsnet.co.uk

🥄 **farm shop**

Free-range seasonal (September to Christmas) geese, bred on the
farm. The geese are grass-fed, supplemented with home-grown grain.
Traditionally dry-plucked and hung for a week, the geese are available
from the farm shop, which is also stocked with local produce.

Homewood Partners

Peach Croft Farm, Radley, Abingdon, Oxfordshire OX14 2HP   T: 01235 520094
W: www.peachcroft.co.uk
🥄 farm shop 🚚 delivery service

Seasonally available free-range geese, reared on grassy paddocks
from slow-growing breeds. The birds are fed a natural diet of grass
and some home-grown wheat and are reared without antibiotics or
additives for growth promotion. The poultry are hand-plucked and
then allowed to mature for up to ten days prior to Christmas.
Available fresh from the farm, via the delivery service or from local
butchers during the month of December. Homewood is a member
of the British Goose Producers Association and accredited by the
Traditional Farmfresh Turkey Association.

Sheepdrove Organic Farm
Family Butchers

3 Lower Redland Road, Bristol BS6 9TB T: 0117 973 4643
W: www.sheepdrove.com

An outlet for the extensively-reared meat and free-range poultry
produced by Sheepdrove Organic Farm, Lambourn. See the Super
Hero Box, opposite, for more details.

Copas Traditional Turkeys

Kings Coppice Farm, Grubwood Lane, Cookham, Berkshire SL6 9UB   T: 01628 474678
📨 farm gate sales

Every aspect of the way Copas turkeys are reared has been chosen
with one goal – to produce a turkey with the best possible flavour
and texture. Old-fashioned breeds are used, which means that
the turkeys can grow to full maturity – a minimum of 25 weeks,
compared to the scant nine most mass-produced birds are
allowed. This enables the turkeys to develop a layer of fat under the
skin, and it is this, along with the traditional dry plucking, that
keeps the meat tasty, moist and succulent during roasting. Hanging
for a full 10 days allows the flavour to develop still further, giving
the turkeys a distinctly old-fashioned quality sadly lacking in
factory-farmed birds. Check the website for your nearest stockist.

Cranleigh Organic Farm Shop

Lower Barrihurst Farm, Dunsford Road, Cranleigh, Surrey GU6 8LG T: 01483 272896
E: organicfarmshop@btopenworld.com

🥄 **farm shop**

Open every day except for Tuesdays, Cranleigh Organic Farm Shop sells home-reared, free-range, organic, traditional-breed chickens. Fed on organic corn and home-produced vegetables, the chickens are reared in small flocks. Processed on site, they are dry-plucked. Geese and turkeys are available at Christmas and there are also home-grown vegetables in season and a full range of groceries. Everything is organic.

The Weald Smokery

Mount Farm, Flimwell, East Sussex TN5 7QL T: 01580 879601
W: www.wealdsmokery.co.uk

✉ **mail order**

Hand-prepared, traditionally smoked meat and fish are all prepared without dyes, additives or artificial preservatives at The Weald Smokery, who have won numerous Great Taste Awards, notably for their smoked duck breast and smoked salmon.

Sheepdrove Organic Farm

Warren Farm, Lambourn, Berkshire RG17 7UU T: 01488 71659
W: www.sheepdrove.com

Sheepdrove Farm produces all types of extensively reared meat, especially free-range chickens, and they welcome visitors. See the Super Hero box, page 368, for more information. There is also a shop, Sheepdrove Organic Farm Family Butchers, in Bristol (see page 369).

Wyndham House Poultry

2–3 Stoney Street, (near Borough Market), London SE1 9AA T: 020 7403 4788

Wyndham House is a poultry specialist, with a fantastic choice of mainly free-range duck, chicken, game birds, goose and turkey,

with all kinds of related products. The birds are usually selected
direct from the producers.

M Feller Son & Daughter, Organic Butchers

54–55 The Covered Market, Oxford OX1 3DY   T: 01865 251164   W: www.mfeller.co.uk

Plenty of Soil Association accredited organic meat is on offer here,
with good-quality, free-range chicken.

Harvest Moon Organic Farm

Dawes Lane, Sarratt, Hertfordshire WD3 6BQ   T: 07776 194241

🥬 **farm shop (Fridays only)** 🛒 **farmers' markets**

Organic free-range chickens from the slow-growing Master Gris
breed range freely over organic, herb-rich pasture at Harvest Moon
Farm. Free-range eggs are also available. Find the produce at
Swiss Cottage, Wimbledon, Pimlico, Islington and Blackheath
farmers' markets.

Wonston Organic Poultry

Upton House Farm, Wonston, Winchester, Hampshire SO21 3LR   T: 01962 760219
W: www.organic-chicken.co.uk

🛒 **farmers' markets** 🚚 **delivery service**

The organic free-range chickens at Wonston are reared slowly
to around 16 weeks – much longer than even organic regulations
stipulate – and this allows them to develop great texture and flavour.
Available from local farmers' markets (check the website for details)
or call to arrange a delivery.

Great Grove Poultry

Whews Farm, Caston, Attleborough, Norfolk NR17 1BS   T: 01953 483216
📮 **farm gate sales**

Free-range geese and free-range Bronze turkeys are available at
Christmas from Great Grove Poultry. Call to place your order.

Munson's Poultry

Emdon, Straight Road, Boxted, Colchester, Essex CO4 5QX   T: 01206 272637
W: www.munsonspoultry.demon.co.uk

 farmers' markets

Free-range Norfolk Black turkeys, pork, beef and lamb, home-made
sausages and eggs (duck, hen, goose, guineafowl, quail and
pheasant) are all available from Munson's stall at the Billericay
farmers' market.

Kelly Turkey Farms

Springate Farm, Bicknacre Road, Danbury, Essex CM3 4EP   T: 01245 223581
W: www.kelly-turkeys.com

 mail order

The free-range organic turkeys and chickens at Springate Farm are
slow-growing breeds, reared for flavour. They are dry-plucked by
hand and the turkeys are hung for around ten days.

Rumburgh Farm

Rumburgh, Halesworth, Suffolk IP19 0RU   T: 01986 781351
W: www.rumburghfarm.freeserve.co.uk

 farm gate sales

Free-range Bronze and Norfolk Black turkeys for the Christmas
season. Slowly matured, for a closely grained, moist texture, the
turkeys are dry-plucked by hand and hung for at least a week.
Turkeys are available to collect from the farm but must be ordered in
advance.

Farmyard Chicken Company
(S J Frederick & Sons)

Farm Office, Temple Farm, Roydon, Harlow, Essex CM19 5LW   T: 01279 792460
W: www.labelanglais.co.uk

 mail order

Slow-growing, free-range chickens from breeds specifically selected for flavour are the speciality here, maize-fed for flavour. The birds are reared in some cases up to 100 days, which is a great deal longer than conventionally reared chickens, and it is this increased lifespan which yields a flavour that broiler chickens can never achieve. At Christmas free-range, dry-plucked turkeys are available.

Morton's Traditional Taste

Grove Farm, Aylsham Road, Swanton Abbott, Norwich, Norfolk NR10 5DL

T: 01692 538067   W: www.mortonstraditionaltaste.co.uk

✉ **farm gate sales**

Seasonal Kelly Bronze and Norfolk Black turkeys, all free-range, are available from November.

Peele's

Peele & Partners, Rookery Farm, Thuxton, Norwich, Norfolk NR9 4QJ   T: 01362 850237

✉ **farm gate sales** ✉ **mail order**

Free-range, rare-breed Norfolk Black turkeys, slowly reared on home-grown wheat, barley and beans, and free-range geese in season are available from Peeles.

super hero

SELDOM SEEN FARM, Billesdon (see page 374)

The free-range geese and Bronze turkeys at Seldom Seen Farm are allowed to grow at their own pace, unforced, raised on grass and home-grown corn. They are processed by hand on the farm, dry-plucked and hung for 12–14 days and are available direct from the farm between October and Christmas. During December, the farm has a Christmas shop, with every kind of food you could possibly need for the season, including their famous Three Bird Roast – a goose, stuffed with a chicken, stuffed with a pheasant, layered with pork and orange – enough to feed 15–20 people. Absolutely everything is done by hand at Seldom Seen Farm and the level of attention to detail really does make the produce stand out from the crowd.

Great Clerkes Farm

Little Sampford, Saffron Walden, Essex CB10 2QJ   T: 01799 586248

📧 **farm gate sales** ✉ **mail order**

Free-range, grass-fed geese, reared slowly and dry-plucked in
the traditional manner. The geese have a home-grown cereal
supplement to their diet, which gives their flesh a golden hue.
They are available from late November.

Seldom Seen Farm   super hero

Billesdon, Leicestershire LE7 9FA   T: 0116 259 6742

📧 **farm gate sales** ✉ **mail order**

Seldom Seen Farm raises free-range geese and Bronze turkeys.
See the Super Hero box, page 373, for more information.

Woodlands Organic Farm

Kirton House, Kirton, Boston, Lincolnshire PE20 1JD   T: 01205 722491
w: www.woodlandsfarm.co.uk

📧 **farmers' markets** ✉ **mail order** 📦 **box scheme**

Woodlands Farm specializes in free-range, organic Bronze turkeys,
which have access to grassy paddocks at all times. They are reared
in small groups and slaughtered on the farm to reduce stress.
Organic vegetables and organic Lincoln Red beef are also available
through the box scheme the farm operates, and at many farmers'
markets throughout Lincolnshire.

W E Botterill & Son

Lings View Farm, 10 Middle Street, Croxton Kerrial, Grantham NG32 1QP
T: 01476 870394

📧 **farm gate sales**

Free-range, dry-plucked geese and Bronze turkeys, along with some
local game, are all available seasonally.

Springfield Poultry

Steen's Bridge, Leominster, Herefordshire HR6 0LU   T: 01568 760270

✉ **farm gate sales**

Using a slowly growing breed from Ireland, the Mee family rear chickens in small groups. The birds are killed at twice the age of conventional broilers, producing well-developed flavour in the meat. Turkeys are available at Christmas – call to order.

food facts

WHAT SHOULD I ASK WHEN CHOOSING POULTRY?

What makes good poultry on the plate is very simple. It comes down to breed, feed, welfare and age at slaughter. Good producers will choose the breed of bird that they rear specifically for good eating qualities; it may not be the fastest growing, but it will taste good. They won't fill their birds with the cheapest high-protein ration from an unknown source, containing all sorts of additives – they'll give them home-produced feed, or a good-quality ration, often organic. The flock will also have access to fresh pasture and will be fit and healthy – meat is muscle, so a fit bird will produce better quality meat. Finally, they'll be allowed to mature at their own pace, and will be slaughtered considerably later than factory-farmed birds, which means that the taste of the meat is allowed time to develop.

Goodman's Geese

Goodman's Brothers, Walsgrove Farm, Great Witley, Worcester WR6 6JJ
T: 01299 896272   W: www.goodmansgeese.co.uk
✉ **farm gate sales** ✉ **mail order**

The geese at Walsgrove Farm are all reared free-range, with a natural diet of grass, corn and straw. Bronze turkeys are also available in season. Geese are available from September to Christmas, turkeys from November to Christmas.

Holly Tree Farm Shop

Chester Road, Tabley, Knutsford, Cheshire WA16 0EU   T: 01565 651835
w: www.hollytreefarmshop.co.uk
⤙ **farm shop**

Holly Tree Farm Shop is a cornucopia of traditional local produce
but the main draws are the free-range geese and ducks, reared by
the shop owner, Karol Bailey. The farm is run with great emphasis
on animal welfare and environmental concern and land is rested
properly between batches of poultry to maintain natural fertility.

The Ellel Free Range Poultry Company

The Stables, Ellel Grange, Galgate, nr Lancaster LA2 0HN   T: 01524 751200
w: www.ellelfreerangepoultry.co.uk
▨ **farm gate sales** ✉ **mail order**

Free-range chickens and guineafowl throughout the year, and
turkeys and geese at Christmas are available here, all reared with
great attention to animal welfare. New for this year is home-
produced Dexter beef, hung for a full four weeks.

Burtree House Farm

Burtree Lane, Darlington, Co. Durham DL3 0UY   T: 01325 463521
w: www.burtreehousefarm.co.uk
⤙ **farm shop** 🏛 **farmers' markets**

Robert and Lea Darling rear free-range chickens very slowly, which
are not killed until 12–16 weeks old, compared to the short 42 days
of conventional broiler chickens, producing a much fuller flavour.
Lea also makes an amazing selection of cakes, some gluten-free,
including 11 different varieties of tea loaf, all made using the free-
range eggs from her own hens. Other local produce is available,
including award-winning dry-cured bacon, guineafowl and Kelly
Bronze free-range turkeys are available in season. Burtree House
Farm produce is available direct from the farm (call first if you want
a chicken) or from local farmers' markets.

Piercebridge Farm Organics

Piercebridge, Darlington, Co. Durham DL2 3SE   T: 01325 374251
E: piercebridgefarm@zoom.co.uk
⏚ **farm shop**

Piercebridge Farm offers traditional, dry-plucked, organic chickens, which are slowly matured and hung. The farm shop also has home-reared organic lamb and potatoes, organic beef, sausages and pork, an excellent range of organic vegetables and fruit, and even an organic coffee shop and is a member of Northumbria Organic Producers.

Highlands Farm

Lindhead Road, Burniston, Scarborough, North Yorkshire YO13 0DL   T: 01723 870048
⏚ **farmers' markets**

All kinds of free-range poultry are reared at Highlands Farm – geese and Norfolk Kelly Bronze turkeys are available at Christmas and ducks and chickens are available all year. The geese and ducks are particularly lucky – access to a river means they live as nature intended. The chickens are killed at 14–15 weeks old, around twice the age of commercial broilers. Suffolk cross lamb, hung for two weeks for flavour and tenderness, is also on offer, available from Driffield, York and Malton farmers' markets.

Thornbeck Farm

Calf Fallow Lane, Norton, Stockton-on-Tees, Cleveland TS20 1PF   T: 01642 365661 OR 07715 023102
⏚ **farm gate sales**

Both chickens and pheasants are raised at Thornbeck farm from day-old chicks on a diet of locally grown corn (including some which is organic), and water from the farm's own spring. Allowed to grow to a minimum age of 12 weeks, the birds develop good flavour and texture, and are processed on the farm and delivered locally for a low-food-miles product.

FOOD HEROES OF BRITAIN

'O' Kane Poultry Ltd

170 Larne Road, Ballymena, Co. Antrim BT42 3HA   T: 028 2564 1111
w: www.okanepoultry.com

Look out for 'O' Kane free-range chickens in Marks & Spencer's stores across Northern Ireland, sold under the Oakham Gold label. They are sourced from small NI farms and are specifically chosen, slower growing breeds. With access to open fields, reared in smaller flocks and fed a GM-free diet that does not force their growth, the chickens develop an old-fashioned flavour and texture. An organic free-range Bronze turkey is seasonally available, too.

Culdrum Organic Farm

Aghadowey, Coleraine, Co. Londonderry BT51 3SP   T: 028 7086 8951 OR 07764 638356   w: www.culdrum.co.uk

🖻 **farmers' markets** 🖾 **farm gate sales** 🖾 **box scheme**

A mixed organic farm, with inspiring principles – the farming is as environmentally sensitive as possible. Free-range chickens are reared in small groups, fed an entirely natural diet of crushed oats, barley and vegetables and allowed to grow at their own pace. There are also plenty of organic vegetables and pork and sausages from the rare Saddleback breed. The vegetables can be obtained through the weekly box scheme the farm runs or at St Georges Market in Belfast, where the chicken and pork are also available.

Mullan Farm

84 Ringsend Road, Limavady, Co. Londonderry BT49 0QJ   T: 028 7776 4157

🖻 **farmers' markets** 🖾 **farm gate sales**

Organic poultry in many different varieties – Black turkeys at Christmas, chickens, ducks and geese – are all reared organically in small flocks at Mullan Farm. The poultry houses are moved regularly, so the birds always have fresh pasture and plenty of space to range. Available from the farm itself or every Saturday at St Georges Market in Belfast.

Maughanasilly

Kealkil, Bantry, Co. Cork   T: 027 66111

➥ **farm shop**

A mixed farm producing organic, free-range poultry and beef, Maughanasilly encourages visitors to get involved; see the Super Hero box, below, for more information.

Ballysimon Organic Farm

Midleton, Co. Cork   T: 021 463 1058

≝ **farmers' markets**

Organic, free-range chickens – a slow-growing French breed, reared to 12 weeks old for a full flavour, eggs and Aberdeen Angus slowly matured organic beef are available at Midleton, Cork, Cobh and Douglas farmers' market every week.

super hero

YVONNE O'FLYNN, of Maughanasilly Farm, Bantry (see above)

Maughanasilly is a mixed farm where attention to animal welfare is a priority. When any of the animals become ill, they are treated with homeopathy, although in such an extensive system of rearing, sickness is very rare – Yvonne couldn't remember the last time she had to call the vet out. Organic free-range ducks, geese and chickens are available and also pork and vegetables in season, cut to order. When children from cities visit her farm when they are on holiday in the area Yvonne is often shocked that they know so very little about where food comes from. The O'Flynns happily let these kids collect eggs from the hen house, feed the animals and generally get a sense of what goes on at a farm, hoping in this way to help bridge the gap between town and country.

Gartmorn Farm

Alloa, Clackmannanshire FK10 3AU   T: 01259 750549   W: www.gartmornfarm.co.uk

farmers' markets   **farm gate sales**   **mail order**

Gartmorn Farm free-range turkeys, chickens, ducks and seasonal geese are reared in open barns and have access to fields and the orchard; the ducks also have their own pond. Produce can be bought directly from the farm, by mail order or from Perth, Cupar, Glasgow and Kirkcaldy farmers' markets.

The Chicken Lady

North Horntowie Free Range Poultry, North Horntowie, Cairnie, Huntly, Aberdeenshire AB54 4TA   T: 01542 870329

delivery service

Liz Jones rears her own free-range chickens, slowly grown for maximum flavour, and delivers them locally to customers. She has got together with a group of other local producers and now offers a range of great local foods – her own chicken, lamb and Aberdeen Angus beef, and from other producers, free-range eggs, salmon, cheese, free-range pork, fresh garlic, dry-cured bacon and quail eggs.

Highland Geese

Corranmor Farm, Ardfern, by Lochgilphead, Argyll PA31 8QN   T: 01852 500609
W: www.highlandgeese.co.uk

farm gate sales   **mail order**

Free-range geese from the farm's own laying stock and day-olds brought in from trusted breeders, fed only on grain and grass. The geese are available fresh at Christmas and frozen for Easter.

Caithness Goose Company

Oliclett Farm, Thrumster, Caithness KW1 5TX   T: 01955 651387
W: www.caithness-goose.co.uk

farm gate sales   **mail order**

Free-range geese are reared traditionally on grass and oats here – the oats impart a robust flavour to the meat. Dry-plucked and hung for two weeks, the geese are available direct from the farm. Islay MacLeod and Guy Wallace, the farmers, are in the early stages of resurrecting an old Caithness speciality – smoked goose – from references to this dish found in an 1824 cookbook. Caithness Goose Company is a member of the British Goose Producers Association.

Madgetts Farm Poultry

Tidenham Chase, Chepstow, Monmouthshire NP16 7LZ   T: 01291 689595

farmers' markets

The Williams family rear free-range chickens and ducks, and geese and bronze turkeys at Christmas. Available from many farmers' markets on the Welsh/English borders, including Gloucester, Cirencester, Stroud, Hereford and Stow-on-the-Wold.

Coedwynog Free Range Geese

Felindre Farchog, Crymych, Pembrokeshire SA41 3XW   T: 01239 820306
w: www.coedwynog-geese.co.uk

farm gate sales

The Careys rear geese from day-old chicks, ranging free on 18 acres of pasture, with the grass they eat supplemented with home-grown wheat. Dry-plucked by hand, the flesh of the geese is a rich honey colour, due to their natural lifestyle. Geese are available direct from the farm in December and from butchers' shops throughout Wales. Goose fat is available all year round.

Wern Poultry Products

Wern Villa, Rhydcymerau, Llandeilo, Carmarthenshire SA19 7RP   T: 01558 685591
w: www.wernpoultry.co.uk

farmers' markets   farm gate sales   mail order

The organically reared chickens at Wern Poultry Products are bred to be slow growing and strong, a breed called the Carmarthen Buff, based on the Cornish Red chicken. They mature slowly without suffering the problems conventional broiler chickens suffer, such as broken legs, due to their skeletons being unable to support their fast, forced growth. The birds here are grown to over 100 days old, well over the minimum stipulated by the Soil Association, and this results in meat with well-developed flavour and texture. Fed on corn, beans and peas, the flesh of the birds has a rich yellow colour. Free-range organic eggs and ducks are also available. Buy direct from the farm (visitors are encouraged) or from Cardiff Riverside farmers' market.

Goetre Farm

Llanllwni, Llanybydder, Carmarthenshire SA40 9SG   T: 01570 480671
E: michael@goetrefarm.co.uk
🚚 delivery service

Free-range ducks and Saddleback pork, free-range Kelly turkeys at Christmas, and non-intensive, barn-reared chickens are available from Goetre Farm by home delivery. All the animals are reared without antibiotics, and the poultry is hung before sale. The pork is butchered on site, and home-made sausages (which won two Great Taste awards in 2004) and home-cured bacon is available. Goetre Farm is a member of the Traditional Farm Fresh Turkey Association, which has strict criteria regarding rearing the turkeys. Call to arrange a delivery, or find the produce at Llwynhelyg Farm Shop (see page 142).

Cefn Goleu

Pont Robert, Meifod, Powys SY22 6JN   T: 01938 500128
✉ farm gate sales

Anne and Michael Moorhouse rear unusual-breed turkeys – Norfolk Black, Bronze, Bourbon Red and Buff. They are reared organically, processed on the farm and hung properly before dressing. Free-range organic table chickens and organic turkey eggs – very unusual! – are also available. Call to arrange an order to collect from the farm.

Cefn Maen Farm

Usk Road, Raglan, Monmouthshire NP15 2HR   T: 01291 690428
✉ farm gate sales

Free-range seasonal Bronze turkeys, dry-plucked and hung for two weeks for an old-fashioned flavour. Customers can visit the farm to see how the turkeys are reared. Call to arrange this or to place an order for collection. Order by mid November to be sure of getting the size you want.

POULTRY

Penucha'r plwyf Farm

Llantrisant, nr Usk, Monmouthshire NP15 1LS T: 01291 620093

 farmers' markets

These organic, slowly reared chickens are available from Usk farmers' market on the first and third Saturdays of the month.

food facts

ANTIBIOTICS AND THE POULTRY INDUSTRY

There is real fear these days among a good number of scientists that the routine use of antibiotics in livestock feed, which is particularly prevalent in intensive poultry rearing, is partly to blame for the failure of antibiotics in human medical use and the rise of 'superbugs' that are resistant to antibiotics. It is interesting to note that instances of salmonella in chickens has increased, not decreased, as the routine use of antibiotics has increased. It is not just chickens that are intensively reared and subject to antibiotic use either, turkeys and ducks are also sometimes reared in these conditions. In Sweden, the routine use of antibiotics in the chicken industry was banned in 1984 and, since then, salmonella has decreased significantly. Farming authorities are at pains to point out that antibiotics are not used as growth promoters but simply as a defence against disease, but the reality is that antibiotics do promote growth and yet don't seem to do much to prevent the spread of disease. If the birds were not kept in such cramped conditions, and if the market hadn't pushed the price of poultry so unrealistically low, then antibiotics would not be needed at all. A well-reared, free-range bird goes a long way towards avoiding these problems and its price represents its real value.

Acknowledgements

In compiling this guide I have been offered invaluable help by the institutions, publications and individuals listed below. I would like to thank them for their support. Many of the organisations have extremely useful websites and I have included them here in case you feel inspired to find out more about the various bodies and what they stand for.

Organisations

Biodynamic Agricultural Association of Great Britain
TEL: 01453 759501 w: www.anth.org.uk/biodynamic

CAIS (Irish Farmhouse Cheesemakers Association)

The Campaign for Real Ale (CAMRA) TEL: 01727 867201
w: www.camra.org.uk

Common Ground TEL: 01747 850820 w:www.commonground.org.uk

Compassion in World Farming TEL: 01730 264208 w: www.ciwf.co.uk

English Wine Producers TEL: 01536 772264
w: www.englishwineproducers.com
(with special thanks to Julia Trustram Eve)

The Food Commission TEL: 020 7837 2250 w: www.foodcomm.org.uk

The Game Conservancy Trust TEL: 01425 652381 w: www.gct.org.uk

Guild of Fine Food Retailers TEL: 01747 822290
w: www.finefoodworld.co.uk

Guild of Q Butchers TEL: 01383 432622
w: www.guildofqbutchers.co.uk

Marine Stewardship Council w: www.msc.org

The National Federation of Fishmongers

Northern Ireland Seafood TEL: 028 9045 2829 w: www.niseafood.co.uk

The Organic Trust TEL: +353 1 853 0271
w: www.iol.ie/~organic/trust.html

Rare Breeds Survival Trust   TEL: 02476 696551
w:www.rare-breeds.com

Soil Association   TEL: 0117 929 0661   w:www.soilassociation.org

The Specialist Cheesemakers Association   TEL: 020 7253 2114
w: www.specialistcheesemakers.co.uk

Sustain – The Alliance for Better Food and Farming   TEL: 020 7837 1228
w: www.sustainweb.org (with special thanks to Dan Keech)

Welsh Development Agency   TEL: 01443 845500   w: www.wda.co.uk
(with special thanks to Mike Caplan-Hill)

Wholesome Food Association   TEL: 01803 866877
w: www.wholesomefood.org

Publications

The Bridgestone Guides www.bestofbridgestone.com – *The Bridgestone Food Lover's Guide to Northern Ireland* and *The Bridgestone Food Lover's Guide to Ireland* (both Estragon Press). With special thanks to Caroline Workman.

British Baker magazine www.britishbaker.net

Thanks also to Avril Allshire from Caherbeg Free-range Pork, Clodagh McKenna from West Cork Slow Food, Giana Ferguson from Gubbeen Farmhouse and Jenny Davies from Llwynhelyg Farm Shop.

FOOD HEROES OF BRITAIN

index by location

✖ BREAD	◯ DRINKS	▽ GAME
✖ DAIRY AND EGGS	◆ FISH	◇ MEAT
✚ DELICATESSENS	◻ FRUIT AND VEGETABLES	✶ POULTRY

ENGLAND

Bath

✖ Bath Soft Cheese Company, Bath (Kelston), 54
✖ Fine Cheese Co., The, Bath, 54
✖ Paxton & Whitfield, Bath, 54
◆ FishWorks, Bath, 176
◇ Real Meat Company, The, Bear Flat, 276
✶ Bath Organic Farms, Weston, 364

Bedfordshire

✖ Cheese Kitchen, The, Bedford, 65
✚ Mrs Huddleston's, Leighton Buzzard, 112

Berkshire

✖ Two Hoots Farmhouse Cheese, Wokingham, 69
✚ County Delicacies, Reading, 116
◯ Valley Vineyard, Twyford, 159
◆ Hand Picked Shellfish Company, Basingstoke, 179
◻ Cross Lanes Fruit Farm, Reading, 226
◇ Ashgood Farm, Slough, 306
◇ Evans & Paget, Thatcham, 308
◇ Fuglemere Rare Breeds, Slough, 307
◇ Ranger Organics, Reading, 305
◇ Swan Inn, The, Hungerford, 302
◇ Whittings Butchers, Reading, 306
✶ Copas Traditional Turkeys, Cookham, 369
✶ Sheepdrove Organic Farm, Lambourn, 368, 370

Birmingham

◇ M Finn Butchers, Great Barr, 314

Bristol

✚ Better Food Company, The, Bristol, 102
◯ K G Consultants, Compton Dando, 146
◆ Club Chef Direct, Barrow Gurney, 176
◻ Arne Herbes, Chew Magna, 212
◻ Jekka's Herb Farm, Alveston, 213
✶ Sheepdrove Organic Farm Family Butchers, Bristol, 368, 369

Buckinghamshire

✖ Bakers Basket, Aylesbury, 25
✖ H P Jung, Beaconsfield, 26
✚ Food Halls, The, Gerrards Cross, 111
✚ Roots Deli, High Wycombe, 112
◻ Home Cottage Farm, Iver, 224
◻ Sustainable Lifestyles Research Co-op Ltd, The, Aylesbury, 221
▽ Castleman's Farm, Woburn Common, 261
▽ Manor Farm Game, Chesham, 260
◇ Fullers Organic Farm Shop, Milton Keynes, 304

Cambridgeshire

✖ Fosters Mill, Swaffham Prior, 34
✚ Cambridge Cheese Company, The, 117
✚ La Hogue Farm Shop and Delicatessen, Ely, 118
✚ Swayfen Herb Farm, Swavesey, 121
◯ Chilford Hall Vineyard, Linton, 160
◻ Waterland Organics, Cambridge, 228
▽ Brown's of Stilton, Stilton, 263
▽ C E Brown, Shudy Camps, 263
◇ Better Beef, Conington, 310
◇ Monach Farms, Huntingdon, 311, 312
◇ P & S Cruickshank, Cambridge, 310

Cheshire

✖ Abbey Leys Farm, Knutsford, 78
✖ Cheese Shop, The, Chester, 77
✖ H S Bourne, Malpas, 78
✖ Ravens Oak Dairy, Nantwich, 79
✚ deFINE Food and Wine, Northwich, 130
✚ Godfrey C Williams & Son, Sandbach, 130
✚ Granthams of Alderley Edge, Alderley Edge, 128
✚ Hollies Farm Shop, The, Tarporley, 131
◆ Cheshire Smokehouse, The, Wilmslow, 194
◻ Eddisbury Fruit Farm, Kelsall, 239
▽ Arley Wild Boar, Northwich, 266
▽ Housekeeper's Store at Tatton Park, The, Knutsford, 265
◇ Brookshaws of Nantwich, Nantwich, 331
◇ R F Burrows & Sons, Tarporely, 333
◇ Steve Brooks Butcher, Sandback, 332
✶ Holly Tree Farm Shop, Knutsford, 376

Cleveland

✚ Red Berry Foods at Station House Tea Rooms, Stockton-on-Tees, 134
◇ Larberry Pastures, Stockton-on-Tees, 340
✶ Thornbeck Farm, Stockton-on-Tees, 377

Cornwall

✖ Carley's, Truro, 24
✖ H M Pearce, Callington, 18
✖ Lydia's Cottage Industry, Redruth, 21
✖ Portreath Bakery, Portreath, 21
✖ Stein's Patisserie, Padstow, 21
✖ Barwick Farm, Truro, 62, 63
✖ Ben's Hens, Truro, 62
✖ Cheese Shop, The, Truro, 63
✖ Cornish Cheese Co., Liskeard, 58
✖ Cornish Country Larder, Newquay, 58
✖ Cornish Farmhouse Cheeses, Treverva, 56
✖ Forge Farm, Bodmin, 54
✖ Helsett Farm, Lesnewth, 57
✖ Little Bosoha, Helston, 56
✖ Lower Bodiniel Farm, Bodmin, 54
✖ Lynher Dairies Cheese Company Ltd, Truro, 64
✖ Pengoon Farm, Helston, 56
✖ Trevaylor, Truro, 64
✖ Trewithen Farm Foods, Lostwithiel, 58
✚ Bre-Pen Farm, Newquay, 105
✚ Di's Dairy and Pantry, Rock, 106
✚ Enys Wartha, Penzance, 105
✚ Oughs, Liskeard, 104
✚ Porteath Bee Centre, Wadebridge, 108
✚ Stein's Seafood Deli, Padstow, 105
◯ Camel Valley Vineyard, Bodmin, 146

○ Haye Farm Scrumpy Cider, Lostwithiel, 146
◆ Bude Shellfish, Bude, 177
◆ Cornish Cuisine, Penryn, 181
◆ Cornish Smoked Fish Company, The, St Austell, 182
◆ Duchy of Cornwall Oyster Farm, The, Falmouth, 179
◆ Falmouth Bay Oysters, Falmouth, 179
◆ Fowey Fish, Fowey, 180
◆ Martin's Seafresh, St Columb Major, 183
◆ Matthew Stevens & Son, St Ives, 183
◆ Mevagissey Wet Fish, Mevagissey, 180
◆ Pengelly's, East Looe, 179, 180
◆ Pilchard Works/Cornish Fish Direct, The, Newlyn, 180
◆ Quayside Fish Centre, Porthleven, 182
◆ Sarah's, Cadgwith Cove, 177
◆ Seabourne Fish, Penryn, 181
◆ Wing of St Mawes, St Columb, 182
□ Boddingtons Berries, Mevagissey, 217
□ Bosavern Farm, Penzance, 218
□ Cusgarne Organics, Truro, 219
□ Gary Dutton Butchers, Wadebridge, 259
▽ Ian Lentern, Penzance, 289
◇ Churchtown Farm, Fowey, 284
◇ Cornish Country Meats, Liskeard, 286
◇ Nancarrow Organic Farm, Truro, 293
◇ Philip Warren & Son, Launceston, 286
◇ Primrose Herd, Redruth, 290
◇ Richard Kittow & Sons, Fowey, 284
✳ South Torfrey Farm, Fowey, 365

County Durham

✖ Cotherstone Cheese Company, Marwood, 80
○ Lanchester Fruit, Lanchester, 166
□ Eggleston Hall, Barnard Castle, 241
□ Herb Patch, The, Ebchester, 243
▽ Teesdale Game & Poultry, Durham, 267
◇ Bowlees Farm Shop, Weardale, 340
◇ F Simpson & Son, Bishop Auckland, 335
◇ Lartington Lamb, Lartington, 337
◇ Westholme Farm Meats, Barnard Castle, 334
✳ Burtree House Farm, Darlington, 376
✳ Piercebridge Farm Organics, Darlington, 377

Coventry

◆ Stephenson's Fishmongers, Coventry, 192
□ Ryton Organic Gardens, Ryeton-on-Dunsmore, 235
✳ Aubrey Allen Ltd, Coventry, 315

Cumbria

✖ Broughton Village Bakery, The, Broughton-in-Furness, 36
✖ Hazelmere Café and Bakery, Grange-over-sands, 37
✖ Moody Baker Workers Cooperative, The, Alston, 36
✖ Staff of Life, Kendal, 38
✖ Village Bakery, The, Penrith, 38
✖ Watermill, The,, Penrith, 37, 38
✖ Cheese Shop, The, Kendal, 78
✖ Cream of Cumbria, Carlisle, 77
✖ Thornby Moor Dairy, Carlisle, 77
✚ 1657 Chocolate House, Kendall, 129
✚ Cartmel Sticky Toffee Pudding Co. Ltd, Cartmel, 128
✚ Country Fare, Kirkby Stephen, 129
✚ Demel's Sri Lankan Chutneys, Ulverston, 131
✚ Low Sizergh Barn Farm Shop, Kendal, 129
✚ Lucy's Specialist Grocers, Ambleside, 128
○ Cowmire Hall Damson Gin, Kendal, 165
○ Strawberry Bank Liqueurs, Crosthwaite, 165
○ Think Drink, Sedburgh, 166
◆ Bessy Beck Trout Farm, Kirkby Stephen, 194
◆ Hawkshead Trout Farm, Ambleside, 193
□ Dawson Fold Farm, Kendal, 239
□ Flodder Hall, Kendal, 240

□ Howbarrow Organic Farm, Grange-over-sands, 239
▽ Sillfield Farm, Kendal, 265, 266
◇ Aireys Farm Shop, Grange-over-sands, 328
◇ Barwise Aberdeen Angus, Appleby-in-Westmorland, 326
◇ Border County Foods, Carlisle, 327
◇ Bromley Green Farm, Appleby-in-Westmorland, 327
◇ Farmer Sharp, Dalton-in-Furness, 330
◇ Greystone House Farm, Penrith, 331
◇ Hallsford Farm Produce, Carlisle, 327
◇ Kitridding Farm Shop, Kirkby Lonsdale, 329
◇ Lune Valley, Kirkby Lonsdale, 330
◇ Old Smokehouse & Truffles Chocolates, The, Penrith, 331
◇ Richard Woodall, Millom, 330
◇ Savin Hill Farm, Kendal, 329
◇ Slacks of Cumbria, Penrith, 332
◇ Steadman's, Sedburgh, 333
◇ Stoneyhead Pork, Penrith, 332
◇ Whiteholme Farm, Carlisle, 328
◇ Yew Tree Farm, Keswick, 329

Derbyshire

✚ Chatsworth Farm Shop, Bakewell, 122
✚ Original Farmers' Market Shop, The, Bakewell, 122
◇ Chantry Farm Shop, Kings Newton, 317
◇ Lower Hurst Farm, Buxton, 315

Devon

✖ Common Loaf Bakery, Honiton, 19
✖ Otterton Mill Bakery, The, Budleigh Salterton, 18
✖ Seeds Bakery & Health Stores, Dartmouth, 19
✖ Seeds Bakery & Health Stores, Totnes, 23
✖ Blissful Buffalo, Holsworthy, 56
✖ Curworthy Cheese, Jacobstowe, 58
✖ Middle Campscott Farm, Illfracombe, 57
✖ Sharpham Creamery, Totnes, 62
✖ West Hill Farm, Ilfracombe, 57
✚ Burts Potato Chips, Kingsbridge, 104
✚ Riverford at Kitley, Plymouth, 106
✚ Riverford Farm Shop, Staverton, 107
✚ Wellswood Village Pantry, Torquay, 107
○ Bramley and Gage, South Brent, 149
○ Country Cheeses, Tavistock and Topsham, 61, 62
○ Grays Farm Cider, Tedburn St Mary, 149
○ Plymouth Gin, Plymouth, 147
○ Sharpham Vineyard, Totnes, 150
○ Tuckers Maltings, Newton Abbot, 147
◆ Barnacle Bill Direct, Brixham, 176
◆ Browse Seafoods, Brixham, 177
◆ Dartmouth Smokehouse, The, Dartmouth, 179
◆ Market Fish, Dartmouth, 183
◆ Ticklemore Fish Shop, The, Totnes, 184
□ Riverford Farm Organic Vegetables, Buckfastleigh, 213
□ Rod and Ben's Food from the Soil, Exeter, 215, 216
□ Bee Organic, Totnes, 219
□ Higher Crop, Exeter, 215
□ Holsworthy Organics, Holsworthy, 216
□ Linscombe Farm, Crediton, 214
□ Orswell Cottage Organic Garden, Barnstaple, 212
▽ Deer Force 10, Buckfastleigh, 258
▽ Palmers of Tavistock, Tavistock, 259
◇ Country Ways, Umberleigh, 294
◇ Dartmoor Happy Hogs, Okehampton, 288
◇ East Hill Pride, Newton Poppleford, 288
◇ Eversfield Manor, Okehampton, 288
◇ Fountain Violet Farm, Kingswear, 286
◇ Fowlescombe Farm, Ivybridge, 285
◇ Gittisham Herd at Combe Estate, Honiton, 285
◇ Haymans Butchers, Sidmouth, 291
◇ Higher Hacknell Farm, Umberleigh, 294
◇ Pipers Farm, Exeter, 283

◇ Smallicombe Farm, Colyton, 282
◇ Wallaces of Hemyock, Hemyock, 285
◇ Well Hung Meat Co., The, Plymouth, 289
◇ Wild Beef, Chagford, 279
✳ Ark Chicken, Exeter, 365
✳ Meat Joint, The, Barnstaple, 364
✳ Providence Farm, Holsworthy, 365
✳ Wixon Farm, Chulmleigh, 365

Dorset

◼ Leakers Bakery Ltd, Bridport, 18
◼ Long Crichel Bakery, Wimborne, 25
◼ N R Stoate and Sons, Shaftesbury, 22
✖ Dorset Blue Cheese Company, Sturminster Newton, 61
✖ Modbury Farm, Bridport, 55
✖ Woolsery Cheese, Dorchester, 55
✚ Honeybuns, Holwell, 103
✚ Tamarisk Farm, Dorchester, 102
✚ Washing Pool Farm Shop, Bridport, 102
◆ Bell's Fisheries, Wimborne, 186
◆ Fish Stall, The, Christchurch, 177
◆ FishWorks, Christchurch, 178
◆ Frank Greenslade, Poole, 182
◆ Hand Picked Shellfish Company, Portland, 185
◻ Dorset Blueberry Company, The, Wimborne, 220
◻ Elwell Fruit Farm, Bridport, 212
◻ Gold Hill Organic Farm, Blandford Forum, 212
◻ Green Valley Foods at Longmeadow, Dorchester, 215
◻ Peppers By Post, Dorchester, 215
▽ Framptons of Bridport, Bridport, 258
▽ L & C Game, Buckland Newton, 258
◇ Becklands Farm, Bridport, 277
◇ Cranborne Farms Traditional Meats, Cranborne, 294, 295
◇ Denhay Farms Ltd, Bridport, 278
◇ Eweleaze Farm, Osmington, 289
◇ Heritage Prime, Lyme Regis, 287
◇ Lagan Farm Meats at Milton Park Garden Centre, Gillingham, 284
◇ Owls Barn, Christchurch, 282
◇ Pampered Pigs Pantry, Tolpuddle, 293
◇ Real Meat Company, The, Poole, 290
◇ Star Farm, Sturminster Newton, 292
◇ West Hembury Farm, Dorchester, 283
◇ Westleaze Farm, Beaminster, 276
◇ Wyld Meadow Lamb, Monkton Wyld, 278
✳ Home Farm Shop, Blandford Forum, 364

East Yorkshire

◻ Barmston Organics, Driffield, 242
✳ Rose Cottage Foods, Driffield, 335

East Sussex

◼ Cyrnel Bakery, Forest Row, 27
◼ Infinity Foods Bakery, Brighton, 26
◼ Real Pâtisserie, Brighton, 26
✖ Golden Cross Cheese Company, Lewes, 67
✖ Nut Knowle Farm, Horham, 66
✖ Sussex High Weald Dairy, Uckfield, 69
✚ Montezuma's Chocolate, Brighton, 109, 110, 111
✚ Trencherman and Turner, Eastbourne, 111
○ Breaky Bottom Vineyard, Lewes, 154
○ Davenport Vineyards, Rotherfield, 157
○ Kent and Sussex Apple Juice and Cider Centre, Hartfield, 153
○ Middle Farm, Lewes, 154
○ Ridgeview Wine Estate, Ditchling Common, 151
○ Ringden Farm Apple Juice, Etchingham, 151
○ Sedlescombe Organic Vineyard, Robertsbridge, 157
◆ Botterell's, Rye, 188
◆ N Sayers Fish Merchants, Brighton, 186

◻ Boathouse Organic Farm Shop, Lewes, 224
◻ Hen on the Gate, The, Mayfield, 225
◻ Simply Wild, Robertsbridge, 226
◻ Sussex Saffron, Hooe, 224
◻ Tendring Fruit Farm, Hailsham, 223
▽ Ashbee & Son, Rye, 261
◇ J Wickens Family Butchers, Winchelsea, 309
◇ Little Warren Farm, Newick, 305
◇ Pounsley Hill Produce, Blackboys, 298
◇ Tablehurst Farm, Forest Row, 301
◇ Wealden Farmers Network, Battle, 296
✳ Weald Smokery, The, Flimwell, 370

ESSEX

✚ Chisnalls Delicatessen, Saffron Waldon, 120
✚ Dedham Gourmet, The, Dedham, 117
✚ Food Company, The, Colchester, 118
✚ H Gunton, Colchester, 118
✚ Hoo Hing, Romford, 120
✚ Manningtree Delicatessen, The, Manningtree, 120
◆ Colchester Oyster Fishery Ltd, Colchester, 190
◆ Company Shed, The, Colchester, 191
◻ Ashlyns Organic Farm Shop, Epping, 230
◻ Audley End Organic Kitchen Garden, Saffron Waldon, 233
◻ Brooklynne Farm Shop, Clacton, 229
◻ Clay Barn Orchard, Colchester, 229
◻ Crapes Fruit Farm, Aldham, 229, 230
◻ Gourmet Mushrooms, Great Bromley, 231
◻ Lathcoats Farm, Chelmsford, 228
◻ Park Fruit Farm, Frinton-on-sea, 231
◇ Buntings Butchers, Maldon, 310, 312
◇ Hepburns of Mountnessing, Brentwood, 309
◇ Monach's Farm, Langenhoe, 312
◇ Steeple Wick Farming Company, Steeple, 313
◇ Weylands Farm, Colchester, 310
✳ Farmyard Chicken Company (S J Frederick & Sons), Harlow, 371
✳ Great Clerkes Farm, Saffron Walden, 374
✳ Kelly Turkey Farms, Danbury, 372
✳ Munson's Poultry, Colchester, 372

Gloucestershire

◼ Authentic Bread Company, The, Newent, 20
◼ Bread Pancheon, The, Chipping Campden, 19
◼ Hobbs House, Nailsworth, 18, 20
◼ Shipton Mill, Tetbury, 23
◼ Sunshine Health Shop, Stroud, 23
✖ Birdwood Farmhouse Cheesemakers, Huntley, 72
✖ Cerney Cheese, Cirencester, 55
✖ House of Cheese, The, Tetbury, 61
✚ Daylesford Organic Farmshop, Kingham, 103
✚ Hampton's Deli, Stow on the Wold, 107
✚ Longborough Farm Shop, Moreton-in-Marsh, 104
○ Benson's Fruit Juices, Sherbourne, 148
○ Minchews Real Cyder and Perry, Tewkesbury, 149
○ Three Choirs Vineyards, Newent, 147
◆ Donnington Trout Farm, Stow on the Wold, 183
◆ Severn and Wye Smokery, Westbury-on-Severn, 185
◆ William's Kitchen, Nailsworth, 180
◻ Camphill Village Trust (Oaklands Park), Newnham-on-Severn, 217
◻ Duchy Home Farm Organic Vegetables, Tetbury, 219
◻ Hayles Fruit Farm, Winchcombe, 220
◻ Organic Farm Shop, The, Cirencester, 214
◻ Slipstream Organics, Cheltenham, 213
◇ Adeys Farm Organic Meats, Berkeley, 277
◇ Allen Hale Butchers, Stroud, 292
◇ Bill and Sue Osborne, Lydney, 287
◇ Butts Farm Shop, The, Cirencester, 282

◼ BREAD   ✖ DAIRY AND EGGS   ✚ DELICATESSENS   ○ DRINKS   ◆ FISH

◇ Chesterton Farm Shop, Cirencester, 282
◇ Country Butcher, The, Huntly, 285
◇ Crooked End Farm, Ruardean, 290

Guernsey

□ Guernsey Organic Growers, St Martins, 218

Hampshire

✖ Winchester Bakery, The, Winchester, 32
✖ Meadow Cottage Farm, Borden, 65
➕ Grapevine Delicatessen, The, Odiham, 116
➕ Lymington Larder, Lymington, 116
➕ Pollen Organics, Bramshott Chase, 109
O Suthwyk Ales, Fareham, 152
O Wickham Vineyard, Shedfield, 158
□ Blackmoor Apple Shop, Liss, 224
□ Fruitwise, Southampton, 227
□ Laverstoke Park Produce, Basingstoke, 221
□ Mrs Tees Wild Mushrooms, Lymington, 225
□ Warborne Organic Farm, Lymington, 225
▽ Manydown Farmshop, Basingstoke, 260
◇ Dairy Barn Farm Shop, Stockbridge, 308
◇ Uptons of Bassett, Southampton, 307
✱ Wonston Organic Poultry, Wonston, 371

Herefordshire

✖ Origin Foods, Royston, 31
✖ Just Rachel Desserts, Ledbury, 73
✖ Monkland Cheese Dairy, Leominster, 73
✖ Neal's Yard Creamery, Dorstone, 71
✖ September Organic Dairy, Kington, 75
✖ Shepherd's, Hay-on-Wye, 72
➕ Ceci Paolo, Ledbury, 124
➕ Country Kitchen, A, Ross on Wye, 126
➕ Silver Palate, The, Harpenden, 111
➕ Taste of the Country, Evesham, Ledbury,
   Long Compton, 123, 124
O Broughton Pastures Organic Fruit Wine, Tring,
   158
O Gregg's Pit Cider and Perry, Much Marcle, 162
O Gwatkin Cider at Abbey Dore Farm Shop,
   Abbey Dore, 162
O Jus, Ledbury, 162
O Oliver's Cider and Perry, Ocle Pychard, 163
O Orchard Hive and Vine, Leominster, 162
◆ Grapevine, Kington, 193
□ Court Farm and Leisure, Tillington, 235
□ Dragon Orchard, Ledbury, 236
□ Fern Verrow Vegetables, St Margarets, 238
□ Henclose Farm Organic Produce, Little
   Dewchurch, 219
□ SoilMates, Ross-on-Wye, 237, 238
▽ Hamblings, Rickmansworth, 261
◇ Eastwoods of Berkhamsted, Berkhamsted, 297
◇ Huntsham Farm – Pedigree Meats, Ross-on-
   Wye, 323
◇ John Miles Traditional Breeds Butcher, Ledbury,
   317
◇ Real Meat Company, The, Wheathamstead, 309
✱ Harvest Moon Organic Farm, Sarratt, 371
✱ Springfield Poultry, Leominster, 375

Isle Of Man

◆ Moore's Traditional Curers, Peel, 194
◇ Manx Loaghten Marketing Co-operative Ltd,
   The, Castletown, 328

Isle Of Wight

➕ Angela's Delicatessen, Yarmouth, 117
□ Godshill Organics, Godshill, 222
◇ Isle of Wight Bacon Company, The, Godshill,
   302

Isles Of Scilly

✖ St Martin's Bakery and Scillonian Fayre, St
   Martins, 22

Kent

✖ Artisan Bread, Whitstable, 32
✖ Marsh Mellow Bakery, Dymchurch, 27
✖ Oscar's Bakery, Faversham, 27
✖ Sarre Windmill, Sarre, 32
✖ Crockham Hill Cheeses, Crockham Hill, 66
✖ Hunts Hill Barn, Tenterden, 68
✖ Lower Basing Farm, Cowden, 66
✖ Tenterden Cheesemakers, Tenterden, 68
➕ Goods Shed, The, Canterbury, 110
O Bearsted Vineyard, Maidstone, 156
O Biddenden Vineyards and Cider Works,
   Biddenden, 150
O Chegworth Valley Juices, Maidstone, 156
O English Wines Group plc, Tenterden, 158
O Neals Place Farm, Canterbury, 150
O Owlet Apple Juice, Lamberhurst, 154
O Pawley Farm Traditional Kentish Cider,
   Faversham, 153
◆ Whitstable Shellfish Company, Whitstable, 188,
   189
□ Allens Farm, Sevenoaks, 226, 227
□ Perry Court Farm Shop, Canterbury, 222
□ Thrognall Farm, Sittingbourne, 226
◇ A J Barkaway Ltd, Faversham, 301
◇ Burscombe Cliff Farm, Ashford, 295
◇ Chandler & Dunn Ltd, Canterbury, 299
◇ Dennis of Bexley, Bexley, 297
◇ Little Omenden Sussex Beef, Ashford, 296
◇ Lower Thorne Farm, Pluckley, 305
◇ Piggybank Farm, Lenham, 303
◇ Sladden Farm, Alkham, 299

Lancashire

➕ Huntley's, Preston, 130
➕ Southport Potted Shrimps, Southport, 194
□ Growing With Nature, Pilling, 240
◇ Jack Scaife, Rossendale, 332
◇ Keer Falls Forest Farm, Carnforth, 328
◇ Mansergh Hall Farm, Kirkby Lonsdale, 330
✱ Ellel Free Range Poultry Company, The,
   Galgate, 376

Leeds

▽ C & G Starkey, Sherburn-in-Elmet, 267

Leicestershire

✖ Paul's, Melton Mowbray, 35
◇ Heards of Wigston, Leicester, 318
◇ Home Farm Organics, Loughborough, 319
◇ Michael F Wood, Leicester, 318
◇ Manor Farm, Loughborough, 320
◇ Picks Organic Farm Shop, Barkby Thorpe, 314
◇ Quenby Hall Organic Foods, Leicester, 318
◇ Real Meat Company, The, Leicester, 318
◇ Stephen Morris Butchers, Loughborough, 321
◇ Seldom Seen Farm, Billesdon, 373, 374
✱ W E Botterill & Son, Grantham, 374

Lincolnshire

✖ Bridge Farm Organic Foods, Gainsborough, 71
✖ Cheese Society, The, Lincoln, 73
✖ Fred W Reade & Sons, Alford, 70
➕ Lincolnshire Organics, Scunthorpe, 127
➕ Special Edition Continental Chocolate, Market
   Rasen, 125
◆ Alfred Enderby, Grimsby, 193
□ New Farm Organics, Boston, 234
◇ Curtis of Lincoln, Lincoln, 319
◇ Elite Meats, Lincoln, 319

| □ FRUIT AND VEGETABLES | ▽ GAME | ◇ MEAT | ✱ POULTRY |

◆ F C Phipps, Boston, 314
✖ Lakings of Louth, Louth, 321
✱ Woodlands Organic Farm, Boston, 374

Liverpool

✚ Seasoned Pioneers, Liverpool, 130

London

■ & Clarkes, London, 29
■ Baker & Spice, London, 28
■ Born and Bread Organic Bakery, London, 28
■ Breads Etcetera, London, 28
■ Celtic Bakers, The, Cricklewood, 29
■ De Gustibus, London, 30
■ Flourish Bakery and Pâtisserie, London, 30
■ Lighthouse Bakery, The, London, 30
■ Neal's Yard Bakery, London, 30
■ Poilâne, London, 31
✖ La Fromagerie, London, 67
✖ Neal's Yard Dairy, London, 67
✖ Paxton & Whitfield, London, 68
✚ Abel & Cole Ltd, London, 112
✚ Artisan du Chocolat, L', London, 113
✚ Brindisa, London, 113
✚ Chocolate Society, The, London, 113
✚ Delectables Fine Foods, London, 114
✚ Forman & Field, London, 114
✚ Gourmet World, London, 114
✚ Oil Merchant Ltd, The, London, 114
✚ Rococo Chocolates, London, 115
✚ Spice Shop, The, London, 116
O Pitfield Brewery (The Beer Shop), London, 155
O Porterhouse, The, London, 156,
◆ FishWorks, London, 187
◆ Fresh Food Company, The, London, 187
◆ H Forman & Son, London, 187
◆ Steve Hatt, London, 188
□ Cool Chile Co., London, 225
▽ Randalls Butchers, London, 261
◇ C Lidgate, London, 303
◇ G G Sparkes, London, 304
◇ Kingsland Edwardian Butchers, London, 303
◇ M Moen & Sons, London, 303
◇ Stenton Family Butchers, London, 304
✱ Old Post Office Bakery Ltd, The, London, 31
✱ Wyndham House Poultry, London, 370

Manchester

✖ Cheese Hamlet, The, Didsbury, 79
▽ Lords of Middleton, Middleton, 265

Merseyside

◇ Broughs of Birkdale, Southport, 333

Middlesex

◇ A G Millers, Teddington, 308

Newcastle Upon Tyne

■ Café Royal, Newcastle upon Tyne, 39
■ Thomson's Bakery, Westerhope, 39
✚ Honey Tree Organic Greengrocers and Good
   Food Store, The, Heaton, 133
◇ George Payne Butchers, Gosforth, 338

Norfolk

■ Metfield Organic Bakery, The, Harleston, 34
■ Mill Bakery, The, Dereham, 33
■ North Elmham Bakery, Dereham, 33
✖ Domini Quality Foods, Diss, 69
✖ Mrs Temple's Cheese, Wells-next-the-sea, 70
✚ Didlington Manor, Thetford, 121
✚ Picnic Fayre Delicatessen, Cley-next-the-sea,
   117

O Crones Cider, Kenninghall, 161
O Old Chimneys Brewery, The, Diss, 160
O Woodforde's Norfolk Ales, Norwich, 161
◆ Cookies Crab Shop, Holt, 191
◆ Crowe Fishmongers, Norwich, 191
◆ Fish Shed, The, Brancaster Staithe, 190
◆ Richard and Julie Davies, Cromer, 191
◆ W J Weston, Holt, 191
□ Abbey Farm Organics, King's Lynn, 232
□ Barker Organics, Norwich, 232
□ Clive Houlder, Fakenham, 231
□ Harvey's Pure Meat, Norwich, 262
□ Plumbe and Maufe, King's Lynn, 232
□ Stable Organics, Norwich, 233
◇ Ash Farm Organics, Derham, 311
◇ Sausage Shop, The, Holt, 311
◇ Tavern Tasty Meats, North Walsham, 312
✱ Great Grove Poultry, Attleborough, 371
✱ Morton's Traditional Taste, Norwich, 373
✱ Peele's, Norwich, 373

North Lincolnshire

■ True Loaf Bakery, Kirton in Lindsey, 34, 35

North Somerset

◇ J C Burdge, Langford, 278

North Yorkshire

■ Davills Pâtisserie, Ripon, 39
✖ Swaledale Cheese Co., The, Richmond, 80
✚ Campbell Lindley's, Harrogate, 132
✚ Chocolate Society, The, Boroughbridge, 131
✚ Garden House, The, Richmond, 133
✚ Garth Cottage Nursery, Northallerton, 133
✚ Organic Pantry, Tadcaster, 134
✚ Rosebud Preserves, Masham, 132
O Black Sheep Brewery plc, The, Ripon, 167
O Wright Wine Company, The, Skipton, 167
◆ Bleikers Smokehouse, Harrogate, 196
◆ Fortunes, Whitby, 198
◆ Kilnsey Park, Skipton, 196
□ Bluebell Organics, Barnard Castle, 241, 242
▽ Hutchinsons, Harrogate, 267
▽ J B Cockburn & Sons, Bedale, 267
▽ Wensleydale Wild Boar, Ripon, 268
▽ Yorkshire Game, Richmond, 268
◇ Happy Piggy Pork, Layburn, 337
◇ Highside Butchers, Ripon, 339
◇ Langthornes Buffalo Produce, Northallerton, 338
◇ Oxford Sandy & Black Pigs, Scarborough, 339
◇ Thornhill Farm, Easingwold, 336
✱ Highlands Farm, Scarborough, 377

Northumberland

■ Jo's Home Baked Bread, Hexham, 39
✖ Doddington Dairy, Wooler, 81
✖ Northumberland Cheese Company, Seaton
   Burn, 80
✖ Wheelbirks Farm, Stocksfield, 80
✚ New Barns Farm Shop, Morpeth, 132
✚ Northumbrian Hamper, Seahouses, 134
◆ Bywell Fish and Game Smokery, Stocksfield,
   197
◆ Lindisfarne Oysters, Belford, 195
◆ Ridley's Fish and Game, Corbridge, Hexham,
   195, 196
◆ Robertson's Prime, Alnwick, 195
◆ Swallow Fish, Seahouses, 196
□ Carroll's Heritage Potatoes, Cornhill-on-Tweed,
   242
□ North East Organic Growers Ltd, Bedlington,
   241
◇ Capri Lodge, Morpeth, 338
◇ Northumbrian Quality Meats, Hexham, 336
◇ Piperfield Pork, Berwick-upon-Tweed, 334

■ BREAD   ✖ DAIRY AND EGGS   ✚ DELICATESSENS   O DRINKS   ◆ FISH

◇ R Carter & Son Butcher, Bamburgh, 334
◇ R G Foreman & Son, Berwick-upon-Tweed, Norham-on-Tweed, 334, 338
◇ Rock Midstead Organic Farm Shop, Alnwick, 333
◇ Well Hung and Tender, Berwick-upon-Tweed, 335

Nottinghamshire

✘ Colston Bassett Dairy, Colston Bassett, 75
✘ Cropwell Bishop Creamery, Cropwell Bishop, 75
✚ Cheese Shop, The, Nottingham, 125
✚ Farmshop Home Delivery, Bingham, 122
◻ Trinity Farm, Cossall, 234
◇ Hockerton Grange Farm Shop, Southwell, 324
◇ Meynell Langley Farm Shop, Kirklangley, 317
◇ Routledge's Butchers, Kirkby-in-Ashfield, Nottingham, 317, 323

Oxfordshire

▣ Bread & Co., Banbury, 25
▣ Old Farmhouse Bakery, The, Abingdon, 25
✚ Wells Stores at Peachcroft Farm, Abingdon, 109
◆ Hayman's Fisheries, Oxford, 188
◻ Brook Cottage Farm, Wantage, 228
◻ Millets Farm Centre, Abingdon, 220
◻ Sarsden Organics, Chipping Norton, 222
◻ Waterperry Gardens, Wheatley, 228
◇ Foxbury Farm, Brize Norton, 298
◇ Gabriel Machin, Henley-on-Thames, 302
◇ J M Walman Family Butchers, Bicester, 297
◇ M Newitt & Sons, Thame, 308
◇ W J Castle, Burford, 299
✱ M Feller Son & Daughter, Organic Butchers, Oxford, 371
✱ Homewood Partners, Abingdon, 369

Reading

◇ Whitings Butchers, Reading, 306
◇ Wysipig, Arborfield, 306

Rutland

◇ Northfield Farm, Oakham, 323

Shropshire

▣ S C Price, Ludlow, 35
✘ Appleby's of Hawkestone, Whitchurch, 76
✘ Chicken Came First, The, Newport, 74
✚ Chocolate Gourmet, The, Ludlow, 124
✚ Deli on the Square, Ludlow, 124
✚ Granary, The, Craven Arms, 123
✚ Greenfields Farm Shop, Telford, 127
◆ Organic Smokehouse, The, Craven Arms, 193
▽ Alternative Meats, Shrewsbury, 264
◻ Augernik Fruit Farm, Hopton Wafers, 236
◻ Five Acres, Shrewsbury, 237
◇ Barkers, Acton Burnell, 313
◇ Corvedale Organic Lamb, Stanton Long, 322
◇ D W Wall & Son, Craven Arms, 316, 322
◇ G & R Tudge, Ludlow, 321
◇ Maynards Farm Bacon, Shrewsbury, 324, 325
◇ Orleton Farm Shop, Ludlow, 321
◇ Ted's Meat, the Traditional Taste of Shropshire, Sherrifhales, 324
◇ Wenlock Edge Farm, Much Wenlock, 322

Somerset

✘ Alham Wood Cheeses, Shepton Mallett, 59
✘ J A & E Montgomery Ltd, Yeovil, 65
✘ Keens Cheddar (S H & G H Keen), Wincanton, 65
✘ R A Duckett, Shepton Mallet, 60
✘ Westcombe Dairy, Evercreech, 60
✚ Emma B Delicatessen, Somerton, 106

✚ Lefktro UK Ltd, Hinton St George, 103
✚ Provender Delicatessen, South Petherton, 107
✚ Sageberry Cheese Delicatessen, Frome, 103
○ Avalon Vineyard (Pennard Organic Wines), Shepton Mallett, 148
○ Hecks Farmhouse Cider, Street, 149
○ Somerset Cider Brandy Company, Martock, 146
◆ Brown and Forrest, Currey Rivel, 178
◆ Phil Bowditch, Taunton, 184
◻ Bell and Birdtable, The, Wellington, 220
◻ Merricks Organic Farm, Langport, 217
◻ West Bradley Orchards, West Bradley, 216
▽ Barrow Boar, Yeovil, 260
▽ Somerset Organics, Bruton, 258
▽ Thoroughly Wild Meat Co. Ltd, The, Wincanton, The, 259
◇ Bill the Butcher, Bruton, 278
◇ Brewhamfield Organic Dairy Farm, Bruton, 279
◇ Brown Cow Organics, Shepton Mallet, 291
◇ Charlton Orchards, Taunton, 218
◇ Clive Downs Butchers, Porlock, 290
◇ Ham Street Farm Produce, Glastonbury, 284
◇ Hindon Organic Farm, Minehead, 288
◇ John Thorner's Ltd, Shepton Mallet, 291
◇ Lyng Court Organic Meat, Taunton, 293
◇ Moorland Farm Shop, Axbridge, 276
◇ Norwood Farm, Norton St Philip, 276
◇ Old Castle Farm, Chard, 279
◇ Pitney Farm Shop, Langport, 286
◇ Swaddles Green Organic Farm, Chard, 280
✱ Dunning Quality Geese, Yeovil, 368
✱ Exmoor Organic, Minehead, 366
✱ Somerset Farm Direct, Taunton, 366

South Yorkshire

▣ Potts Bakers, Barnsley, 38
◇ Real Meat Company, The, Sheffield, 339

Staffordshire

▣ High Lane Oatcakes, Stoke-on-Trent, 36
✘ Staffordshire Cheese Company, Leek, 78
✘ Staffordshire Organic Cheese, Newcastle-under-Lyme, 79
◻ Essington Fruit Farm, Wolverhampton, 238
◻ Field 2 Kitchen, Gailey, 239
▽ Bradshaw Bros Ltd, Burntwood, 263
◇ A Johnson & Son, Burton-on-Trent, 315

Suffolk

▣ All Natural Bakery, Bury St Edmunds, 33
✘ Suffolk Meadow Ice Cream, Saxmundham, 70
✚ Alder Carr Farm, Ipswich, 119
✚ Fruits of Suffolk, Ipswich, 119
✚ Jules and Sharpie, Stradbroke, 120
✚ Tastebuds, Woodbridge, 122
✚ Thorpeness Village Store, Thorpeness, 121
○ Shawsgate Vineyard, Woodbridge, 161
◆ Aldeburgh Fish Stall, Aldeburgh, 189
◆ Butley Orford Oysterage, Woodbridge, 192
◆ Carley and Webb, Woodbridge, 192
◆ John's Fish Shop, Southwold, 192
◻ High House Fruit Farm, Woodbridge, 234
◻ Hollow Trees Farm Shop, Ipswich, 231
◻ Laurel Farm Herbs, Kelsale, 232
◻ Longwood Farm, Bury St Edmunds, 309
▽ Brampton Wild Boar, Beccles, 262
▽ K B Stannard & Sons, Saxmundham, 262
▽ Wild Meat Company, Saxmundham, 262
◇ Baylham House Rare Breeds Farm, Ipswich, 311
◇ Emmett's Store, Saxmundham, 312
◇ Five Winds Farm Smokehouse and Butchery, Woodbridge, 313
◇ Red Poll Beef, Saxmundham, 313
✱ Rumburgh Farm, Halesworth, 372

| ◻ FRUIT AND VEGETABLES | ▽ GAME | ◇ MEAT | ✱ POULTRY |

Surrey

- ✖ Flour Power City, Guildford, 28
- ✖ Pâtisserie, The, Cobham, 26
- O Denbies Wine Estate, Dorking, 151
- ☐ Kingfisher Farm Shop, Dorking, 222
- ▽ George Arthur Ltd, Lightwater, 260
- ◇ C H Wakeling Ltd, Godalming, 301
- ◇ F Conisbee & Son, East Horsley, 300
- ◇ Head Fine Foods, New Malden, 304
- ◇ Kenneth J Eve, Epsom, 300
- ◇ Osney Lodge Farm, South Godstone, 307
- ◇ Real Meat Company, The, Carshalton Beeches, 299
- ✱ Cranleigh Organic Farm Shop, Cranleigh, 370

Warwickshire

- ✖ Paxton & Whitfield, Stratford-upon-Avon, 75
- ✚ Kim's Cakes, Nuneaton, 125
- ✚ Meg Rivers, Shipton-on-Stour, 127
- ☐ Field 2 Kitchen, Atherstone, 234
- ◇ Berkswell Traditional Farmstead Meats, Coventry, 316
- ◇ G N F & G A Browning, Rugby, 323

West Midlands

- ✖ Ram Hall Dairy Sheep, Berkswell, 71
- ✚ Montezuma's Chocolate, Solihull, 109, 110
- ◇ Hopwood Organic Farm, Solihull, 237
- O S & A Rossiter, Bournville, 314

West Sussex

- ✖ Slindon Bakery, Slindon, 32
- ✖ Horsham Cheese Shop, The, Horsham, 67
- ✖ Old Plaw Hatch Farm, Sharpthorne, 68
- ✖ Twineham Grange Farms Ltd, Haywards Heath, 66
- ✚ Montezuma's Chocolate, Brighton, Chichester, 110, 111
- O Gospel Green Cyder, Haslemere, 153
- O Lurgashall Winery, Petworth, 156
- O Gran Stead's Ginger Wine, Shoreham-by-sea, 157
- O Nyetimber Vineyard, West Chiltington, 159
- ☐ Costrong Fruit Farm, Billingshurst, 221
- ◇ Rudgwick Organic Beef & Veal, Rudgewick, 306
- ◇ Shiprods Farm, Horsham, 302
- ◇ Sussexway Meat, Pease Pottage, 305

West Yorkshire

- ✚ Rocky Valley Deli, The, Ilkley, 132
- O Leventhorpe Vineyard, Leeds, 166
- ☐ Brickyard Farm Shop, Pontefract, 243
- ☐ E Oldroyd and Sons Ltd, Wakefield, 244
- ☐ Goosemoor Organics,, Wetherby, 244
- ☐ Swillington Organic Farm, Leeds, 243
- ◇ Blacker Hall Farm Shop, Stockton-on-Tees, 340
- ◇ Lishmans of Ilkley, Ilkley, 336, 337

Wiltshire

- ✖ Ashmore Farmhouse Cheese, Salisbury, 59
- ✖ Berkeley Farm Dairy, Swindon, 61
- ✖ Lyburn Farmhouse Cheesemakers, Salisbury, 59
- ✚ Truffles, Salisbury, 106
- ◆ Mere Fish Farm, Warminster, 185
- ◆ Purely Organic, Warminster, 184, 185
- ☐ Coleshill Organics, Swindon, 218
- ☐ John Hurd's Organic Watercress, Warminster, 219
- ☐ V & P Collins, Chippenham, 213
- ☐ Westwood Farm, Chippenham, 214
- ◇ Boyton Farm, Warminster, 295
- ◇ Eastbrook Farms Organic Meat, Swindon, 293
- ◇ Hazelbury Partners, Corsham, 283
- ◇ Hill End Farm, Chippenham, 278
- ◇ Langley Chase Organic Farm, Chippenham, 280
- ◇ Marshfield Organic Farm, Marshfield, 280
- ◇ Real Meat Company, The, Bradford-on-Avon, Calne, Warminster, 277, 279, 367
- ◇ Sandridge Farmhouse Bacon, Chippenham, 281
- ◇ Temple Farming, Marlborough, 284
- ◇ Thornham Farm Shop, Melksham, 287
- ◇ Vowley Farm, Wooton Bassett, 295, 296
- ✱ Withyslade Farm, Tisbury, 366

Wirral

- ☐ Church Farm Organics, Thurstaston, 240

Worcestershire

- ✖ Tony's Bakery, Kidderminster, 34
- ✖ Ansteys of Worcester, Worcester, 76
- ✖ Keys Hill Poultry Farm, Bromsgrove, 71
- ✖ Lightwood Cheese, Worcester, 76
- ✖ Mar Goats, Worcester, 76
- ✚ Berrow Honey, Martley, 128
- ✚ Plantation Cottage Herbs, Pershore, 126
- O Astley Vineyards, Stourport-on-Severn, 164
- O Avonbank, Pershore, 164
- O Talbot at Knightwick, The, Knightwick, 164, 165
- ☐ Walsgrove Farm, Spetchley, 237
- ◇ Checketts of Ombersley, Droitwich, 316
- ◇ Curradine Angus, Shrawley, 324
- ◇ Detton Beef and Lamb, Kidderminster, 316
- ◇ Hampton Farm Shop, Evesham, 235
- ◇ Happy Meats, Stanford Bridge, 325
- ◇ Malvern Country Meals, Malvern, 322
- ✱ Goodman's Geese, Worcester, 375

York

- ✚ Henshelwood Deli, York, 134
- O York Beer and Wine Shop, York, 168
- ◆ Cross of York, York, 198

Anglesey

- ☐ Porthamel Organic Farm, Llanfair PG, 252
- ▽ Owen Roberts & Son, Anglesey, 272
- ◇ Beef Direct Ltd and Lamb Direct Ltd, Llanerch y Medd, 358

Bridgend

- ✖ Lewis Fine Foods, Porthcawl, 48, 51

Cardiff

- ✖ Allen's Bakery, Roath, 48
- O Seidr Dai, Cardiff, 171, 172
- ◇ J T Morgan, Cardiff, 355

Cardigan

- ✖ Clover Jerseys, Llangoedmor, 96

Camarthenshire

- ✖ Llanboidy Cheesemakers, Whitland, 99
- ✖ Nantybwla, Carmarthen, 97
- ☐ Glyn Fach Farm, Llanelli, 253, 254
- ◇ Albert Rees, Carmarthen, 355
- ◇ Eynon's of St Clears Ltd, St Clears, 360
- ◇ John James, Carmarthen, 355
- ◇ Maestroyddyn Organics, Llanwrda, 360
- ◇ May Organic Farms, The, Lampeter, 357
- ✱ Goetre Farm, Llanybydder, 382
- ✱ Wern Poultry Products, Llandeilo, 381

| ✖ BREAD | ✖ DAIRY AND EGGS | ✚ DELICATESSENS | O DRINKS | ◆ FISH |

Ceredigion

- ✖ Caffi Patio, Cardigan Bay, 96, 98
- ✖ Caws Cenarth, Boncath, 95, 96
- ✖ Gorwydd Caerphilly, Tregaron, 99
- ✖ Teifi Cheese, Llandysul, 98
- ✚ Llwynhelyg Farm Shop, Llandysul, 142
- ✚ Treehouse, The, Aberystwyth, 141
- O Bragdy Ceredigion Brewery, Pentregat, 173
- O New Quay Honey Farm, New Quay, 173
- ◆ Fish on the Quay, Aberaeron, 208
- ◆ New Quay Fresh Fish Shop, New Quay, 209
- ◻ Nantclyd Organics, Aberystwyth, 252
- ◇ Cambrian Organics, Llandysul, 358, 359
- ◇ Julia Coviello, Lampeter, 357

Conwy

- ✚ Blas Ar Fwyd, Llanrwst, 142
- O Natural Mead Company, The, Corwen, 172
- ◇ Edwards of Conwy, Conwy, 356

Gwent

- ✖ Bower Farm Dairy, Abergavenny, 95
- ◻ Berryhill Fruit Farm, Newport, 254

Gwynedd

- ✖ Popty'r Dref, Dolgellau, 48
- ◻ Llangybi Organics, Pwllheli, 255
- ◻ Savages, Bethesda, 252, 253

Mid Glamorgan

- ◇ Penrhiw Farm Organic Meats, Treharris, 360

Monmouthshire

- ✖ Wigmore's Bakery, Monmouth, 49
- ◆ Minola Smoked Products, Abergavenny, 209
- ◻ Carrob Growers, Llanrothal, 254
- ◻ Ty Mawr Organics, Abergavenny, 251
- ◇ Daren Farm, Abergavenny, 354
- ◇ N S James & Son, Raglan, 360
- ✳ Cefn Maen Farm, Raglan, 382
- ✳ Madgetts Farm Poultry, Chepstow, 381

Pembrokeshire

- ✖ Golden Crust Bakery, The, Pembroke, 50
- ✖ Pantri Nolwenn, Haverfordwest, 49
- ✖ Y Felin, St Dogmaels, 51
- ✖ Caws Caerfai, Haverfordwest, 98
- ✖ Drim Farm, Narberth, 98
- ✖ Llangloffan Farmhouse Cheese, Fishguard, 97
- ✖ Pant Mawr Farmhouse Cheese, Clynderwen, 97
- ✚ Popty Cara, Lawrenny, 141
- ✚ Wendy Brandon Handmade Preserves, Boncath, 141
- ◆ Celtic Dawn, Haverfordwest, 209
- ◻ Spring Meadow Farm, St Davids, 255
- ◇ Bumpylane Rare Breeds, Haverfordwest, 356
- ◇ Knock Farm Organics, Haverfordwest, 356
- ◇ Rose Park Organic Farm, Llanteg, 359
- ◇ Welsh Hook Meat Centre, Haverfordwest, 357
- ✳ Penucha'rplwyf Farm, Raglan, 383
- ✳ Coedwynog Free Range Geese, Crymych, 381

Powys

- ✖ Bacheldre Watermill, Montgomery, 49
- O Gellirhyd Farm, Crickhowell, 172
- ◻ Cwm Harry Land Trust, Tregynon, 255
- ▽ Welsh Venison Centre, The, Brecon, 273
- ◇ Edward Hamer, Llanidloes, 358
- ◇ Graig Farm Organics, Llandrindod Wells, 358
- ◇ New House Farm, Builth Wells, 354
- ◇ Penmincae Welsh Black Beef & Lamb, Builth Wells, 354
- ◇ Pentre Pigs, Welshpool, 361

- ◇ Pigs Folly, Builth Wells, 355
- ✳ Cefn Goleu, Meifod, 382

Swansea

- ◆ Coakley-Greene, Swansea, 209

Vale of Glamorgan

- ✚ Foxy's Deli, Canarth, 143
- ◻ Fruit Garden, The, Cardiff, 253

NORTHERN IRELAND

Antrim

- ✖ Causeway Cheese Company, Ballymena, 81
- O Hilden Brewing Co., The, Lisburn, 168, 169
- ◆ Morton's, Ballycastle, 198
- ◻ Kelly's, Lisburn, 246
- ◇ Ballylagan Organic Farm, Ballyclare, 341
- ◇ Wysner Meats and Restaurant, Ballycastle, 340
- ✳ 'O' Kane Poultry Ltd, Ballymena, 378

Armagh

- ◇ A Flanigan & Son, Armagh, 341
- ◇ John R Dowey & Son, Lurgan, 343
- ◇ T Knox & Sons, Portadown, 344

Belfast

- ✖ Café Paul Rankin (Roscoff Bakery), Belfast, 40
- ✖ Knotts Cake and Coffee Shop, Newtownards, 42
- ✚ Chocolate Room, The, Belfast, 135
- ✚ Feasts, Belfast, 135
- ✚ Olive Tree Company, The, Belfast, 135
- ✚ Vineyard Delicatessen, The, Belfast, 114
- O Vineyard Belfast Ltd, The, Belfast, 168
- ◆ Walter Ewing, Belfast, 198
- ◻ Four Seasons, Belfast, 245
- ◻ Michel's Fresh Fruit & Veg, Belfast, 245
- ▽ Coffey's Butchers, Belfast, 268
- ◇ Owen McMahon, Belfast, 341

Down

- ✖ Camphill Organic Farm Shop & Bakery, Holywood, 41
- ✖ Corn Dolly Home Bakery, The, Newry, 41, 42
- ✖ Country Kitchen Home Bakery, The, Lisburn, 41
- ✚ Heatherlea, Bangor, 40
- O Whitewater Brewery, Kilkeel, 168
- ◆ Cuan Sea Fisheries, Killinchy, 198
- ◆ Helen's Bay Organic Gardens, Helen's Bay, 246
- ◻ Home Grown, Newtownards, 246
- ▽ Finnebrogue Venison Company, Downpatrick, 268
- ◇ McCartney's, Moira, 344
- ◇ Pheasants' Hill Farm Shop, Comber, 342
- ◇ David Burns Butchers, Bangor, 341

Derry

- ✖ Ditty's Home Bakery, Castledawson/Magherafelt, 40, 42
- ✖ Hunter's, Limavady, 41
- ✖ Kitty's of Coleraine, Coleraine, 40
- ✚ Belfry Deli and Café, The, Coleraine, 136
- ◻ Sperrin's Organic Wholefoods, Claudy, 245
- ◇ Arkhill Farm, Garvagh, 342
- ◇ J E Toms & Sons, Portstewart, 344
- ◇ McKees Butchers, Maghera, 343
- ◇ Moss Brook Farm, Magherafelt, 343
- ◇ Norman Hunter & Son, Limavady, 343
- ◇ O'Kane Meats, Claudy, 342

| ◻ FRUIT AND VEGETABLES | ▽ GAME | ◇ MEAT | ✳ POULTRY |

FOOD HEROES OF BRITAIN

✱ Culdrum Organic Farm, Coleraine, 378
✱ Mullan Farm, Limavady, 378

Tyrone

☐ Organic Doorstep, Castlederg, 245
◇ Mr Eatwells, Omagh, 344

Cavan

✖ Corleggy Cheese, Belturbet, 83

Clare

✖ Cratloe Hills Sheep's Cheese, Cratloe, 84
✖ Inagh Farmhouse Cheese, Inagh, 86
O Biddy Early Brewery, The, Inagh, 170
◆ Burren Smokehouse, Lisdoonvarna, 202

Cork

◗ Arbutus Bread, Montenotte, 43
✖ Organico, Bantry, 43
✖ Ardrahan Cheese, Kanturk, 87
✖ Ardsallagh Goats' Products, Carrigtwohill, 83
✖ Coolea Farmhouse Cheese, Macroom, 88
✖ Coturnix Quail, Dunmanway, 85
✖ Durrus Farmhouse Cheese, Bantry, 82
✖ Glenilen Farm, Drimoleague, 85
✖ Gubbeen Cheese, Schull, 88
✖ Milleens Cheese, Beara, 82
✖ West Cork Natural Cheese Co., The , Schull, 88
O Franciscan Well, The, Cork, 169
◆ Belvelly Smokehouse, Cobh, 199
◆ Kinsale Gourmet Store, Kinsale, 201
◆ K O'Connell Ltd Fish Emporium, Cork, 200
◆ Ummera Smoked Products, Timoleague, 202
◆ Woodcock Smokery, Castletownshend, 199
☐ Caroline's Home Grown Veg, Bandon, 247
☐ Garden, The, Cork, 247
☐ Peppermint Farm & Garden, Bantry, 247
◇ Caherbeg Free Range Pork, Rosscarbery, 347
◇ Gubbeen Smokehouse, Schull, 347
◇ Krawczyk's West Cork Salamis, Schull, 348
◇ On The Pigs Back, Cork, 345
✱ Ballysimon Organic Farm, Midleton, 379
✱ Maughansilly, Bantry, 379

Donegal

☐ Donegal Organic Farm Produce, Glenties, 248

Dublin

◗ Bakery, The, Dublin, 44
✖ Sheridans Cheesemongers, Dublin, 85, 86
O Llewellyn's Orchard Produce, Lusk, 171
O Messrs Maguire, Dublin, 169
O Porterhouse, The, Dublin, 170
◆ Caviston's Seafood, Sandycove, 200
◆ Nicky's Plaice, Dublin, 200
▽ Molloys of Donnybrook, Dublin, 269
◇ O'Toole's Butchers, Dublin, 345

Galway

◗ Goya's, Galway, 44
✖ Sheridans Cheesemongers, Galway, 85, 86, 88
✚ McCambridges of Galway Ltd, Galway, 136
◆ Connemara Smokehouse, The, Ballyconneely, 199
◆ Kinvara Smoked Salmon, Kinvara, 202
◆ McDonagh's Seafood House, Galway, 201
◆ Michael Kelly (Shellfish) Ltd, Kilcolgan, 201
☐ Brooklodge Nursery, Ballyglunin, 246

◇ McGeogh's Butchers, Oughterard, 347
◇ Tormey's Butchers, Galway, 346

Kerry

✖ Killorglin Farmhouse Cheese, Killorglin, 87
✖ Murphy's Ice Cream, Dingle, 84
◇ Continental Sausages, Killarney, 346

Kilkenny

✖ Lavistown Cheese, Kilkenny, 87

Laois

✚ Kitchen and Food Hall, The, Portlaoise, 137

Louth

✖ Glyde Farm Produce, Castlebellingham, 84

Meath

✚ Aines Chocolates, Oldcastle, 137

Offaly

◇ Tormey's Butchers, Tullamore, 348

Sligo

✚ Tir na nOg, Sligo, 137

Tipperary

◗ Barron's Bakery, Cappoquin, 43
✖ Cooleeney Farmhouse Cheese, Thurles, 89
✖ J & L Grubb, Fethard, 85
✚ Country Choice, Nenagh, 136
☐ Apple Farm, The, Cahir, 247
◇ James Whelan Butchers, Clonmel, 345
◇ Michael Hickey, Cashel, 344

Waterford

✖ Knockanore Farmhouse Cheese, Knockanore, 87
◆ Helvick Seafood, Dungarvan, 200
◇ John David Power, Dungarvan, 346
◇ McGrath's Butchers, Lismore, 346

Westmeath

◇ Tormey's Butchers, Mullingar, 346

Wexford

✖ Carrigbyrne Farmhouse Cheese, Adamstown, 81
✖ Croghan Goat Farm, Blackwater, 83
✚ Farmer Direct, New Ross, 136

Wicklow

◗ Stoneoven, The, Arklow, 43
O Porterhouse, The, Bray, 169
☐ Ballinroan, Kiltegan, 249
☐ Marc Michel, Kilpedder, 248

Aberdeenshire

◗ Newton Dee Bakery, Bieldside, 44
✖ Ken Watmough, Aberdeen, 202
☐ Croft Organics, Daviot, 250
☐ Huntly Herbs, Huntly Herbs, 250
☐ Lenshaw Organics, Inverurie, 250
▽ Forbes Raeburn & Sons, Huntly, 270
✱ Chicken Lady, The, Huntly, 380

| ◗ BREAD | ✖ DAIRY AND EGGS | ✚ DELICATESSENS | O DRINKS | ◆ FISH |

Argyll and Bute

- ✖ Kintaline Farm, Oban, 93, 94
- ✚ Isle of Colonsay Apiaries, Colonsay, 138
- ◆ Cockles, Lochgilphead, 206
- ◆ Inverawe Smokehouse, Taynuilt, 208
- ◆ Loch Fyne Oysters Ltd, Clairndow, 203
- ◇ Ormsary Farm, Lochgilphead, 352
- ◇ Saulmore Farm Shop, Oban, 353
- ✱ Highland Geese, Lochgilphead, 380

Ayrshire

- ✖ Dunlop Dairy, Kilmarnock, 93
- ✖ Hand Made Cheese Co., The, Dalry, 90

Berwickshire

- ◇ R G Foreman & Son, Coldstream and Eyemouth, 350, 351

Clackmannanshire

- ✱ Gartmorn Farm, Alloa, 380

Dumfries and Galloway

- ✖ Galloway Farmhouse Cheese, Newton Stewart, 93
- ✖ Loch Arthur Creamery, Dumfries, 90
- ◆ Colfin Smokehouse, Stranraer, 208
- ▽ Galloway Smokehouse, The, Newton Stewart, 271
- ▽ Old Knockelly Smokehouse, Thornhill, 271

Edinburgh

- ▧ Au Gourmand, Edinburgh, 46
- ▧ Engine Shed Bakery, The, Edinburgh, 46
- ✖ Iain Mellis (The Cheesemonger), Edinburgh, 90, 94
- ✚ Plaisir du Chocolat, Edinburgh, 138
- ✚ Valvona & Crolla, Edinburgh, 131
- ◆ Eddie's Seafood Market, Edinburgh, 205
- ◇ Findlays of Portobello, Edinburgh, 350
- ◇ Pentland Hills Produce, Hill End, 353

Fife

- ▧ Adamson's Bakery, Pittenweem, 47
- ✖ Iain Mellis (The Cheesemonger), St Andrews, 94
- ◆ Lobster Store, The, Crail, 204
- ◻ Pillars of Hercules Organic Farm, Falkland, 249
- ▽ Fletchers, Auchtermuchty, 269, 270
- ▽ Hilton Wild Boar, Newburgh, 271
- ◇ J & M Stewart, St Andrews, 353

Glasgow

- ▧ McPhies, Glasgow, 46, 47
- ▧ Star Continental Bakery, Glasgow, 46
- ✖ Iain Mellis (The Cheesemonger), Glasgow, 92
- ✚ Heart Buchanan, Glasgow, 139
- ◆ MacCallums of Troon, Glasgow, 205
- ▽ Robertson Jeen, Glasgow, 270

Grampian

- ▧ J G Ross, Inverurie, 47

Highland

- ◻ Earthshare Ltd, Nairn, 251
- ◻ Really Garlicky Company, The, Nairn, 250
- ✱ Caithness Goose Company, Thrumster, 380

Inverness-Shire

- ✚ Gourmet's Lair, Inverness, 140
- ◆ Andy Race Fish Merchants, Port of Mallaig, 206, 207
- ◆ Crannog, Fort William, 205
- ▽ D J MacDougall, Fort Augustus, 269

Isle of Arran

- ✖ Island Cheese Company, The, Brodick, 89

Isle of Mull

- ▧ Island Bakery, The, Tobermory, 48
- ✖ Isle of Mull Cheese, Tobermory, 95
- ◆ Tobermory Fish Company, Tobermory, 208
- ◇ Ardalanish Farm, Bunessen, 350

Isle of Skye

- ◆ Anchor Seafoods, Portree, 207
- ◆ Isle of Skye Seafood, Broadford, 203
- ◻ Glendale Salads, Glendale, 249

Kincardineshire

- ◻ Burnarrachie, Stonehaven, 251

Lanarkshire

- ✖ H J Errington & Co., Carnwarth, 89
- ◻ Briarneuk Nursery, Carluke, 249

Moray

- ✖ Wester Lawrenceton Farm, Forres, 92
- ✚ Phoenix Community Stores, Findhorn Bay, 139
- ◇ Macbeths, Forres, 351
- ◇ Speyside Organics, Aberlour, 349

Orkney

- ✖ Grimbister Farm Cheese, Kirkwall, 93
- ◇ Orkney Organic Meat, Holm, 351, 352

Outer Hebrides

- ◆ Hebridean Smokehouse Ltd, Locheport, 207
- ◆ Salar Smokehouse Ltd, Lochcarnon, 206

Perth and Kinross

- ▧ Campbell's Bakery, Crieff, 45
- ▧ McDonald's Cheese Shop, Blairgowrie, 89
- ◇ Aberfeldy Butchers, Aberfeldy, 348
- ◇ Brig Highland Beef, Bridge of Earn, 353
- ◇ Jamesfield Organic Farm, Abernethy, 349
- ◇ Lurgan Farm, Aberfeldy, 349

Ross-Shire

- ✖ Highland Fine Cheeses Ltd, Tain, 95
- ✖ West Highland Dairy, Stromeferry, 94
- ✚ Gillies Fine Foods, Strathpeffer, 140
- ✚ Struan Apiaries, Conon Bridge, 139
- ◆ Keltic Seafayre, Dingwall, 204
- ◆ Summer Isles Foods, Achiltibuie, 203
- ▽ Highland Wild Boar, Alness, 269

Shetland

- ◆ Hand-Made Fish Company, The, Bigton, 203
- ◇ Globe Butchers, Lerwick, 352

South Lanarkshire

- ◇ Ramsay of Carluke Ltd, Carluke, 350

Stirling

- ◯ Beers Scotland Ltd, Stirling, 171

Sutherland

- ◆ Cowie's of Helmsdale, Helmsdale, 205
- ◆ Helmsdale Smokehouse, The, Helmsdale, 206

| ◻ FRUIT AND VEGETABLES | ▽ GAME | ◇ MEAT | ✱ POULTRY |

alphabetical index

& Clarkes, 29
1657 Chocolate House, 129
A Flanigan & Son, 341
A G Millers, 308
A J Barkaway Ltd, 301
A Johnson & Son, 315
Abbey Farm Organics, 232
Abbey Leys Farm, 78
Abel & Cole Ltd, 112
Aberfeldy Butchers, 348
Adamson's Bakery, 47
Adeys Farm Organic Meats, 277
Aines Chocolates, 137
Aireys Farm Shop, 328
Albert Rees, 355
Aldeburgh Fish Stall, 189
Alder Carr Farm, 119
Alfred Enderby, 193
Alham Wood Cheeses, 59
All Natural Bakery, 33
Allen Hale Butchers, 292
Allen's Bakery, 48
Allens Farm, 226, 227
Alternative Meats, 264
Anchor Seafoods, 207
Andy Race Fish Merchants, 206, 207
Angela's Delicatessen, 117
Ansteys of Worcester, 76
Apple Farm, The, 247
Appleby's of Hawkestone, 76
Arbutus Bread, 43
Ardalanish Farm, 350
Ardrahan Cheese, 87
Ardsallagh Goats' Products, 83
Ark Chicken, 365
Arkhill Farm, 342
Arley Wild Boar, 266
Arne Herbes, 212
Artisan Bread, 32
Ash Farm Organics, 311
Ashbee & Son, 261
Ashgood Farm, 306
Ashlyns Organic Farm Shop, 230
Ashmore Farmhouse Cheese, 59
Astley Vineyards, 164
Au Gourmand, 46
Aubrey Allen Ltd, 315
Audley End Organic Kitchen Garden, 233
Augernik Fruit Farm, 236
Authentic Bread Company, The, 20
Avalon Vineyard (Pennard Organic Wines), 148
Avonbank, 164

Bacheldre Watermill, 49
Baker & Spice, 28
Bakers Basket, 25
Bakery, The, 44
Ballinroan, 249
Ballylagan Organic Farm, 341
Ballysimon Organic Farm, 379
Barker Organics, 232
Barkers, 313
Barmston Organics, 242
Barnacle Bill Direct, 176
Barron's Bakery, 43
Barrow Boar, 260
Barwick Farm, 62, 63
Barwise Aberdeen Angus, 326

Bath Organic Farms, 364
Bath Soft Cheese Company, 54
Baylham House Rare Breeds Farm, 311
Bearsted Vineyard, 156
Becklands Farm, 277
Bee Organic, 219
Beef Direct Ltd and Lamb Direct Ltd, 358
Beers Scotland Ltd, 171
Belfry Deli and Café, The, 136
Bell and Birdtable, The, 220
Bell's Fisheries, 186
Belvelly Smokehouse, 199
Ben's Hens, 62
Benson's Fruit Juices, 148
Berkeley Farm Dairy, 61
Berkswell Traditional Farmstead Meats, 316
Berrow Honey, 128
Berryhill Fruit Farm, 254
Bessy Beck Trout Farm, 194
Better Beef, 310
Better Food Company, The, 102
Biddenden Vineyards and Cider Works, 150
Biddy Early Brewery, The, 170
Bill and Sue Osborne, 287
Bill the Butcher, 278
Birdwood Farmhouse Cheesemakers, 72
Black Sheep Brewery plc, The, 167
Blacker Hall Farm Shop, 340
Blackmoor Apple Shop, 224
Blas Ar Fwyd, 142
Bleikers Smokehouse, 196
Blissful Buffalo, 56
Bluebell Organics, 241, 242
Boathouse Organic Farm Shop, 224
Boddingtons Berries, 217
Border County Foods, 327
Born and Bread Organic Bakery, 28
Bosavern Farm, 218
Botterell's, 188
Bower Farm Dairy, 95
Bowlees Farm Shop, 340
Boyton Farm, 295
Bradshaw Bros Ltd, 263
Bragdy Ceredigion Brewery, 173
Bramley and Gage, 149
Brampton Wild Boar, 262
Bread & Co, 25
Bread Pancheon, The, 19
Breads Etcetera, 28
Breaky Bottom Vineyard, 154
Bre-Pen Farm, 105
Brewhamfield Organic Dairy Farm, 279
Briarneuk Nursery, 249
Brickyard Farm Shop, 243
Bridge Farm Organic Foods, 71
Brig Highland Beef, 353
Brindisa, 113
Bromley Green Farm, 327
Brook Cottage Farm, 228
Brooklodge Nursery, 246
Brooklynne Farm Shop, 229
Brookshaws of Nantwich, 331
Broughs of Birkdale, 333

Broughton Pastures Organic Fruit Wine, 158
Broughton Village Bakery, The, 36
Brown and Forrest, 178
Brown Cow Organics, 291
Brown's of Stilton, 263
Browse Seafoods, 177
Bude Shellfish, 177
Bumpylane Rare Breeds, 356
Buntings Butchers, 310, 312
Burnarrachie, 251
Burren Smokehouse, 202
Burscombe Cliff Farm, 295
Burtree House Farm, 376
Burts Potato Chips, 104
Butley Orford Oysterage, 192
Butts Farm Shop, The, 282
Bywell Fish and Game Smokery, 197

C & G Starkey, 267
C E Brown, 263
C H Wakeling Ltd, 301
C Lidgate, 303
Café Paul Rankin (Roscoff Bakery), 40
Café Royal, 39
Caffi Patio, 96, 98
Caherbeg Free Range Pork, 347
Caithness Goose Company, 380
Cambrian Organics, 358, 359
Cambridge Cheese Company, 117
Camel Valley Vineyard, 146
Campbell Lindley's, 132
Campbell's Bakery, 45
Camphill Organic Farm Shop & Bakery, 41
Camphill Village Trust (Oaklands Park), 217
Capri Lodge, 338
Carley and Webb, 192
Carley's, 24
Caroline's Home Grown Veg, 247
Carrigbyrne Farmhouse Cheese, 81
Carrob Growers, 254
Carroll's Heritage Potatoes, 242
Cartmel Sticky Toffee Pudding Co. Ltd, 128
Castleman's Farm, 261
Causeway Cheese Company, 81
Caviston's Seafood, 200
Caws Caerfai, 98
Caws Cenarth, 95, 96
Ceci Paolo, 124
Cefn Goleu, 382
Cefn Maen Farm, 382
Celtic Bakers, The, 29
Celtic Dawn, 209
Cerney Cheese, 55
Chandler & Dunn Ltd, 299
Chantry Farm Shop, 317
Charlton Orchards, 218
Chatsworth Farm Shop, 122
Checketts of Ombersley, 316
Cheese Hamlet, The, 79
Cheese Kitchen, The, 65
Cheese Shop, The, 125
Cheese Shop, The, 63

Cheese Shop, The, 77
Cheese Shop, The, 78
Cheese Society, The, 73
Chegworth Valley Juices, 156
Cheshire Smokehouse, The, 194
Chesterton Farm Shop, 282
Chicken Came First, The, 74
Chicken Lady, The, 380
Chilford Hall Vineyard, 160
Chisnalls Delicatessen, 120
Chocolate Gourmet, The, 124
Chocolate Room, The, 135
Chocolate Society, The, 113, 131
Church Farm Organics, 240
Churchtown Farm, 284
Clay Barn Orchard, 229
Clive Downs Butchers, 290
Clive Houlder, 231
Clover Jerseys, 96
Club Chef Direct, 176
Coakley-Greene, 209
Cockles, 206
Coedwynog Free Range Geese, 381
Coffey's Butchers, 268
Colchester Oyster Fishery Ltd, 190
Coleshill Organics, 218
Colfin Smokehouse, 208
Colston Bassett Dairy, 75
Common Loaf Bakery, 19
Company Shed, The, 191
Connemara Smokehouse, The, 199
Continental Sausages, 346
Cookies Crab Shop, 191
Cool Chile Co., 225
Coolea Farmhouse Cheese, 88
Cooleeney Farmhouse Cheese, 89
Copas Traditional Turkeys, 369
Corleggy Cheese, 83
Corn Dolly Home Bakery, The, 41, 42
Cornish Cheese Co., 58
Cornish Country Larder, 58
Cornish Country Meats, 286
Cornish Cuisine, 181
Cornish Farmhouse Cheeses, 56
Cornish Smoked Fish Company, The, 182
Corvedale Organic Lamb, 322
Costrong Fruit Farm, 221
Cotherstone Cheese Company, 80
Coturnix Quail, 85
Country Butcher, The, 285
Country Cheeses, 61, 62
Country Choice, 136
Country Fare, 129
Country Kitchen Home Bakery, The, 41
Country Kitchen, A, 126
Country Ways, 294
County Delicacies, 116
Court Farm and Leisure, 235
Cowie's of Helmsdale, 205
Cowmire Hall Damson Gin, 165
Cranborne Farms Traditional Meats, 294, 295
Cranleigh Organic Farm Shop, 370
Crannog, 205
Crapes Fruit Farm, 229, 230
Cratloe Hills Sheep's Cheese, 84
Cream of Cumbria, 77
Crockham Hill Cheeses, 66
Croft Organics, 250
Croghan Goat Farm, 83
Crones Cider, 161
Crooked End Farm, 290
Cropwell Bishop Creamery, 75
Cross Lanes Fruit Farm, 226

Cross of York, 198
Crowe Fishmongers, 191
Cuan Sea Fisheries, 198
Culdrum Organic Farm, 378
Curradine Angus, 324
Curtis of Lincoln, 319
Curworthy Cheese, 58
Cusgarne Organics, 219
Cwm Harry Land Trust, 254
Cyrnel Bakery, 27

D J MacDougall, 269
D W Wall & Son, 316, 322
Dairy Barn Farm Shop, 308
Daren Farm, 354
Dartmoor Happy Hogs, 288
Dartmouth Smokehouse, The, 179
Davenport Vineyards, 157
David Burns Butchers, 341
Davills Pâtisserie, 39
Dawson Fold Farm, 239
Daylesford Organic Farmshop, 103
De Gustibus, 30
Dedham Gourmet, The, 117
Deer Force10, 258
deFINE Food and Wine, 130
Delectables Fine Foods, 114
Deli on the Square, 124
Demel's Sri Lankan Chutneys, 131
Denbies Wine Estate, 151
Denhay Farms Ltd, 278
Dennis of Bexley, 297
Detton Beef and Lamb, 316
Di's Dairy and Pantry, 106
Didlington Manor, 121
Ditty's Home Bakery, 40, 42
Doddington Dairy, 81
Domini Quality Foods, 69
Donegal Organic Farm Produce, 248
Donnington Trout Farm, 183
Dorset Blue Cheese Company, 61
Dorset Blueberry Company, The, 220
Dragon Orchard, 236
Drim Farm, 98
Duchy Home Farm Organic Vegetables, 219
Duchy of Cornwall Oyster Farm, The, 179
Dunlop Dairy, 93
Dunning Quality Geese, 368
Durras Farmhouse Cheese, 82

E Oldroyd and Sons Ltd, 244
Earthshare Ltd, 251
East Hill Pride, 288
Eastbrook Farms Organic Meat, 293
Eastwoods of Berkhamsted, 297
Eddie's Seafood Market, 205
Eddisbury Fruit Farm, 239
Edward Hamer, 358
Edwards of Conwy, 356
Eggleston Hall, 241
Elite Meats, 319
Ellel Free Range Poultry Company, The, 376
Elwell Fruit Farm, 212
Emma B Delicatessen, 106
Emmett's Store, 312
Engine Shed Bakery, The, 46
English Wines Group plc, 158
Enys Wartha, 105
Essington Fruit Farm, 238
Evans & Paget, 308
Eversfield Manor, 288
Eweleaze Farm, 289
Exmoor Organic, 366
Eynon's of St Clears Ltd, 360

F C Phipps, 314
F Conisbee & Son, 300
F Simpson & Son, 335
Falmouth Bay Oysters, 179
Farmer Direct, 136
Farmer Sharp, 330
Farmshop Home Delivery, 122
Farmyard Chicken Company (S J Frederick & Sons), 372
Feasts, 135
Fern Verrow Vegetables, 238
Field 2 Kitchen, 234, 239
Findlays of Portobello, 350
Fine Cheese Co., The, 54
Finnebrogue Venison Company, 268
Fish on the Quay, 208
Fish Shed, The, 190
Fish Stall, The, 177
FishWorks, 176, 178, 187
Five Acres, 237
Five Winds Farm Smokehouse and Butchery, 313
Fletchers, 269, 270
Flodder Hall, 240
Flour Power City, 28
Flourish Bakery and Pâtisserie, 30
Food Company, The, 118
Food Halls, The, 111
Forbes Raeburn & Sons, 270
Forge Farm, 54
Forman & Field, 114
Fortunes, 198
Fosters Mill, 34
Fountain Violet Farm, 286
Four Seasons, 245
Fowey Fish, 180
Fowlescombe Farm, 285
Foxbury Farm, 298
Foxy's Deli, 143
Framptons of Bridport, 258
Franciscan Well, The, 169
Frank Greenslade, 182
Fred W Reade & Sons, 70
Fresh Food Company, The, 187
Fruit Garden, The, 253
Fruits of Suffolk, 119
Fruitwise, 227
Fuglemere Rare Breeds, 307
Fullers Organic Farm Shop, 304

G & R Tudge, 321
G G Sparkes, 304
G N F & G A Browning, 323
Gabriel Machin, 302
Galloway Farmhouse Cheese, 93
Galloway Smokehouse, The, 271
Garden House, The, 133
Garden, The, 247
Garth Cottage Nursery, 133
Gartmore Farm, 380
Gary Dutton Butchers, 259
Gellirhyd Farm, 172
George Arthur Ltd, 260
George Payne Butchers, 338
Gillies Fine Foods, 140
Gittisham Herd at Combe Estate, 285
Glendale Salads, 249
Glenilen Farm, 85
Globe Butchers, 352
Glyde Farm Produce, 84
Glyn Fach Farm, 253, 254
Godfrey C Williams & Son, 130
Godshill Organics, 222
Goetre Farm, 382
Gold Hill Organic Farm, 212
Golden Cross Cheese Company, 67
Golden Crust Bakery, The, 50
Goodman's Geese, 375
Goods Shed, The, 110
Goosemoor Organics, 244

Gorwydd Caerphilly, 99
Gospel Green Cyder, 153
Gourmet Mushrooms, 231
Gourmet World, 114
Gourmet's Lair, 140
Goya's, 44
Graig Farm Organics, 358
Gran Stead's Ginger Wine, 157
Granary, The, 123
Granthams of Alderley Edge, 128
Grapevine Delicatessen, The, 116
Grapevine, 193
Grays Farm Cider, 149
Great Clerkes Farm, 374
Great Grove Poultry, 371
Green Valley Foods at Longmeadow, 215
Greenfields Farm Shop, 127
Gregg's Pit Cider and Perry, 162
Greystone House, 331
Grimbister Farm Cheese, 93
Growing With Nature, 240
Gubbeen Cheese, 88
Gubbeen Smokehouse, 347
Guernsey Organic Growers, 218
Gwatkin Cider at Abbey Dore Farm Shop, 162

H Forman & Son, 187
H Gunton, 118
H J Errington & Co., 89
H M Pearce, 18
H P Jung, 26
H S Bourne, 78
Hallsford Farm Produce, 327
Ham Street Farm Produce, 284
Hamblings, 261
Hampton Farm Shop, 235
Hampton's Deli, 107
Hand Made Cheese Co., The, 90
Hand Picked Shellfish Company, 185
Hand-Made Fish Company, The, 203
Happy Meats, 325
Happy Piggy Pork, 337
Harvest Moon Organic Farm, 371
Harvey's Pure Meat, 262
Hawkshead Trout Farm, 193
Haye Farm Scrumpy Cider, 146
Hayles Fruit Farm, 220
Haymans Butchers, 291
Hayman's Fisheries, 188
Hazelbury Partners, 283
Hazelmere Café and Bakery, 37
Head Fine Foods, 304
Heards of Wigston, 318
Heart Buchanan, 139
Heatherlea, 40
Hebridean Smokehouse Ltd, 207
Hecks Farmhouse Cider, 149
Helen's Bay Organic Gardens, 246
Helmsdale Smokehouse, The, 206
Helsett Farm, 57
Helvick Seafood, 200
Hen on the Gate, The, 225
Henclose Farm Organic Produce, 219
Henshelwood Deli, 134
Hepburns of Mountnessing, 309
Herb Patch, The, 243
Heritage Prime, 287
High House Fruit Farm, 234
High Lane Oatcakes, 36
Higher Crop, 215
Higher Hacknell Farm, 294
Highland Fine Cheeses Ltd, 95
Highland Geese, 380

Highland Wild Boar, 269
Highlands Farm, 377
Highside Butchers, 339
Hilden Brewing Co., The, 168, 169
Hill End Farm, 280
Hilton Wild Boar, 271
Hindon Organic Farm, 288
Hobbs House, 213
Hobbs House, 18, 20
Hockerton Grange Farm Shop, 324
Hollies Farm Shop, The, 131
Hollow Trees Farm Shop, 231
Holly Tree Farm Shop, 376
Holsworthy Organics, 216
Home Cottage Farm, 224
Home Farm Organics, 319
Home Farm Shop, 364
Home Grown, 246
Homewood Partners, 369
Honey Tree Organic Greengrocers and Good Food Store, The, 133
Honeybuns, 103
Hoo Hing, 120
Hopwood Organic Farm, 237
Horsham Cheese Shop, The, 67
House of Cheese, The, 61
Housekeeper's Store at Tatton Park, The, 265
Howbarrow Organic Farm, 239
Hunter's, 41
Huntley's, 130
Huntly Herbs, 250
Hunts Hill Barn, 68
Huntsham Farm – Pedigree Meats, 323
Hutchinsons, 267

Iain Mellis (The Cheesemonger), 90, 92, 94
Ian Lentern, 289
Inagh Farmhouse Cheese, 86
Infinity Foods Bakery, 26
Inverawe Smokehouse, 208
Island Bakery, The, 48
Island Cheese Company, The, 89
Isle of Colonsay Apiaries, 138
Isle of Mull Cheese, 95
Isle of Skye Seafood, 203
Isle of Wight Bacon Company, The, 302

J & L Grubb, 85
J & M Stewart, 353
J A & E Montgomery Ltd, 65
J B Cockburn & Sons, 267
J C Burdge, 278
J E Toms & Sons, 344
J G Ross, 47
J M Walman Family Butchers, 297
J T Morgan, 355
J Wickens Family Butchers, 309
Jack Scaife, 332
James Whelan Butchers, 345
Jamesfield Organic Farm, 349
Jekka's Herb Farm, 213
John David Power, 346
John Hurd's Organic Watercress, 219
John James, 355
John Miles Traditional Breeds Butcher, 317
John R Dowey & Son, 343
John Thorner's Ltd, 291
John's Fish Shop, 192
Jo's Home Baked Bread, 39
Jules and Sharpie, 120
Julia Coviello, 357
Jus, 162
Just Rachel Desserts, 73

K B Stannard & Sons, 262
K G Consultants, 146
K O'Connell Ltd Fish Emporium, 200
Keens Cheddar (S H & G H Keen), 65
Keer Falls Forest Farm, 328
Kelly Turkey Farms, 372
Kelly's, 246
Keltic Seafayre, 204
Ken Watmough, 202
Kenneth J Eve, 300
Kent and Sussex Apple Juice and Cider Centre, 153
Keys Hill Poultry Farm, 71
Killorglin Farmhouse Cheese, 87
Kilnsey Park, 196
Kim's Cakes, 125
Kingfisher Farm Shop, 222
Kingsland Edwardian Butchers, 303
Kinsale Gourmet Store, 201
Kintaline Farm, 93, 94
Kinvara Smoked Salmon, 202
Kitchen and Food Hall, The, 137
Kitridding Farm Shop, 329
Kitty's of Coleraine, 40
Knock Farm Organics, 356
Knockanore Farmhouse Cheese, 87
Knotts Cake and Coffee Shop, 42
Krawczyk's West Cork Salamis, 348

L & C Game, 258
L'Artisan du Chocolat, 113
La Fromagerie, 67
La Hogue Farm Shop and Delicatessen, 118
Lagan Farm Meats at Milton Park Garden Centre, 284
Lakings of Louth, 321
Lanchester Fruit, 166
Langley Chase Organic Farm, 280, 281
Langthornes Buffalo Produce, 338
Larberry Pastures, 340
Lartington Lamb, 337
Lathcoats Farm, 228
Laurel Farm Herbs, 232
Laverstoke Park Produce, 221
Lavistown Cheese, 87
Leakers Bakery Ltd, 18
Lefktro UK Ltd, 103
Lenshaw Organics, 250
Leventhorpe Vineyard, 166
Lewis Fine Foods, 48, 51
Lighthouse Bakery, The, 30
Lightwood Cheese, 76
Lincolnshire Organics, 127
Lindisfarne Oysters, 195
Linscombe Farm, 214
Lishmans of Ilkley, 336, 337
Little Bosoha, 56
Little Omenden Sussex Beef, 296
Little Warren Farm, 305
Llanboidy Cheesemakers, 99
Llangloffan Farmhouse Cheese, 97
Llangybi Organics, 255
Llewellyn's Orchard Produce, 171
Llwynhelyg Farm Shop, 142
Lobster Store, The, 204
Loch Arthur Creamery, 90
Loch Fyne Oysters Ltd, 203
Long Crichel Bakery, 25
Longborough Farm Shop, 104
Longwood Farm, 309
Lords of Middleton, 265

Hearing the latest gossip

DESIGN FOR A WILDERNESS

Phil Drabble

Illustrated with photographs
by S. C. Porter

PELHAM BOOKS

First published in Great Britain by PELHAM BOOKS LTD
52 Bedford Square, London, WC1B 3EF
1973

ISBN 0 7207 0706 4

Set and printed in Great Britain by
Tonbridge Printers Ltd, Peach Hall Works, Tonbridge, Kent
in Baskerville eleven on twelve-and-a-half point on paper supplied by
P. F. Bingham Ltd, and bound by James Burn at Esher

CONTENTS

Preface 9

CHAPTER ONE Purpose 11

CHAPTER TWO Pressures 23

CHAPTER THREE Prototype 40

CHAPTER FOUR The Plan 67

CHAPTER FIVE Perks 93

CHAPTER SIX People 120

Index 137

ILLUSTRATIONS

Hearing the latest gossip — *frontispiece*

Between pages 48–49
Jess comes through the garden gate. Froggatt's forty acre in the background
Dunstal pool from the study window
Annie Moonie helps to feed Honey, the white fallow fawn
The mistle thrushes I saved from the crows
Mandy, Fly, me, Tick and Spider in the wood
Tick loves ferreting
Fred, the barn owl

Between pages 80–81
Roe buck by Dunstal Pool
Twelve Sunday lunches! Silkie bantam and Aylesbury ducklings
Grey squirrel. The one that got away!
The vole that ate the strawberries till Fred ate him
Making a pool
The pool we made in Primrose Dell
The Canada goose on the study window-sill
The Bewick's swan that stayed four years

Between pages 104–105
The ride to Primrose Dell from the study window
The last of the nuthatches
Swallows on a thumb stick in the garage
A great spotted woodpecker nests in the birch by the hen pen

Mallard ducks nest right by the house
Turtle doves are so much nicer than collared doves
Wrens in the binder twine in the goat shed

Between pages 128–129
Spotted flycatchers nest by the kitchen window
Pouter pigeons and collared doves at bird bath
The author's pigs provide free labour in the woods
Roe buck in velvet
The kestrel that roosted on the dogs' chair
The weasel that catches the mice
Swallows on the cross cut saw in the garage
Pied wagtails in the garage

Preface

It is common for those who are fettered to a factory bench or office desk to dream of escaping to work for themselves. But after more than twenty years in industry, I took the plunge to earn my living with my pen. When I succeeded in buying a cottage and ninety acres of secluded woodland, where I could create a wildlife sanctuary, it seemed to be the pinnacle of my ambition.

I soon found that there is no such thing as 'balance' in nature but only perpetual change. I discovered that my beloved wilderness was a wasting asset: that, left to itself, it would deteriorate until it was no longer attractive to many of the threatened species I wanted to encourage.

The only way I knew to prevent this was to evolve a practical plan for its conservation – which is the modern jargon word for what gamekeepers have been doing for generations!

Sportsmen and naturalists have so much in common that they are stupid to alienate each other by allowing their lunatic tails to wag such reasonable dogs. So I hope that the design I have evolved for the management of my wilderness will be of some service to both camps.

P.D.

CHAPTER ONE

Purpose

My desk is so narrow and so close to my study window that I often get the illusion of working outside. Our oakwood merges with an unfenced paddock and, about fifty yards away to my left, the trees sweep down to a large pool. Beyond that are the green fields of superb dairy country.

It is a panoramic view because my nose is never more than eighteen inches from the window pane, so that the slightest movement on the pool or in the paddock or at the edge of the wood cannot fail to catch my eye. Such delightful distractions are multiplied because three wide grassy rides have been cut radially half a mile or so into the wood in such a fashion that each 'points' at my study window.

I work at the hub of the activities of a whole spectrum of wildlife – so that, as I glance up, I cannot fail to see not only what is at the edge of the paddock, but also deer and hares and pheasants in the rides or foxes and birds crossing from one compartment of trees to another, deep in the heart of the wood. I live the sort of life I used to day-dream about for the twenty-odd years when I was in industry, working for other people, and gaffered by the clock.

Every morning my car got snarled up in the same traffic jams at the same traffic lights. My guts were filled with the same stench of diesel and no bird could sing loud enough to drown grumbling exhausts and whining gears. The same face seemed to peer through every windscreen, as apathetic and expressionless as every other face. The only signs of animation in these faces were transient glares of hate at whoever had the initiative to jump the queue.

I passed away such frustrations by projecting myself to the next week-end when I could escape and lose myself in quiet country; when time would no longer matter, and the neuroses induced by irate customers or bloody-minded shop stewards would shrink into perspective.

There is nothing unusual about day-dreaming about being one's own boss, able to choose whom one works with, or about escaping to some never-never land where the sun always shines and the comforts of life appear without effort. But converting such ambitions to reality is quite another matter. Having scrabbled for a reasonable standard of living in one field, it comes hard to start at the bottom of another.

I had planned for this by writing and broadcasting as much as I could in my spare time, convincing my company that it was not bad publicity to have an employee who was known to people who might not be directly interested in buying springs or weighing machines.

I found it impossible to get home from work at six and to start writing immediately, but when I had wound down for about three hours, I found no great difficulty in doing another two or three with my pen. Especially work I loved. So I wrote my first three books between nine at night and one in the morning, and managed to average a broadcast about once in three weeks from 1947 to 1961.

This obviously took a certain amount of company time, but I compensated for it by taking my annual holiday as odd days in the studio. For almost thirteen years I introduced a monthly sound programme called 'In The Country', and my friend Paul Humphreys, who produced it, so arranged it that we did most of the studio work after 6 p.m.

A change is as good as a rest, they say, and this writing and broadcasting not only refreshed me after the chores of factory life, but also introduced me to a whole host of friends with similar interests, whom I should never otherwise have met.

Eventually I worked myself into a position where I could afford to step out of the engineering industry to earn a living with my pen, without starting again from the breadline. By then I was doing a regular column for the Birmingham *Evening Mail*, which I still do as 'Country Scene'; I also had a regular radio programme, occasional books, and whatever else I could scratch for.

I never expected to earn as much as I had in industry, but my whole philosophy was based on the concept that some things matter more than money. I yearned to do something creative where I could choose as my partners people with whom I had something in common and liked. I wanted to be able to take a day off for a ploughing match or field trial, and to eat and work and sleep and laze, however the spirit moved me. And it suddenly seemed important to own a bit of England, where I could create a sanctuary for myself and the wild creatures which I found so irresistibly attractive. This urge for land of my own was as basic as a badger's primitive jungle that had never been cultivated.

It seemed important to look out of my own window on to my own soil, and to see wild creatures so regularly that we would get to know each other as intimately as a shepherd knows his sheep.

I described in *My Beloved Wilderness* how I put the first part of this plan into effect; how, after months of wrangling, we bought Goat Lodge and about ninety acres of woodland. 'Wilderness' was a fair description for it. Half the wood was neglected, and the other half in the process of being chopped down.

The standing timber on about forty acres had been sold before I came on the scene, and the Forestry Commission had a 999-year lease on this patch. They planted it with pine trees shortly after we came, but it did not look like doing much good.

My wife, Jess, is as fond of gardening as I am of wildlife, and she had re-created a paradise at our last house of a neglected old garden which had become a desert of weeds.

But it is one thing to start with dignified old trees and mature azaleas and rhododendrons, and quite another to face a primitive jungle that had never been cultivated.

Neither of us minded, though. We both believe that nothing worthwhile is easy, and were overjoyed at our luck at getting a place so isolated. And every time that we went into the wood we saw something exciting we hadn't seen before. Sometimes it was large and spectacular, as when we came up on two fallow bucks fighting for possession of a herd of does, and sometimes inconspicuous – the first snowdrop, or a tree creeper hunting for insects on a trunk within arm's reach meant more to me than it had done to be made a director of my firm.

Nobody who has not spent years in a nine-to-six job with all the boring routines of endless conferences, fixed meal breaks and set times to do a job can understand the joy of no longer owning the clock to be one's master. Nevertheless, for months I never got used to the fact that it no longer mattered if I was wandering in the wood during 'working hours'.

I nearly always go round the wood when I feed the stock in the morning, which is sometimes before breakfast and sometimes after, depending on what work there is to do. Jess comes, too, after lunch, and we are often there for about an hour, and sometimes around dusk as well. I rarely go down the same paths twice running, and I vary the times according to my whim, so that I am gradually getting to know every hillock and hollow, and what I am most likely to see there.

Even so, it tooks months to get over the vague feeling of guilt at taking pleasure in the wood when I would previously have been 'working'. This feeling was aggravated because people used to say, and some still do, how lovely it must be to live in retirement in such a lovely spot – although I am well aware that I do more work in 'retirement' than they do for a living!

After a morning's chores in the kitchen even Jess sometimes

says how lovely it must be to be able to mess about outside –
even when I've been doing mauling toil in sweaty weather.
The fact is, I work as hard or harder now than at any time
in my life. As a freelance writer I cannot control the input of
my work, so I have usually either too much ahead, or too
little. Most often too much, I am glad to say. Press dates
have to be met, and they have an awkward way of coin-
ciding.

There is, too, always a mountain of work to be done out
in the wood. Hard physical work – clearing thickets or cleaning ditches, or mowing weeds or cutting logs. Short-term,
this brings in no return, so I do it in the gaps between
writing assignments. When there is some exceptionally interesting nest to watch, or the deer are rutting, or there is a
litter of fox or badger cubs above ground, I *make* the time to
stand and stare. And 'make' is the operative word. Work still
has to go on, and it often has to be done at inconvenient
times, perhaps before breakfast, or after supper.

In total I have less spare time now than I ever had, and I
am rarely away from home for more than a night at a time.
I take no holidays, except four days before Easter for the
annual conference of the Mammal Society. But I *need* no
spare time, because I love writing, and I love doing and
seeing the things I write about.

It is great fun making a living in such a pleasant way.
As a kid I was a natural wheeler-dealer, and I have always
got a kick out of driving a good bargain. While at prep
school I kept a few tame mice at home, and, at the end of
the holidays, I fitted up a mouse box in the hen pen, where
they would be warm and safe from cats while I was away.
I arranged it so that they could get out and scrounge their
own food from what the hens discarded, so that they caused
no trouble while I was away. By the time next holidays
came around, they had bred and increased, so that I
could sell the surplus at the local pet shop for my pocket
money.

The only losers in the deal were the kids who bought them,

because the young mice had never been handled, and could bite as sharp as rattle snakes!

This innate commercial streak has stood me in good stead. Since I can't afford the luxury of running a wildlife reserve as a hobby, I cost out every project before I start it to check its viability. There is not always an end product such as timber or young trees to sell, but every idea must show promise before I put it into practice, even if it does no more than supply original copy for articles or broadcasts.

This is, perhaps, because I was brought up to believe that a sound way of making a mark in life is to have an unusual combination of knowledge. My father was a doctor, and wanted me to read medicine at university – but, instead of joining in his practice, he then wanted me to qualify in law as well. He said that the fees to be earned by the few people having such dual qualifications were utterly out of proportion to their intrinsic worth. I should have hated either doctoring or law even more than industry, but I have never forgotten the principle.

Few naturalists have commercial minds, and not many industrialists know a blackbird from a starling. Writers on natural history, too, often live by scissors and paste, drawing upon other writers' work, because they have no practical experience of their own to draw upon. But at first it seemed that there was copy wherever I looked, saleable stories in every direction, so that all I had to do was to keep my eyes skinned, and report the plots as they developed.

I remember going into Primrose dell just as the sun was setting one night. It is described as a marlpit on the ordnance map, and you can't get much more unromantic than that, but its attractions depend on the way you look at it.

At some time in the past hundreds of tons of marl had been dug here by hand for spreading on the acid clay to grow more corn. The hole that was left has steep sides about twenty feet deep, and in summer it is covered in thick vegetation as token of the fertility of its soil. Late in the season it grows the most lush giant mare's tail that I ever saw.

But the time to go to the dell is in spring, just before sunset. There is a carpet of primroses then, so delicate and pure that, as the sun sinks below the marlpit rim, they blush for a few seconds in its reflection; then, as daylight fades, they rival the moon for pallor.

Some of the girls from the school of St Mary and St Anne, which is a mile away in the village, had built a fox earth here with the boys from Denstone, but they didn't muster enough brute force to dig it deep enough to be very effective. It was well sited and it should have been ideal, because it is in a corner of the wood about as far from human habitation as is possible in the midlands. Although it hasn't attracted a breeding fox or badger, I have so much faith in it that I am going to have another go with a mechanical digger instead of picks and shovels.

The wood is now much quieter than when we came because there was a bit of poaching at first, which I have been able to stop because I am out at such irregular hours. One of the benefits has been that we are blessed with an exceptional variety of birds, animals, insects and plants. So much so that the Nature Conservancy scheduled it as a Site of Special Scientific Interest, largely because of the wild daffodils on Daffodil Lawn and the heronry in Holly Covert and Dunstal Pool Plantation.

Nuthatches are among my favourite birds and, when we came, it was not uncommon to see four or five together on the fat that we hung out for the tits. They are very beautiful, a little less in size than a starling, with similar-sized yellow bills. They have blue-grey plumage on their backs and wings and crowns, elegant buff waistcoats, yellow legs and black stripes through their eyes.

Not least of their attractions is a limpid piping call with a variety of notes. Bird books describe them as common, but they are only common in the right sort of country, and it had been a red-letter day to see one before we came here. As the years ticked on we have gradually seen less and less of our nuthatches till, last year, not a single pair nested in the wood.

This was in marked and most unwelcome contrast to most other species, which prospered – presumably because I was controlling their predators, increasing their food supply and providing a sense of security.

When I realised that nothing I was doing was effective in maintaining the numbers of nuthatches, it brought me up with a jolt. It is very daunting, when you are confident you are a success, to discover that an audit of your figures does not substantiate your optimism.

When I escaped from industry and took sanctuary in this seclusion, I did not consciously set out to do a job at all, except in the limited sense of writing enough to buy my victuals. For the first year or so my cup overflowed with delight simply to have no master on my back. The clock urged 'hustle on' no more, so that I was free to go out for as long as I liked in conditions I used to regard as perfect for holidays. I did every day the sort of things I had had to work hard for five days a week in order to do on the remaining two.

The disappearance of our nuthatches drove home the unpleasant truth that it is not necessarily easy to increase what species you like simply by playing the part of a gamekeeper. There may be nothing new about nature conservation that keepers haven't known for years, but even their skill is not omnipotent in the countryside. What had failed to dawn on me was not so much that nothing in nature ever stands still, as the fact that changes are extremely rapid if you leave things to themselves.

The reason that there was such a wonderful variety of wildlife when we came was that it so happened that there was an exceptional range of habitat. By the house there was a mature oak wood with silver birch, ash, sycamore and alder. Below this were hazels, blackberry, hawthorn, honeysuckle, bilberry, bracken and fern. A five-star choice of food and shelter!

Daffodil Lawn at the far end of the wood is a seven-acre clearing which has been used to grow hay for the deer and the Bagot Goats for generations. Daffodils grew there, as it name implies, and wild violets and cowslips and wood anemones and a luxury of simple English wild flowers which are becoming scarcer in areas where intensive husbandry is practised.

At 'our' end of the wood there is Dunstal pool, of an acre and a half, and a paddock by the house. At the far side, to the south-east, about forty acres had been clear felled and replanted with Corsican pines by the Forestry Commission before we came on the scene. It was bare and open when we arrived, and the young trees were surrounded by a blanket of bracken and rough or feggy grass that was ideal for grasshopper warblers and nightjars and hares and partridges.

Lords Coppice, the first part of this area to be replanted nine years ago, has since grown up beyond recognition. The Forestry Commission pines are between nine and twelve feet high and too dense to battle through where they have taken well. There are thickets of birch saplings which, in areas where the pines didn't thrive, seem to stand close as ears of corn. In some patches the bracken grew so rank that it smothered the young trees, while in others, where the trees took hold, they got their revenge by shading the bracken until it died.

Living in the wood, as we do, we didn't at first notice what was happening because the change crept up on us so slowly. It was only when the nuthatches disappeared that it dawned on us how little resemblance there would soon be to the original place we bought.

The discovery prompted closer analysis. At the moment the birch is thick and ideal for many birds to nest. Yellowhammers and tree pipits love it. So do the deer. They come from miles around to scrump our acorns and, when they have filled their bellies, they melt away into the birch scrub until they have slept off their meal and it is time to come out to feed again.

At the moment the mixture must be ideal to encourage the optimum variety of both birds and beasts, but it is obvious that this will not last for long. The pines will grow and crowd out the birch and bracken; the wild rose and young oak seedlings, the grass and bilberry will be shaded out as the treetops knit into an opaque canopy that will exclude light from the whole woodland floor. Then there will be no food and no cover. Few birds or insects will thrive in the sterile carpet of pine needles so typical of Forestry woods. It will degenerate into what the experts are pleased to term a monoculture.

This is precisely what I want to avoid. The joy of this place is its variety, and when we came I was optimistic enough to dream that I could cosset the wildlife here to make a bird sanctuary which should be a model for bird sanctuaries for miles around. I believed that, with good management, I could encourage such a high density of wildlife in my sanctuary that there would be a surplus to overspill into surrounding areas more troubled by disturbance.

With a little modification of my original plan, I still believe I can. The critical thing will be to maintain diversity of habitat. Woodland is always growing or maturing or dying, and each phase is important to something, so that I set about designing a scheme where there would always be some part of the wood in each of the varying phases. I wanted to evolve a plan to create a constantly changing mosaic of glades and open patches and thickets and boggy areas with woodland rides for access and observation points.

This was not possible when we came, because I could not do as I liked with my own wood since it was leased to the Forestry Commission for almost the next thousand years!

Pressures on the countryside are so great due to the hunger for escape to wild places, combined with high wages and easy transport, that it will not only be necessary to manage reserves to act as reservoirs to restock their surroundings. It will also be necessary to establish populations of plants and insects and animals which did not exist there before.

This is controversial. Purists, especially botanists, are often violently opposed to moving any plant, not because they dislike taking seeds or specimens from their 'natural' habitat, but because they dislike introducing them where they were not established before. These enthusiastic recorders have spent years searching the countryside, yard by yard, cataloguing all the plants they find and marking them on their maps. If someone dares to plant a cowslip where they have not recorded the presence of cowslips, they see red.

I think this is rubbish. It is just another symptom of collector's mania. Such folk are more concerned in inflating their egos by being known as the man who discovered a hitherto unrecorded site for a plant than they are about its survival. Each new species on their checklist adds a notch to their reputation, till he who has most shouts 'Conker!' with all the puerile gusto of a schoolboy with a chestnut on a string.

They equate 'nice' with 'rare', and I find that some specialists who call here get all steamed up about our wild service tree, which is not a common species in Staffordshire. I don't really know why they should, because service trees are often indicative of the antiquity of woodland, and this was once part of the forest of Needwood. The fact remains that few service trees have been recorded for Staffordshire so the experts exclaim 'How nice!'

For my money there are lots of nicer things. Thickets of blackthorn which grow the sloes we use for sloe gin at Christmas, for instance. And if you know a nicer liqueur than that, I should be grateful for the recipe! Or blue tits feeding from the nut basket within a yard of my head as I write this, or fallow deer tame enough to trust me not to harm them, or cock pheasants or mallard drakes glistening in the sun. All these are nice but, because they are also common, the boffins sniff at them.

I believe that the important thing is not the cult of rarity but the culture of as many native fauna as it is possible to persuade to thrive here. I stress 'native' because I am unattracted by foreign immigrants, whether they be animals or men. But I believe that pressure on the countryside is such that it is a service to provide conditions so that it is possible to enter a wildlife sanctuary and to see as much in a few acres as would be seen in as many miles if everything was left to the mercy of intensive farming or the interests which scrabble to turn the countryside into a bumper 'sports complex'.

So when a neighbour was about to plough up an old pasture, I lifted some of the cowslips which flourished there and transplanted them to our paddock. They fill my eyes with pleasure when I look up from my desk; they are secure against selective weed killers and, with luck, will scatter their descendants far and wide.

The prospect of owning a bit of England where I could wander at will, proved as attractive in reality as it did in a dream. But it would have palled when the novelty wore off because the role of spectator cannot long be satisfactory to anyone who is mentally and physically active.

Worse still, I soon saw that, by the time I had provided seclusion, my wilderness would probably have passed the peak of its potential as a sanctuary. Left to itself, it was doomed to be a wasting asset. The fauna would diminish as the newly planted wood matured and the tree tops shaded out the food and cover plants which were at their peak within five or six years of our arrival.

So when the honeymoon was over, I was determined not to let my treasure depreciate. I was determined to formulate a management plan that would improve its potential as the years went by, so that, when the time came to topple off my perch, something more worthwhile than an inscription on a tombstone would remain to mark my passing.

CHAPTER TWO

Pressures

Good intentions do not convert day-dreams to realities. Before launching such a scheme I felt it reasonable to assess the opposition. The most vital stratum of society to convince would be the planners – and they are not a species with which I have much in common. They are often so constipated with dogma that they sieve every decision through a mesh woven to catch votes.

One stroke from their pesky pens can turn a woodland paradise, stuffed with the sweetest singing birds, into a concrete jungle or a picnic site where pop music from parked cars obliterates every other sound. The next stroke can turn the wintering ground for waterfowl and waders into a sports complex where nothing survives but racing speed boats and yelling water skiers.

The with-it doctrine of multi-use of our resources is jargon to deceive us that it is sensible to encourage almost any leisure activity on any stretch of water or land. But a moment's reflection demonstrates what nonsense it is to suppose that bird watchers will see anything around a motor race track, or fishermen catch much in a speedboat's wake.

It is useless trying to photograph wildlife (except the human variety) at a pop festival, or to go grouse shooting in the middle of a bunch of orienteerers. I am more interested in wild birds than bird watchers, but unfortunately birds don't vote – so they don't impress the planners.

So far as my prototype reserve is concerned, I cannot afford to pour money into it, so shall try to make it self-supporting. I shall try to improve the habitat by cropping it in rotation so that there is a constantly changing pattern of food and cover. As one patch grows too thick, I aim to sell the surplus to pay for planting the next.

If this design for my wilderness turns out to be successful, it might then be possible to persuade the planners to take similar steps in areas of low commercial and amenity value so that they can improve their wildlife facilities without cost to rates or taxes.

There are plenty of dedicated conservationists who would be only too pleased to supply both the expertise and most of the manpower to build up a chain of such secluded sanctuaries. These could be the reservoirs to stock surrounding amenity areas which would not be viable alone.

In 1970 Prince Philip launched a campaign under the title of 'European Conservation Year' to turn the spotlight of publicity on to the dangers that hung over wildlife and even gracious buildings. The results were spectacular, with press and TV and radio jumping in the boat until it almost sank with good intentions. For the first time it dawned on ordinary urban people that there really was a danger that birds and butterflies and animals might be poisoned by pesticides to the point of extinction.

Public opinion waxed so strong that it became socially unacceptable to pick wildflowers or take birds' eggs or throw up spoilbanks on beautiful skylines. Conservation and pollution became in-words, unfortunately repeated so often that uncommitted folk, who could have helped most, grew bored, although it was the dedicated cranks who pushed their theories to extremes who were most to blame. By the end of Conservation year the idea had been almost done to death.

That didn't detract in the least from the validity of the original concept and the harsh fact remains that unless practical steps are taken to preserve threatened species, their numbers will decline to the point of extinction. European Conservation Year had underlined the need; all that remained was to find people able and willing to convert the theory to practice.

The obvious first choices were natural history and conservation societies, already composed of people passionately interested in wildlife. But even these societies often contained people whose interests conflicted! The bird watchers stamped around, heads in the air looking for nests – and trampled on the flowers. Botanists were so involved with plants that some didn't appreciate the disturbance they caused.

Too often both suffered under the delusion that only what is rare is nice, so that they were more interested in conserving a site famous for rarity than creating a reserve that would do most good to most things. By no means all of them admit the necessity for positive management – perhaps because they do not realise that competition is often so fierce that thugs survive at the expense of the weak. In any case, management costs money.

There is a hard core in most societies who bear the brunt of raising the wind to buy nature reserves and manage them. This is done by films and lectures and the deadly dull do-gooding of sales of work and bun fights.

In my view it should not need charity to raise money to save our national heritage. It should be possible to devise commercially viable alternatives. Only a dedicated minority of eager beavers are happy to beg their fellows to dip into their pockets for no return, but thousands would probably help if they had something to show for the outlay.

The nostalgic urge to own land goes so deep that it struck me that there must be thousands of potential buyers if there was any chance of owning or being partner in a nature reserve.

I know one nature reserve of about thirty odd acres which is bounded on one side by a public footpath. It was bought by a county conservation trust, partly with their own money and grants, and partly with borrowed cash which they must pay back. There is nothing that the trust could do to prevent any member of the public standing on that path to revel in the beauty of the wild flowers or bird song, so I suggested that they made the best of a bad job by cashing-in on the path.

If the people who stand there bought the bit they stood on, they would quadruple their pleasure! If the trust was prepared to sell a strip a yard wide along the footpath it could be divided into tiny plots of, say, one yard square to which access could be gained directly from the path. Attractive deeds could be drawn up for each plot, which the owners could frame and hang over the mantelpiece to prove that they were part-owners of a nature reserve, without in any way detracting from the value of the reserve. And the trust would come out of the deal the richer by £5 or £10 a plot towards the purchase of their next venture.

The added advantage would be that, in the event of the land being subject to possible compulsory purchase, any authority would find it so complicated to deal with such a multiplicity of owners (who might be difficult to trace) that they would probably try for alternatives!

There is nothing new about the idea, for Americans have been buying bits of Stratford for years, but the officials of the trust were too stuffy. They thought 'it might spoil their image'!

The necessity for such reserves is partly due to the fundamental changes in the countryside caused by an agricultural revolution which has toppled ancient skills. Farm wages are so high, though still below urban rewards, that it makes economic sense to do with machines what men once did. A man with a tractor can plough in a day more than a man with a team of horses could do in a week. A combine harvester can eat into a field at an acre every ten minutes or so, but the rub is that such machines tie up so much capital that it is vital to lay out the farm to suit the machines, instead of buying machines to suit the farm, as our forefathers did.

Hedges have to be grubbed out and stubbles ploughed immediately so that there is less food and cover available than there used to be. Sprays will be used to kill 'pests' and doubt-less some of the innocent will suffer at the same time. 'Pretty' grey squirrels will be poisoned or trapped to safeguard grow-ing timber.

It is no use kicking against such pricks because nature lovers who have tried to out-canute Canute in the past have been labelled 'cranks' and damaged the chances of their more objective fellows. The alternative is to formulate a practical policy for providing alternative habitats and food for at least a nucleus of threatened creatures. This is not as difficult as it sounds. In our affluent society the pseudo-intellectuals now worship the golden calf, not of lucre but of leisure. They believe that, instead of being the larder which provides our food, the countryside should be the play-ground of the people.

Generations ago, when the only way to get to work was to walk, neighbours were naturally only too happy to allow their friends freedom to walk across their land. In any case, rural populations were then so sparse that the numbers want-ing to do so would have been insignificant.

The network of footpaths that were formed usually fol-lowed hedgerows, which may now have disappeared so that the old lines run through crops. The change that has taken place, due to easy transport and the fashion of using the country as a dormitory, is as psychological as physical. No place can stay secluded because of the motor-car, and there are those who cry for the whole countryside to be thrown open as a playground where they have every 'right' to romp across the private property of others, because long usage had devalued paths cut as a neighbourly privilege into rights of way for strangers.

In our urban society politicians have been tempted to sub-scribe to the view, because that is where the mass votes lie. But, whatever the doctrinaire arguments, the fact is that too much human pressure on the countryside is not simply peri-lous to shy creatures, it is extremely dangerous to farm stock which is vital for our larder.

Foot-and-mouth disease, brucellosis, swine vesicular disease and sheep scab are among the complaints which are highly contagious or infectious and which can easily be spread from infected farms to 'clean' land. Animal husbandry is now so intensive that epidemics can all too easily be brought on innocent peoples' boots.

I know one farmer with a pedigree herd of brucellosis-free cattle who was greatly incensed when he saw a gang of ramblers walking through his in-calf heifers and he made it plain that their arrival was unwelcome. The ruck-sacked leader thereupon read him a lecture on his selfishness, adding that the farmer 'over there' was kind and considerate, and that he had given them a conducted tour of his cowsheds.

It so happened that the 'considerate' farmer's cattle had brucellosis, which is a dangerous form of undulant fever transmissible to man, and one spot of vaginal discharge of afterbirth carried on a boot could have infected the whole clean pedigree herd.

A sensible compromise might be to utilise leisure as a cash crop. Many small farms which are undercapitalised are being squeezed out of business and it could well be that the farmers might welcome paying guests. Many such unprofitable farms are situated in the wildest and most beautiful country, so that it would not seem unreasonable for campers and ramblers and orienteerers to pay for their pleasures where they could be sure of a welcome, instead of intruding where they are not wanted.

A fringe benefit would be that farmers who wished to cultivate them as a cash crop would compete for their custom by offering facilities, instead of insisting they keep to the narrow confines of a footpath. They might find that many of their visitors were keen naturalists and, if these were prepared to pay a fair price for their pleasure, as shooting men and fishermen are, it would suddenly become possible to employ wardens to preserve wildlife for nature lovers to photograph or enjoy simply watching them living normal lives without fear of execution.

Some injection of capital is as necessary to wildlife conservation as it is to build up a shoot. Success may well depend on accepting reasonable self discipline ourselves, as well as imposing the discipline of control on species which thrive to the extent that they are a peril to the weak and a hazard to crops.

Keepers and naturalists traditionally regard each other with mutual distaste, and it is a fact that bad examples of either are a menace to the countryside.

There is nothing new about nature conservation, which keepers have been practising for centuries – though in the interests of a very restricted range of creatures, often at the expense of almost everything else. The general principles that have guided them apply equally to shoots and nature reserves, and it is worth remembering that it is only in comparatively recent times that naturalists have looked with disfavour on killing any rarity they see! No Victorian drawing-room was complete without its cases of stuffed birds and animals.

It may be significant that the remaining really destructive keepers seem mostly to be the old-fashioned ones, who cannot believe that any bird with a hooked bill or animal with canine teeth should be allowed to live.

A farmer phoned me recently to see if I wanted to photograph a badger which had been snared in his boundary hedge the night before. A self-lock snare had caught it round the middle and 'practically cut it in two. It must have died a frightfully slow and painful death,' he said.

I could have done nothing about it even if I had got a picture because there is nothing illegal about it and many of the anti-blood sport brigade would rather foxes and badgers died by such slow torture than that they were hunted. The man I really blame is the owner of the land who employs the keeper without supervising what he does.

Not all keepers even stay within the law, because it is almost impossible to prove what goes on in the secret fastnesses of deep country. One old lady fed waterhens at her bird table, and was not a little surprised to see a stranger also feeding them by throwing bread over the garden fence. She was even more surprised to see her pets roll over when they ate it, so she sent for the R.S.P.C.A. inspector who arrived with a policeman. The stranger unwisely returned to collect them and was subsequently convicted of poisoning them with alfa chloralose.

The important thing about this is not that some of the worst type of keepers will kill anything but game with ruthless impartiality. What matters most is that the poison he used was alfa chloralose. It is the substance at one time recommended to control wood pigeons by the Ministry of Agriculture. Before that, I doubt if one keeper in a thousand had heard of the stuff.

With typical bureaucratic double-talk, the Ministry claimed that alfa chloralose was 'not a poison but a narcotic'. They said that all it did was to stupefy its victims temporarily. If smaller birds took a dose and died, the ministry said it was an overdose! But they couldn't explain to me the difference between a fatal overdose of a narcotic and a lethal dose of poison!

The scheme for woodpigeons was eventually dropped, but the Forestry Commission are now working on its use for control of grey squirrels. They are shyly reticent about the side effects on predators which catch the doped squirrels, or smaller animals which can enter the containers baited for squirrels.

The worst aspect of the Ministry's abortive scheme for wood pigeons has been the publicity that alfa chloralose has received. It is now being used illegally for magpies and crows, and one respected consultant on shooting management told me that it is 'wonderful' for foxes!

Such irresponsible actions do reputable sportsmen irreparable harm, just as the fuddy-duddies amongst conservationists get reasonable naturalists bracketed with cranks. There is plenty of scope for give and take, and the small bird population on a well-run shoot, where crows and other predators are reasonably controlled, is far higher than in similar but unkeepered country.

I know more keepers who are good naturalists than bad keepers. They do not harm barn owls or badgers or any rare hawks. Surprisingly enough, most of them are ruthless on hedgehogs, although it has been demonstrated conclusively by hundreds of post mortems that the amount of game eaten by hedgehogs is insignificant. As with badgers, the harm they do is far outweighed by the good, and I am quite convinced that badgers are of positive benefit to pheasants.

Pheasants are stupid birds and, left to themselves they will often roost or 'jug' on the ground in coarse grass or rushes. Here they are easy prey to foxes, which locate them accurately by scent, as a pointer will, and then pounce on them in the darkness.

I have watched badgers working in the dusk and have several times had the opportunity of seeing what happens when they come across a sitting hen. Their diet is mainly earthworms and beetles and vegetables and insects, and they do not pounce on their prey as a fox will. They bumble into it and prod it with their snouts to see if it is edible. Even a slothful domestic hen will not stand for this, so she cackles away to safety, leaving the badger surprised but empty jawed. No pheasant puts up with this fright twice, so it avoids the same shock next evening by flying up to roost, not only out of reach of badgers but foxes too.

Sparrow hawks have been hit so hard by pesticides that intelligent keepers spare them, and I know one who boasts of the number of pairs that rear young on his estate, where he genuinely believes that they do good by culling ailing game and putting greater fear into the black hearts of carrion crows than he can.

But there are still a minority who are ruthless with hawks. It is useless to argue with some of them because their bigotry is too ingrained, but others are open to reason, though fanatics, who are obviously trying to ban everything a keeper earns his living from, are unlikely to get a very sympathetic hearing.

Flexibility is vital, and there are borderline cases. As a conservationist, I happen to be very fond of weasels. I know that they kill a few small birds, including game, and that they raid my tit boxes. But they also kill a great many young rats which would do far more damage if they had been spared.

I keep tunnels set with Fenn traps at strategic spots around the yard and buildings and reckon to catch nearly every rat as he arrives. I don't catch them all though, as a tragedy revealed. I found a weasel dead in one of my traps, accidentally executed in the act of dragging out a three parts grown rat he had killed by biting it behind the ear. The weasel had died with the victim in his jaws. I can normally avoid this by setting the traps 'hard' so that a weasel can pass across the treadle without springing the trap. I never bother to trap at all if I know there is a weasel about because he is so much more efficient than I am.

I don't mind an odd pair of foxes about because I love to watch them, and they do as much good as harm by culling the weak and sickly of most species before catching the healthy, and there is no sight in nature prettier than a litter of fox cubs at play. And I positively welcome owls and other predatory birds.

As naturalists we tend to bellyache at keepers who are tough with whatever interferes with game, but if we want their co-operation, it is only fair to give as well as take. In many nature reserves it is the policy to let the 'balance' of nature sort itself out. Even from the wildlife's point of view, it would be difficult to formulate a more short-sighted policy because, left to themselves, the bully boys and thugs triumph in nature just as they do if given too much freedom in our own society.

It is perfectly true that, centuries ago, there were neither keepers nor naturalists and that, even last century, naturalists were as bad as anybody for shooting rarities instead of conserving them. But centuries ago England was a wild and wooded country, and there was room and cover for heavy stocks of wildlife to survive. That woodland has since been eroded and grubbed out, so that more acres can lie under the plough, and competition to live in the shrinking cover is now so fierce that it is vital to take active steps to discipline the thugs and vandals, and to improve the quality of food and shelter for the rest.

Nature reserves where crows and grey squirrels and foxes and jays and magpies swarm are reservoirs to infest surrounding shoots where keepers are working night and day to improve their stocks of game. As fast as these men catch resident crows, they are replaced from the adjacent reserve as surely as water finds its own level.

Not unnaturally, keepers regard giving sanctuary to vermin as an unfriendly act. They know that threatened species in the reserve are put at the same risk as their pheasants and partridges, and they write off the wardens who encourage such thuggery as ignorant cranks. I know this only too well, because it so happens that my wood is a major winter crow roost. The woodpigeons drift in to Dunstal Pool plantation just before dusk and, when they have settled, the crows take it as a signal that all is well.

Quite suddenly, as if at a sign from a leader, flocks of jackdaws leave their vantage points and fly into our wood for the night. When they settle undisturbed, and only then, the leading crows follow them in.

This seems to pass some telepathic signal to hordes which have been waiting in safety out of sight and out of earshot. As if by magic, the darkening sky is black with crows, and I have estimated that a flock of over a thousand inflict their unwelcome presence on my grudging hospitality.

I am well aware that to allow them sanctuary must be deemed a hostile act by every shooting man for miles around, but I have so far failed to find a remedy which will banish the crows without scaring everything else out of the wood.

It is ironic that they probably do the creatures in our

wood less harm than they do miles away. They arrive at dusk and leave at dawn, and few remain to spend the day, when they would be doing most damage. I am around so much that the stragglers soon find that there are considerable risks involved in dawdling anywhere within reach of my rifle.

The result is that the wood supports a good population of pheasants, which benefit from the treatment meted out to creatures less able to look after themselves. I love to see them feeding round the house, for no wild bird is lovelier, and there are one or two exceptionally tame old cocks which come to greet me as soon as they hear my feed can. Every spring I trap up a few hens in box traps, held open by a hazel wand for trigger, and I pen them up to lay eggs which I can hatch and rear under my silkie bantams.

If I didn't pen the hens so that I could collect their eggs to rear under controlled conditions, the few remaining crows would do the job for me. They often take the eggs they steal to the same spot to eat them, as a thrush will use the same stone to crack her snail shells, so that it is not difficult to see precisely where to wait at dawn to knock the survivors off with my rifle.

There is no great skill required, for it is efficient execution more than sport, but I find it fascinating to discover just how inconstant the villains can be. Within twenty-four hours the survivor has usually found another mate which sits up on high, as his predecessor did, until I get him in my telescopic sight and tip him off his perch.

Last year I found a mistle thrush nest in a hazel fork at the edge of the paddock, not because I saw the thrush building, which is how I find most of my nests, but because I saw a pair of carrion crows mobbing her.

Every time a crow went near, the cock thrush dive bombed him and drove it off, so the other crow tried. They were baiting those thrushes as surely as bulldogs ever baited a bull, but it was done to an obvious sinister pattern. As I watched, I could see that one crow was trying to taunt the thrushes to drive him further, and further away so that his mate would be able to nip in and steal the eggs just as the guardians thought they had successfully routed the foe.

The result of this macabre ritual was a foregone conclusion. Or it would have been without my intervention. I eased my study window gently open, inched the muzzle of my rifle through the crack, lined up the cross wires of the telescopic sight – and gently squeezed the trigger.

I hung the black carcass on a twig to serve as his gibbet about five yards from the thrushes' nest and, though the mistle thrushes took no notice of it after an hour, it acted as an effective scarescrow to its fellows until the eggs were hatched and the youngsters fledged.

I was born in a generation where sportsmen-naturalists were common, and I have always loved to see dogs work. Indeed I spent most Sunday mornings for over twenty years bolting rats with ferrets and catching them with dogs. I would rather have a good day's ratting than a week's holiday by the sea.

I learned a great deal of my natural history from keepers and poachers, so that I am in a position to know from experience how much they have in common. It seems madness to me that they should so often range themselves in opposite camps to naturalists.

Next to shooting men, I suppose that huntsmen have as much influence on the wildlife of their country as anyone I know. Whether it is for good or bad depends on the individual, and I have met some at each end of the scale. I mentioned in *My Beloved Wilderness* the early troubles we had with the hunt that was operating here at the time. They were a pretty urban lot and I had no respect for their expertise or indeed their manners, since they neither gave warning of their coming nor apologies for disturbance when they had gone. It got to the pitch of ordering them off with a rifle, which is rated uncivilly eccentric in decent county circles!

Fortunately they disappeared in some sort of takeover bid

by the Meynell, which is hunted by Dermot Kelly, who is a different kettle of fish. We walked round each other a bit stiff-legged for a while, but at last we got down to constructive talking. I know perfectly well that, if his hounds get away on a screaming scent, and the fox makes our way, there is precious little he can do about it. And he knows that, if hounds do get among the deer here, they can do me a lot of damage, and that having relatively tame creatures here is not just my fad, it is my living.

So we agreed that he would keep out as much as he could and warn me before he came. And if hounds did get in, he would get them out as soon as they ceased to hunt their fox before they got wrong ideas about the deer.

It didn't work, of course, because, when hounds did get in he wasn't around, although I told him where they were; so I caught them up and put them in a dog kennel. There is nothing like mutual respect as the basis for agreement, so we arrived at a sensible working arrangement. When I know that hounds are going to be in the district, far from shutting out the hunt, I unlock the gates to give them easy access. Then, if there is trouble, I know they will get hounds out as soon as they can.

Even that may not be quick enough to prevent them from scattering 'our' deer to the four points of the compass, dispersing the pheasant, and undoing, in a few minutes, work that may have taken months to do. It hasn't yet happened because the master has managed to whip hounds off when they point their noses in our direction.

If I wanted to get awkward, I could in effect sterilise a sizeable area of hunting country, which is in any case shrinking because of motorways and all the pressures that threaten the wildlife in which I am specially interested. But we have so much in common that compromise seems far more reasonable.

The hunt can have even more effect on the local badger population than keepers do, because a bad keeper is confined to one estate, or at most to two or three, while the country hunted by one pack can span many square miles. It is therefore well worth while both sides giving a fair bit in order to achieve co-operation which is mutual. A really fanatical huntsman hates all badgers simply because their scent may distract hounds when they are on a fox's line and, worse still, because they open up earths which were 'stopped' the night before.

It is common practice in hunting circles to send a man round the fox earths in the area hounds are expected to hunt next day. This earth stopper blocks up the holes with a bunch of faggots or a spadeful of turf so that if a hunted fox tries to escape by taking shelter in the earth, he finds the entrance barred and sets off for a distant earth which gives hounds a better run.

Foxes are suspicious creatures which will not interfere with an earth that was only stopped the night before, but badgers are not so easily deterred, and may even excavate a fresh entrance or exit hole. So huntsmen who think the world revolves around their sport are sometimes quite ruthless in eliminating the badgers over the whole area they hunt, simply to avoid the chance of having a potentially good run spoiled.

Most, however, are prepared to give and take. They know that some people get at least as much joy from simply watching badgers going about their normal inoffensive business as they get from chasing foxes, so they spare the badgers. Only a small minority of shooting and hunting men cause damage to wildlife in general, but they drag their fellows with them into disrepute – to the point where they risk rousing public opinion to lobby to have their sports declared illegal.

Yet fishermen, who are quiet and peaceable by comparison, probably cause far more damage to nesting birds and otters by accident than either keepers or huntsmen do by design. The coarse fishing season already starts before many wild birds have finished nesting and there is a proposal to abolish the close season altogether. If anything comes of this, the banks of pools and reservoirs and rivers will suffer serious disturbance right through the nesting season.

They do no deliberate harm and, ironically, if they were there every day instead of mainly at week-ends, they might well do less damage. Birds would realise that bushes and trees and undergrowth were untenable close to the water's edge, and would choose safer alternative sites. As it is they have five days of the week to build and lay their eggs in peace, but are liable to be scared away long enough to allow the eggs to be cooled or stolen by predators on the sixth and seventh.

Otters are such shy creatures that they will leave their holts in hollow roots or old rabbit warrens by the water's edge with far less disturbance than is caused by the quietest fishing club. Their plight has been aggravated by the current trend for water boards to cut down the trees along river banks to convert rivers into drains which can be dredged by mechanical diggers. It is a process designed to allow rain water to flow straight to waste in the sea, which seems a little short-sighted in view of the rapidly rising consumption of water.

It would be impractical to prevent thousands of fishermen enjoying their sport for the sake of a few rare birds, but it might be as sensible to compromise with them, as with shooting and hunting men. It ought to be possible, with a little good will, to leave some stretches of the bank undisturbed, perhaps on the inside of loops, where short cuts would avoid the need of passing close to thickets reserved as sanctuaries.

Cycling and riding and gliding and golf have minimal effect for good or ill on the wildlife of a district, and planning authorities do immense good by siphoning off vast numbers of urban visitors into deliberately contrived 'honey pot' zones. They choose a pleasant spot with scenic views, or open areas where children can play, and provide car parking and picnic facilities, lavatories and stalls to sell ice creams and hot dogs. A great many people from towns simply want to 'get away from it all' and have no great desire to walk far. They are more than satisfied if they can see vast areas of open sky instead of city streets, and breathe in God's fresh air instead of polluted fug.

Such folk are more gregarious than a flock of starlings, and they soon grow bored by solitude. They seem to trust their own judgement so little that they cannot credit that they have arrived at a pleasant place unless crowds of other visitors around them provide visual proof that it is popular. Honey pot sites, which they find so satisfying, relieve pressures which would otherwise squeeze quieter spots to destruction.

Television and radio and country books have multiplied the people interested in birds almost beyond belief, so that bird watchers have become important to all who are interested in catching votes. For many dedicated bird watchers the satisfaction is the basic urge to collect something. Instead of stealing eggs, as their grandfathers did, they tick off the names of the birds they see on a check list. They will motor miles to see a rarity and 'bag' him on their little lists, and they will shiver hour after bitter hour in a lakeside hide, counting wild ducks on the water. A minority of them satisfy the instinct to discover something new. They are the bird watchers who put numbered rings on the legs of fledglings or adult birds which they catch in nets, so that they can trace their future movements or fate when the birds they ringed are caught again or picked up dead.

They have unearthed new facts about migration and longevity, about breeding habits and feeding grounds. At the same time they have probably experienced the same instinctive thrills as sportsmen feel when they capture quarry with apparently different motives.

Conservationists and sportsmen have much in common, but a tiny minority of cranks among the naturalists, or vandals among the sportsmen, are all that it takes to divide the two camps. The majority in each faction would be well advised to prevent their silly tails wagging reasonable dogs.

CHAPTER THREE

Prototype

I have had as much enjoyment from common birds and animals around my own house and garden as from all the exotic creatures on show in stately homes. The advantage of living amongst wild creatures, instead of catching fleeting glimpses of them during visits to the country, is that you get to know them individually. It is fascinating to watch precisely how they acquire and defend their territory, and which vantage points birds choose for singing posts. It is even more interesting to try to analyse what motivates their choice; why one high perch should be preferable to another.

I get a great deal of fun compiling a time table, because wild creatures follow routine even more slavishly than we do. In January, for example, our pheasants come out of the wood to the deeply strawed patch where I throw wheat down for them at a quarter to nine and half past three. If I put it down much earlier, the collared doves scoff the lot before the pheasants arrive, because the doves will hang around on the off-chance of easy food.

The sun just clears a stand of oak by the pool at midday in winter and, the moment the warm rays light up the ride, a moorhen comes out to lie spreadeagled in luxury with all the abandon of a blonde on the beach.

I find it more rewarding to be intimate with local wildlife than only to enoy a nodding acquaintance with inaccessible rarities.

Precisely the same principles apply to wildlife management in a few square yards of a suburban garden as to a status-symbol shoot costing hundreds of guineas a year for each gun, or to a National Nature Reserve. You may not have curlews or lesser spotted woodpeckers as neighbours, but you will be astonished what pleasant things you have got if you take the trouble to look. What is more, if there were enough small gardens where birds and animals could find sanctuary, they would do as much to help threatened species as official nature reserves.

When we came to Goat Lodge, nine years ago, it had been empty for two years and I doubt if the garden had been touched for ten. There were nettles higher than my head between the house and the earth closet, and a tangle of brambles and birch saplings where the lawn once was. The trees in the orchard had been ring barked by the Bagot goats and long since died and rotted.

We had to bulldoze the scrub away before Horace Deakin, our builder, could start and the first thing he did was to erect an open-fronted cedar shed 30 ft. x 20 ft., initially for his material store but later for the garage.

Horace and his father were in and out of this shed all day and every day, and they had a brilliant petrol vapour lamp so that they could carry on when dusk had fallen. The sudden din and glaring light in what had been a silent, isolated spot created conditions about as unsuitable as you could dream-up for a sanctuary. Yet, within a few weeks the first pair of birds were nesting in a deep recess over the open doorway.

They were not sparrows or starlings or any of the birds I would have expected. They were a pair of redstarts. Redstarts are among the most strikingly beautiful birds I know They are also very shy.

The cock bird was immediately obvious in flight because he had a fiery chestnut tail as obvious as a rear light, and we thought he would have been more appropriately named red-finish than redstart. He had a black throat, white forehead and delicate grey mantle. Delighted as we were to see him, we were puzzled as to why he had honoured us with his company when there were so many alternative nesting sites, with far greater privacy, in the wood. Then, almost before the redstarts had settled in, a pair of swallows built their mud nest on a beam at one end of the shed and a pair of pied wagtails under the eaves at the other.

'Three pairs of nice birds,' my ornithologist friends remarked, though I regard most birds as nice.

But they were three surprising species to have moved in to what amounted to a noisy, busy workshop, and within a few weeks of its erection. I can claim no credit, because the management which caused the invasion was quite fortuitous. The hard fact was that our shed was the best of a bad lot of sites. Although there were, as I had noticed, scores of apparently desirable residences, in the wood, there were also platoons of predators which would not pluck up courage to chance their luck poking around for prey in a busy workshop.

This theory has since been substantiated, as I will show later, because less birds now nest around the house since I have improved the potential of more secluded places and set about the predators. Precisely the same applies to most suburban gardens, where neighbours' cats may be even more trouble than our carrion crows.

Redstarts lay one, or sometimes two clutches of five or six pale blue eggs, and sometimes more, while blackbirds and thrushes, common even in urban gardens, produce four or five eggs, two or three times a year. Each pair could theoretically produce eight or ten fully fledged young annually, but their population does not increase. It is, therefore, not unreasonable to calculate that 70 per cent or 80 per cent young birds hatched do not survive to breed next season. Most of them die by accident or predation.

This gives some idea of the odds against survival. If predators can be controlled, as keepers control them, or conditions supplied which offer reasonable safety, as I had done by accident with our cedar shed, breeding birds will accept the invitation with open wings.

It is obviously not possible to control your neighbour's cats, as I cull out the crows and rats and squirrels, although I would rather have a litter of stoats or fox cubs in my wood than one domestic cat. The alternative is to supply nesting sites which cats and crows and magpies cannot reach. This is easy enough for those species which will accept artificial nest boxes, and there are a great many of them. Great tits and blue tits are perhaps the commonest in suburbia, though cole tits and marsh tits, willow tits and redstarts, pied flycatchers and tree sparrows can all be attracted. So can nuthatches, if you are lucky enough to have a home in wooded country, provided they haven't been decimated by some mysterious complaint, as ours have.

The British Trust for Ornithology, whose headquarters are at Beech Grove, Tring, Herts, supply an excellent booklet, giving precise dimensions for nest boxes, which are easy and cheap to make at home. The Royal Society for the Protection of Birds, The Lodge, Sandys, Beds are equally helpful.

I cannot stress too strongly how critical these dimensions are. For example a box with an entrance hole $1\frac{1}{16}$ in. diameter is ideal for blue tits, cole tits and marsh tits; great tits like $1\frac{1}{8}$ in., tree sparrows $1\frac{1}{4}$ in., starlings 2 in., and so on. They are all in the little B.T.O. booklet, with results backed by years of experience.

Bird boxes are expensive to buy, so I always make my own. I lay no claims to being a cabinet maker nor even a decent joiner, but birds are no connoisseurs of craftsmanship and they accept my rough-and-ready standards without demur. When there is nothing better to do, I knock up a few bird boxes out of whatever old bits of board are lying about. They have cracks and gaps, but I try to make the top waterproof; I don't mind a crack or so at the bottom so that, if a drop of rain does seep in, it soon drains out again.

Bird boxes have two advantages for the birds and one for me. They are predator-proof, so that, once inside, birds and eggs and nestlings are far safer from cats and crows and magpies than they might otherwise be, and I naturally erect them where the risk is least.

Weasels will sometimes run up and raid them, since weasels can squeeze where most birds can get; and woodpeckers will often enlarge the hole or make a new one and filch the nestlings. Although I know this perfectly well, it never ceases to give me a nasty surprise to discover such beautiful birds are no better then they should be.

I take great care to erect the bird boxes where I can watch results without any need to disturb the birds, which I consider quite unjustified. The general rule with tit boxes is to put them at about eye level on walls or trees where they are not subject to direct sunlight which might turn them into miniature ovens when crammed with young on a hot day. They should obviously be out of reach of children, since human predation is often the most difficult to control!

We get immense fun with all sorts of nest boxes, ranging from splendid, expensive professionally made samples which sometimes arrive unasked, to old kettles and my own rough efforts.

We are situated on the edge of a belt of woodland which extends for thousands of acres to the north and north-west, with a thousand acres of plough on the far side of the wood and pastures rolling away to the Trent basin in the south. As a result, our small birds have far more food than they can eat, but so many natural enemies that safe nesting sites are at a premium. The pioneers discovered, even during the bedlam of building, that they were safer putting up with the proximity of humans around the homestead than searching for solitude out in the wood.

When we moved in we soon realised that it was a fool's paradise which wouldn't last unless we took positive steps to make it last. At the time we were hanging great hunks of fat from the knacker's yard on trees at varying distances from the house because our first objective was to discover the potential.

We put sultanas and biscuit meal and canary seed on the bird table and seed in hoppers hanging from the window. I made baskets for shelled peanuts and threaded strings of monkey nuts to hang beside them. All the old apple and tomato skins and fruit that went a bit soft landed on the bird table rather than in the dust-bin, and I put corn down in the paddock for the wild duck and pheasants.

I discovered that, if I put the corn in the long grass growing round the young trees in a spinney we planted, the ducks and pheasants saved me weeding it because they continually scuffled for corn where the weeds were trying to gain a foothold.

News of our free hospitality seemed to spread all through the wood, because almost everything payed us a social call. The snooty herons and long-tailed tits and tree creepers, which do not normally bother with bird tables, were about the only exceptions. We even had bramblings waiting patiently on the study step, directly under the nut hopper, picking up the crumbs spilled by the feather-bedded tits.

We were also popular with less desirable guests. Magpies and jays ventured right on to the bird table by the window, and carrion crows hung around the outlying feeding points, dive bombing anything which managed to crack off a sizeable bit of fat. Worst of all, we got rats under the bird table.

I opened the study window a couple of inches and, when I knocked off a few crows and magpies with my rifle, the survivors took the hint and took their custom elsewhere. And, as I have always kept a ferret since my rat-catching days, it was quite like the best of old times to have half an hour's ratting every time the dogs marked one to ground.

I keep a trap line of Fenn tunnel traps set for squirrels in the wood and look them twice a day when I am out with the dogs. Or I did when I came. Now the dogs have cottoned on to the idea and do my job for me by going on ahead and marking any trap that has been sprung, however cold and stiff the victim is.

45

Fenn traps work on the same principle as the old-fashioned gin, except that they are made of strong wire rod, instead of having steel-toothed jaws, and they are designed to grip around the body and kill instead of catching alive by a leg. When gins were made illegal in England, several years ago, (they were legal in Scotland till April this year) they were replaced by various types of lethal traps, which had to be set in tunnels to avoid catching larger quarry accidentally, which could be maimed instead of killed cleanly. They don't need baiting for squirrels. All that is necessary is to site the wooden tunnel, about two feet long and six inches square, at the foot of a tree where squirrels feed and play. Their curiosity will impel them to enter the tunnel on a fatal exploration. I have accounted for just under a thousand squirrels since we have been here by trapping, and shooting with a rifle. Some have been caught in the open by the dogs although they would obviously have been perfectly safe if they had stayed aloft.

This has taken a great deal of pressure off small birds' nests and eggs, besides preventing damage to trees by barking. The campaign has been so successful that, for two years, I don't think a single pair of squirrels have nested in the wood.

It fired my ambition to reintroduce red squirrels, which were here until the greys arrived, bringing with them the disease which is fatal to reds but not, alas, to greys. I thought how wonderful it would be to have a thriving colony of breeding reds, but I fear it will never be possible.

However successful I am at culling the greys in winter and spring, we are invaded by next year's crop when the corn is cut in August. They come drifting in, in family parties, as if I'd issued an invitation to bid them to feast on hazel nuts and acorns before they are properly ripe.

I get cracking as soon as they arrive, but it is well after Christmas before I have accounted for the last, though this is still in plenty of time for the welfare of the birds that breed in spring. The annual tally is now somewhere between fifty and seventy, depending on the season, so that, if I did re-introduce red squirrels, it would be impossible to cope with the grey without risking the red. And if I left both in peace, the grey would infect the red as well as doing great damage to small birds.

When I discovered the rats around the bird table, I went up the wood for a couple of tunnel traps and placed them in strategic positions so that the rats would dive through them for cover if they were disturbed. It was so successful that I have since gone to the trouble of building permanent brick-and-mortar tunnels, of the correct size to take a Fenn trap when set, with two loose bricks on top for inspection and easy setting.

I have built one of these near the corn store, fowl pen, pig pen, fruit cage, bird table and anywhere else that rats appear. It may sound a lot of trouble, but my brick-laying is any-thing but professional, I used secondhand bricks and they only took about a quarter of an hour apiece to slap together. I don't put traps in them until I see evidence that there is a rat or two about the place, so that early arrivals use them and taint them with their scent, and when I do load them with traps, I catch the lot before they have time to grow suspicious and trap shy.

With these traps I reckon to catch every rat within a week of his arrival, and the annual bag is somewhere in the region of fifty. The winters of 1971 and 1972 were so mild that we had quite a plague, but I caught about thirty one week and had to finish the survivors off with with Warfarin rat poison.

My other way of dealing with rats is particularly popular with the dogs – and I enjoy it too. I have placed several lengths of four-inch cast-iron heating pipe from an old greenhouse on known rat runs as far from buildings as possible. Rats hate crossing open country on their way from one feeding point to another and soon get in the habit of using these pipes as intermediate shelter points. The dogs know this and, when I go out last thing before bed to feed them, they sniff up every pipe to see if a rat has taken refuge there.

I know at once if one has dived up one of these funk holes because all four dogs will be jostling around the pipe, taking it in turns to shove in their muzzles in vain attempts to reach their quarry. All I have to do is to make them stand back while I push an old line prop up the pipe to bolt the rat, or block him in with a couple of bricks till daylight breaks.

Not everyone who likes to see birds in his garden wishes to take up ratting, but if the bird table is mounted so that it overhangs its support, rats will not be able to climb over the edge and steal the food, even if they manage to scale the legs. All other food should be placed carefully out of reach, because rats will not stay unless they have access to food, and our rats are really attracted by the pigs and poultry, which are more difficult to feed without waste.

If an odd rat does appear, bait a drain pipe, four inches diameter and three feet long, with Warfarin, or put it under a concrete paving slab set on four bricks so that there is room for rats to forage underneath. If the Warfarin is placed in a little plastic bag, it will stay dry and appetising until a rat does come along and gnaws a hole in the bag to eat the fatal meal.

Warfarin has the advantage of being less dangerous than other poisons if it is accidentally taken by a domestic animal. It is a cumulative anti-coagulant which has to be taken several days running before it is lethal. So if a dog, for example, picks up an odd dose, it will have little effect. Some people say that it will only poison rats, but this is not true. If other animals get repeated doses it will kill them as surely as the rats for which it was intended. The advantage with rats is that the effect is so remote from the time it was taken that they do not associate it with danger, and become 'poison shy'.

Many cat owners like cats as well as birds, so that cats

Jess comes through the garden gate. Froggatt's forty acre in the background

Dunstal pool from the study window

Anne Moonie helps to feed Honey, the white fallow fawn

The mistle thrushes are saved from the crows

Left to right: Mandy, Fly, me, Tick and Spider in the wood

Tick loves ferreting

Fred, the barn owl

are less easy to deal with than other common predators. They have to be deterred instead of culled.

Because my experiment here is also my profession, I have gone to the extreme of surrounding six acres, which includes the paddock, pool, house and some scrub woodland, with wire netting six feet high. In theory, both cats and foxes could scale this, but in practice, I find that they do not, provided they cannot see something very tempting lying close to the netting. So I walk round the inside boundary periodically at dusk and disturb any pheasants or ducks which are squatting there so that they choose less disturbed spots – where they are incidentally safer.

The netting was very expensive, but it serves to keep my hand-reared deer inside, and a pair of badgers lived in an artificial sett quite happily for a number of years, coming and going to the wood at will through a swinging 'badger gate' which was too much like a trap for suspicious foxes. I can rear my wild duck and pheasants and keep them safe within the enclosure until they are strong enough to fly, and the netting keeps the rabbits away from my wife's cherished garden. But whatever advantages the fence may have, I am bound to admit it was a bit extravagant!

For some small gardens, a wire netting fence need not be so prohibitive, for it will not only keep cats away from the birds, but it will keep strange dogs out and the house dogs from straying. It need not be in the least obtrusive if the whole roll is dipped in black bitumen before erection, for this not only gives the netting about double the life, it makes it practically invisible when once the bitumen goes dull. It is well worth making the top foot overhang at right angles, which will be practically unclimbable for cats.

There are not many effective ways of deterring cats from hunting birds, which is their nature, though some dogs take such delight in seeing off strange cats that it becomes almost an obsession. The snag is that they often become unbearably noisy about it and, in any case, they are rarely around at the vulnerable hours of dusk and dawn. However, we are lucky to live a mile from the nearest village, and our nearest neighbour is a farmer who is such a keen pigeon flyer that we do not suffer from cats at all.

Half the fun in feeding and protecting birds close to the house is that, with any luck, they will nest where it is possible to observe them at any time one likes. And I have found from experience that rough old boxes are as effective as expensive ones, and one of my favourites is a clumsy, open-fronted affair screwed right close to the side door, about six feet from the kitchen window.

Jess spends a lot of time at the sink or kitchen stove and she is at least as fond of birds as I am, so I put this box where she could see right inside from the kitchen window, on the off chance that fate would be kind.

Soon after our first pair of spotted flycatchers arrived in spring I knew we'd hit the jack pot. The cock bird was conspicuous in his immaculate spotted waistcoat, sitting on the electric cable that feeds the outhouses across the yard. We dawdled over breakfast, watching him launch himself on a flight of a few yards, out and back, as rhythmic as a yo-yo on a string. Each time he shot out, a passing insect paid the price as surely as if he had been a lizard's tongue.

Breakfast dragged on and on as we watched, because, when he had eaten his fill, his flights grew longer as he prospected the yard in search of a nesting site. He first found what apparently suited him under the eaves of the old wash house, which is now the dog kennels. Time after time he sat on the twigs of the clematis, which was just beginning to climb the roof, and I believe he would have nested there if Mandy, the old lurcher, hadn't come out at a critical moment. She froze in her tracks, nose questing until she spotted where he perched, then she sat purposefully down and stared him out. The idea of a nest of young birds immediately over the entrance to her kennel apparently did not hold out much appeal.

She is a kind-natured old dog, and wouldn't harm anything but rats and rabbits and hares and squirrels because I teach all my dogs from early puppyhood that the wild birds and pheasants and ducks and domestic fowl are about the place for our benefit, not theirs. It is far easier to train a dog that chasing stock is not allowed before he starts than after bad habits have been formed, and I reckon to get my pups steady by the time they are twelve weeks old.

In any case, old Mandy was doing no more to the fly-catcher than make it plain to him that she didn't remember him asking permission to share the yard of her pen. So he took the hint and began to prospect the yard once more. During the next few days, he tried a cleft in the old yew tree, the wisteria over my study window, and, most determined of all, the ledge in the garage where the redstart had nested the year before. He spent so much time here that we made certain that he'd made his final decision – when, for no apparent reason, he changed his mind and settled for the birdbox by the side door.

We noticed him here about a week after we'd first seen him, and it was fascinating to watch him at such close quarters going right inside and 'trying it out for size'.

Time and again he hopped in and out, crouched down and turned round and round, as a dog does before settling on the hearthrug. He obviously liked what he found because he then kept it under his eye almost continuously for several days. Presumably this was an instinctive check that there was no likelihood of danger at some time he hadn't noticed.

One advantage of living here is that practically no one calls. Nobody delivers milk or bread or papers. We have to fetch them from the village. The butcher doesn't call, and our only regular visitors are the postwoman in the morning and the grocer once a fortnight. Nobody uses the front door and we very rarely use the side door by the bird box because we and all our friends go in and out through the back door.

The flycatcher would have found it difficult to choose a spot subject to less disturbance. The one thing which puzzled us was that he seemed to be alone. If he had got a mate, he kept her discreetly hidden.

This didn't last for long. Within a day or so there were a pair, flying in and out, beginning to build a nest. They didn't work all the time. I could see them busy at it from the bathroom above, when I was shaving early in the morning, but they'd stopped by breakfast time. Then they did several shifts during the day, though I couldn't make up my mind if they regulated them by the clock or if they simply worked when there was no one about.

Nothing gives us more possessive pride than being able to watch 'our' birds at breakfast. They bring this normally silent meal alive with civilised conversation. But then, once the nest was built, they seemed to desert it entirely. The hen called stealthily at intervals to lay her clutch of eggs and all we could see was the glint of her eye as she sat motionless on her nest. But we never saw her arrive or leave because she was so secretive.

She laid her clutch and hatched them and, as the fledglings grew they became more and more insatiable until the old birds were too busy to take any more notice of us at all. From first light to dusk, they stuffed their young, which grew almost visibly. The joy we got for the price of a little trouble knocking up that rough box and putting it where we could see it couldn't be measured in terms of cash.

The young grew and fledged, and spent most of the next week or so in the garden on the other side of the house, learning their lovely aerobatics as they launched themselves at passing flies and returned to their perch to consume them.

When they had gone, I cleaned the nest box out and squibbed it with a few puffs of insecticide, because one of the greatest hazards to young birds is to get infected with lice before they are old enough to bathe or dust bath to get rid of them.

I shall never forget seeing a brood of house martins grow to fledgling size but flutter helpless to earth on their maiden flight. I picked them up to examine them and found the flesh at the base of their feathers literally black with lice, which had sucked their living blood till they were too anaemic to survive. So when old birds nest in previously used nests, their young often pay dearly for their sloth.

While the flycatchers had been delighting us at their nest by the kitchen window, a pair of pied wagtails had been bringing off a successful brood in a nest perched on a pick axe hanging from a nail in the garage. When they fledged, the young were even more droll than the flycatchers, because they seemed to be able to run as fast as other birds flew. They to came round on to the lawn because Jess's garden is already mature and shady enough to supply cover and food which scores of small birds find irresistible.

While the flycatchers were using every inch of three-dimensional air space, the wagtails caught their prey within inches of the level lawn. I often scoff at my own clumsiness at swatting a fly, but these wagtails made me humbler still. They could sprint yards across the open lawn and catch a fly in their beaks before he knew what had hit him. They worked close enough to the window for us to observe every detail, and we sat after supper until the light faded, entranced by their adroitness. They came casually in from any angle, but never seemed to miss.

Suddenly the old cock bird grew agitated and scolded off to the far end of the lawn. His alarm infected a blackbird which flew into a rhododendron, uttering the slow, staccato, limpid cry that I usually associate with a blackbird swearing at a cat.

I knew it wasn't a cat because the fence is cat-proof and, anyway, we are not within the territory of any hunting cat. I didn''t think it was an owl they had discovered at his daytime roost, because owls usually provoke more of a chatter and, anyway, the wagtail's antics indicated that the object of his distaste was somewhere at ground level.

Suddenly I caught a glimpse of russet amongst the herbacious plants on the border – and a weasel gambolled on to the lawn, and off again as the wagtail approached, as if birds scared the daylights out of him.

All was still for a while and then the weasel reappeared on

the lawn nearer to us. The wagtail wheeled and repeated his threat display, so the weasel dived for cover again.

The pantomime continued as a sort of game of Russian roulette with the weasel cartwheeling out from ever changing angles until the wagtail got close enough to see him off.

The act certainly fooled the wagtail – and it nearly fooled me! It really did appear that the lithe animal was not pre-pared to mix it with an adversary buoyed up with the courage of paternal protection.

Common sense told me to open the window and to go out to scare the weasel off, but curiosity triumphed. If things were as they seemed and a heroic small bird drove a blood-thirsty villain off his young, that would be news indeed. It would be as good as if the man had bitten the dog.

That only happens in cloud-cuckoo land, and I was soon to chastise myself for knowing no better. The weasel left the lawn as stage and continued his antics half hidden behind a clump of lupins in the wings. Emboldened by his success, the wagtail ran on to the bed to get a better vantage point to chatter from. Before he realised anything was amiss, the weasel had popped round the other side of the lupin and sprang on him from behind. The comedy had turned to tragedy – and we were one wagtail less, though much the wiser should the act ever be get an encore, with a fresh actor for the victim.

As if determined to ensure sufficient numbers for future survival, the widow paired again immediately and, as soon as she was in breeding condition again, she tried another nesting site.

Wagtails are larger than flycatchers, but this time she left the garage and took to our box by the kitchen window that I had just cleaned out after the flycatchers had done with it. It looked most uncomfortable because her tail was about twice as long as the flycatchers and the 'trying to fit' routine proved such a farce that we had to revise our theories.

Perhaps they are not trying to fit at all. Perhaps it is just a measurement technique to decide what thickness of wall the nest will need to provide maximum comfort? Perhaps it is a form of self imprinting to produce subconscious attachment to the site, as a spur to its defence?

Whatever the basis for their ritual, the fact was that they laid and hatched and reared as successfully as the flycatchers had done, and this time, so far as I know, neither of them chanced their wings in encounters with opponents out of their class!

That box has been a widow's cruse of enchantment because it never seems to be without a tenant during the nesting season. The only logical explanation must be that our local small birds have discovered that they are safer within arm's reach of us than in apparently secluded spots in the wood where predators hold sway.

It may be significant that the redstarts never nested in the garage after that first season. It wasn't because we caused more disturbance in subsequent years, for we didn't go in and out of the garage half as much as the builders had. I believe that the explanation was that my campaign against predators was beginning to bite, and that they were going further away from the house into the wood, so I tried the effect of putting two open fronted boxes and several ordinary tit boxes on trees fringing the wood across the paddock opposite my study window.

The tit boxes were taken within days, and so was one experimental open-fronted box of my own design. Instead of being taller than it is wide, this box fits on to the tree horizontally, with a vertically sliding door at one end. This opens downwards to give an entrance slit of variable depth, depending upon how far the door is opened.

To our great delight it was taken at once by redstarts which reared a brood successfully. I have no means of knowing if it was the same pair which had nested in the garage the year before, one of their young, or a strange pair which had come to this territory by coincidence. We do not ring our birds because I do not think the risk and discomfort justified, except for very special projects which promise benefit to the birds as well as pleasure for the ringers.

I had noticed in the winter that a great tit was roosting in this experimental box and I have no doubt that, left alone, he would have defended it against the redstarts when they arrived from their winter migration. So, when he was out during the daytime, I slid the door to and shut him out for the rest of the winter, so that he had to find another roosting hole which would do to breed in next spring.

When I did open it, tits at once signified their intention of nesting there, which was not what I had in mind. So I shut it again and kept it shut till the redstarts arrived and began prospecting for breeding sites. Only when they were going over the area where the box was with a tooth comb did I throw it open. Sitting at my desk, I kept glancing up to see what happened and was soon delighted by the vision of a redstart's flashy backside as he hawked for insects within yards of the box. He contented himself for a while but it was not long before there were a pair and within hours they had taken possession of the box.

It was the old story of possession being nine points of the law. If the tits had got there first, I have no doubt at all that the redstarts would have had no chance. But, once the redstarts were installed, they proved quite capable of defending it against all comers, and they reared their brood successfully.

Boxes which are designed to be kept shut until the desired birds are in breeding condition can be particularly useful for persuading selected species to nest where it is convenient to observe their behaviour or to photograph them. All the same, I have never managed to get the redstarts to choose it again, in spite of keeping tits out until the redstarts are around – because, as my gamekeeping in the wood has had more and more effect, I have made larger areas relatively safe so that the shyer birds are no longer so keen to integrate with the likes of me.

I have also had a lot of fun with another specialist box with one glass side. Apart from that, it is normal in every way except that I use an entrance hole of one and a quarter inches diameter to increase the variety of potential tenants.

If it was kept permanently open to the light, I do not think that many birds would use it. So I fix it to my study window so that the glass side of the box is against the glass of my window, with the entrance hole at right angles to the side. I then hinge a piece of wood to the inside of the window so that it can close down flat on the pane, to give the effect of a fourth solid side to the box, which is then only lighted through the entrance hole. Occasionally, on winter evenings, I lift the hinged wood in the study and peep inside to see if anything is roosting there.

Although it is large enough for great tits, blue tits take to it most freely, for there is a major surplus of blue tits to potential suitable sites. Anyhow they like to roost there in winter and nest there in spring so that it is possible to inspect the progress of the nest without disturbance, simply by lifting the flap inside my study window.

I do this sparingly, so as not to make them nervous, but if I want to carry out sustained observations on feeding the young at very close quarters, all that is necessary is to black out my study, so that I peer at them from darkness which makes me invisible.

I have done precisely the same thing with starlings, in a box with a two-inch diameter hole. I am sure that those who cannot escape to the country, as I have done, could derive the greatest pleasure from doing the same thing in suburban gardens.

Starlings, because they are 'common' instead of 'nice', are greatly maligned. If they were rare, the wonderful iridescent sheen on their feathers would inspire more poems than the sweetest singing nightingale. Next time you are close to a starling, observe him objectively with no preconceived prejudices about how dirty or noisy he is. Admire the cheeky brilliance of his eye and his delicate yellow dagger of a bill. Take note of his virtuoso mimicry, for he can kid you that a curlew or woodpecker or plover or duck has taken a pitch on your patch.

No talking budgerigar has a vocabulary to touch a humble starling, no Elizabethan dandy had a ruff to match the undulations of his throat while he pours out his heart in song. If I was condemned to be banished to a town, I could derive more pleasure from taming city starlings than from keeping the most exotic birds confined in cages.

The first year or so here, while I was working hard to endow the wood with a sense of security, we were constantly delighted by the birds around the house. Swallow nests in the outbuildings gradually increased from one in the garage to seven spread around every available site. There were nests in the tractor shed, one in the wood shed and, most extraordinary of all, one in the ferret pen.

This was a brick built earth closet when we came but, when we installed water closets in the house, we ripped out the ancient two-seater from the earth closet and concreted the floor. Never having been forced to use an earth closet, I am ignorant about the mechanics, but our last house before Goat Lodge also had a closet in the garden with an immense bench seat in which had been cut twin seats. What friendly chaps our grandfathers seem to have been!

When ours had been concreted and fitted with a wire mesh door it made an ideal ferret pen, or an admirable place to shut a hen and chicks safe from rats at night. When I wasn't using it for a time, I left the door open and, before I realised what was happening, the swallows had built a nest there.

I wanted to put a hen and pheasant chicks in, so the only solution was to cut a gap in the wire netting at the top of the door and nail a steel sheet below it so that nothing could climb up.

It didn't seem to worry the swallows in the least and, within half an hour they were skimming through their entrance flap as if it had been there when they decided to build.

When the pheasant chicks were big enough to be safe from rats, I moved them into the paddock and wedged the coop for the broody hen in the fork of a tree. She called them up to her and they were soon roosting safely aloft instead of jugging on the ground.

Meanwhile the closet was available for the ferret, which had by this time got a litter of kittens, but I was worried they might make the swallows desert. So I sat around to watch what happened when the swallows saw the ferrets on the floor below them, so that if they were worried, I could have to find somewhere else for the ferrets.

The swallows seemed less worried than their potential foes. They dive bombed whenever one stuck its head out of the box, but soon took no notice of each other although the birds naturally did not alight in the danger area. The proof of the pudding was that the swallows did not go away when their young were fledged, as they would if they had been seriously disturbed. They reared two more broods that season and have been back (or other swallows have) each year since.

There were no house martins when we came so I bought an artificial nesting box especially designed for martins. It was rather expensive, so I copied it but got the entrance holes a little too big and the house sparrows took over.

I have had a great deal of trouble with sparrows bullying both swallows and martins because putting out as much food as I do does attract a mob of scrounging sparrows. I wouldn't particularly object if they didn't compete so successfully with gentler species, so I catch what I can in cage traps.

They soon get wise to these though and I have found that the only efficient, although time-consuming way is to knock off selected offenders with my air rifle, before they have time to drive swallows or martins from their nests. In any case, I believe that any necessary control should be as selective as possible. The fact that sparrows are so wily helps rather than hinders. As soon as they see their fellows being sorted out, the rest get excessively gun-shy and go away to find more congenial quarters, relieving me of the unpleasant task of culling them.

I have had great success with tits and wagtails, redstarts

and flycatchers, owls and jackdaws in nest boxes and nearly every upturned bass broom or roll of wire netting is used to support a nest almost before my back is turned. The most charming of all was a wren which built in a hank of binder twine accidentally (or untidily) left dangling over a beam in the goat shed.

At the far end of the wood, by Daffodil Lawn, there is a corrugated steel sheet pen where the Bagot Goats shelter in winter. They spend the summer at Blithfield Hall, which is open to the public, and, in winter, their owner, Lady Bagot, sends them back here to the woods where their ancestors roamed for centuries. This rests their paddock at The Hall, so that it is free from parasites when they return, and it allows them to have their kids under my supervision. I give them a daily ration of sheep nuts and as much hay as they want, and I put it in racks from which they can only pull off a mouthful at a time to limit the waste.

When I fill the hay racks, I hang the twine, that bound the bales, over a beam out of the goats' way. By the end of winter there is a great hank of this binder twine, and I noticed, three springs ago, that a wren was building a nest in it. It was a most beautiful spherical nest, about as big as a croquet ball, entirely interwoven with twine. But any hopes of making him pay rent by allowing us to photograph him were doomed to failure because it was a 'cock nest'.

Cock wrens must be pretty keen because they stake out their territory and select possible sites for several nests. Instead of taking his mate on a conducted tour and making her decide on which site she would like to live, he builds the nests first and then shows them to his mate.

Those that she doesn't choose remain untenanted cock nests, although I have known them to be used later in the season. We were not so lucky. The craftsman-built creation in our binder twine found no favour and was still untenanted at the end of the season.

The next year I took as much trouble to arrange the twine as if I had been creating an exhibition bird box. Once more the cock bird built a most desirable nest which seemed to me to have every modern convenience. It could not possibly get wet, it was safe from predators, because I had taken care to hang the twine where rats or weasels could not climb, and the goat shed was at the edge of mixed woodland which must have offered bounteous free food. I do not know where they did nest, but it certainly wasn't there.

Last year I tried again and took even more trouble. I arranged the hanging twine with the dedication of a film star's personal dresser, adroitly sited both to suit the wrens and to be easy to photograph. Having been twice bitten, I contained my enthusiasm when dry, dead bracken began to 'grow' amongst the twine, but this time my patience was rewarded. When the nest was approved, the little hen obliged by laying a clutch of eggs which she hatched and reared.

There have been lots of other successful nests where wrens have built in forks of trees, the space where a brick was knocked out of the tractor shed wall, behind the diesel tank and under the eaves by the corn store. But all those were built with no help of mine, while the binder twine nest in the goat shed gave me deep satisfaction because it was a joint effort!

Apart from completely artificial nesting sites, Jess and I take great pride in using our influence. She is passionately fond of gardening and has created a lovely cottage garden from the wilderness of scrub which was here when we came. Luckily for me – and indeed for the birds as well, she is no fanatic prepared to sacrifice everything for some cherished plant.

She has the knack of encouraging tender plants with her green fingers, but not at the expense of the wildlife which shares her borders. If her roses get blight, she would rather spray them with old-fashioned soapy water than put insectiverous birds at risk by using a more efficient but poisonous pesticide.

She knows that the larvae of many attractive butterflies

love nettles, so she is prepared to turn a blind eye on the nettles I allow to thrive just over the paddock fence. And she will take endless trouble festooning flowering shrubs with black cotton rather than ask me to get the rifle out to the bullfinches. I think that, as a result, she gets far deeper joy from her garden than any specialist with a one-track mind.

The drive up to the farm beyond us overlooked the garden when we came, so we planted a hornbeam hedge along the boundary and a rhododendron hedge inside that. Nine years later the hornbeam is thick and over six feet tall, and the rhododendrons not quite as high but even thicker.

The wire netting rabbit fence is on the outside of the hornbeam, so the double hedge within is not only safe but also a beautifully warm winter roost for a wide variety of birds. It gives nesting cover in summer for greenfinches and blackbirds and thrushes.

The greenhouse is screened from view by broad-leaved holly; old hawthorn stumps are decently clad in clematis, and there is a matt of honeysuckle and wisteria on the walls of the house. The garden is completed by a thick yew hedge from the house to the drive and shrubs around the lawn and flower beds. Deliberate planting to attract birds and butter-flies is as effective as a method to increase wild populations as artificial nest boxes, and it can be done by anyone with the smallest garden.

We are lucky in having natural advantages too. The drive has a jungle of blackberry scrub for more than half a mile – and it is far more use to me like that than if some status-conscious dandy were to turn it into neat lawn edged with geraniums. The whole thing is topped off by my neighbour who grows a wonderful crop of thistles, which are not every-one's idea of modern farming, but greatly appreciated by goldfinches – which we know as 'seven-coloured linnets' in this part of the world.

As a result, the garden is not just colourful with roses and azalias and a multitude of flowers, it is stuffed with birds besides, which repay us not only with colour and song and movement, but also by limiting the insect pests before they can increase to plague proportions.

Not all our birds would be welcome everywhere, of course, but oddly enough about the only two species unlikely to be found in suburban gardens would probably be least welcome. They are pheasants and wild duck, which are popular in the countryside either for the sport they give or because they are such delicacies.

A cock pheasant or a mallard drake glinting in the sun are about as beautiful as any bird I know. If they were rare, misers would shell out their hoarded brass to go on uncomfortable safaris to photograph them in colour.

We've got lots of both species, and one of my extravagances is to feed them in the paddock and on a straw patch at the edge of the wood where they delight us with their colourful displays. The tame mallard duck give confidence to a wonderful variety of wild duck which fly in to share their food, and it is not uncommon to see a winter flock of a hundred and fifty feeding within a few yards of the windows.

Many of them stay to breed, and the old predator trouble crops up once more. Those which lay eggs in the reeds on the island or in the cover along the banks almost invariably lose every egg before it hatches.

They are very regular in their habits, as most wild creatures are, and when they are incubating eggs, the ducks fly off at the same time every morning to bathe and feed. When they have laid a full clutch, they pull tiny feathers out of their breasts and 'feather their nests' by making a sort of eiderdown to blanket the eggs while they are away. This keeps them warm and, in theory, hidden.

The snag is that it doesn't fool the crows. For one thing mallard drakes are attentive mates and, about half an hour before the duck is due to leave her eggs to feed, her drake flies from the pool and hangs around, usually within about fifty yards of the nest.

This may be anything up to half a mile from water, so that the sight of a mallard drake, sticking out like a sore thumb in some unlikely spot, is a fair indication that it is probably worth waiting around to see where the duck shows up.

I find nearly all my duck nests like this and, when I want a few hand-reared ducklings as decoys for wild birds or presents for my friends, I do not have to comb the country-side to find them.

The old crows know just as much. I watch them from my window, perched on high, scanning the horizon for signs of movement. When a mallard drake flies off the pool, they shift their look-out post in order not to lose him. The drake settles down, patiently waiting for the duck to leave her eggs, and even if she is out of his line of vision, he seems to know by instinct the instant she gets up off her eggs. When he cranes, to catch a glimpse of her, the crows and I do too, and it is often possible to see her tail poking out from under a bush as she bends to pull the feathers over her eggs with her flat bill.

It is usually possible to get a fair idea of where she has come from when she leaves cover, so that it does not take long to find the nest while she is away. She goes to the water not only to feed but also to bathe, so that, when she returns, her wet feathers moisten the eggs and the shells gradually grow more brittle, and the tiny ducklings can chip their way out when the time comes for the eggs to hatch. That is if the time does come! Eggs that are near the pool, far from human disturbance, are nearly all found and de-voured by carrion crows. One of our fringe benefits is that the duck trust us so much that we always have several nests in the garden.

They lay under rhododendron bushes or right up against the oak boards by the house; there is nearly always a nest at the foot of the clematis which enshrouds the hawthorn stump, one under the prostrate juniper by the front porch and an-other on top of a board, six feet above the ground by the yew hedge.

This board is covered by a clematis I dislike because it

64

grows into the yew and deforms the top of the hedge, but Jess says she doesn't want a garden as disciplined as a public park. My sympathies are with the yew which is accosted by such an unwelcome embrace. But whatever we feel about the clematis, it certainly makes ideal cover for a duck nest, and we always wait with bated breath to watch the mother entice her ducklings down.

We can predict pretty accurately when this is going to be. When I calculate that it is about the last week, I wait until the old duck goes off to the pool and then take her eggs out of the nest. I float them in a bowl of tepid water.

As the time approaches for them to hatch, the embryo absorbs some of the nourishment, excreting gas which makes the eggs float some time before they hatch. The duckling stirs, as a human embryo will kick inside its mother's belly, and as it stirs, it rocks the floating egg to dance a weird fandango in the lukewarm water. From this it is possible to predict with accuracy how many eggs are alive and how many addled, so that counting chickens before they hatch is not as foolish as it sounds.

On about the last day but one the egg shells chip as the ducklings hammer for their freedom. This message is communicated to the mother, who refuses to leave the nest at all the day before her eggs hatch out.

She sits motionless, crooning contentedly, listening intently to the voices of her young and 'talking back' to them so that, by the time they hatch, her voice is imprinted on their minds and their voices on hers. Perhaps these are the most important moments in a duckling's life because, thereafter, he will be able to distinguish the commands of 'his' duck from all other ducks, and she will know him from all the other ducklings on the pool.

The old duck still sits on her nest for yet another day after her youngsters hatch to let them dry out and gain strength. They do not need food because, as they are drying out after their immersion in the egg, they absorb the nourishment that saturated them.

Next morning is the time we have been waiting for. The old duck flies down on to the hard brick terrace, leaving her ducklings in the nest. Not only have they learned her voice by now they know by instinct the commands it conveys.

So she utters a babel of quiet and seductive quacks calling her young so irresistibly that they launch themselves in an apparently suicidal leap into space, crashing down on to the terrace below.

Crashing, of course, does not describe their fall. If she called them too soon, while they were still wet and soggy, I reckon that they would hit the ground hard enough to sustain serious hurt. By delaying their journey, to water before the vital twenty-four hours have elapsed, she gives their down time to dry and get fluffy, so that their feathers act as a parachute on the way down and as a mattress when they land. They don't even seem to notice the bump, but cluster beneath her, waiting for the next command. This does not come till the last duckling has left the nest.

We have watched this drama through the window at close quarters several times, but still cannot decide whether she knows when the last arrives or whether she waits until there are no more tiny squeaks in answer to her call.

Next year, I have decided to rig a microphone up within inches of a nest to try to discover the answer by tape-recording the dialogue, although, if my experience with wild creatures runs true to form, next year will be the first time the ducks will give their high nest a miss!

CHAPTER FOUR

The Plan

Most of our successes so far could have been achieved in almost any small garden by carefully siting nest boxes, planting suitable cover and regular feeding. And, although I was ready to make long term plans for the wood, even here the steps that I intended to take to improve its potential are equally valid for small private gardens.

Naturalists are frequently bitter if a landowner alters a site on his own property to improve his financial prospects if, at the same time, he disturbs the wildlife there. Yet they are prepared to do far less than game keepers to improve or even maintain conditions for the creatures in which they are interested.

Sportsmen have always been ready to pay for their pleasures, although they are usually hard-headed enough to do all they can to get value for their money. To this end, some of their keepers are over-zealous in controlling predators, just as naturalists underrate the value of subsidiary feeding to encourage animals or birds to congregate in areas where they will be least threatened and most easily observed.

The keepers who cull out predators too harshly often do more harm than good by allowing weaklings to spread disease which could have been avoided if predators had culled the weaklings naturally, before they could pass their malady on. It is a question of striking a sensible balance. Naturalists are interested in both predators and prey, but many nature reserves would have greater variety if predators were kept in check.

Where we have most to learn from keepers is in feeding. Every keeper knows that it is pointless to rear 1,000 pheasants if his beat only carries enough food for 500, unless he supplies sufficient artificial feed for the other 500. So he spreads thick layers of straw at strategic patches of his rides, and feeds enough grain by hand to sustain the surplus that would otherwise have wandered over his boundary in search of a living. Unscrupulous keepers cash in on this, and allow their rich neighbours to rear birds which they then entice on to their beats with a carefully selected menu.

Artificial feeding is obviously expensive, so sportsmen always try to obviate the need for hand feeding by planting their covers with plants which will mature until they grow enough natural food to maintain the stock they want throughout the season. They plant snowberry and cotoneaster and berberis and holly and hawthorn and other trees and bushes which will provide a constant succession of food.

In the old days, stubbles were left unploughed until spring so that there was enough grain to be had for the scratching to feed birds until nesting time came round again. Game covers were sited cunningly so that pheasants would naturally retire there when full fed, to roost, and would not have far to go for food next morning.

That is all finished now, because farming has become such a mechanised business that corn is reaped by combine harvesters, which spill far less grain, and the straw and stubble is often burned before autumn is over.

Sportsmen, rich enough to pay several hundred guineas for the privilege of having a gun in a syndicate, would indeed be penny-wise to quibble about a few tons of corn to keep their birds around. So their keepers take short-term action to compensate for the lack of stubble by sowing patches of game-mixture especially for their birds. This is sown in narrow strips, from which their quarry can easily be flushed to the guns and the seed sown includes rape, canary, sun flower and buck wheat, which are equally attractive to a host of other birds besides pheasants.

This perfectly standard game-keeping practice is equally applicable for threatened species. *It should be* of great interest to conservationists, who might profitably spend some of their members' subscriptions on doing precisely what keepers have done for generations.

So far as I am concerned, I decided to 'improve' the potential of my wood. It already has the natural advantages of mature stands of oak which attract pheasants and deer from miles around when acorns fall. And the mountain ash and bilberry bring flocks of squabbling thrushes and field-fares, mistle thrushes and blackbirds. The hazel and birch and ash and sycamore are attractive to a whole spectrum of small animals, as well as to birds, but the Corsican pine that the Forestry Commission planted will have far less attractions as soon as it grows enough to canopy over.

I have always found the Commission far more co-operative than most bureaucrats, and when we came they were busy planting it. I didn't want the whole place turning into a clear felled desert, so I asked them to leave a few standing birch and was agreeably surprised to discover how helpful they were. For a while it was perfect country for grasshopper warblers, nightjars, reed bunting and stonechats, with even an occasional curlew. The isolated stands of birch they left made ideal launching posts for tree pipits to start their songs as they descended like parachutes.

There were very few pheasants because the crows had all the early nests of eggs, and the foxes took so many sitting hens that a stranger could have been excused for thinking we culled hens selectively and left the cocks.

In Holly Covert and Dunstal Pool Plantation, the mature deciduous area, there were a lovely lot of tree creepers, nut-hatches, tits of all sorts and most of the woodland birds that we'd hoped for and expected. After half a lifetime gaffered by the clock, it was perfect paradise. Jess and I wandered round whenever we felt like it. Often enough we saw something we weren't used to, beetles or caterpillars or moths which we had to look up when we got in to identify, in spite of the fact that it had been our hobby for so long.

Observing wildlife in one's own patch, however small, is quite different from catching fleeting glimpses on hurried expeditions to strange places. Instead of seeing *a* goldfinch, or long-tailed tit, or weasel, we began to recognise them as individuals. We began to wonder if we should see *our* goldfinch on *that* patch of thistles again or *the* rabbit that goes through *that* gap in the fence.

It was usually impossible to do more than guess with birds but, when nesting time came round, they began to stake out their territory. I never see as much when I am walking as when I am standing still, so we developed the habit of pausing every now and then for perhaps half an hour or so. Often enough nothing stirred when we stopped so that the wood seemed as empty as a desert until we had merged with our surroundings and been forgotten.

There are quantities of snails on Ley Close, above Primrose Dell, with pink spiral shells, edged with a brown line. I see them feeding in the open only very rarely but, in various places in the wood, there are patches thick with their shells. There is always a tree root or a large stone in the centre of each collection of shells. These are thrushes' anvils and, when we stayed still to observe one, the odds were that we would soon see the thrush arrive with a whole snail held in its beak, especially if we were out early in the morning.

When it reached its anvil, it put the shell down and looked round for a while to make certain that no predator lay hidden, waiting to pounce as soon as it became absorbed in its work. It would then start to hammer its victim unmercifully till the shell shattered and exposed the defenceless, succulent body, which the thrush swallowed like an oyster.

Such little dramas were no less exciting because they were not rare. Similar things had probably gone on under our noses all our life, but we had had no eyes to see them because we were always in a hurry. We found hairy caterpillars and brilliant moths, iridescent beetles, and yellow-bellied newts.

Things we hadn't had time for since our childhood suddenly took on new significance because we appreciated them better.

Ten years ago we were enchanted for the first time by the continuous buzzing song of grasshopper warblers in summer. They are small and dainty, with very pointed beaks and, for a while, we didn't know what they were because there had been none where we came from. We wrote them off among the ubiquitous 'little brown jobs', which was our name for all the birds we didn't know, and we did not even associate them with their song at first.

It is a most extraordinary sound, not unlike the wheel of a bicycle freewheeling fast downhill. It is emitted continuously from the same spot until, just as you think you've located it, it moves twenty yards away. This is not the masterpiece of some ventriloquial virtuosity, but a duet between two cocks, each singing from concealment near his nesting site.

The sad thing is that I can't hear them any more because the quality of my hearing has deteriorated with advancing years. The pitch of a grasshopper warbler's song is at the upper limit of normal human hearing and, as the eardrum thickens with age, it grows too insensitive to respond to such a dainty orchestra.

Unwilling to admit to myself that I was going back, I did try to persuade myself, for a while, that it was not my hearing getting dull so much as a decline in the numbers of grasshopper warblers, but the theory didn't hold water, because younger people could still hear them. All the same, it wasn't a bad bit of self-deception, because the habitat really was changing remarkably fast. The area had started out with very little undergrowth because the canopy of mature trees our predecessors had chopped down had shaded out most of the plants at ground level. For the first year or so after the felling there were plenty of foxgloves, a little wispy bracken, feggy grass and a few brambles. It was open tussocky country well suited to partridges and small, ground-nesting birds which needed both light and cover.

Then, as the seasons passed, this mat of vegetation thickened and prospered, forming a miniature jungle, more suited to voles and shrews than small birds needing to be able to get suddenly airborne to escape from predators.

Meanwhile the Forestry Commission continued to plant the forty acres up with Corsican pine in rows about five feet apart, which competed with the rank natural vegetation for survival. The Commission helped them for a year or two by weeding round each young tree by hand. It wasn't weeding in the loving sense that Jess cherishes her garden, for there was no question of removing encroaching plants until the naked earth was visible.

This weeding consisted in walking, bent double, along each row with a razor-sharp sickle, slashing down the grass and bracken that threatened to suffocate each weakling tree. The result was that the trees grew, so that, in about four years, their crowns lorded it high above the common weeds and nothing could stop their further progress. For those intervening years, the physical act of weeding provided enough open spaces and variety of cover for all sorts of wildlife to prosper.

But when it dawned on me how precarious were the conditions necessary for plentiful variety, I was filled with despair. I did not see how I was going to cope on my own, nor was it practicable to invite our friends round on 'weeding parties'. They are earthy and common sense enough for the novelty to have worn off before it began.

Even if I could dream up some practical alternative, I couldn't have put it into practice because the Forestry Commission lease ran for nine hundred and ninety-nine years, and their job was to make their trees pay, not to act as a philanthropists in the interests of the birds and the bees and the flowers.

Still, I do not readily take 'No' for an answer. Having worked hard all my life to own a bit of England that really did belong to Jess and me, I was determined that the reality should prove at least as attractive as the dream. I was damned if I was going to let half of it slither through my fingers to fetch up as forty acres of miserable softwood sterility where nothing prospered but nasty little pines.

All the Commission paid for its use was a miserly rent of half-a-crown an acre a year. Twelve and a half niggardly washers that masquerade as our fine New Pence.

They didn't need to sell many trees to make a profit on that, so I didn't anticipate that they would part up with it easily. I decided that there was no commercial way to justify the transfer, so that I must dream-up something which could be mutually beneficial. The policy of the Commission towards wildlife and the use of their land for amenity had recently changed. So I decided to try to enlist their sympathy for the work that I was doing by creating a reservoir to restock surrounding areas with wildlife.

It so happened that 1970 was European Conservation Year when there had been great publicity for such schemes, and public bodies, conservation societies and private people had been invited to compete for awards, to be presented by Prince Philip for 'outstanding contributions to the countryside'.

There were only a hundred awards for the whole country and large bodies such as planning authorities, the National Coal Board, the Central Electricity Generating Board, the Forestry Commission, and so on, were eligible to compete. The awards might be for anything from landscaping a colliery spoil heap to the creation of a National Nature Reserve, so competition was obviously going to be fierce.

I decided to have a go because, if I could get my nose among the winners, it would add authority to the work I was doing and it might be more difficult to 'obstruct an outstanding contribution to the countryside' than it would otherwise have been to write off just another day-dream of an eccentric naturalist. Accordingly, I composed a thesis with this always at the back of my mind, and was lucky enough to be among the only four private individuals to win an award, most of which went to large societies and public bodies.

So I was summoned (along with the other ninety-nine!) to Guildhall in London, where Prince Philip presented me with a very pleasant inscribed bronze plaque. I now had the evidence to try to persuade the Forestry Commission to disgorge my lease. I wrote and explained that I was working on wildlife management and, as evidence that the work I was doing was in line with the Commission policy on the fauna of their woods, I sent a copy of the thesis which had won me the award.

As usual, I got nothing but co-operation. They agreed to turn the lease over to me if I was prepared to pay them for the labour and young trees they had put into my land. Although it was a considerable capital sum, it made commercial sense. When I had bought the place originally the forty acres that was let at half a crown an acre had obviously not been worth more than the capital sum which would bring in £5 a year. Something less than £100 the lot. So although I didn't get much rent, I hadn't paid much for it.

Under my own control, it could be sold with vacant possession, which would add a very considerable amount to the value of the whole. And as I have no intention whatever of selling, it will at least grow with inflation, which is more than the rent would have done. The trees that I bought are also growing into money, and as I thin them out to give the clearings and glades I need for a nature reserve, I can sell the thinnings to pay for at least some of the labour.

So that countryside award has worked according to plan, and has been of very material help in turning my daydreams into reality.

Most of the wild creatures in a wood live near the edge. When trees mature and grow together, they form a dense canopy which shades out most life at ground level, so that most of the food, insect and vegetable, is in the areas where light can penetrate.

Life is also most uncomfortable if it is impossible to have

74

easy access to fresh air which is free to circulate to dry out sodden fur or feathers after rain, or after pushing through soggy grass or bushes. The first thing, therefore, was to create additional 'edge' to the wood, which could most simply be done by cutting rides through it, or by making clearings and glades.

The snag with straight rides is that they may funnel wind and draught so that some of the advantages of woodland edge are lost. So I decided to make as few straight rides as possible, subject to my somewhat selfish desire to watch anything that moved by being able to see as far as possible into the wood.

It is astonishingly difficult to cut down a swath of trees so that the gap they leave emerges anywhere near the spot you planned and, when I had visited any of the stately homes where the grounds had been laid out by Capability Brown, I used to wonder how he did it.

I found it quite hopeless to try to cut a ride when the leaf is on because it can be guaranteed to kink into a dog's leg and come out where you least expect within ten yards. So I possessed myself in patience till winter came, and marked a ride on my map where it would emerge above Primrose Dell, in the diagonally opposite corner of the wood from the house.

It so happened that this was almost due east and west, so I worked backwards from the house going east by the compass, cutting a narrow path, about four feet wide, so that as I looked back along the cutting I made, I could always see the study window. But I soon came to a halt because there were more than enough protruding twigs to obscure my view.

I was loth to widen the path because the first part of it passed through mature oak trees in Dunstal Pool Plantation, and I was determined to fell no more timber than I had to. So I tried working at dusk, leaving a bright light in the study window which I could home on like a guiding star. This was relatively effective because by moving my head a

75

foot or so right or left, it was possible to spot the light and chop down whatever had obscured it. The danger was that it was all too easy to cut down something which should have been left and would take centuries to replace. The narrow path gradually lengthened until it disappeared over the brow of the hill on Ley Close, leaving the ride, as I had planned, looking into the infinity of open sky, without a building or tree in sight. After that it wasn't so difficult to nip a tree or two out at a time to widen the ride and give the sense of perspective I hankered for.

There has been a ride opposite the study window since the first year we were here, but now that I could do what I like with Lords Coppice, I could see that a small nudge would double its length. All that I had to do was to take a few trees out of the right-hand side to be able to look right through the young plantation I had just got back into my possession.

To complete the job, I cut a third ride over the pool and right to the far corner of Lords Coppice, which is around a thousand yards. All three are cut radially, and 'point' at my study window, although we can also see along them from the sitting room next door.

They are my greatest luxury. Whenever I raise my eyes from my desk, I can look right along whichever I choose. If I pause for a while in thought, absently looking along one of them, the odds are that something will move and attract my attention. I keep a pair of 15 x 60 Zeiss binoculars on a shelf within arm's length of my desk, and with them I can pick out a creature as tiny as a stoat at the far end of the wood.

Birdwatchers would say that such a magnification is far too much, because the power exaggerates the slightest tremor of the hand until the image leaps and dances. This may well be so if you are standing outside with nothing solid to steady you. But I have the desk to lean my elbows on and, when I am seated beside it, my elbows make a tripod with my body which disciplines the shakes. I persuade myself that all writing should be creative and that creative work is not possible without thought. Such self-deception gives me leave to spend countless happy hours looking out of my window gathering copy to write about!

I am gradually trying to seed the new rides with grass and white wild clover to attract deer and hares and rabbits to come out and feed where I can see them, and it is surprising what a lot of birds are fond of clover too.

Inside the wood there are several patches of bracken of between one and two acres in extent. Some bracken is good. Pheasants nest in it and deer drop their fawns. Nightjars like the same sort of cover, and rabbits and hares use it for shelter, while there is a carpet of bluebells in spring before the bracken wakes again. The snag is that it shades out and kills young trees and, in time, it will weaken and smother the bluebells unless I get down to the task of doing something about it.

It is supposed to be far more difficult to eradicate than I have found it, although when quite large areas are cleared, they are inclined to be reinvaded from surrounding bracken brakes.

I mow the rides we made when we came with the old tractor and an ordinary farm hay-mowing machine. About once a month from May to September is all they need. If I leave longer intervals, it takes longer to shift the grass I cut than it does to mow it. And sitting comfortably on a tractor seat is really very pleasant, because everything around gets used to regular mechanical noise, and I see all sorts of creatures that would have hidden if I had walked around.

The bonus for cutting so often is that I don't have to clear the grass because it is short enough to wither away where it is, and an old country saying is that, if you cut bracken four times in three years, you will eradicate it.

It is also almost as effective to roll it while the young fronds are tender. I bought an old horse roller for £3 at a farm sale and I pull it behind the tractor where there are too many old roots which would snag the knives of the mowing machine. But for the last two years I have been using something easier than either and far more effective. Pigs.

We used pigs to clear the patch for Jess to start her garden nine years ago, and it occurred to me that they would do just as good a job in the wood. The cost of labour would put the task of making clearings by hand quite beyond my pocket unless there was some end-product that I could sell to pay the wages. Clearing it myself with the old tractor was also out, because of the roots and stumps left when the timber had been felled, and to do it by hand would leave no time to earn my living with my pen.

But pigs go round the roots; they consume everything green and then uproot it, and they keep turning the roots over till the soil drops off them and they die. When the task is done, they leave the perfect tilth for a seed bed – and they are the only woodmen I know that I can put in the deep freeze when they are redundant!

I chose the breed for the job with great care. Modern, intensively kept pigs are susceptible to virus pneumonia and lung worm and all the complaints that scientists have induced in their passion for quick growth and lean meat.

I managed to find a farmer who breeds pigs on a large scale out of doors. Many pig breeders say that if you keep two boars together, they will fight to the death. They say that if one sow finds another's litter, she will eat them, and that pigs behave as badly as human beings. But the farmer I discovered knew the secrets. He runs about forty sows together all their lives, and they establish their own social order, within which they live quite amicably.

He raises two boar piglets together and they are never apart, from the time they are weaned until they are slaughtered, so one establishes precedence, and they don't fight.

He then introduces both boars into the field with the forty sows at the same time. The master of the two, the one highest on the social scale, serves any sows in season and he goes on serving them until he is spent. This, then, is no time to quibble about orders of precedence, so the other boar, the humbler of the two, takes over where his partner left off.

Between them, they serve the whole bunch of sows in a very short time, so that they all fall due to pig close together. Before that happens, the boars are removed and a simple corrugated iron shelter is put in the field for each sow, spaced in even rows.

The master (or mistress?) sow takes her pick of these farrowing huts and establishes herself in it with her territory around it. Each of the other sows then picks hers, those at the upper end of the social scale having first choice, the humbler ones taking what is left. The vital thing is to place food and watering points so that every sow can get directly to them without having to pass close to the shelter, and so through the territory, of another sow. Each must be able to feed without trespassing on her neighbour.

Pigs are passionately fond of grazing, given the chance, poor things, and each sow grazes the grass in her territory and wanders on to the subsidiary feeding points as she chooses. In due course, each has her piglets in her own hut, and a low fence, like a fender, is put across the entrance to keep the piglets in for ten days, although the mother can step over it and continue to wander where she likes.

A fringe benefit of having all the sows pigging at about the same time is that piglets from large litters can be stolen by the pigman their first day and fostered on to sows with small litters, so that all the youngsters get a fair share of the whole communal supply of milk.

At ten days old the barriers are removed so that the little pigs can run all over the field with their mothers. The extraordinary thing is that, at this stage, the sows seem to bear no animosity either to each other or to their neighbours' young which are soon running at will all over the place, as fancy takes them, joining first with one litter then with another.

No one who has witnessed the degradation of sows cramped in farrowing crates, or piglets reared without ever seeing the light of day, can fail to be moved by the spectacle of four hundred little pigs running at liberty with forty sows. They take sensual joy in galloping around, and are as happy and dignified as if they were wild.

They graze the sweet grass as avidly as a herd of cows, and chase each other in play like energetic rugby footballers. When they are replete and weary with their pleasure, the old sows stretch themselves out in rows to sunbathe, udders pointing skyward, as abandoned and shapeless as trippers on a holiday beach.

The stupidity is that, because it is natural, so many believe it cannot be profitable as well, and it is true that a hardier type is needed than the poor creatures bred for generations to mature as rapidly as hot-house flowers in the humid conditions of an intensive piggery.

The pigs I buy are Wessex saddle-back half-breds, the result of crossing a Large White boar on to Wessex sows, though the first bunch I bought last year were pure bred Wessex hogs, discarded when their sisters were retained for breeding stock. They were lively and hardy, and the moment they got in the wood, it was obvious that it was the habitat for which pigs were originally designed. It delighted my eyes to see them set about their task.

They went round the boundary of their enclosure, to establish the size of their territory, and then they beach-combed it yard by yard, scoffing the titbits first, leaving the rest to be picked over later. They ate the honeysuckle and browsed the leaves of birch and nut saplings and any succulent grass and clover they could find.

If you have never watched at close quarters a pig's snout grubbing for food, you wouldn't credit that anything so strong could be so sensitive. To begin with, I have come to the conclusion that a pig's sense of smell is as delicate as a pointer's. I have seen these hogs stop rooting and stand rigid for a moment, testing the breeze when something strange was about.

They knew if wild deer or strange men or dogs were approaching long before the sharpest eye could pierce the

Roe buck by Dunstal pool

Twelve Sunday Lunches! Silkie bantam and Aylesbury ducklings

Grey squirrel. The one that got away!

The vole that ate the strawberries till Fred ate him

Making a pool

The pool we made in Primrose dell

The Canada goose on the study window-sill

The Bewick's swan that stayed four years

thicket or the keenest ear could hear twigs crack or mud squelch. Yet, a moment before, that same perceptive organ had been turning over huge clods or prizing out roots as if it were a burglar's jemmy.

It suddenly became obvious why pigs ears are so shaped, because, when their snouts probed amongst the roots and thorns, their leathery ears flapped over their eyes to provide a natural curtain of protection.

I fenced them in a patch roughly fifty yards square, each side being the length of a roll of Weldmesh netting and, inside this run, I made a simple hovel of three vertical iron hurdles, with corrugated iron sheets for roof and sides. I chucked a few straw bales under this twelve-foot square shelter, and left the open side pointing south-east, to catch the morning sun.

In fine weather they didn't bother to use it and, if we walked by late in the evening dusk, they were lying in rows, touching each other for warmth and company, but as open to the sky as the wildest wild animals. If it rained, they were only too pleased to accept the hospitality of my straw under the civilised roof of the hovel. No creatures love their comforts more dearly than pigs, so that to inflict on them the squalor of sweat pens, where they have to lie in their own dung, and eat food from patches of their urine, is barbarous torture.

Within a day or so, their enclosure looked as if it had been hit by a tornado. Grass was eaten, turves uprooted, bracken trodden flat and rolled under its own roots, sapling birch and nut torn out, and all their greenery consumed. No gardeners with spades would have done a better job and, as choice of food was limited, they turned the ground over and over in search of morsels they had missed until they had worked the soil into a tilth as fine as a field that had been harrowed. This seed bed can either be planted naturally with seeds blown on the wind or carried by birds, or it can be replanted with young trees which will have some chance to get established before it is necessary to weed them.

I planted the first patch they cleared at the back of Dunstal Pool with a mixture of kale and rape and turnip and buckwheat to attract the pheasants and deer as far as possible from danger, towards the centre of the wood, where I could see them cross the centre ride from my study window.

This season I am clearing – or the pigs are for me – a patch of two or three acres right in front of the windows but about two hundred yards from the house. I intend to sow half of this with game mixture and half with grass alternate years until I get it properly clean. After each crop I shall let the pigs grub it up again until it is bracken-free and fertile, after which I shall keep it as a clearing in the centre of the wood.

By controlling the pigs in movable, fifty-yard squares, bounded by netting, it is possible to keep them away from specimen trees and to keep them there just long enough to clear the vegetation without getting the choicest patches puddled while less palatable bits are still stiff with weeds.

A fifty-yard roll of heavy-gauge netting needs a stout and rigid straining post at each end, but only light support posts in between, and the modern weld mesh netting is so much more rigid that the old-fashioned woven stuff, that there is no trouble with the pigs getting underneath it. Each roll can be shifted in a matter of minutes, when the time comes to move them over a patch, so that the capital cost of starting with a unit of ten pigs worked out at well under £4 a head.

I feed pig nuts as supplementary diet and they have about three pounds a head a day and four pounds for the last month before they are sold as bacon pigs or heavy hogs. This saves about a pound or a pound and a half for each pig, each day they live in the wood, as compared to the weight they would need if they could get no natural food for themselves. So foraging in the wood, which they obviously enjoy, saves £7 or £8 a head in food over the time they are here, which goes a long way to subsidising my own inefficiencies.

The ham and pork are absolutely superb. The natural

food and unlimited exercise produce incomparably firm yet succulent meat of a quality that money can't buy from a factory farm. So we always buy the best pig back from our butcher to put in our own deep freeze and, last year, it worked out at only 20 pence a pound – including the hams!

I intended initially to use the pigs only as a once-off operation; simply to get the patches I'd earmarked as glades and clearings into suitable condition. But it was so successful that I shall make the process continuous.

A glade does not remain a glade for many years without choking up with bramble and rose and bracken, followed by a crop of seedling trees. So I have decided to clear patches in rotation as a farmer would rotate his crops. I shall thus have a wood patterned like a draft board with a mosaic of different densities and types, ranging from stands of mature pine, ripe for the axe, to patches of bare soil that have only just been cleared by pigs.

This would be quite uneconomic if it had to be paid for, but with the help of the pigs I not only get my glades for nothing but also cheap food as well.

A ten-acre square of Lords Coppice was cleared and planted by the Forestry Commission before we came and thickets of birch have shot up among the Corsican pine as close as stems of corn. These stems are about twice as thick as a man's thumb and ten feet high, and in patches they are so dense that it is physically impossible to force a way through them.

At the moment they form superb cover for fallow deer which instinctively search out secret paths through them to secluded bowers where they lie undisturbed. The snag is that, as time goes on, their tops will grow together and competition for light will wax so fierce that the strong will strangle the weak which will die and crumple and rot on the ground. Patches of birch have already done this in Holly Covert, with the result that only a spatter of weedy little trees survived, about three or four inches across the trunk.

They don't let in enough light to allow a shrub layer to

thrive, yet they are not thick enough to form cover themselves. It is a copybook example of how habitat can deteriorate when left to itself and, when I have time, I shall take out most of these little trees and leave some decent open spaces for the bilberry to recover and prosper.

I certainly don't intend to let Lords Coppice degenerate into such a state, and have discovered that racecourses use a great deal of birch to make the jumps. They want it in bundles about as large as a man can span with both arms, made up with saplings about nine or ten feet tall and inch and a half at the base.

Skilled foresters can slice these off at a single blow, just above ground level and they tie them into bundles with binder twine, which comes off bales of hay before they are fed to cattle. Not many men want the physical work involved nowadays, so they can command a piecework price almost as much as the racecourse can pay. But, even if there isn't much in it for me, the task of thinning out the birch at least pays for itself, and I plan to crop mine on a six year rotation, about six acres at a time.

This will mean that I shall always have a bare patch ready to be cleared by pigs, and a patch so dense that its turn will come next year. Between these extremes there will be grades of density to suit the tastes of most of the creatures we could hope to attract.

Hazel is better coppiced periodically too, because deer are particularly fond of the young shoots as they regenerate. There is a sensible market for the thinnings here too, in the form of bean sticks and a few selected stocks for walking sticks.

Perhaps the biggest potential in this type of wood is for growing trees. Garden centres have developed a tremendous demand for growing trees from two to ten feet high, and 1973, being Plant a Tree Year, has focussed the attention of planners and roadmakers on the possibilities of 'instant' trees to improve amenities without waiting for them to grow. The snag is that the purchaser not only wants the tree, he wants a good rootball of soil with it, which leaves a water-logged depression if the soil is as heavy clay as ours.

But it is fairly simple to shove a bit of adjacent soil in the hole with a tractor and fore-end loader, and the leafmould that goes in makes an ideal plot to plant a young replacement. A side effect is that the wood gradually accumulates a chain of swampy patches that weren't suitable for young trees, which will grow types of vegetation which were not there before.

The highest area in the wood is a hill brow on Ley Close, above Primrose Dell. There is virtually nothing here but bracken and the bluebells, which flower before the bracken shoots. I want to try an experiment here on two patches. One will be cleared by pigs, and I want to check if they kill all the bluebell bulbs in the process; I shall mow the bracken on the other with the tractor mower set about six inches above ground level to miss the bluebells.

In both cases I shall plant with spruce when the bracken is under control, and crop the spruce at five or six years for instant trees which would fetch in excess of £1 a foot, even at present prices. This will provide another gradation of cover, quite different from anything else in the wood.

Water is amongst the most precious attractions of any sanctuary. Dunstal Pool, within eighty yards of the house, is an acre and a half, with some nice boggy patches on the northern side. The main ditch which feeds it goes right up the centre of the wood before making a right-angle turn and then following the edge of the wood to Bagots Park, where the ordnance map is marked with a well at the topmost corner of our land. But when the ditch was cleaned out to help drain the park, it turned out that the map was wrong. What it showed as a well was only a horse trough, fed by drainage or a spring, somewhere off our ground up on Squitch Bank.

The difference that draining the park has made is very marked. When we came, the thousand acres next to us was sodden, feggy grass and reed and bracken, spattered with stag-headed oaks which were really the rejects from the saleable timber that had been felled in the 1930s.

There were no drains, so that, when it rained, the water seeped slowly into the heavy soil and took days to percolate down to our ditch. It came through so slowly that there was very little increase in flow after a thunderstorm, but still a steady trickle after weeks of drought.

Any ideas that our ground had many springs soon disappeared after the park was drained. In the park they dug trenches four or more feet deep at about a chain apart and these led from Squitch Bank to the horse trough in our ditch.

Within a couple of hours of a storm, water cascades into our pool on one side – and out of the overflow on the other. Unfortunately, it drops the silt it carries down from the wood as it crosses the pool!

Drainage is now so good (or so bad, from our viewpoint) that we get these sudden flushes after a storm and the supply dries altogether after only a few days of drought. By the end of summer the level in our pool has fallen by about eighteen inches.

The primitive urge to play with fire and water still fascinates me. I feel that there is tremendous scope to fit sluices in the deep ditches cut, by Herculean labours, through Holly Covert. As soon as I get a few days to spare, I hope to put in crude sluices to back up flood water into the lower parts of the wood, so that I can feed it back to the pool gradually as it used to flow in the past.

The fringe benefit of this would be that odd peaty patches in the lower levels of the wood would get waterlogged and marshy which, although it might not fill a forester's heart with joy, would add another dimension to the variety of habitat. But putting in such sluices is back-breaking graft, compared to one we got for nothing in Cockshutt Close.

By the time I got the lease back from the Commission, the fence they put up when they planted it, was corroded and rotten. I didn't want packs of stray dogs trespassing after our deer, and it was obvious that trespass by the deer on to neighbouring farmland would be equally unwelcome.

So I decided to start off right by fencing the whole boundary. This involved about sixty rolls of netting, each fifty yards long, which would be a major expense I should have to write off, as I could see no way to recoup it. But it would at least make me cock of my own midden.

It so happened that the British Reinforced Concrete Company was just breaking into the fencing field, so I persuaded Dan Ledbetter, their Managing Director, that we might be mutually helpful. I would be delighted to give extended field trials if he was prepared to subsidise the experiments in any way.

The fence they were making was square mesh but with welded joints instead of the usual hinged or woven joints. It was far more rigid than the old-fashioned stuff, and would obviously make a far stronger fence when stretched up tight. The flexible stuff collects lime and artificial manure as it is spread on arable land, and this corrodes it at the joints, from where the rusting starts, so that the welded fence would be less susceptible to corrosion. Unfortunately it was said to be difficult to erect on anything but level ground. It wasn't flexible enough to 'give' over hills and hollows.

This difficulty proved quite easy to overcome. All that was necessary was to anchor one end to a really solid straining post and stretch the whole length with a really powerful strainer. The intermediate posts were put in afterwards and the finished fence will twang like a banjo. It looks as good or as bad as the workmanship that erected it, but put up right, there is nothing to touch it.

It would have been impossible to put up a fence of any sort at all when we started, because the hedge that was once round the wood had been breached in places and great tangles of blackthorn and hawthorn and bramble formed a skirt round its edge. So I decided to invest the money I should have spent on a holiday and to do the job in such a fashion that I could forget all about boundary fences henceforth.

A man poking around with a sledgehammer and bill hook would grow a king-sized crop of blisters before he'd got half-way through such a task, and I reckoned a man with an earth-moving machine would take the irk out of such work and probably be cheaper in the end (The argument drugged my conscience if it fooled nobody else!).

The first job was to bulldoze a path right round the edge of the wood so that a tractor could follow with a circular saw on the end of a hydraulic arm. This wouldn't have been necessary on a farm that had a normal boundary, but it would give a 'clean' side to the wood so that it would be possible to work near enough to the hedge to erect the fence.

The crawler that came to blaze the trail was squat, powerful and fitted with steel tracks like a tank. It looked as if it could claw its way up the side of a ravine, shattering and uprooting anything that thwarted it. It proved unstoppable, and it left a flat brown scar of earth in its wake as naked as a new-ploughed field – until it came to one little valley at the far side of the wood which had a deep ditch at the bottom to drain Cockshutt Close across our boundary to Mr Charles' land.

The sides of the valley were far too steep for a rubber-tyred tractor, but the crawler treated it with contempt. I asked Dennis, the driver, to shove a bit of the bank into the bottom so that I could cross with my old tractor. For, if I am to sell the produce of the wood and feed my pigs when they are clearing patches for replanting, it is vital to be able to get anywhere on the tractor to cultivate and harvest it.

The grunting machine was pitiless. Clumps of dainty blue-bells meant no more to it than soulless stones. A tickle of soil spilled over the steel teeth of the bucket and was swallowed and disgested beneath the next great bite. And as the bucket was repeatedly filled and emptied, the valley sides were eroded and tamed into gentle slopes, and the valley floor rose up to meet them, damming the waters outlet.

I was delighted. A barrowful of crumpled bluebells might jerk a few tears from the starry-eyed, but my earthy mind is too practical for that. I calculated that my bonus would be a crystal-clear pool where there had been nothing but a deep ditch before, and it turned out even better than I'd hoped.

The limpid water welled up as I watched, and I visualised the newts and sticklebacks and water hens that would enliven next year's crop of bluebells with their animation. Dennis was pleased, too, and I fancied that even the phlegmatic crawler was a bit skittish in its triumph, but our jubilation was short-lived. I calculated that, if we could remove just one more hump from the valley bottom, we'd have a wonderful instant pool.

No knight, spurring on his battle charger, could have out-manoeuvred Dennis as he urged his steed towards the offending foe. Then I thought my eyes were playing me tricks, but there was no shadow of doubt that the elephantine machine was not going where he aimed it, but was cavorting sideways instead. One second it was irresistible, the next it was slithering round as helpless as a dinosaur on roller skates.

Dennis, perched, impotent on top, suddenly realised he wasn't going where he was looking. The whole contraption lurched round out of plumb, slewed to a crazy angle and slithered down the ditch. He couldn't goad or flog it, so he savagely opened the throttle and filled its guts with diesel gas. It snorted with rage, and its tracks flailed round in vain as it dug itself into a watery grave. Nothing could be done and, as the throttle eased its punishment, the convulsions subsided into a pitiful mechanised death rattle – and then silence.

Sadly the driver climbed down and, abandoning his vanquished monster, he shrouded it in a tarpaulin winding sheet. There it stood, a mute symbol that Nature is not always slave to the whims of auto-mechanical Man, until an even bigger monster came next day to haul it out on the end of an undignified chain.

Less than three months later the pool had filled and gone

turgid with an overgrowth of algae which flourished until, overcome by its own success, it clouded the water and poisoned itself with its own fecundity. It died and sank to the bottom, eventually creating a natural balance as the water in a newly planted aquarium thickens before settling to limpid maturity.

My one regret was that the water has risen round the butt of an old hornbeam tree which I fear will 'drown' and die in consequence. Although I normally hate killing trees, this one is not really so bad because it wasn't a very good specimen and will now be taken over by wood-boring insects and provide a rich hunting ground for woodpeckers and tree creepers and other insectivorous birds.

The pool is already a sanctuary for flamboyant dragon flies and the wild duck fly in to feed at dawn and dusk. But the greatest thrill was at first light one morning when I had taken the dogs for a walk before breakfast. I am not sure what sharpened my perception, but I was suddenly aware of a sense of anticipation, although I couldn't, for the moment, pinpoint the cause.

It is normally the dogs who give prior warning. Tick, the pointer, will slide forward, nostrils dilated so as not to miss the faintest whiff of promise. A sibilant whisper is all it needs to warn her to freeze in her tracks, so that she is always an asset and never a liability. But this time the dogs didn't give a quiver of interest to substantiate my premonition, and it was I who first saw the flash of gaudy green which could only mean one thing. Stiffening into immobility, I hissed a command to 'drop' and, although I made so small a sound, the dogs obeyed mechanically and crouched silent at my feet.

On a branch overhanging the pool, a kingfisher perched motionless as we were. For a few seconds it seemed that we were staring each other out, but then it dawned on me that he hadn't seen us at all. He was absorbed in his search for fish and, as I watched, he cocked his head slightly and plopped into the water in a vertical dive.

It was so clear that I could see him deep beneath the surface before he returned to his branch. As he shook himself, a shower of droplets rainbowed in the morning sun, but even his brilliance couldn't disguise the fact that he was an ungainly bird in silhouette. Then he broke the magic spell and darted off down the valley towards Ash Brook.

I breathed a prayer of thanks to the benighted bulldozer, because such a bird, almost 'in hand' in a pool of my own devising, was worth a flock on any one else's bushes.

Such physical changes as rides and pools, large clearings and deer-proof fencing are equivalent to the capital expenditure necessary to start a little factory. So far as I am concerned, I trust the outlay will be called for only once in a lifetime. Nevertheless I was not anxious to create something static that I could relax and enjoy, I wanted to begin something which could develop as long as I lived, not just to see it, but to help it. I had spent a year or so 'learning my territory', as a wild creature would and, for the first time in my life I experienced the sensation of utter content.

Not being cut out for spectator roles, the novelty soon wore off, so that the discovery that I had acquired a wasting asset was more of a challenge than a shock. It came as a relief to have to get stuck into something creative that would tax my capacity to get results, and I greeted with pleasure the fact that it was a task without end.

As one patch of birch is cleared and sold for foolhardy men on horseback to fall over, the next will be maturing. Patches to follow must be laid out and planned as a mosaic around the wood to provide kaleidoscopic patterns to attract the creatures which will leave if I don't succeed. Stands of pines chopped down for Christmas trees at eight new pence a foot can be replaced by spruce, which should be saleable, dug up for instant trees, at a hundred pence a foot in five years time. And I want to encourage young oak and mountain ash which has seeded naturally, by slashing away adjacent pines, so that some can remain to provide acorns for the deer and rowan berries for the birds while the surplus is sold to provide a spot of ready cash.

There are endless theories I want to test. I want to discover how much wild animals' fear of man is basic instinct and how much is derived from unpleasant experience. I am already convincing myself that if there was no reason to be afraid, a great many creatures would grow as tame as penguins on the frozen wastes, which have never had the chance to learn how dangerous man is.

Certainly because I walk round the rides in our wood, instead of through it, our fallow deer have acquired enough confidence in me to allow me to approach within twenty or thirty yards.

I want to create additional swampy patches to attract wading birds, because I know less about them at first hand than any of the other species that are likely to use the reserve. And by no means least of the things I want to try is to provide physical proof to both sportsmen and naturalists that they have nothing to lose by collaboration, and much to gain.

Shooting men who trap and snare all the badgers 'in case' they kill a pheasant, and shoot owls and hawks, have nobody but themselves to blame for all the adverse publicity they will get from a handful of strident 'antis', who would be rightly labelled cranks if no one gave them ammunition.

Naturalists will have to compromise over the control of vermin which does serious harm to the game other folk have spent hard-earned cash to rear. So I want to show here that it *is* possible to have pheasants and foxes, herons and fish, hawks and partridge, simply by exercising common-sense control. What is more, I want to spend the rest of my life converting my theories into practice.

CHAPTER FIVE

Perks

Managing a woodland reserve brings endless pleasure from laying plans which result in improved conditions for a whole range of threatened creatures. I get a tremendous kick from persuading a completely wild animal to do something I have planned it should do, without it ever being conscious that I have influenced it in any way. I enjoy combining this with wangling a little income from the sale of trees or undergrowth I would have otherwise have had to pay to get rid of. And, most of all, I enjoy writing and broadcasting about what I do. Words are such amusing playthings that, if I am not pressed, a perfectly straightforward article will take me an uneconomic time to write; not because it is difficult, but because I can amuse myself for hours doodling with words to see what unexpected nuances emerge from rephrasing the simplest ideas.

It often occurs to me that I get far more pleasure from writing than ever my readers get from the products of my pen, and this pleasure is multiplied by the fact that I couldn't choose a more congenial place for my composition if I tried.

Sometimes I write for five minutes in the hour – and then look out of the window, thinking what I going to write about next, for the other fifty-five. I see dramas unfolding before me, as when two fallow bucks were fighting or a hawk caught its prey in full view; I can watch the mechanics of precisely how the herons get the first twig to stay in the tree while they go away to collect more to build their nest. I see little things at close quarters – starlings hunting for leather-jackets, or how the tits do a Houdini act by pulling a whole nut from the nut cage, when the mesh is theoretically too small to allow the passage of anything so large.

In the course of twelve months I spend literally hundreds of hours sitting at my window, which is as good as sitting right at the heart of the reserve. Indeed it is sometimes better because, for all practical purposes, I am invisible from outside, so that my subjects go about their normal business completely unselfconsciously. And when I grow too old to get out in all weathers and at all times, as I do now, I shall be able to continue to enjoy the fruits of my labours from the same window where I planned so many of them.

In addition to such intangible pleasures, my work brings a fair share of benefits in kind. I keep a few silkie bantams to hatch eggs from pheasant and wild duck nests deserted by their owners – and sometimes eggs I steal from undeserted nests!

These bantams run with half a dozen barnyard hens we keep for the good of the house. Naturally I don't keep any of them intensively, nor sell their produce – if only because there is not enough surplus. They range free all summer in a paddock on the far side of Dunstal Pool and in the wood by the house when the evenings draw in. They get all the exercise they want, fresh green grass and clover, and as many insects as wild birds would scratch for and catch. The quality of their eggs is superb because the yolks are golden, the shells strong and the whites firm and pure. Compared with the anaemic abortions squeezed out of artificially fed battery captives, existing without fresh air or light, or without access to any natural food, our eggs are a feast for gourmets.

I often get soaked through feeding them or baulmed-up with muck, cleaning out their pens. My fingers sometimes stick to frozen bucket handles in mid-winter, but we have never bought an egg in more than thirty years of marriage and, judging by the insipid mush served up for hotel breakfasts, we shan't start while I have strength to feed my hens.

Pullets are fairly expensive to buy anywhere near the point

of lay, so we get a few day-olds every year from a breeder who keeps pedigree Rhode Island Reds on free range. The cost is slightly higher than cross-bred birds produced for intensive laying houses, but one of my extravagances is that highly bred stock never fails to delight me.

It would be wasteful to put only half a dozen chicks with a broody hen, so I get a few cock chicks to keep them company and rear them all on free range. By doing them well, I can get the cocks to about nine pounds weight at seven months and, as soon as I do, I kill the lot for Jess to feather and dress and put in the deep freeze.

The advantage of this is that they do not pass their prime and get tough, nor go on eating their heads off after they reach optimum weight. I rear a dozen Aylesbury ducklings under silkie bantams and, usually, two or three geese, and we buy back one of our home-fed pigs for less than half the price it would cost over the counter.

This pork is as different from factory-fed stuff as free-range eggs from the product of a battery. Part of the reason is obviously that the pigs get enough exercise to put on firm flesh, and they are free to select their own fresh greens and other natural food. But I sometimes wonder if part of the secret is not the way they die as well.

They live here in the wood in utter contentment and, when their time is up, I do not send them to the cattle auction. Our own butcher, Mr Wilson, sees how they are kept and fed, so that he knows that they will produce pork beyond compare. He is only too pleased to buy the lot at top market price. He turns up for them one Sunday morning and they walk quietly into his van, lured by a feed of pig nuts. Within an hour they are dead.

They are never chivvied by strangers nor bullied by their own kind, nor trundled for miles to market in a cattle truck. They are never beaten by drovers nor prodded by prospective purchasers. They are never goaded through the sale ring nor yammered over by slick-tongued auctioneers. Nor are they kept for twenty-four hours or so in the lairage of a public abbatoir, reeking of carnage and resounding with the screams and death rattles of their relatives. Our pigs live natural lives, and die humanely so soon after they are taken from the wood that their flesh never has time to grow toughened and stringy from stress.

Some people couldn't eat the animals they had fed. So long as I know they have lived happily, and naturally and suffered no indignities in the slaughterhouse I would rather eat the products of my craft than creatures which others forced for profit not for pride.

The same applies to the wild things in the wood. Ours is the only standing oakwood left from the original Bagots Wood of more than a thousand acres. The rest has been felled and replanted with pines. The result is that there is little more than standing room in ours when the acorns fall. Deer come in from all around and the undergrowth positively crackles with pheasants.

Nothing is lovelier than a glistening cock pheasant, so I straw an open patch of woodland in front of the windows and feed it with the sweepings from a cornmill floor so that we can sit and enjoy the colour and movement. When spring arrives, there is no more randy brute in all creation than a cock pheasant and, if more than one is left to every five hens, he will fight interminably with his rivals and harry the hens till their fertility is impaired. All shooting men know this, and the sportsmen amongst them spare the hens after Christmas shoot only cocks for the last few weeks of the season in an effort to end up with the right ratio of cocks to hens.

I don't shoot ours but catch them up alive in box traps so that I can set my favourite cocks, which are almost tame enough to eat out of my hand, free again, to squire as many hens as I want in the wood. The surplus cock birds finish in the deep freeze. I make no secret about this, and heard indirectly that a local shooting syndicate grumbled because they said I enticed 'their' birds over my boundary and knocked them off. It is an interesting point of view, since they regularly sow several acres of game mixture just inside their boundary, which certainly entices 'my' birds to be shot at by them!

The cards are stacked in my favour because, if I put down no feed at all, the wild birds would come across in search of acorns and, if I was so minded, it would be simple enough to catch up the lot.

To make quite certain that I have less, not more, than my fair share, I catch up a few hens in spring and pen them with a cock so that I can collect their eggs and hatch them under silkies. I usually rear fifty or so, some of which undoubtedly stray into their game mixture and are shot, so that any I cull for the deep freeze are more than made good by those I turn down.

Fallow deer increase naturally by about fifteen per cent a year, so that, if left to themselves, the wild stock in the wood would soon grow too great to be sustained by the natural food supply.

The wild deer here spend some of their time in my wood and some in the big wood across the drive. There are normally between eight and fifteen here, including a delightfully tame old dark doe which has been around for five years and become almost a household pet. Perhaps 'pet' is an exaggeration because she is anything but affectionate and is really a very uncivil old hag, but we forgive her bad manners because she is so fearless.

She comes daily to the salt lick, but the fact that she has taken our salt does nothing to improve her behaviour as a guest. The moment I throw down a bucket of grain for the pheasants, she turns up uninvited to guzzle it. She and her little clique (herd would flatter her) accept my hospitality with regular displays of bad manners. When I take the dogs out in the wood, she stands her ground and stamps her forefoot with insolent bad grace. She follows us, always at a safe distance but near enough to be abusive, and sees us off 'her' territory with staccato barks and belches to warn the rest of her kind that intruders are about.

Such provocative behaviour is really a compliment. It means that she is so secure in the knowledge that she will come to no harm in my wood that she can afford the bravado of warning me off. If I called her bluff by making the least move towards her, she would melt away into the shadows.

Gerald Springthorpe, the Commissions game warden, manages the deer for Brian Dale and me as if it were still one estate, and we have agreed that we will allow no one else to cull them.

Gerald is nationally known as an authority on fallow deer, and his approach is entirely professional. He assesses the numbers that the habitat can carry, and takes out only the minimum to leave the optimum numbers at the correct sex ratio. While he is at it, he takes positive steps to improve the quality of the survivors by carefully selecting the worst specimens to cull. He has been a personal friend of mine for over twenty years so that I have had plenty of time to prove by experience just what a good all-round naturalist he is, and that shooting deer is the one part of his job that he finds distasteful.

The alternative method of keeping the deer in check would be through a deer control society. These societies are formed of groups of amateurs who will go out on request to shoot surplus deer, and doubtless some of them are very good. But I should be very chary of employing them myself because of the obvious difficulty of guarding against people joining simply for free sport, which would have otherwise cost a great deal of money to rent. Many of them might be more interested in taking 'specimen' heads, so that they could leave the worst to breed instead of the best; and if a black sheep crept into their flock, he could easily use his opportunities to see where the pheasants are roosting – and call uninvited later!

Gerald Springthorpe has forgotten more about deer than such amateurs will ever learn, so it is a great comfort to be able to rely implicitly on his judgment of how they should be cropped in their own best interests.

As the woodland owners we get what venison we need for the deep freeze, and the poultry and game the place supplies allows us to keep a good table at a very modest cost. Jess grows peas and beans and strawberries and raspberries, so that we can often eat a meal which is home-produced from chicken soup to the sloe gin to top it off.

Although I like good food, there is one perk of my profession which I prize even more highly. Among the joys – and penalties! – of being a naturalist are the waifs and strays left on his doorstep. For some obscure reason, the most unlikely people lumber themselves with the most unsuitable pets. They 'rescue' young birds, 'find' leverets which they persuade themselves have been abandoned by their mothers; and they buy badger and fox cubs. The sportsmen who make a lucrative, tax-free profit out of this enterprise spend the breeding season destroying badger setts.

If these wretched pets do not die at once, their new owners soon get bitten or baulmed-up with excreta or decide that life is no longer possible without a foreign cruise. Their pet becomes a burden, and the more unscrupulous or unimaginative manage to convince themselves that they will be doing it a kindness if they 'return it to the wild'.

The fact that it has never been wild since its eyes first opened, so that it would not have the smallest chance of fending for itself, does not percolate their addled minds. They are too ignorant to know that turning a wild creature adrift in another's territory can more often cause fatal battles than turning it loose among species with nothing in common. More sensible and kindly folk seek an alternative home that is likely to provide conditions at least as good as they could, and the fact that I often write and broadcast about similar experiences, encourages them to pass it on to me.

I often refuse because I know only too well that it is kinder to destroy some young things than to try to rehabilitate them. Foxes are a case in point. Hundreds of cubs are dug out every spring by men axious to test the mettle of their working terriers against a fox or badger nursing young.

99

Their working terriers have hearts as big as their brains are small and they often suffer far greater punishment than their quarry, especially when they are working to badger.

Any bulging-muscled fool or loud-mouthed dog can dig out a litter of fox cubs and the very helplessness of the woolly cubs sometimes kindles such dolts' innate chivalry. They will stand and watch their own dog's muzzle cut to the bone by a badger – and express their delight at what a 'game 'un' he is! 'Dead game to fox, badger and otter,' they will boast. In the next breath they will say they couldn't harm an innocent cub – but will sell him to children as a plaything!

Foxes are easy enough to rear but they never grow truly tame. There is always a faraway look in their eyes, for ever pining to be free. Such a hand-reared cub will kill instinctively, but it needs a vixen's training to teach it to stalk its quarry and catch wild prey. Having once lost its fear of man, it will find it far simpler to tackle poultry and tame pheasants and domestic creatures, whose death will only add to foxes' reputation as a pest.

Hand-reared cubs are therefore doomed to imprisonment for life (I know one poor wretch which has been chained to a barrel for over eight years). The alternative is an unpleasant death choking in a wire snare, eating a bellyful of poison, or collecting a skinful of lead shot. My reply to those who try to foist their fox cubs on to me is to tell them to destroy them themselves – and never to take another.

As I write this, my study reverberates to the rhythmic snores of deep and innocent sleep. Two sow badger cubs were brought to me five years ago and I reared them on the bottle as companions – and I hoped mates – for the boar I had reared the year before. One sow died in a snare when she went too far off our land, but the other lives in an artificial sett I built within sight of the sitting room window.

The reason my study is so filled with sound is that the Natural History Unit of the B.B.C. fitted a microphone in the sett which is wired to my study so that I can hear what is going on inside and gradually compile a glossary of badger vocabulary on my tape recorder.

This causes not the slightest inconvenience to the sow who is emitting the snores because she is unaware of it. She is as free as any completely wild badger to come and go to the world outside, passing in and out of the wood through a swinging badger gate. It is far too like a trap for foxes to risk it so that the badgers can return from the wood to the enclosure with no risk of foxes following and catching the ducks or pheasants.

That little sow badger has given me pleasure beyond riches. I have kept nightly records of her times of activity, and she has taught me much that would have been impossible either in the dessiccated atmosphere of a scientific laboratory or even sitting in a hide where anything she did during the hours of darkness would have remained a secret. Because I had reared her and she trusted me, I was able to watch her root for beetles and worms without the least sign of self-consciousness and to observe how the tempo of her activity in winter slowed down almost to the point of hibernation – but never quite.

It is flattering to be greeted by a display of affection nor-mally reserved only for other badgers – and almost as in-teresting to watch truly wild instincts gradually gaining supremacy over the unnatural fixations so common with young creatures which have known only the companionship of man instead of their own kind. By the time she was two she had reverted and was as wild and timid as the wildest wild badger.

Some visitors have been particularly difficult to rehabilitate – Fred the barn owl for example. I have always been in-tensely fond of barn owls and sad that their numbers are suffering such a decline. I think that part of the cause is the poisonous pesticides used on farms, which affect the small rodents barn owls prey upon, and poison the owls that eat the afflicted voles and mice. Even more important is the modern way of dealing with rats and mice on farms, which are now poisoned instead of being caught by traps or ferrets, as skilled rat catchers used to do.

Barn owls are far worse affected than tawny owls because little poison is put down in woodlands, where the tawny owls hunt, but barn owls, which are found more on agricultural land and around farm buildings, catch mice poisoned by pesticides in the fields and mice poisoned by unskilled pest officers around farm buildings.

Fred was hatched in an ancient barn at Lea Marston, in Warwickshire. The whole of the top section of the barn roof had been enclosed to make an impressive owl cote especially to attract barn owls to roost and nest. In ancient times farmers rightly regarded a nest of owls round the buildings as a better insurance against rats and mice in their ricks than a whole colony of cats.

In autumn 1971 an owlet fell from this owl cote and was taken into the house by one of the farm cats. The Breeden family, who farm there, hand-reared the owlet and fed him mainly on wood pigeon, which was torn into chunks of suitable size and fed with feathers attached for roughage to make his pellets during digestion. He lived perfectly free in the kitchen, roosting on the dresser, and when he was old enough to fly he went in and out through the kitchen window as the fancy took him. As things turned out, he didn't stay away for long because the wild owls failed to recognise their relative and mobbed him as a stranger. The Breedens didn't worry because he seemed perfectly happy indoors, and all went well until he developed a violent dislike for the cat which had introduced him to her owners. Whenever she came into the kitchen, Fred launched himself into the attack and banged and buffeted her until she fled.

Mrs Breeden is keener on cats than I am, so, instead of banishing the cat, she decided that Fred it was who must go. I was the beneficiary, and little did I know what I had taken on. I knocked a hole in the gable over the dog kennels and built a luxurious owl cote inside. Then I concocted a temporary aviary with some scaffold poles and a roll of wire netting. This was plenty large enough for him to fly and high enough for him to get above roof level so that he could grow accustomed to all of the territory which surrounded him. I also made a pleasant cage over the filing cabinet in my study where he could roost by day. The purpose of this was for him to develop complete confidence in me so that, if anything did go wrong when the time came to set him free, he would be tame enough to trust me implicitly and come back to be fed.

One of Jess's greatest worries in spring and summer is the multitude of wood mice and voles which infest her garden to gorge on fruit and bulbs. I normally cope with them by catching them alive in Longworth traps, and usually set them free in dense cover somewhere at the far end of the wood. When Fred arrived, their luck was out. I fed them to him instead.

This was where I really got a nasty jolt. I discovered that he had not the least idea how to catch them, so that it was immediately obvious that, if I did set him free, he would most certainly starve before he could learn to look after himself. To train him to be self-supporting proved to be a long and arduous job.

I intended to pay the cost of his aviary and owl cote out of articles and broadcasts about him, so I decided, while I was at it, to give as much publicity as I could to the fact that barn owls are on the schedule of protected species and that it is illegal to disturb adults at nest, even for photography, or to take young birds into captivity without a special permit from the Nature Conservancy. So I wrote and explained that a foundling had come into my possession and asked for formal permission to keep him in captivity until I could return him to the wild and he could catch his own food and could fend for himself. The Regional Officer for the Conservancy informed me that he had passed my request on to the officer in Scotland who dealt with permits – or who did not deal with them, as it turned out!

That was in March 1972. Not having heard a whisper by

the end of June, I wrote, a trifle testily perhaps, saying that I was doing my part by trying to publicise and strengthen the laws designed for protected species, a little co-operation would be appreciated. A reply to my letter, for instance.

A letter from Scotland, a fortnight later, explained that it was no offence to take a 'disabled' bird and tend it and release it 'when it was no longer disabled'.

He added that this was a loophole in the law which he was not anxious to advertise too widely, though my opinion is that it is such nonsense that it should get the full blast of publicity in order to force a sensible alteration of the law.

But there was worse to come. He went on to point out that *possession* of a protected bird is not an offence unless it can be proved that it was illegally taken. The offence is solely in the *taking*.

As so often happens, the law is an ass, and I should like to see the spotlight directed on such bumbledom until the law is given enough teeth to bite those who harm what it acknowledges are species in need of protection. If this is really impracticable, it seems a waste to pay bureaucrats who cannot reply to reasonable requests in case they expose a loophole in the law.

While this was going on, Fred thrived, oblivious, in his aviary, which I had mouse-proofed by nailing sheets of galvanised steel inside the bottom of the netting, not to keep mice out but to keep them in. I fixed funnel entrances, which converted the aviary into an outsize cage mouse trap and baited it to attract as many unwary rodents to enter as I could. I supplemented these with whatever I could catch in the strawberry bed and around the pig pens and fowl house.

It was astonishing to see just how inept Fred was. He would sit on his perch, watching a mouse on the floor below and dive down with talons outstretched. Time and again he dived and, time and again, he missed.

A tawny owl, plopping down on to the woodland floor would have scored a winner every shot. Of course, barn owls don't hunt like that. They skim silently along, more like a

The ride to Primrose dell from the study window

The last of the nuthatches

Swallows on a thumb stick in the garage

great spotted woodpecker nests
the birch by the hen pen

llard ducks nest right by the
ise

Turtle doves are so much ni
than collared doves

Wrens in the binder twine in
goat shed

sparrow hawk quartering than a kestrel pouncing, and he obviously could not change from hereditary methods. But it did convince me that the odds against his survival, if he had simply been set free, were a certainty to nothing.

He did get better in the end, so I took the netting off the top of his aviary. He was now free to go where he liked, but I was hoping that he would settle permanently in his owl cote and I encouraged this by supplying food in the bottom of the aviary as I had done while he was a captive. He roosted in the owl cote as I had hoped, and delighted us by hunting at dusk over the paddock and garden and pool. He ate whatever food I put out, and was safely roosting when I went to see him in the morning.

I had pipe dreams of him returning with a wild mate and breeding there so that we could enjoy the rare luxury of watching the two ghostly figures quartering the paddock and my neighbours' fields as they hunted for prey for their young. But such dreams do not materialise easily. A week after I set him free, he was absent for the first time in the morning, though he returned at dusk for the food I put in his aviary. As time went on, his absences got longer and more frequent, but I did have the satisfaction that I was hacking him back to the wild successfully. That is the falconer's jargon for flying a hawk at liberty until it is self-supporting and flies away. Clever falconers hack their birds for as long as they dare, to get them strong and free-flying, but they catch them up at the last minute for training, just before they claim their independence.

I had no wish to confine Fred again – and it would have been illegal if I had, even by the present sloppy law – so I saw less and less of him for the next six weeks till he felt capable of living by his own talons, when he disappeared for good. Although I didn't see him again, there was the satisfaction of having taught him to be self-supporting and I have had better luck in the past with other birds of prey.

A delightful little kestrel arrived one day with an odd cockscomb of feathers sticking out of her skull at right-angles to the way a normal cockscomb grows. Although she was harmless – and legally protected – some lout had shot her, and the man who brought her to me had rescued her and nursed her back to health.

One pellet had cut across the scalp above the eyes, leaving a gaping wound that had to be cleaned and dressed. When it healed up, the feathers did not lie flat but stuck up in a stark line which distinguished her for the rest of her life. But having cured her, her benefactor dared not let her go where he found her, because he knew the shooter who had wounded her would finish off the job if he could. So he asked me to release her in our wood.

I kept her in a cage in my study for a couple of weeks and fed her on mice and sparrows to be sure she was healthy and casting proper pellets of the indigestible components of her diet. Although she started in a cage, she wasn't in it long because she had grown so tame that she was perfectly safe loose in the room. Instead of bashing herself into the window or knocking the ornaments off the shelves, she took up her stance on the back of the dogs' chair, and amused herself all day by watching every movement through the window.

She was as affectionate as plenty of dogs, so that it was quite a wrench to open the window and let her go. The instant when a tame creature passes from captivity to freedom is somehow very moving. It is an odd emotional experience of mixed-up feelings of hope and good wishes, and the faint regret of parting with a friend. Things will never be the same again but, if all goes well, a potential casualty is on her way to freedom again. The snag is that if all does not go well, it is my judgement or my expertise which must take the rap.

This cockscombed kestrel was a saga of success. She planed out of the window only as far as the edge of the wood where, in full view, she perched on a rotten willow and preened herself from top to tail as if cleansing her fastidious feathers of any taint of man. She then flew off into the wood, but it was not the last we saw of her because her feathered fringe distinguished her from all others of her kind. As I worked at my desk by the window I saw her perched, replete and idly digesting the prey she had caught, or hovering over the rough grass by the pool, waiting to pounce on a vole.

She had a great advantage over young hand-reared birds because she had been reared in the wild and was quite capable of catching her own dinner by the time a charge of shot had so nearly put paid to her account. Seeing her hunting around by day repaid much of the trouble for earlier failures, but the real thrill came when Jess and I were having tea in the sitting room just as the light was fading.

Dusk had almost fallen when we saw a shadow skim the whole length of the window from the direction of the wood towards the house. Although the light had almost gone, I was pretty certain from the silhouette that the bird had been a hawk. Not wishing to disturb it, we curbed our curiosity and stayed where we were.

Next night, at the same time, we saw the bird again, and this time we were certain that it swept up towards the gable over the hall. Perhaps it was 'our' hawk cashing-in on our hospitality by nabbing a sparrow going to roost on the house? Tawny owls often raid our eaves, but we had never seen a kestrel so close to the house. The same thing happened for several nights but we could only see a tantalising few yards of flight without ever seeing the end of the drama.

It was too much for my curiosity so, the following night, I went out about half an hour before our visitor was due and hid in a rhododendron clump at the far end of the lawn, armed with a pair of binoculars. My patience was rewarded when the little cockscombed kestrel flew in, not to catch a sparrow but to roost on an oak beam under the gable over the hall. I stayed in my bush as quiet as a mouse till darkness fell, in case I disturbed her, before returning to the house to enjoy my tea.

She roosted there regularly all through the winter from November till early March, then she paired with a wild hawk and tried to nest in the stag-headed oak across the paddock. But the carrion crows would have none of this, and dive-bombed them till they gave the black villains best and went to nest in a hollow oak at the far end of the wood in Ley Close.

I saw her from time to time for eighteen months after I set her free – which was a pretty good span with so many vandal trigger fingers around. She was a rare success, which makes all the trouble of restoring animals and birds to the wild worthwhile.

Early summer is the peak time for such experiments. Young birds, as soon as they leave the nest, wander a few yards – and yell for food. Their reflex is to open their gapes as soon as a shadow passes overhead, hoping their parents will stuff them with food. Well-intentioned strangers, seeing a bottom-less gullet hearing cries of hunger, not unnaturally assume the fledgling has been abandoned and is starving. They take it home to try to rear it, although if they left it where it was, the odds are that the old birds would return within minutes and cram it so tight it couldn't squawk. Such ama-teurs soon find that they have neither the time nor access to the special food to make a job of young birds or animals, so they bring them to me.

A young mistle thrush arrived one day which had been 'rescued' and reared by the children at a primary school until his appetite grew beyond their ability to satisfy. He was perfectly delightful. He was so accustomed to being sur-rounded by a class of squalling kids that sudden noise or movement didn't fluster him in the least. When I ran out of worms for him I discovered that he did very well on shredded raw meat and liver, and would sit for hours digesting his last meal on my study bookcase. When he could fly strongly, I set him free and he hung around for weeks, flying down when I went out for the slivers of meat he knew I would be bringing.

I had no means of identifying him subsequently because I do not put rings on the legs of the birds that pass through my hands except for very special reasons. I learned this lesson years ago with a plover I had reared, which turned out to be one of the most delightful creatures it has ever been my luck to know. When he was getting strong on the wing, I decided to ring him so that I might get news of his subsequent fate from some birdwatcher whose hobby is catching and ringing birds.

Fanatical bird ringers are dead against putting their numbered rings on anything but truly wild birds, because the unnatural behaviour of hand-reared birds might give misleading results to scientists studying bird behaviour. But I managed to find a 'blackleg' ornithologist who was prepared to stretch a point, and he snapped an authentic metal ring on my young peewit's leg.

Had it been put on a wild bird, that is the last we should have seen of it, so we should have had no means of knowing whether it caused any discomfort. As it was, my bird was around next day and the days that followed that. Within a week, he was standing on one leg, miserably holding the other in the air. Although he was at liberty, I had no difficulty in picking him up to see why he was so listless.

It needed no skilled diagnosis to establish the cause of his trouble. Even after so short a time, the edge of the ring had chafed the scales on his leg, which now appeared to be chapped. I have no idea if the leg would have become calloused, to resist the ring's wear or if discomfort would have been prolonged, because I removed it. But, however curious I have been since, I have not repeated the experiment.

This is such good mistle thrush country that I was never able to be sure whether the bird I liberated stayed with us or not. I went into the yard one February afternoon and heard a mistle thrush chatter. There was nothing odd about this because they were establishing their nesting territory so that they were touchy enough to swear at their own shadows if there was nothing more tangible to annoy them.

As I glanced up, the cock bird dived off his perch in obvious retreat instead of the more usual attack. His pursuer

was a bluish bird about twice his size, with a longish tail
and pointed wings. It could easily have been mistaken for a
cuckoo in summer.

'Our' mistle thrush side-slipped under the telephone wires,
skimmed the wire netting which joins the yard gate to the
garage, and practically looped the loop through the tangle
of branches of the old hawthorn tree.

He had the advantage of course. He had served several
weeks apprenticeship chivvying every trespassing rival which
had dared stick a beak over our boundary. He knew every
twig and every hazard in his territory, and he was not simply
trying to give his pursuer the slip but to lead him such a
perilous dance that, with luck, he would pile into an invisible
wire and break his unfriendly neck.

It was no good relying on ill luck or ill wishes. His aggres-
sor was no out-of-season cuckoo, but a hungry sparrow hawk.

We know them as 'blue hawks' in Staffordshire, and their
habit is to cruise along the edge of woodland, skimming
adroitly among the trees, until they surprise a flock of small
birds feeding in a clearing or a singleton, like our mistle
thrush, which can be panicked into open flight instead of
diving for safe cover.

Fear spurred our thrush on until he flew almost as fast as
the hawk, side-slipping as deftly as a rugger player sells the
dummy, so that, time and again, the hawk overshot her
target and seemed in imminent danger of crashing.

The crazy chase continued in and out of the trees and
round the yard until, at last, the thrush crossed the open
space over the fowl run. It was a fatal error, for the hawk
closed in so fast that there was only a puff of feathers,
hanging as still as anti-aircraft smoke, as evidence that their
courses had coincided. The hawk never paused in her flight
but, as she disappeared, I could see the bedraggled corpse of
our mistle thrush dangling limply from her talons.

I suppose the whole drama lasted no more than ten or
fifteen seconds, but it seemed an hour to me and, I imagine,
a lifetime to the victim. Even those of us lucky enough to

live and work in deep country rarely have such a chance to watch the plot unfolding to its bitter end.

Some birds which come as casualties stay a long time but leave no real impression, and others are gone within minutes. We were coming home late one evening across the reservoir from Blithfield, and noticed a bird, apparently disabled, wandering in the road. There is an ugly concrete viaduct splitting the water into two, so that there was little room for anything which couldn't fly to get out of the way of traffic.

I eased the car to a standstill beside the bird, opened the door and hooked him into the car by his neck, intending to take him home and assess the damage. It was an impressive neck to catch hold of, with a bill as sharp as a javelin, and the fact that he allowed me to pick him up was all the confirmation I needed that his injuries must be pretty bad.

When I got back, I examined him all over with my finger tips but could feel no broken bones, so I shut him in a shed to rest till morning. Next day he allowed me to enter and pick him up with nothing worse than a threatening jab from his bill – and still I could find nothing wrong. So far as I could see he was a great crested grebe in perfect health.

I should have found it difficult to get enough small fish for him, so I launched him gently on the pool to see what would happen. He swam strongly to the middle, performed a fastidious toilet, as if I had defiled the feathers I had touched, flew straight into the air and set course for the precise direction from which I had brought him.

I have never seen a great crested grebe get airborne from land, so I assume the explanation for his docility was that headlights on the road had fooled him into the belief that the viaduct was not tarmac but water. When he landed he would discover that his mistake had prevented him getting airborne without some help from me, because his legs are set far back for swimming under water, but are of little use on land.

Several years earlier my neighbour Edward Froggatt had brought in a Bewicks swan that had crashed into the electricity pylons and shattered a wing. It was a compound fracture of the knuckle joint and jagged splinters were sticking out grotesquely, so that there was nothing I could do about it but amputate.

The wing healed easily enough but the swan wouldn't feed, so I put him on the pool, thinking he would come out with the ducks for corn, but he skulked in the middle, and for some reason became waterlogged and nearly died before I could recapture him.

I was in two minds whether to destroy him, But I hate being beaten when once I have started, so I began to force-feed him. Within a few days he was tame enough to feed from my hand and, after that, he never looked back. So, when I let him go next time, he was confident enough to come up and feed as I had hoped at first. He had no option about staying, poor chap, because he could never fly, and for two winters he called down wild Bewicks flying over on migration. They didn't stay, of course, and it was very sad to see him left entirely alone again when he would so obviously have loved to go off with them. When he died, four years later, I was not sorry to see him go.

Apart from my badgers – which have had a whole book to themselves* – I have enjoyed the companionship of deer as much as any creatures which were not entirely wild. My tame roe deer lived happily for over ten years and, when she died, I decided to find out more about fallow deer.

The fallow in our wood tend to be dark, partly I imagine because black is a dominant colour, and partly because they are inconspicuous and the menil (which retains its spotted coat in winter) and normal spotted deer are in danger of getting shot first.

I decided to try to get a white fawn to rear on the bottle. It would be impossible to mistake her in the wood, and I calculated that it might be possible to persuade even those who feel undressed without a gun not to take pot shots at her if she did happen to stray on to their land. But although

* Badgers at my Window

several midland deer parks have a few white deer in their herds (which they do not normally like) a fawn of the right age proved exceptionally difficult to come by, and I had to wait several years.

At last, on June 19th last year, Gerald Springthorpe turned up with a female fawn. She was strong, too strong for my peace of mind, and she certainly wasn't white. Her coat would have been the envy of the most glamorous red-headed film star. Her eyes were brown and the cleaves of her feet a contrasting fleshy pink. She was the most difficult creature I have ever tried to rear by hand, and it needed every ounce of my patience and experience to gentle her.

The real trouble was that she was about a week too old so that it was too late for her to become imprinted on me, because she had already rivetted all her affection on her dam. To make matters worse, the fact that she was already so strong added to the danger of injury because she flew into blind panics at the slightest strange movement.

If I had put her outside, I should never have seen her again until she was so faint with hunger that I could pick her up. So I put her in a small shed where I thought she would be easy to catch and hold until she was used to the bottle and came for it willingly.

The first time I approached, she ricochetted from rough wall to rough brick wall faster than a squash ball driven by a master's racquet. The first time round she grazed the skin from her tender nose, so I slid out, and shut the door before she did herself a serious injury. I returned to catch her when it was pitch dark, and set about converting her shed into what amounted to a padded cell. I lined the walls and door with perspex, too smooth to graze her skin and not rigid enough to bruise her.

I am experienced enough at handling animals to sneak in and 'field' her the instant her panic set in, so I sat down on the hay, guided her on to my lap and inched the teat into her mouth. Then, the moment the life-giving liquid touched her tongue, she subsided into peace and fed greedily. It was mechanically simple to catch her after that, so that she no longer battered herself about and she fed freely enough, provided always that I used a teat with a hole to suit her rate of consumption.

The treatment obviously suited her physically because she grew so fast, but she showed no signs of getting tame. Most of the creatures I have bottle-reared have soon associated me with pleasurable food and showed no fear after the first few days. But this fallow fawn was different. Each time I entered her pen, she stood up, staring and rigid. If I approached her, she leaped up the nearest corner or dived for the door, though I had no difficulty in forecasting the instant when her terror would explode into action. By leaving a tempting gap, I found that I could always trick her into leaping neatly into my arms.

Even when she was lying peacefully feeding, she was still subject to illogical qualms, so that it was necessary to be constantly on the alert to forestall her efforts to escape. Each feed took about half an hour and she had four feeds a day, so that it was reasonable to expect that we would soon get to know each other fairly well; but she was as wild as the day she first came at the end of a month. I was dispirited and distressed, but at last I triumphed over her obstinacy.

The sixth week after her arrival, she gave a tiny squeak of welcome when I approached. I kept perfectly still, holding out the bottle towards her and, very gingerly and stiff-legged, she came towards me, of her own free will, and began to suck. I slid my hand beneath the bottle and, when I caressed her, she relaxed instead of flexing her muscles. The feeling of relief at breaching her defences by kindness was almost indescribable.

Even after that it wasn't all plain sailing. She was still subject to panics, but I now felt justified in taking a chance by giving her more freedom. I made a little wire-netting enclosure outside her pen where she had green grass to nuzzle and lie on and, far more important, where she could look round and see the normal movement of the place. She could see wild duck come up from the pool to be fed and the dogs and cars in the yard, and roe deer grazing in the paddock.

As soon as I dared, I fenced about an acre of the paddock off for her and, quite suddenly, her whole nature changed. It dawned on her that she had nothing to fear from me, and she turned overnight from the wildest wild creature to one of the most friendly and confiding animals that have ever shared our lives. No cade lamb is bolder or more greedy, for she will go straight up to strangers and nuzzle them for food. She bucks and kicks her heels higher than a cowboy's bronco, and gallops round the paddock with the dogs without any sign of fear.

When my study window is open, she calls for biscuits, as my old roe did, and I hope that next year she will mate with a wild buck and produce a fawn, so that I can make observations of its development at close quarters.

There is little more satisfying than winning the confidence of anything so wild and shy, because I knew in my bones that the least bungle on my part would have shattered her trust irrevocably. She might have injured herself in her blind efforts to escape, and would almost certainly have suffered psychologically so that her affections could never have blossomed.

We still argue about her colour. She matched a red-head when she came, but her coat faded to the shade of a Guernsey cow in autumn, and has since gone lighter still. When she moults into adult pelage there seems a fair chance that she will be cream, it not pristine white. She is already very photogenic, and stands out marvellously against sombre woodland shade. It will be interesting to see how far she wanders, and the time scale of her movements.

I am scrupulous in never attributing anthropomorphic qualities to animals, but it is useful to know individuals by name when writing about them in popular, as opposed to scientific, media, and when I first mentioned the arrival of my fallow fawn in my weekly column in the *Evening Mail,* I said I thought of calling her Spook.

Although readers heaped coals of fire on my head for suggesting anything so unsuitable for such a delightful creature, I had my reasons. There are white fallow deer on the next estate to the park where she was bred, and there is also a ghost story. The legend is that an ancient lord of the manor was growing old without an heir, when it at last became obvious that his wife was that way inclined. But, shortly before the child was due, the mother contracted smallpox, so the husband asked his physician what the chances were of his coveted heir catching it from her.

The reply was that he might well get it when he was born, but that his safety could only be procured by an unacceptable risk to the mother. Such landowners are jealous of their heritage, and the doctor was told 'Cut down the tree but save the branch!'

The park has been haunted ever since by the disembowelled mother, groaning horribly, and it may well be no coincidence that white deer roam there in the moonlight, and that her cries are remarkably like the groans of a fallow buck at his rutting stand.

I can vouch neither for the truth nor the accuracy of the story, but my journalistic mind latched on to it as a reasonable peg on which to hang a name for the loveliest sprite that decorates our wood.

The one inhabitant which takes exception to her is the Canada gander. A pair of Canada geese have visited us every March for several years, and have taken possession of the pool. This would be fine except that, having spent several weeks here, driving off the deer and the dogs if they go too close, to say nothing of other Canada geese which come later, they go on to Edward Froggatt's pool to nest.

Last year, I got fed up with this, and stole their eggs and hatched three goslings under bantams. They grew up so tame that they spent hours a day sitting on my study window sill, plastering it with goose guano, and peering at me from a range of about three feet. They reminded me of an old school gaffer who used to put me off by watching over my shoulder while I wrote his essays.

One got airborne in a November gale, and I assume was blown off course until he was lost, because that was the last that I saw of him. The remaining pair have been an endless source of predictions by the local birdwatchers, who were confident that they would leave me to join up with flocks of wintering Canada geese. But they were wrong, for our geese stayed till February, and I don't think they would have gone then if we hadn't chopped a tree down on the edge of the pool.

It was a big old oak, blocking the view of the new ride I was cutting into Lords Coppice, and it made a terrific crash when it came down. The geese had taken no notice of the chain saw's yowling, but the tearing timber was too much for their nerves. They flew off low over Jolliffes' farm, turned east, and flew away low down the valley.

That was the last we saw of them for a month, and it was an inconclusive end to the argument. The ornithologists claimed that they were right, and I thought they would probably have come back if only they had flown away high enough to get proper bearings. All was well though, at the beginning of March. They returned with an orchestration of honkings, settled at once and chose a spot in the reeds for their nest. The only change in their behaviour was that their sojourn amongst strangers had made them a little less tame.

One of my pleasantest childhood memories is a wonderful sermon I sat through while on holiday at Braunton in Devonshire. I say 'sat through' deliberately, because I never heard a word. We had hardly got inside the church before I spotted a long-eared bat flying high among the ancient figures in the vaulted ceiling. I don't know if he had been disturbed, or if the gloom up there was right for nocturnal insects, or if the whole place was alive with deathwatch beetles. What I do know is that the aerobatics of that bat were more inspriring to me than anything that the preacher droned about.

Bats have always had an irresistible attraction for me, and when an old poacher taught me how to catch them coming from their roost I put his method to the test. There was a large colony of pipistrelles in an old stone archway a few miles away, and I asked the owner if I could catch a few to try to found a colony here.

The method worked beyond my wildest dreams. One hundred and fifty-seven bats came out of that roost, and I caught every one. Having satisfied myself how well the trap worked, I liberated all but thirty-five within a few feet of their roost. I brought the rest home and put them in our roofspace, having blocked up all the exit holes. Twenty-four hours later, I prized the lead flashing away from the chimney to leave a slit I trusted would be to their liking.

I have no means of knowing whether those bats 'homed' to their original roost, three or four miles away, because I did not put identification rings on them. Specialists on bats think that the probability is that they would return where they came from.

The fact is that we have since had a colony of bats in our roof, which covers the new extension we built when we came. They could be some of the bats I introduced, because there is a limitless supply of insects along the edge of the wood which must make it a desirable residence. Or perhaps the introduced bats tainted the roof with their smell, which attracted strange bats to choose it for themselves. Or perhaps it was coincidence.

Whatever the source of the colony, we have since been delighted on summer evenings watching 'our' bats hawk flies and moths around the house and yard, and the original pipistrelles have since been joined, at intervals, by a much smaller colony of long-eared bats.

If your curiosity was aroused about my method of capture, I am sorry, but it will have to stay that way. Bats are

threatened species, at least as much as most scarce birds. I
told the secretary of the Mammal Society bat group what I
had learned, but wild horses wouldn't drag it out of me for
strangers in case it got into the hands of a pest destruction
officer, or a parson who doesn't like such competition in his
sermon.

CHAPTER SIX

People

Not least among the pleasures of my occupation is the joy that I get from people who I might never otherwise have met. I am not thinking of distinguished naturalists because nothing is more boring than name-droppers who bask in the reflected glory of their famous friends. I am thinking of people, often shy and very retiring, whose paths cross inevitably with mine because of our mutual interests.

Years ago, now, Jess and I were invited out to lunch expressly to meet Beatrice Eatough, the 'squirrel woman'. It was a hilarious lunch because, long before the ice had been broken, Jess asked her where she lived and was told 'about four miles outside Newport, on the Whitchurch side.'.

'Funny,' said Jess, 'that's where I've got a perfectly delightful house.' This was an obvious winner so she went on to describe 'her' charming little warm stone house beside a wood with two Wellingtonia trees in front.

'What a funny thing,' was the reply, 'I've lived in that house for years.' The explanation was that, while I was shackled to industry, we were always on the lookout for ideal escapes, pipe-dreaming about what we could do 'when we got them.

Together we built a fantasy world where, all over the country 'our' houses waited for us to buy them when I won the pools or, even less likely, when I wrote a best seller after coming home from work.

We soon discovered that, in precisely the same way, the Eatoughs had regarded the same little house as 'their' house too, for years. The only difference was that they got it and we didn't!

As a sequel, we were invited to see it. 'Come and have a squirrel tea,' Bee said. It turned out to be one of the most memorable days of my life. I have always had a natural affinity for badgers but I could be equally content in good red squirrel country, although I know only too well that they have now become so rare that it will remain an unrequited yearning.

We drove across a field and into the cottage garden, to be welcomed by a beautiful red squirrel which was sitting calmly at the foot of the Wellingtonia on the lawn. Red squirrels have always been rarities in my experience, and it etched itself into my mind because it had already made my day. If we hadn't seen another, I should have gone home happy. But we had seen nothing as yet. We were taken into a sunny little sitting room and seated while our hostess opened the window. Holding a walnut in each hand, she rattled them together and called out a loud invitation to unseen guests.

Within seconds, one squirrel ran down the Wellingtonia, another appeared from the depths of the hedge and one out of the herbacious border. They all ran across the lawn towards the house, up the creeper and on to the window sill. Without the slightest hesitation, taking no notice of us, they hopped on to a chair, across the carpet and clambered on to Bee's hands and arms. Then they retired to the windowsill to eat their booty, still inside the room, to be followed by what appeared to be a queue of the most delightful fairy relatives it is possible to imagine.

They were all completely wild, for none of them had been hand-reared or spent an instant in captivity. They had been tamed simply by unremitting patience and kindness, and the natural bond of sympathy which some people are lucky enough to have with wild animals.

They were so tame that they even trusted strangers, and took nuts from our hands as freely as if we'd been friends for years. Jess was even told to hold on to her nut to see how strong red squirrels are. She never discovered because her squirrel took it as a slight to have food offered and then withdrawn. So he bit her thumb and made her drop it altogether!

We had lots of squirrel teas after that, and have been firm friends ever since. I once saw eleven wild red squirrels in that sitting room at the same time and one let me hold a microphone so close while he splitting a nut that the tape recording sounded like a fat woman waltzing on a gravel drive.

Alas, the whole colony succumbed to the foul disease with which grey squirrels are thought to infect them. The symptoms are rather similar to myxomatosis in rabbits, and it seems to be as infectious and fatal.

But the grey stone house is still there, and so are the Eatoughs. Bee's gift is not confined to squirrels, and I have seen her call nuthatches to eat cheese from her fingers, and her whole garden is full of all sorts of birds as tame as robins. And although she is so gentle, she is no slushy sentimentalist, as any stoat or rat which casts covetous eyes on the tree-creepers which roost in the Wellingtonias soon find out. She is a crack shot with a rifle, and any stoat which sits up to reconnoitre is likely to stop a bullet which will crack his skull.

The school of St Mary and St Anne down in the village of Abbots Bromley is a widow's cruse of embryo naturalists. It is a leading girls' boarding school and, in theory, the Upper VI biology group can come up here to do projects which will be of help to them in their exams. Some choose to do population studies of small mammals, or examine the effect on surrounding vegetation of damming a ditch and making a pool.

This year Shiela Fletcher and Christine Evans have come regularly all through the year to try to establish whether herons are double-brooded, and to record the effects of clearing patches of the wood with pigs. They took a census by metre squares to record what was there before the pigs were introduced. Then they repeated it when the pigs had just finished, and will monitor the regeneration next season.

When their predecessors, Liz Moonie and Lois Millar, were observing herons, Douglas Thomas, who was producing *Animal Magic*, asked me to put up a hide so that he could get some close-ups of herons feeding young. I always enjoy working with Johnny Morris, who introduces the programme, so did my best to comply.

The nests were in tall oaks and I could only find one low enough to be overlooked from an adjacent tree. We lashed ladders to the trunk with wire and, the higher we got, the less I liked it. At last we got a ladder to the top and fixed up a corrugated plastic sheet hide integral with the ladder. It was now possible to perch up there, seeing but unseen, so I reported that all was ready.

When the camerman arrived, he took one look and said it was too high for him. I said it was too high for me too, but I'd been up there to help lash it together, in spite of the discomfort. Goaded into trying, he was no more than half-way up before he had convinced himself that herons' nests were not for him, so he packed up his cameras and shuffled off home.

When the girls heard about it they subsided in cascades of giggles and asked if they could go up themselves. I had no intention of allowing them to fall out of a tree to break their necks without a written permit either from their parents or headmistress, whatever they said about me being a crusty old square, so they had to retire with their passion for pinnacles unsatisfied.

It so happened that Miss Roch, the headmistress, was here to lunch on the following Sunday, and when I told her the story, she asked to see the hide. She took one look and then, to our intense surprise, she shinned up like a sailor to the yardarm. She stayed awhile to watch the young birds and when she came down, she gravely told me that I had been quite right not to let them go up. 'It did sway about a bit,' she said. So much for intrepid cameramen.

Although the theory is that the girls do projects for their academic benefit, I do not really worry about that angle. To allow all five hundred girls into the wood would defeat its own object by driving out everything else. So I limit the numbers by inviting only those who are specifically interested in biology. Having done that, I don't mind what they do so long as they enjoy it and it does not interfere with the work in the reserve. I remember that chapel and Shakespeare were such chores at school that I have avoided both since, and I see no point in stuffing them with dry and uninteresting facts.

I enjoyed our school natural history society, the 'Bug Soc.', mainly because it gave me the chance to sneak off for an illegal smoke. But I did do just enough serious natural history to leave me with a thirst for more – a thirst that grows more unquenchable the older I grow. So I feel that, if only a few of the girls who do projects up here look back on it with pleasure, as the years go by, they will defend such places in the future with a fervour that should vanquish any threats.

The only other school with which I have had much contact is equally good but at the opposite end of the educational scale. There is no sixth form there for the simple reason that it is a State primary school which passes on its pupils when they reach the age of eleven. Mary Sheward, the headmistress, retired last summer and now that she is no longer there to breathe fire into its guts, there is the risk that it will revert to anonymity or be absorbed by the kind of glass-and-concrete emporium which dispenses academic knowledge without discipline or culture.

We met many years ago because of our mutual interests, and I was fascinated to discover what and how she taught. Within sight of her school room the great nests of a heronry are clearly visible, and succeeding generations of the children have kept records of annual breeding results for twenty years or so. They collect egg shells and discarded food pellets cast out of the nests. They analyse the pellets for food content, by teasing them apart to their basic components, and

look at the powder on the moulted feathers and make skeletons from the corpses of fledglings that fall from the nests.

Their herons do not only teach them natural history. They
teach arithmetic as well. They look at the nests through the
window and guess how far they are away. Some think a mile
and some ten yards, so they go outside and count the paces
from the school to the heronry, which may vary from four
to five hundred, depending on the individual length of little
legs!

This not only teaches them to bracket their guesses, it also
teaches them how inaccurate guesses are. So they have their
first go at scientific measurement. They roll a wheel, which
turns one revolution a yard, and count the revolutions, and
then they learn to cross check that with a surveyor's measur-
ing chain. They discover by this that the heronry is just a
quarter of a mile from their schoolroom window and, by the
time that they have guessed and paced and measured it
scientifically, a quarter of a mile *means* something to them.

Then they are provided with a stop watch with which they
time how long it takes the herons from the instant they rise
from the nest until they fly directly over the schoolroom.
That is the elapsed time it takes to fly a quarter of a mile,
from which they learn to calculate how many miles an hour
it is, which gives them a visual idea of speed as well as an
insight into arithmetic. To drive the lesson home, they count
the wing beats and calculate how far each flapping stroke
propels them.

At the back of the school is a little paddock seventy yards
square. The kids guess and measure and calculate the hedges
until they can also visualise seventy yards, and simply by
multiplying seventy by seventy, they also know what an
acre looks like, give and take a few square yards! They are
better equipped at the age of eleven to assess the size of a
field than most people are when they leave university.

When I called one day to see Mary, all the little ones
were playing in a hollow tree on Enville common, and telling
her what they thought had happened there in days gone by.

Theories ranged from violent death to gentle love; one little girl thought it was where Shakespeare wrote his sonnets, and a more practical lad was certain that that old tree was the refuge where generations of sly foxes had given hounds the slip.

How wonderful it must be to be taught the art of abstract thought in an ancient tree in deep countryside! The whole teaching there was based on rural life and every child planted a tree when he arrived as a toddler, weeded and tended it as he passed through the school, and could take it home to transplant as a memento of a happy childhood when the time came for him to leave. 'There is no vandalism in our village,' Mary Sheward said.

I saw the proof of the pudding when she brought a bus-load of her children over here to see the sanctuary. Their eyes were as sharp as hawks and they moved with the stealth of poachers. My tame roe deer, who normally reckoned three a crowd, accepted them with confidence. They walked round so quietly that they all saw wild deer and a stoat hunting and their discipline was such that they could all file past a bird sitting on eggs without startling her off the nest.

When they got home, they wrote civilised little bread-and-butter letters of appreciation, many of them illustrated by coloured drawings which they did of their own accord. One little lad confided 'when you took us up the ladder to the observation tower, you trod on my finger. You didn't know, but I did!'

What a primary school, and what a character to run it! They were the only school kids I ever envied.

A few months ago, I was invited to take part in a *Look Stranger* programme on B.B.C. 2, based on the work I am doing here. It is probably the only time I shall ever have twenty-five minutes to myself on the box, and Derek Trimby, the producer, said that the film could include my friends who share my life.

I met him through his wife Dily Breese, for whom I have worked a lot on sound, and I have enjoyed her programmes more than any I have done. It seemed a golden opportunity in prospect but, as so often happens, reality only dawned as the time approached and I was forced to face the fact that, if success depended on the producer, it would be all too easy for me to be the architect of failure! He could take pictures as pretty as you please, but my words had to fill them in!

Filming the animals was fine. We started in the summer, when I was just ready to give the barn owl Fred his freedom. He was spending his days in my study and he was as co-operative as if he had been hatched under an arc light. The cameraman could have been his oldest friend and he sat on my shoulder and gently groomed my shaggy eyebrows with his lethal bill. The general madhouse atmosphere with whirring cameras and commands of 'hold it' or 'do it agin', or 'inch to the left', or 'don't look so bloody miserable' disturbed me far more than Fred.

When the time came to set him free, the camera was focussed to record the moment of truth. Would he fly up to his owl cote, where he had been confined in his temporary aviary? Or would he cock a snook at my naturalist zeal and fly off into the blue, leaving me looking a fool, to talk my way out of that?

He behaved perfectly, even when the cameraman wanted us to do it all over again, from the reverse angle, so that the sequence could be cut to whatever length the producer wanted. There was some risk that he would fly away if asked to do it again, but the background of television is a series of repeats and endless waits and against my better judgement, I took him out of the sanctuary of his owl cote and let him go again.

This time he didn't fly straight in. He flew instead to the top of the scaffolding which had supported his aviary netting and stood statuesque to survey his surroundings.

This was too much for the swallows, who were nesting in the garage, so they dive bombed him one after another, swooping so low they made him duck. It was a shot we couldn't have set up in years and I decided that, if this film was no better than the rest, it would at least be different. But the cameraman said I might as well forget it. His film ran out just before the swallows attacked.

Filming animals is like that. All the best chances come when the film is being loaded or the lens is being changed or the light is drawing in. It is also unbelievably slow, because top-class producers are perfectionists or they wouldnt be top class.

Even a simple thing like filming the dogs going over a five-barred gate can take half an hour or more. The lurchers are all superb fencers and will go over a gate without checking in their stride. Tick, the German pointer is stockily built, a stong little dog bred for endurance more than speed. She has far too much guts to let this put her at a disadvantage, so she went over with the others. If she did have to try a bit harder, no stranger would have known.

Dogs have given me such pleasure all my life that I never feel quite complete without them. They lie in idle comfort, as I'm working at my desk, and by the fire when work is done; Tick sleeps in a dog box in our bedroom. Except when I am trying to make tape recordings or waiting in the wood to watch something specific, they are almost always with me. I felt that making a film about the place would not paint a fair picture without them and, being an extrovert myself, I wanted them to show themselves to advantage.

Before we could begin, there was a conference to decide exactly where to place the camera, so that the light would give a dramatic background, with the dogs and gate silhouetted against the sky. We then had to have a run-through so that the cameraman could check that he could hold them in focus from take-off to land fall. He couldn't, so he had to shift and we went through it all again!

This time all was well but there was another last minute conflab to decide whether to speed up the camera so that it could be filmed in slow motion. When, at last, I gave them the word to go over, Mandy had discovered an easier spot in

Spotted flycatchers nest by the kitchen window

Pouter pigeons and collared doves at bird bath

The author's pigs provide free labour in the woods

Roe buck in velvet

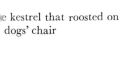

e kestrel that roosted on
dogs' chair

e weasel that catches the
e

Swallows on the cross cut saw in the garage

Pied wagtails in the garage

all her rehearsals; she ran wide so I had to recall them, get them back out of sight of camera, and do it all again.

Even when we did succeed, we had to repeat it as usual, once with them coming towards the camera and once going away so that the film could be cut to any length. Considering the permutations against getting four lively dogs in the air two or three times simultaneously, in the same relative positions, it is marvellous that we are not at it still.

Filming the wild creatures was even worse. The camera battery went flat in the middle of the heron sequence and an otherwise perfect shot of seven deer, feeding in the ride by the house, landed on the cutting room floor because there was a scratch on it. And the deer and herons proved less co-operative than the dogs about rehearsals and retakes.

It is almost impossible for any but professional actors, which none of us were, to go over and over the same sequence without getting more wooden every time, so the result was about three hours film, after twelve days filming, which had to be edited down to twenty-five minutes. So most of our star performances joined the herons, with their flat battery, and the deer with a vertical scratch, on the cutting room floor!

Temperamental film stars have always seemed stupid and petty to me, but now I can understand their tantrums. Working under such pressure is a tetchy business, and I was lost in wonder at how Derek kept his temper cool.

Smooth-running features which distil a story until it has a theme that flows, *apparently* naturally, are not just luck. They are the product of craftsman's skill and endless patience and imagination. Like most other things which test one to the limit, they may be exciting or fun in prospect or to look back on, but they are hell at the time. By the time we had finished I am sure that none of us ever wanted to see any of the others again. When it was transmitted, I was simply delighted with the performances of 'my' animals, and Derek had every reason to take pride in his handiwork. We could have founded a mutual admiration society!

I enjoy working on sound far more than television. A film crew, even for quite a small job, usually consists of a director, cameraman, assistant cameraman, sound engineer, continuity girl or secretary and often a lighting engineer. The whole business is getting terribly union-ridden and the chances of disagreements obviously increase as numbers grow. It is impossible, with even the best intentions, for any one member of the team, including the chap in front of the camera, to be more than a small cog in a big, impersonal wheel.

Sound is very different. It is often only necessary to have the producer and the man in front of the microphone, so that it is possible to combine to produce creative work which is obviously far more satisfying. But, even with sound, luck plays its part in missing situations as well as capturing them.

I was working here with Dilys Breese on a radio nature trail for her programme *Living World*, and we wanted to discuss the bog bean that grows in Dunstal Pool. Although it is a sound programme, and listeners would have been none the wiser if we talked from the comfort of the local bar parlour, she is as meticulous in making it authentic as if every move was shown on film. So, when we were ready, she asked me to go and pick a bit of bog bean so that we could see what we were talking about to make our words more vivid. It was a bitter winter day and when I went down to the pool, I couldn't find any very near the edge. There was just one clump I might reach if I stooped down and bent over as far as I dared.

I judged the distance right but overlooked the fact that I am subject to sudden bouts of cramp. At the critical moment my thigh muscles seized up in agonising rigour and, swinging as leisurely as a pendulum, I toppled slow-motion into the freezing drink. Thankfully the microphone was out of earshot so Dilys couldn't hear what I said.

When Gerald Springthorpe comes to Bagot's wood or up here, he often calls for me. Some people think that a Forestry game warden is simply a professional killer of deer, but the truth is that stalking occupies a comparatively small proportion of his time. He spends countless hours out in the wood assessing the populations and available food supply, and has pioneered methods of sowing 'deer lawns' in the centre of the forests to attract the deer away from vulnerable farmland on the periphery. By providing additional feed, he can increase the number of deer a given forest will sustain.

This is the part of his job that I have so enjoyed sharing. You can't sit for hours in a secluded high seat and see nothing but deer. You see everything else that moves as well. By sucking air through his lips, in imitation of a rabbit's squeal, he can call foxes from deep cover out into the open, and they will come right along the ride almost near enough to spit on them. We've watched owls and nightjars at dusk, and badgers going home at dawn. We've seen whole parties of long-tailed tits and goldcrests foraging over the birches as ruthless as a swarm of locusts. But instead of leaving a trail of destruction, they kill insect pests and leave the trees more healthy than they were.

We like to set out about half an hour before it gets light in the morning so that we can be posted in a vantage point in time to see the dawn break. We spend the next two or three hours sitting there, or wandering round quietly in the wood, seeing but unseen. We discover which blackthorn brakes yield the best sloes for Christmas sloe gin, and which pools can be relied on if I want a few newts in a hurry. We find birds nests and watch fox and badger cubs and, because he loves fishing and is an artist at casting a fly, he is as interested in the small creatures in the wood as the large.

Creatures that are active at dawn and dusk usually lie up in the middle of the day, so we reckon to pack up and go home about nine or half past. Three or four hours out at that time of day is always enough to give me a mammoth appetite so we have a fry-up when we come in. A real man's fry-up, with eggs new-laid that morning, and rashers of sizzling bacon from the pigs that spent the last summer out in the wood.

They are memorable breakfasts to crown vigils spent in

quiet places while city slickers were still asleep in frowsty beds; breakfasts made all the more delicious because time is not the master and we have leisure to discuss the pleasant things we've seen. It is such a civilised contrast to the days when I should have been clocking-in at that time for another boring factory stint. This escape from the tyranny of time was a blessing matched only by the chance to cut loose from convention too. The artificial world of commerce puts a false value on appearance so that smart clothes and plush houses and shiny cars are a necessity for credit-worthy rating.

The oldest and most comfortable clothes now meet my needs, for it makes no difference to me what anybody thinks. I wear out two or three pairs of rubber welly boots to every pair of leather shoes, and it is years since I bought a new jacket or suit. Holidays cost me nothing because I know nowhere I would rather be.

The greatest change has been to our family life. Routine work in a factory meant that there were only two days in a week, and not always that, to do what we chose. Although Jess and I are lucky enough to have much in common, it did mean that if I wanted to spend my half-day making a chicken run and she wanted a lift with something heavy in the garden, we each felt we were poaching the other's precious time. In rush times now, when a book is due at the publishers or there is a build-up in radio or TV work, we get less time still because I work seven days a week instead of five. And it is not uncommon for her to spend longer hours in the kitchen than a factory inspector would approve because she is a superb cook and we both enjoy entertaining both social and professional friends.

But somehow working for yourself, however hard, is quite different form working for a master. Economies for the bene-fit of somebody else can't compare with pennies saved out of our own pocket and we manage to live remarkably cheaply with the honey and game and poultry and pork and fruit produced on the place, and we find our friends prefer such home-grown grub to exotic expense-account dishes mucked about by foreign chefs.

Even in busy times, from the writing point of view, the stock still has to be fed, fences looked and dogs exercised. However busy I am, I go round the wood at least twice a day and usually three times, the dogs are constant companions and Jess comes once if not twice.

But I am not always busy. Money is now a tool instead of a master, and so long as there is enough for our needs, it seems stupid to grind out my guts for a surplus to be scooped by the tax man. So, although I love writing and broadcasting, I try to do less in spring and summer than in autumn and winter. I like plenty of time to see to my broody hens and tend the chicks and cosset the young waifs and strays I inevitably get lumbered with. And that is also the time when Jess and I can both spend a lot of time in the wood, because she loves birds nesting and will sit motionless for hours with a pair of binoculars, watching for the tell-tale signs of feeding birds and the clues they leave when they are building their nests.

In pleasant summer weather we often take sandwiches up the wood, or eat most of our meals, including breakfast, on the old stone slab on the terrace outside the sitting room window. After supper, we go out to listen to the grasshopper warblers, which are now almost too high-pitched for my ears to catch. When they die down, with luck, the nightjars take up their melody in deeper key, so we stay to enjoy them while daylight fades and the moon gets up.

It is a rich reward for the scheming and labour of managing the sanctuary for our benefit as well as theirs, and it makes us appreciate just how lucky we are to be able to share their wilderness.

INDEX

Index

Alfa chloralose, 30
Alien species, 21
Anti-blood sports, 29, 30

Badger digging, 99, 100
Badgers and fox hunting, 36, 37
Badgers and pheasants, 31
Badger sett, 100
Bagot goats, 19
Barn owl, 100–104, 127, 128
Bats, 117, 119
Bewick's swan, 111, 112
Binoculars, 76
Bird gardening, 61–3
Bird ringing, 39
Bracken control, 85
British Trust for Ornithology, 43

Cost of conservation, 29
Crows, 33, 35, 63, 64

Daffodil lawn, 19
Dale, Brian, 98
Deer, fallow, 112, 116
Deer management, 98, 130, 131

Eatough, Beatrice, 120–2
European Conservation Year, 24, 73, 74

Evening Mail, 13

Fishermen, damage by, 37, 38
Fly catcher, spotted, 50–2
Foot-and-mouth disease, 28
Forestry Commission, 30
Fox cubs, 99
Fox hunting, 35–7
Foxproof netting, 49

Gamekeepers, 29–31, 35, 67
Geese, Canada, 116, 117
Glades and clearings, 83–5
Grebe, great crested, 111

Habitat improvement, 69
Hedgehogs, 31
Home grown food, 94–7
Humphreys, Paul, 12

Instant pool, 87

Kelly, Dermot, 36
Kestrel, 105–8
Kingfisher, 90, 91

Living World, 130
Look Stranger, 126–9

Mammal Society, 15
Meynell Hunt, 36
Ministry of Agriculture, 30

Mistle thrush, 34, 35, 108, 110
Modern farming methods, 26, 27
Mortality among young birds, 42
Monoculture, disadvantage of, 20
Morris, Johnny, 123

Nature Conservancy, 17, 103
Nature reserve finances, 24, 25, 67
Nest boxes, 43, 44, 52, 55–7, 60
Nuthatches, 17

Otters, 37, 38

Pheasants, 34, 63, 96
Planners (honey pots), 38, 39
Pigs, 78–82
Plover, 109
Predator control, 32, 33, 45–7
Primrose dell, 15
Prototype reserve, 24
Public footpaths, 27, 28

Rats, 47, 48
Redstart, 41, 42, 55, 56
Reserve, plan for, 91, 92
Rides, woodland, 75, 76
Roch, Muriel, 123

School of St Mary and St Anne, 17, 122
Sheward, Mary, 124–6
Small garden nature reserves, 41, 42
Sparrow hawk, 31, 110
Springthorpe, Gerald, 98, 113, 130–2
Squirrels, 46, 121, 122
Starlings, 57, 58
Swallows, 42, 58, 59
Swine vesicular disease, 28

Thomas, Douglas, 123
Thrush's anvil, 70
Transition from industry to journalism, 12
Trimby, Derek, 126–30

Venison, 97
Vermin, 32, 33

Wagtails, pied, 42, 53, 54
Warbler, grasshopper, 71
Weasel, 32, 53, 54
Weldmesh netting, 81, 82, 87, 88
Wheeler dealing, 15, 16
Wild duck, 63–6
Woodpecker, 44
Wren, 60, 61